Pitman'S
Shorthand Writing Exercises
And
Examination Tests

Pitman'S Shorthand Writing Exercises

And

Examination Tests

A Series Of Graduated Exercises on Every Rule in The System and Adapted for use by the Private Student or in Public Classes

BY

Isaac Pitman

GYAN

Published by

GYAN

Gyan Publishing House
5, Ansari Road
Daryaganj, New Delhi-110002
Phone: 011-47034999, 9811692060
E-mail: books@gyanbooks.com

Distribution Network
gyanbooks.com
India, USA, Canada, UK, Australia

ISBN: 978-93-6280-003-9 (HB)
First Published, 1906

2nd Impression 2024

Printed at: Gyan Press, Delhi.

Pitman'S Shorthand Writing Exercises And Examination Tests
Author: Isaac Pitman

PITMAN'S SHORTHAND WRITING EXERCISES

Pitman's
Shorthand Writing Exercises
and
Examination Tests

A Series of Graduated Exercises on Every Rule in the System and Adapted for use by the Private Student or in Public Classes

EIGHTH EDITION

London
Sir Isaac Pitman & Sons, Ltd., 1 Amen Corner, E.C.
Bath and New York.

PREFACE

THE chief object of this work is to provide the student of Pitman's Shorthand with a series of exhaustive Exercises on every rule in the system. An examination of the arrangement of the Exercises will show that they have been prepared in such a way that the student may not only thoroughly master each principle as it is reached in the course of his study, but that he is enabled *at the same time* to acquire a very extensive knowledge of words and the outlines for them, and also to commence the practice of writing from dictation almost from the beginning of his study of the theory. Facility in writing and in reading shorthand may therefore be obtained *along with* a perfect mastery of the principles, and thus the student will be saved a good deal of valuable time.

It is scarcely necessary to say that this work is not intended to take the place of "Pitman's Shorthand Instructor" or any of the other text-books of the system. It is supplementary to those, and the Exercises herein contained will be most correctly written, and with the greatest benefit to the student, if he will take care always to refer to his text-book before commencing to work the Exercises on any rule. Attention to this, and to the brief directions at the head of the Exercises, will enable the student to work through the various sections with few or no mistakes.

It is probable that the student will meet in these Exercises with some words that are unfamiliar to him. He is recommended in such a case invariably to refer to the dictionary for the meaning of the words, remembering that transcription of shorthand notes is all the more easy when the meaning of the words is perfectly understood by the writer.

It may be pointed out, too, that the Exercises contain very many illustrations of the principle of Word-Building, and that the student will be able to construct innumerable other outlines on the plan suggested by the examples referred to. The total number of words in the sentence exercises is given in the figures in parenthesis at the end of each

CONTENTS

EXERCISE		PAGE
1–6	LONG VOWELS	9
7–12	SHORT AND LONG VOWELS	12
13–17	DIPHTHONGS	16
18–23	CIRCLE *s* AND *z*	20
24–29	LOOP *st* AND *str*	24
30–35	CIRCLES *sw* AND *ss* OR *sz*	30
36–41	VOWELS AND *s* AND *t*	35
42	CONTRACTIONS	40
43	HOOK *l* ADDED TO STRAIGHT LETTERS	41
44	HOOK *r* ADDED TO STRAIGHT LETTERS	42
45–50	INITIAL HOOKS TO STRAIGHT LETTERS	44
51	HOOK *l* ADDED TO CURVES	48
52	HOOK *r* ADDED TO CURVES	51
53–57	INITIAL HOOKS	54
58–64	CIRCLES AND LOOPS PREFIXED TO INITIAL HOOKS	57
65	CONTRACTIONS	64
66	*n* HOOK	64
67	*f* OR *v* HOOK	66
68–72	THE HOOKS *n*, AND *f* OR *v*	69
73–79	CIRCLES AND LOOPS ADDED TO FINAL HOOKS	72
80–86	THE *-tion* HOOK	79
87–92	ADDITIONAL DOUBLE CONSONANTS	87
93	CONTRACTIONS	93
94–99	THE ASPIRATE	94
100–105	UPWARD AND DOWNWARD *l*	101
106–111	UPWARD AND DOWNWARD *r*	109
112–114	UPWARD AND DOWNWARD *sh*	118
115	CONTRACTIONS	122
116–127	THE HALVING PRINCIPLE	123
128–133	THE DOUBLE-LENGTH PRINCIPLE	141
134	CONTRACTIONS	149
135–141	VOCALIZATION OF *pl*, *pr*, ETC.	150
142–147	*w* AND *y* DIPHTHONGS	158
148	CONTRACTIONS	169

EXERCISE		PAGE
149–154	DISYLLABIC DIPHTHONGS	170
155–160	PREFIXES	177
161–166	SUFFIXES	185
167	CONTRACTIONS	195
168–173	GRAMMALOGUES	196
174–179	OMISSION OF CONSONANTS, ETC.	202
180–184	CONTRACTIONS	208
185–186	PHRASEOGRAPHY	214
187–188	PUNCTUATION, ETC.	217
189–190	WRITING IN POSITION	219
191	FIGURES	221
192	NEGATIVE PREFIXES	222
193–196	REPORTING GRAMMALOGUES	223
197–199	REPORTING CONTRACTIONS	226
200–203	ADVANCED PHRASEOGRAPHY	229
204–206	BUSINESS PHRASES AND CONTRACTIONS	233
207	POLITICAL PHRASES	236
208	LAW PHRASES	237
209	THEOLOGICAL PHRASES	238
210	INTERSECTED WORDS	239

WRITING EXERCISES

EXERCISE 1.

Long Vowels.

Vowels placed at the left side of an upright or sloping consonant, or above a horizontal, are read before the consonant. Vowels placed at the right side of an upright or sloping consonant, or below a horizontal, are read after the consonant.

The student is directed by small capital letters when to write the consonants *sh*, *l*, *r*, and *h* downward. Grammalogues and contractions are printed in italic.

1 pa, palm, paw, pall, pawnee, pawed, pay, paid, pale,
2 page, paRe, pooh, ope, pope, poke, pole, poRe, bay, babe,
3 bake, bait, bale, bailee, bathe, baRe, beau, boat, bowl,
4 boRe, boo, bee, bought, eat, ate, oat, tea, toe, toad, tome,
5 toll, tollage, toRe, Tay, tape, take, tame, tail, taRe, awed,
6 ode, day, date, dado, dame, dale, daRe, do, doe, dote,
7 dodo, dole, dome, dooR, donate, donee, aid, Dee, each,
8 chew, choke, jay, Jake, jail, jaw, Joe, Job, joke, Jew, age,
9 caw, Coe, cope, code, coach, coke, comb, coal, coRe, cocoa,
10 coo, Kay, cape, Cato, Cade, cage, cake, came, kale, oak,
11 ache, eke, auk, key, gay, gape, gate, gauge, game, gale,
12 goat, goal, goRe, Gaul, fay, fade, faith, fame, faiL, faRe,
13 fee, faLL, foe, folk, foam, foaL, foRe, foRego, eve, vague,
14 veiL, vote, vogue, voLe, oath, thaw, thee, they, ace, say,
15 saw, so, sew, see, ooze, ease, owes, Zoo, SHah, SHape,
16 SHade SHake, SHame, SHaRe, SHaw, SHow, SHowed, SHoRe,
17 SHoe, SHe, ma, may, make, maim, mail, maRe, maw,
18 maul, mow, mope, mole, aim, moo, nay, nape, name,
19 naiL, knee, gnaw, no, knoLL, NoRe, e'en, own, ail, eel, awl,

20 lay, laid, lake, lave, lame, laiR, lee, law, laud, low, lobe,
21 load, loaf, loth, loathe, loam, loRe, loo, aiR, eaR, oaR, ray,
22 rate, rage, rake, raiL, rare, re, raw, wrought, roe, rope,
23 robe, rote, rode, roach, rogue, roam, roLL, roar, rue, way,
24 wade, wage, ware, we, woe, woad, wore, woo, wee, ye,
25 yew, yea, Haw, Hay, Hake, Haigh, Hoe.

EXERCISE 2.

Long Vowels (continued).

A third-place vowel, between two strokes, is written before the second stroke.

1 beet, deep, cheap, keep, sHeep, neap, leap, reap, weep,
2 heap, eat, beat, keyed, feed, lead, reed, weed, heed, each,
3 peach, beach, teach, leech, reach, liege, eke, peak, beak,
4 teak, meek, leek, reek, league, thief, leaf, leave, teeth,
5 Keith, Meath, wreath, heath, wreathe, beam, team, deem,
6 theme, ream, eel, peel, deal, keel, meal, feeL, veaL, kneeL,
7 reeL, eaR, peeR, beeR, teaR, deeR, jeeR, gear, feaR,
8 veeR, SHeaR, leeR, meRe, rear, weir, boom, tomb, doom,
9 loom, room, poop, coop, loop, rupee, hoop, pool, cool,
10 Goole, fooL, ruLe, boot, jute, root, chewed, food, rude,
11 wooed, pooR, booR, mooR, retail, Nero, oatmeal.

EXERCISE 3.

Long Vowels (continued).

GRAMMALOGUES.

all, *be*, *he*, *the*, *who* (down).

1. *He* may load *all the* Hay. 2. *Who* may take *the* meal? 3. *Who* may *he be who* rode *the* bay maRe? 4. Paul may go *all the* way. 5. *He* may take *the* oRe. 6. SHe may weep *all the* day. 7. *The* Pawnee may take *the* wreath. 8. Joe Booth may vacate *the* poop. 9. May Ruth Cope read *the* tale?

10. Joe Bate may teach me *the* polo game. 11. We feaR *the* thief may locate *the* rare peach. 12. May we go forth ? 13. *All who* read *the* theme may weep. 14. SHOW me *the* bailee *who* came. 15. We *all* say *the* leech may see *the* deep meRe. 16. May Paul Booth lead *the* SHeep ? 17. We may *all* aid pooR Paul. 18. We hope *the* day may *be* faiR. (118)

EXERCISE 4.

Long Vowels (continued).

1. May we SHOW *the* pale hero *the* way we weed ? 2. *He* may take heed. 3. Paul Page may take *the* mail coach. 4. May *he* read *all the* way ? 5. We feaR *the* rogue may peach. 6. *Who* may lead *the* maRe, Joe ? 7. SHe may faLL. 8. We *all* hope SHe may reach *the* mooR. 9. We saw *the* rude rogue *who* rowed *the* boat take *the* boot. 10. *He* may *be the* thief *who* beat Dame Bate. 11. May we take *the* peeR *the* faRe ? 12. We hope pooR Joe Beach may keep *the* cape we bought. 13. We feaR *he* may leave *the* meal. (96)

EXERCISE 5.

Long Vowels (continued).

1. Joe Hague may keep *all the* change. 2. Who saw *the* meek deeR move o'eR *the* mooR ? 3. They may reach *the* deep pool. 4. Paul may see *the* game. 5. *He* may take *all the* oatcake. 6. SHOW me *the* way they rode. 7. *The* rude foe may retake *the* gate. 8. *Who* may take *the* knave ? 9. *All who* know *the* way may take *the* lead. 10. We feaR Joe may pay *all the* faRe. 11. *He* may do so. 12. Paul Peel may pay *the* faRe *he* owes. 13. Joe Beach may read *the* tale, though *he* may teaR *the* page. 14. *Who* may *the* tall dame *be ?* 15. Move *the* coach, so we may *all* see *the* game. 16. *The* sea foam may make *the* cape fade. 17. *The* rogue may mooR *the* boat eRe we reach *the* SHoRe. 18 May we *all* go ? (131)

EXERCISE 6.

Long Vowels (concluded).

1. We may *all* see *the* meek sHeep feed. 2. *Who* may *the* rude thief *be who* rowed *the* boat ? 3. We *all* say *he* may reach Goole. 4. *The* tall Pawnee may also take *the* cocoa. 5. They *all* saw *the* pooR lame maRe eat *the* Hay. 6. May we make *the* rogue sHaRe *the* cake ? 7. They say Job Meek may take *the* boat. 8. May *he* pay *the* toll ? 9. We feaR *the* page may teaR *the* leaf. 10. Move *the* boom, so they may take *the* boat. 11. May Job Cope change *the* food ? 12. We both saw *the* faiR dame take *the* gay cape. 13. *The* rogue *who* wrote *the* page may take *the* wreath. 14. May we lead *the* way ? 15. We may *all* reach *the* cool sHade. 16. *He* paid *all he* owed 17. *Who* bought *the* cheap ball ? 18. May they keep *the* cage ? 19. Make Keith pay *all the* faRe. 20. They may *all* know *the* name. 21. sHow *the* leech *the* faiR page. 22. We feaR they may retake *the* boat. 23. *Who* may take *the* peach ? 24. They may teach *all the* pooR folk *the* game. 25. *The* coach may take *all the* fouR. 26. sHow me *the* maRe. 27. They may keep *all the* cocoa. 28. *Who* paid *the* faRe ?

(194)

EXERCISE 7.

Short and Long Vowels.

Second-place short vowels and third-place long or short vowels, between two consonants, are written before the second consonant.

(*a*) bet, debt, jet, jetty, get, Ted, fed, sHed, meadow, Neddy, led, red, ready, head, heady, etch, ketch, fetch, wretch, edge, kedge, ledge, wedge, hedge, peck, beck, deck, check, neck, wreck, egg, peg, beg, keg, leg, legacy, legate, legatee, levy, reveRe, heavy, gusH, musH, lusH, rusH, husH, dumb, chum, gum, thumb, mum, mummy, mummery, numb, rum, punch, bunch, munch, lunch, hunch, funny, money, honey, penny, Jenny, Kenny, many, length, lengthy, lenity, bench, wrench, wench, pulp, pulpy, dull, cull, colouR, gull, gully, gullied, gulp, gulf, pell, bell, bellow, bellowed, Tell, dell, delta, delay, jelly, Kelly, fellow, mell, mellow, mellowed, melody, relay, yellow, Perth, birth, dearth, girth, mirth, bung, tongue, chunk, junk, monk, monkey, lung, rung, hung, among, tub, dub, chub, chubby, cub, rub, hub, tuck, duck, chuck, lucky, ruck, pug, tug, dug, jug, mug, nugget, lug, luggage, rug, Hug, budge, judge, fudge, nudge, putty, cutty, nutty, rut, perry, berry, Terry, Derry, cherry, Jerry, Kerry, ferry, verity, SHerry, merry, burrow, curry, furrow, furry, thorough, thoroughly, Murray, lurry, hurry.

(*b*) pill, pillow, billow, till, dill, chilly, jill, kill, filly, mill, milk, milky, lily, riLL, pip, tip, dip, chip, kip, SHip, nip, lip, rip, hip, nib, rib, pity, bit, ditty, Kitty, writ, kid, giddy, middy, lid, rid, hid, pitch, ditch, niche, rich, richly, witch, hitch, midge, ridge, pick, tick, chick, kick, thick, nick, lick, rick, pig, big, dig, jig, gig, fig, rig, fifty, live, livelong, dim, dimly, chimney, vim, limb, rim, tinny, finny, ninny, pinch, lynch, winch, pink, chink, link, rink, wink, ring, wing, pull, pulley, bully, bullied, fully, book, took, SHook, nook, look, Hook.

(*c*) appal, apology, appeal, appeaR, apeak, abaSH, abate, abbey, ability, abet, atom, atomic, attic, ado, agility, academy, agony, afaR, aveR, acid, aSHORe, anatomy, anatomic, anchovy, allay, alb, album, aRm, aRmouR, aRmada, aRRay, aRRow, aRk, away, aware, ebb, ebbing, ebony, effect, evict, edit, Emily, enough, envy, envelop, envenom, elf, elope, eRR, eaRl, eaRly, Italy, italic, Islam, image, inch, indulge, ink, inky, opera, operetta, oblong, oddly, offaL, offing, olive, oRb, oRchid, up, uprear, uproar, ugly, unpack, undo, unfaiR, unfaiRly, unveiL, uneasy, uneasily, unmake, unmarried, unLucky, unrobe, unaware, unwary, unwearied, unworthy.

(*d*) pal, pallid, palloR, pack, back, tack, Jack, knack, lack, rack, Hack, Hackney, patty, bat, chatty, fatty, vat, natty, rat, tap, chap, gap, map, nap, lap, rap, hap, tab, dab, cab, sHabby, nab, path, bath, lath, wrath, pad, padlock, caddy, fad, faddy, sHadow, lad, laddie, patch, batch, catch, thatch, match, latch, hatch, pod, body, bodily, toddy, cod, sHod, sHoddy, rod, hod, pop, top, chop, cop, fop, sHop, mop, lop, hop, dock, chock, sHock, mock, knock, lock, rock, rocky, Hock, Hockey, toffee, coffee, lofty, policy, doll, jolly, collie, folly, volley, Mollie, loll, rollick, rot, rob, robbery, dot, domino.

EXERCISE 8.

Short and Long Vowels (continued).

GRAMMALOGUES.

a, an, *and* (up), *are,* *but,* *it,* *of,* *to.*

1. Date *the* cheque *a* month ahead, *and* pay *the* debt *to the* milleR. 2. They wrote *to* say they laid *the* lead in *the* rut at *the* bottom *of the* road. 3. *The* rude village lad sHowed Fanny Finch *the* route *he* took *to* reach *the* sHade *of the* sHed at *the* edge *of the* lake. 4. *The* lame lamb licked *the* pooR limb, *and* feLL eRe *it* got *to the* gate. 5. We *are to* take lunch in *the* dell; *but* we may get no food if we *are* delayed in *the* wood. 6. We hope Mary Beach may marry Philip Murray. 7 If so, we may *all* go *to the* wedding. (107)

EXERCISE 9.

Short and Long Vowels (continued).

1. May we appeal *to* Tom Murray *to* take *a* sHaRe in *the* game, *and* lead us *to* victory ? 2. *The* pick *of the* party *are* away ill ; *but* we hope *to* make *a* faiR game *of it*. 3. If we onLy manage *to* get Tom into *the* team, we may pull off *the* match easily. 4. We own *to an* uneasy feeLing in *the* affaiR 5. Ask NeLLie *to* fetch me *a* big cake, *a* peaR, *and a* cup *of* coffee. 6. *The* sea aiR may make us feeL ready *to* eat 7. We *are to* take lunch in *the* leafy sHade at *the* bottom *of the* lovely valley. 8. Polly *and* Annie *are to* go in *the* gig. 9. They

hope *to* catch up *to* us eRe we reach *the* weir. 10. *The* Yankee wore *a* lovely ruby ring. 11. *He* sHowed rare ability in *the* comic opera, *and* we hope *he* may tarry in *the* village *all the* month. 12. We rarely see so funny *a* fellow. 13. Both Philip *and* Jerry say they see no ability in *the* fellow; *but* they *are* fuLL *of* envy *and* vanity, *and* so they *are* unfaiR. 14. May they sHake off so fooLish *a* feeLing, *and* make *a* thorough apology *to the* chatty Yankee! (200)

EXERCISE 10.

Short and Long Vowels (continued).

1. We may easily take *a* cheque *and* pay *the* debt. 2. *Are* we *to* knock in *the* head *of the* tub? 3. *It* may *be a* dirty job, *but* we may manage *it*. 4. We feaR *to* talk *of the* ability *of the* lad. 5. Ted MilleR may *be* fuLL *of* envy. 6. If we take *the* narrow path aLong *the* meadow, we may readily get *to the* sHop in *the* village. 7. *The* lad may catch up *to* us on *the* way, *and* so we may *all* reach *the* dock eaRly enough *to* take *a* look at *the* big sHip. 8. *It* may *be* many *a* long *and* weary month eRe we see *the* merry fellow *who* came *to the* village *to* see us. 9. *The* memory *of the* jolly party may live many *a* long day. (130)

EXERCISE 11.

Short and Long Vowels (continued).

1. Take *a* cheque *and* pay *the* bill *to the* deaLeR. 2. We hope *the* colouR may keep. 3. They say *the* calico may *be* ready *to* sHip *to*-morrow. 4. We *are to* sHip *the* big keg *of* rum eaRly in *the* month *of* March. 5. We may leave *the* bale *of* twiLL. 6. *It* may *be* ready *to* go eaRly in May. 7. Do they know *the* rate *to* charge? 8. They say so, *but* we feaR they may *be* wrong. 9. Do they know *the* length *and* width *of the* big boat at *the* back *of the* dock? 10. Go *to the* bank; casH *the* cheque; *and* fetch *the* money *to* me. 11. Ask Bennett *and* Murray *to* sHip *the* merino. 12. Take *a* foRm *of* policy, *and* insuRe *the* bale *of* fuR. 13. *Are* we *to* redeem *the* bill

to-day, oR may we leave *it* ? 14. Ask Tom Bailey *to* mark *the* package in red ink. 15. Do they say they guarantee *the* colouR *of the* red robe ? 16. We feaR *it* may easily fade in *a* month. 17. Take *the* bill, *and* ask *the* notary *to* mark *it*. 18. We hope *the* fiRm may deal faiRly, *and* pay *the* bill. 19. Take no cheque, *but* ask *the* fiRm *to* pay *the* bill in ready casH. 20. *The* sHip " Baltic " may load at *the* big dock *to*-morrow. 21. Ask *the* fellow in *the* barge *to* pack *all the* luggage in *the* bottom *of the* boat. 22. *He* may get *a* lad *to* carry *the* bag *to the* sHip. 23. They *all* took *a* thorough look at *the* big sHip. 24. *The* butt of sHerry may *be* ready *to* sHip *to*-morrow oR Monday. (261)

EXERCISE 12.

Short and Long Vowels (concluded).

1. *The* bill may *be* unpaid, *and the* fellow may *be* rude *to* Tom Parry. 2. We rang *the* bell, *but* no lad came *to the* dooR. 3. May *be the* family were away. 4. We *all* appeaR *to* feaR *the* fellow may *be a* sHam. 5. If so, *he* may carry *the* game faR enough *to* take in many pooR folk in *the* village below. 6. *He* may *be* infiRm, *but* we *all* faiL *to* see *it*. 7. *He* may sHock *the* pooR lady at Birch Villa. 8. sHe may *be* ill *and* laid up many *a* month. 9. Tom *and* Adam may both go in *the* coach, *and* ask *the* lady *to* beware *of the* rogue. 10. *He* may easily take away *all the* money. 11 We hope they may pay heed *to all* we may say. (128)

EXERCISE 13.

Diphthongs.

The diphthong *oi* is written in the first place, and the diphthong *u* in the third place. The diphthongs may be joined to a consonant where convenient.

1 (*a*) pie, pipe, piety, pied, pile, pyRe, piracy, bite, bile, byRe,
2 type, tied, tidy, tidily, tithe, timely, tiny, tile, tiRe,
3 attiRe, retiRe, tyro, die, diet, dyke, dime, diRe, chide,

chime, china, gibe, fie, purify, terrify, defy, verify, vilify mollify, indemnify, rarefy, horrify, fife, five, fiLe, fiRe, fiery vie, Viking, viLe, SHy, SHied, SHiny, SHiRe, mighty, mile, miRe, miry, nigh, knife, ninety, deny, demy, denied, NiLe, lie, lied, like, liked, likely, life, life-time, life-long, lively, lithe, lime, lyRe, rye, ripe, right, rightly, ride, riding, writhe, rhyme, riLe, wire, wiry, wired, wiring, hide, item, idle, idly, ivy, ivory, ice, icy, icily, ice-boat, eyes, iRe, IRiSH, iRony, iRonic.

(*b*) pouch, couch, vouch, avouch, avow, outlaw, outlawed, outlawry, outlay, dowry, owl, owliSH, cow, cowed, cowl, cowry, loud, loudly, lounge, rowdy, bough, toweR, county, endow, doughty, pow-wow, bout, toweL, toweLing, downy, doweL, chow-chow, jowl, Gow, gouge, fowL, fowLing, voweL, voweR, SHowery, mouthing, loutiSH, rout, rowel, howdah.

(*c*) boy, boyiSH, boileR, buoyant, buoyancy, toil, toileR, toyed, doily, coy, coyed, coil, coinage, foiL, moil, alloy, joy, enjoy, envoy, oil, oiled, oileR, oily, annoy, annoyeR, aHoy, Hoy, hoideniSH.

(*d*) pue, puke, puma, puny, pule, Bute, beauty, bureau, rebuke, tue, tube, tumoR, tunic, due, endue, adieu, dupe, duty, duke, duly, unduly, cue, askew, cupola, occupy, cube, cubic, cuRe, curacy, ridicule, few, feud, fume, perfume, assume, fury, view, purview, review, sue, pursue, tissue, ensue, mew, mule, muraL, demuRe, new, anew, renew, venue, avenue, Hew, huge, eulogy, EuRope, youth, usurp, usury, value, valued, vacuity, voLume, vicuna, Wight, wide, wideR, widely, wife, wifely.

EXERCISE 14.

Diphthongs (continued).

GRAMMALOGUES.

can, *have*, *how*, *I* or *eye*, *our* or *hour* *was*, *why*, *you*.

1. Both *you and I* know *it was* right *to* ask *the* new duke *to*

rebuke *our* nephew, Tom Boyle. 2. *The* idle fellow *can* admiRe no toil. 3. *He* may annoy *and* ridicule us now, *and* idle away many *an* hour; *but* we know *the* value *of* time, *and*, if we *have to* use *our* poweR *to* do so, we hope *to* make Tom know *it* also. 4. *How* fooLish *to* allow *the* time *of* our youth *to* go idly by, *and* hope *to* retiRe at *a* ripe age, rich, fuLL *of* poweR, *and* liked by *all who* know us! 5. *Why* do *you* take so wrong *a* view *of* life? 6. *I* ask *you to* do youR duty manfully; *to be* genuine; *to* aspire *to a* life *of* utility; *and to* defy *the* idle youth *who* may hope *to* lead *you* aside. 7. If *you* do so, *you* are likely *to* have *a* High name among *all who* know *you*.

(155)

EXERCISE 15.

Diphthongs (continued).

1. *How can I* daRe *to* occupy *an hour of* youR time each day? 2. *You have* so much *to* do, *and* so many *to* take *you* away. 3. *Why was* Tom Abbott allowed *to* leave *our* room *to* go *to* annoy *you*. 4. My *eye* may appeaR dim *to you; but I* am *all* right, *and I* hope *to* enjoy my tea in *the* new room. 5. *The* duke may like *to* take my nephew *to* Cuba in July; *but I* hope *to be* in time *to* make *the* boy retiRe. 6. *I* may *have to* assume *an* authority unLike my own feeLing; *but* if *I* am *to be* loyal *to* my duty *I* may have *to* wire my nephew *to* keep back *an hour* oR so. 7. *You* may know *how to* foiL *the* duke. (130)

EXERCISE 16.

Diphthongs (continued).

1. *Why have you* allowed youR big dog *to* bite my white cow? 2. *How was it he* came *to* terrify *the* pooR animal? 3. *I* may make *you* pay *the* damage, *and it* may *be* youR duty *to* see *the* duke *and* avow *the* injury. 4. If *you* faiL *to* make me *a* fuLL apology *I* may pursue *you* at law, *and* make *you* rue youR idle joke. 5. *How can you* decoy *our* boy Hugh *to the* annuaL faiR at Newcome? 6. We feaR *he* may become *an* idleR,

and so faLL into penury. 7. We see no beauty in *the* type *of* youth *you* sHow *the* boy, *and* we hope *you are* loyal enough *to* review youR life *and* daRe *to* take *a* new path *to the* right. 8. *Have a* High aim in life ; pursue *it* right loyally ; *and* sHow *the* county *all you can* do if *you* like. 9. We hope *you* may leave *the* viLe few *who* value youR money onLy. 10. FeaR no ridicule; *but* aspire *to* become *a* poweR in youR cwn county. 11. Do youR duty like *a* hero, *and* allow no rowdy fellow *to* terrify *you* into *a* wrong path. 12. *You* know we *have to* rebuke *you*, though we love *you*. (200)

EXERCISE 17.

Diphthongs (concluded).

1. *How can I* hope *to* sHip *the* wire by July ? 2. *I* hope *to have the* china ready in time *to* go by *the* boat due *to* leave *on* Monday. 3. Do *you* know *how* much *you are to* allow *the* buyeR ? 4. *Why was he* so much in aRReaR ? 5. Hugh Doyle may take up *our* agency in New York. 6. *I* hope *he* may aRRive in time *to* see *the* buyeR. 7. *I have a* new range *of* vicuna, *of* rare beauty, *to* sHow *you*. 8. Do *you* know *the* value *of the* tunic *he* sHowed *you?* 9. *He* may ask *to* see *a* pure white calico. 10. *The* failuRe *of the* oil fiRm may affect us. 11. Ask *the* dealeR *to have a* pipe *of* sHerry ready *to* sHip by *the* fourth *of* July. 12. Take *a* cab, *and* ride *all the* way *to the* faR dock. 13. *I have to* assume *you are* right in *the* view *you* take *of the* affaiR. 14. *I* hope *you* may thoroughly enjoy *the* voyage *to the* Cape. 15. *Can you* guarantee *the* accuracy *of the* tale ? 16. Ask *the* buyeR *to* view *the* new china. 17. If *you are* wide-awake, *he* may buy *all you have to* sHow. 18. *Why was he* so long in *the* sHop ? 19. If we annoy *the* fellow, *he* may leave us aLone, *and* go *and* buy *of* Boyle *and* Nephew. 20. *The* fellow sHowed rare ingenuity in *the* escape. 21. *He* may eventually take refuge in *the* wood. 22. *He* owes no money *to* our fiRm, though they say so. 23. *I* may go *and* see *the* envoy to-morrow oR Monday. 24. *Be* back in *an hour*. (261)

EXERCISE 18.

Circle S and Z.

The circle *s* is written backward to a straight line ; inside a curve ; and outside an angle formed by two straight lines. In this exercise, and in Exercises 19 to 23 inclusive, italic *s*, *c* or *z* (in words other than grammalogues) signifies that the stroke *s* (or *z*), and not the circle, must be written. Write *ks* for *x*.

(*a*) CIRCLE *s* ADDED TO A STRAIGHT LETTER :—

1 pies, spies, spied, spade, speech, speeches, speaks,
2 sparrow, sparrows, sob, sobs, Sabbath, boys, eats, seats,
3 cites, suits, sty, stew, stews, sat, satiRe, side, sides, sawed,
4 sowed, sighed, sued, cheese, choose, pitches, ditches, riches,
5 witches, pages, badges, dodges, images, nudges, lodges,
6 ledges, wedges, hedges, sieges, ekes, peaks, cheeks, jokes,
7 cakes, fox, invokes, sHakes, mix, nooks, licks, aRks, rakes,
8 awakes, Hoax, soaks, six, pigs, begs, tags, dogs, jugs, kegs,
9 gags, figs, mugs, lags, aRgues, rags, Hags, sago, rose,
10 barrows, tyros, furrows, sorrows, morose, wise, unwise,
11 lengthwise, ways, by-ways, sideways, sways, yes, hues,
12 pass, pass-book, bespeak, busby, baseball, teas, testy,
13 tacit, tacitly, Tacitus, days, decide, decides, disturb,
14 audacity, case, casks, cassock, cascade, race, racer, razors,
15 resource, woes, wiser.

(*b*) CIRCLE *s* ADDED TO A CURVE :—

1 safe, safes, unsafe, pacify, pacifies, sieve, sieves,
2 passive, deceives, extensive, effusive, evasive, massive,
3 missives, receives, thaws, seethes, *s*ues, is*s*ues, pur*s*ues,
4 tis*s*ues, en*s*ues, oozes, asHes, pusHes, busHes, gasHes,
5 gnasHes, lasHes, rusHes, sHoes, alms, palms, calms, lambs,
6 mass, mask, masks, miseR, miseRs, miseRly, same, seams,
7 smokes, smoothes, smasHes, smiles, smeaRs, nose, snows,
8 snooze, snaps, snatches, snakes, sniffs, snaiL, snaiLs,
9 sneeRs, sing, passing, basing, tossing, enticing, dozing,
10 chasing, causing, encasing, guessing, fusing, diffusing,
11 suffusing, infusing, refusing, voicing, invoicing, massing,

12 racing, rising, summarizing, authorizing, signs, designs,
13 ensigns, resigns, ails, sails, soles, slays, slap, sleeps, slides,
14 slouch, sledges, slake, slag, self, sleeves, slums, slings,
15 sluR, sluRs, oRes, soRes, siR, passeR, baseR, teaseR, chaseR,
16 loseR, loseRs, siRe, desiRe, desiRes.

(*c*) CIRCLE *s* WRITTEN OUTSIDE AN ANGLE :—

1 passage, beseech, exchange, episode, beside, besides,
2 oxide, reside, resides, wayside, opposite, paucity, beset,
3 bestows, chastise, justice, excites, sixty, sixth, custom,
4 customeR, costume, gazette, gusset, russet, recites receipts,
5 recede, dispose, expose, gossips, rasps, wasps, hasps, pasch,
6 basks, tasks, dusky, desks, discuss, risks, rusks, hassock,
7 husky, hyssop, pastel, pasture, basic, basset, besot,
8 bestir, tusky, desirous, despair, disburse, duskiness,
9 gesture, reposit, rescue, restoRe, caustic, yeasty.

(*d*) CIRCLE *s* IN MISCELLANEOUS WORDS :—

1 sight, sightless, unsightly, physic, fiscaL, muse, music,
2 musical, excuse, chasms, saRcasm, wisely, sense, senseLess,
3 incense, news, nuisance, series, Saxons, spills, sagacity,
4 satisfy, appetize, scoRe, secuRes, scaRce, scaRcely, silks,
5 suppose, sponge, sadly, salad, satirize, scoops, seediness,
6 service, sincerity, sixpenny, slouches, soups, souRness,
7 spacing, succeeds, suffice, succumbs, surges, syllogism,
8 syllabus, absence, absolve, absorb, advise, anaLyzing,
9 assassin, backslide, canceL, ceiling, damson, demoralize,
10 libellous, lisps, obtuse, uprise, villainous, tyrannize,
11 toilsome, pipe-case, opposing, nominees.

EXERCISE 19.

Circle S and Z (continued).

GRAMMALOGUES.

any, or *in*, *as*, *has*, *is*, *his*, *give*, or *given*, *him*, or *may*, *me*, or *my*, *on*.

See Note at the head of Exercise 18.

1. *Any of my* boys *may give him a* nice slab, if *he* oNLy looks

in at *our* house *on* Tuesday. 2. *I have given* many *a* choice piece away *to the* lads *in the* village. 3. If *he has his* own way, *and* stays *to* take tea, *he may* faiL *to* catch *the* omnibus. 4. *It is* time *to* go now, if *he* desiRes *to* reach *the* castle by six. 5. *As it is, I* feaR *he* may *have to* use *his* top speed, oR *he may* miss *the* bus. 6. *He* seems *to have a* chill ; *he was* sneezing *an hour* ago. 7. If *he* takes *my* advice, *he may be all* right by Saturday. 8. UnLess *he is in* foRm, *he may have to* stay out *of the* team. 9. *In* this case we *may* lose *our* match. 10. *He* takes *a* chill easily ; *he is* so reckless *in his* games. 11. *He is a* superb bat, *and* if *he is in the* team we *may have a* big scoRe. (162)

EXERCISE 20.

Circle S and Z (continued).

See Note at the head of Exercise 18.

1. Keep *the* seal *of* justice *on* thy lips, *and* say no wrong *of* thy fellows. 2. This *is my* advice, *and I* know *it may* save *you* many sorrows. 3. *A* loose tongue *can* easily *give* offence, *as it has given* offence *to* many eRe now. 4. *Any* silly gossip *may* upset *the* wisdom *of a* sage. 5. Decide *to* speak *but* seldom, *and* onLy *in* season. 6. *My* son, Listen *to me, and* take counseL *of him who is* slow *of* speech, *but* fuLL *of* wise maxims. 7. *It may be* amusing, *but it is* unsafe *to* pass *all* youR spaRe time *in* loose reading. 8. *How can* such books *give you* Lessons *in* sagacity ? 9. Do *you* suppose *you can* satisfy youRself *and* absorb wisdom by such reading ? 10. *How* many youths mismanage *and* abuse *the* time they *have to* spaRe by passing *it* away *in the* study *of* fooLish books. 11. *I* beseech *you* resolve now *to* leave such books aLone ! 12. They *can* make *you* no wiser, *and* they *may* disturb youR love *of* genuine reading. 13. Yes, *you may* smile at *the* counseL *you* dislike, *and* say *it is* offensive *to you ; but I* know youR smile *is* onLy *a* sign *of* youR innocence oR youR fancied wisdom, *and I* feeL no annoyance at *it*. (208)

EXERCISE 21.

Circle S and Z (continued).

See Note at the head of Exercise 18.

1. *My* advice *to you and to him is to* peruse youR books slowly, *and give* heed *to the* safe business ruLes *and* maxims *I have given you* both. 2. *I have given the* same counseL *to* Joseph Sparrow, *and he* sHows *his* wisdom by Listening *to me and* following *the* advice *I give him.* 3. At *the* office, *and in* business *hours,* speak onLy *of* business affaiRs. 4. Take heed *of me, and* leave *all* gossip *of* operas, picnics, tennis parties, *and* such like topics *to* youR spaRe time. 5. *To* lounge, *as* some do, *on the* desk, *and* discuss rides aLong *the* Highroads *and* byways *to* lovely villages *and* views *of* rustic beauty, faR outside *the* dismal smoke *of the* city, *is a* loss *of* time, *and it is* nonsense *to* think *you can* make up *the* time *you* lose *in* this way. 6. Besides, *it is an* injustice *to* those *who* pay *you* youR salary. 7. Watch jealously *the* small items; *you can* easily keep *an eye on the* big bills. 8. Satisfy youRself *of the* honesty *of* those customeRs *who* refuse *to* pay ready casH. 9. *A* sleek rogue *has a* way *of* seeming rich, so *as to* hide *his* designs *and* lull *his* victims into *a* faLse security. 10. *A* knave *may* amuse *you on* purpose *to* deceive *you.* (214)

EXERCISE 22.

Circle S and Z (continued).

See Note at the head of Exercise 18.

Joseph Smith.

SiR,—If *you* decide *to* take up *the* agency *to* sell *my* soap *in* youR city, *I* hope *you may* do *an* extensive business. *You can* see *me on* Wednesday *the* 7th, *as* eaRly *in the* day *as you* like. *I have given you* this long notice so *as to give you* nice time *to* get ready. *I* wrote *to the* dealeR *you* spoke *of on* Saturday. *He* says *his* rooms *are* fuLL, *and he has* no space *to* pack *a* solitary box. *He* says if *you* choose *you* may see *him as you* pass *on* Tuesday *the* 10th, *and he may* spaRe *a* few minutes *to* look at youR case *of* soaps. YouRs sincereLy, Maurice Bates. (119)

EXERCISE 23.

Circle S and Z (concluded).

See Note at the head of Exercise 18.

James Mason & Sons.

SiRs,—*In* answer *to* youRs *of* Tuesday, *I have* seen MessRs. Higson *and* Lawson, *of* this city, *but I* am sorry *to* say they refuse *to* buy *any* soap oR soda this time. They say business *is* so slack, *and* money so scaRce, *it is* unsafe *to* buy. I saw this *was an* evasive reason, *given as an* excuse *to* mislead *me and* get rid *of me. I* hope *to* secuRe *the* custom *of* this fiRm *in* time; but *my* feeLings *may have to be* callous, if *I* am *to* succeed. YouRs, Thomas Battison. (98)

EXERCISE 24.

Loops ST and STR.

The loops *st* and *str* follow the same rule of writing as the circle s. The st loop is used finally for either *st* or *zd*. In this exercise, and in Exercises 25 to 29 inclusive, the loops should be employed (in words other than grammalogues) for the representation of the combinations of letters printed in italic. Write *kst* for *-xed*, and *kster* for *-xter*.

(*a*) The Loop *st* used Initially :—

1 *st*op, *st*oppage, *st*upid, *st*upidity, *st*upefy, *st*epson,
2 *st*ub, *st*out, *st*outness, *st*outly, *st*ate, *st*ately, *st*atues, *st*aid,
3 *st*ewed, *st*itches, *st*agey, *st*ucco, *st*ocks, *st*ockade, *st*ags,
4 *st*igma, *st*igmatise, *st*uffy, *st*iffly, *st*iffness, *st*oves, *st*ammeR,
5 *st*eameRs, *st*eamboat, *st*eamsHip, *st*eam-gauge, *st*amina.
6 *st*arch, *st*ench, *st*anza, *st*enciL, *st*ainLess, *st*ingy, *st*inginess,

7 stung, style, stylisH, stoles, stalls, stalled, stolid, stolidly,
8 staR, stoRmy, staRling, staiR, staiRcase, story, storied,
9 storage, sturdy, sturdily, stagnancy, staineR, stalky, staR-
10 gazing, statuRe, status, stealeR, stemless, steRilize, stetho-
11 scope, stirrup, stimulus, stomach, stoneware, stoRk, stud,
12 stuffeR, stultify, stun, stylist, stylus, stop-watch, stoled,
13 stoneR, stillness, stillage, stevedore, stet, stelliFoRm,
14 steerage, stealthily, static, staRlike, staccato.

(*b*) THE LOOP *st* USED FINALLY :—

1 pest, deepest, cheapest, ripest, post, deposed, disposed,
2 exposed, opposed, supposed, appeased, unappeased, beast,
3 biassed, abused, disabused, test, detest, soundest, fastest,
4 slightest, latest, noticed, neatest, fattest, dentist, faddist,
5 saddest, maddest, oldest, boldest, eldest, loudest, widest,
6 induced, reduced, dazed, dozed, chest, joist, rejoiced, just,
7 unjust, adjust, cast, outcast, downcast, encased, boxed,
8 fixed, vexed, mixed, unmixed, caused, accused, excused,
9 guest, biggest, gazed, fast, safest, infest, roughest, fused,
10 diffused, suffused, infused, refused, voiced, invoiced, devised,
11 advised, revised, amethyst, assist, sized, sauced, ceased,
12 soused, zest, mist, pessimist, dismissed, chemist, lamest,
13 topmost, mused, amused, epitomised, victimized,
14 macadamized, apostatized, dogmatized, stigmatized,
15 rhapsodized, catechised, apologized, anaLogized, canonized,
16 latinized, fossiLized, vitalized, vulcanized, anaLyzed,
17 memorized, mesmerized, summarized, authorized, polarized,
18 cauterized, fenced, unfenced, evinced, minced, lanced,
19 balanced, silenced, Licensed, finest, honest, announced,
20 denounced, renounced, lest, palest, tallest, dullest, vilest,
21 solaced, stalest, molest, list, oculist, enList, anaLyst, released,
22 roost, raised, roused, wrist, diarist, aRRest, aRoused, eRased,
23 paRsed, buRst, foRced, enfoRced, endoRsed, unrest, waste,
24 west, south-west, yeast, hypnotized.

(*c*) CIRCLE *s* ADDED TO THE LOOP *st* :—

1 posts, repasts, chests, jests, casts, gusts, fasts, infests,
2 invests, assists, masts, nests, lists, rests, aRRests, buRsts,
3 wastes, apologists, pests, beasts, boasts, texts, tastes, toasts,

dus*ts*, denti*sts*, dive*sts*, dige*sts*, disaffore*sts*, adju*sts*, catechi*sts*, coa*sts*, colori*sts*, gue*sts*, fea*sts*, foi*sts*, fore*sts*, fossiLi*sts*, violini*sts*, satiri*sts*, sophi*sts*, *st*yli*sts*, mole*sts*, manife*sts*, maCHini*sts*, mesmeri*sts*, Methodi*sts*, monopoli*sts*, anaLy*sts*, anatomi*sts*, latini*sts*, aLchemi*sts*, aRchivi*sts*, roo*sts*, reca*sts*, reservi*sts*, rhymi*sts*, hypnoti*sts*.

(*d*) THE LOOP *st* USED MEDIALLY :—

robu*st*ness, methodi*st*ic, fanta*st*ic, te*st*ing, atte*st*ing, dete*st*ing, te*st*ifies, toa*st*ing, toa*st*ing-foRk, adju*st*ing, ju*st*ifies, ju*st*ness, eulogi*st*ic, va*st*ness, ve*st*ry, enLi*st*ing, ela*st*ic, ineLa*st*ic, logi*st*ic, syllogi*st*ic, pugili*st*ic, la*st*ingLy, bapti*st*ery, boa*st*ingLy, denti*st*ic, dige*st*ing, di*st*ich, je*st*ing, je*st*ingLy, sugge*st*ing, joi*st*ing, ju*st*ifieR, te*st*ifieR, schoLa*st*ic, sophi*st*ry, sugge*st*ive, sugge*st*ively.

(*e*) THE LOOP *str* :—

pe*ster*, pe*ster*s, tip*ster*, tip*ster*s, Web*ster*, alaba*ster*, lob*ster*s, atte*ster*, ta*ster*s, road*ster*, road*ster*s, Che*ster*, Manche*ster*, Winche*ster*, Ilche*ster*, ju*ster*, adju*ster*, sugge*ster*, sugge*ster*s, regi*ster*, coa*ster*, ca*stor*s, Donca*ster*, Ba*xter*, de*xter*, fo*ster*, fe*ster*s, inve*stor*, ma*ster*, payma*ster*, sHipma*ster*s, taskma*ster*, riding-ma*ster*, mu*ster*, team*ster*, team*ster*s, deem*ster*, bani*ster*, cani*ster*s, sini*ster*, min*ster*, Beamin*ster*, Axmin*ster*, Westmin*ster*, mon*ster*s, Mun*ster*, ance*stor*, ance*stor*s, song*ster*s, pila*ster*, bol*ster*s, malt*ster*, Ul*ster*, la*ster*, lu*stre*s, roo*ster*, barri*ster*, chori*ster*s, fore*ster*, aRRe*ster*, buR*ster*, Worce*ster*, Huck*ster*, Huck*ster*s.

EXERCISE 25.

Loops ST and STR (continued).

GRAMMALOGUES.

first, *put*, *shall*, *should* (up), *them*, *these*, *this*, *those*.

See Note at the head of Exercise 24.

1. *You should put* youR visitor *first, and* youRself la*st*.
2. *This is the* be*st* way, *and those who* refuse *to* follow *it* mu*st*

be stupid. 3. Who shall teach them these rules of the feast? 4. I suggest some robust, pugilistic master of the customs of society, who is heedless of the stare of those opposed to him. 5. Should he excite a feeling of the deepest disgust in those he teaches, they can scarcely dare to molest so stout a fellow, lest they may be chastised. 6. The master of the steamship "Manchester" is just now on a visit to Winchester. 7. He is a shipmaster of rare skill, and has carried many cargoes in sailing vessels, steamers and coasters, since he first took to the sea. 8. Centuries ago, in the days of masts and sails, ere the power of steam was forced into the service of the sailor, his ancestors were stout masters of ships, and fearless sailors on the stormy seas. 9. The master of the "Manchester" says his ship is the finest and fastest vessel out of Belfast. 10. She must be a masterpiece of speed and beauty, if she is all he says she is. 11. It may be he boasts, like most sailors, of the ship he loves. 12. He is an honest fellow, of rare stamina; stout of limb and capacious of chest, and I should say he has no unmanly fear of the many perils of the sea. (236)

EXERCISE 26.

Loops ST and STR (continued).

See Note at the head of Exercise 24.

1. You should put no faith in the stories of a boaster. 2. He has an elastic tongue, and to bolster up his tales and make a stir, he stops at no barefaced lie. 3. He likes to see modest folk amazed or amused at his recitals, and he is rejoiced if he is noticed. 4. He is master of the loudest and fastest style of speech, and he feels the deepest disgust if his stale stories are refused. 5. In fact, he soon stops his stupid tales if you cease to admire them. 6. This is the best way to stem the talk of these silly fellows. 7. As you have noticed, those sturdy heroes who have calmly gazed into the eyes of some savage monster of the forest, or who have faced death on the storm tossed sea,

are most modest in speech. 8. If you ask them to state some of the sights they have seen, they desire to be excused; and if at last they are roused into speech, they give the story in an honest, but summarized, form. 9. It is the boaster who is the first to speak, and the last to stop. 10. He talks of his supposed abilities; of his ancestors, and the lustre they shed on his name; of his perilous voyages to the west coast; of his guests and his jests; of his tastes and distastes; and so on. 11. He has a store of stories, and he gives you no rest. 12. He is a nuisance at any feast or party, and we shall be best advised if we leave him alone. (261)

EXERCISE 27.

Loops ST and STR (continued).

See Note at the head of Exercise 24.

1. We shall first take the boys to the dentist, who should have seen them long ago. 2. Those who took charge of them should have seen to this; but the teeth of poor lads like these are seldom seen to in time. 3. May I suggest the dentist who lives in the last house in Stanley Avenue? 4. He seems a nice fellow, who may be supposed to know his business thoroughly. 5. His eldest son hopes to be a barrister some day. 6. I can testify to the son's taste in books, as I have sold him dozens of the best volumes. 7. He detests the cheap nasty styles, and selects those likely to last longest. 8. James Chester, who was his headmaster a long time since, says he tantalized and victimized some of the fellows. 9. If so, he shows a change now. 10. I can scarcely take in such a story. 11. If he were guilty of this shabbiness in the past, he has renounced his errors, and is now thoroughly honest, and liked by all who know him. 12. We hope he may succeed in the tests he has to face, and be first in the pass list. (191)

EXERCISE 28.

Loops ST and STR (continued.)

See Note at the head of Exercise 24.

Thomas Simi*ster*.

SiR,—We *are in* receipt *of* youRs *of the* 4th, *and shall put the* te*st* case *to* MessRs. Ba*xter and* Web*ster*, ju*st in the* way *you* desiRe. We hope *to* see *them on* Wednesday, *and should* they sugge*st any* change *in the st*yle *of the* foRm we *shall* write *you on* Saturday at *the* late*st*. *As* soon *as* we *have* fi*xed* up *this* business *to* suit *you*, we *should* like *to have* youR views *on the* case *of* MessRs. *St*ead *and St*eel. We scaRcely know *how to* manage *these* folk. They *are* aRous*ed* at *the* lea*st* annoyance. They *have* tantali*zed* us *the* la*st* six months. They seek *to* induce us *to* receive back *those st*aiR-rods *you* sold *them in* Augu*st*. We *have* refu*sed to* do so, *and the* invoice *is st*ill unpaid. We *shall* po*st you our* monthly summary *of* sales *on* Saturday. YouRs, De*xter & Fo*ster*. (150)

EXERCISE 29.

Loops ST and STR (concluded).

See Note at the head of Exercise 24.

MessRs. Schu*ster &* Sons.

SiRs,—We *have to*-day invoic*ed the* la*st of the st*uffs *you* bought *in* May, *and shall* sHip *them* by *the st*eamsHip "Duke *of* Mun*ster*," sailing *on the first of* Augu*st*. *The st*yles *are all* new, *and the* be*st to be* got at *the* exceedingLy low sum *you* were dispo*sed to* pay. We sincereLy hope *the* sales *may* ju*st*ify *our* choice *of* designs. We *shall* regi*ster the* new designs *of* ladies' capes, *as you* sugge*st*. YouRs, *St*ubbs & Mawson.

(82)

EXERCISE 30.

Circles SW and SS or SZ.

These circles follow the same rules of writing as the circle *s*. In this exercise, and in Exercises 31 to 35 inclusive, the large circles should be employed (in words other than grammalogues) for the combinations of letters printed in italic. *k-ses* should be written for *-xes*. Note paragraphs (*e*) and (*f*).

(*a*) THE *sw* CIRCLE:—

*Sw*eep, *sw*eeps, *sw*eepstake, *sw*op, *sw*ipe, *sw*ab, *sw*eat, *sw*eets, *sw*eetish, *sw*eetest, *sw*eetly, *sw*eetness, *sw*eet-smelling, *sw*ayed, *Sw*ede, *Sw*edish, *sw*addle, *sw*addling, *sw*itches, *sw*age, *Su*akim, *sw*ag, *sw*igs, *sw*iftest, *su*ave, *su*avely, *su*avity, *su*avify, *sw*athes, *Sw*iss, *sw*iSH, *sw*aSH, *sw*um, *sw*immeRs, *sw*ans, *sw*ains, *sw*ooning, *sw*ine, *sw*iniSH, *sw*inge, *sw*ings, *sw*ingeR, *sw*ung, *sw*ells, *sw*eal, *sw*ealing, *sw*allows, *sw*allowed, *sw*allowtail, *sw*illed, *sw*aRm, *sw*eaR, *sw*iRl, *sw*iRled, *sw*iRling, *Sw*iRe, *sw*arth, *sw*arthy, *sw*arthily.

(*b*) THE CIRCLE *ss* USED FINALLY:—

po*ses*, oppo*ses*, depo*ses*, dispo*ses*, expo*ses*, suppo*ses*, repo*ses*, lap*ses*, relap*ses*, collap*ses*, enti*ces*, addu*ces*, indu*ces*, redu*ces*, godde*sses*, cha*ses*, jui*ces*, a*xes*, bo*xes*, ta*xes*, parado*xes*, fi*xes*, ve*xes*, si*xes*, se*xes*, HOa*xes*, mi*xes*, ga*ses*, ga*zes*, gui*ses*, disgui*ses*, fa*ces*, pale-fa*ces*, surfa*ces*, offi*ces*, suffi*ces*, vi*ces*, advi*ces*, devi*ses*, novi*ces*, revi*ses*, si*zes*, assi*zes*, sau*ces*, cea*ses*, sou*ses*, mi*sses*, mu*ses*, ma*sses*, ma*ces*, mo*sses*, oun*ces*, denoun*ces*, announ*ces*, allowan*ces*, fen*ces*, evin*ces*, essen*ces*, min*ces*, lan*ces*, balan*ces*, silen*ces*, sen*ses*, roman*ces*, la*ces*, pala*ces*, chali*ces*, sola*ces*, mola*sses*, lea*ses*, relea*ses*, la*sses*, lo*sses*, lo*ses*, ra*ces*, terra*ces*, care*sses*, choru*ses*, rou*ses*, carou*ses*, ru*ses*, peru*ses*, ro*ses*, ri*ses*, authori*zes*, mesmeri*zes*, aRi*ses*, eRa*ses*, foR*ces*, faR*ces*, hou*ses*, noti*ces*, spi*ces*.

(*c*) THE VOWEL SIGN SHOULD BE PLACED WITHIN THE LARGE CIRCLE IN THE FOLLOWING AND SIMILAR WORDS:—

ap*sis*, adipo*sis*, synop*sis*, ellip*sis*, ba*sis*, exege*sis*, a*xis*,

2 ALe*x*is, phas*is*, emphas*is*, thes*is*, parenthes*is*, parenthes*es*,
3 synthes*is*, phthis*is*, Nemes*is*, diagnos*is*, amanuens*is*,
4 Genes*is*, paralys*is*, anaLys*is*, dialys*is*, pyros*is*, soros*is*,
5 amauros*is*, dieres*is*, laps*us*, Petas*us*, Pegas*us*, ne*x*us,
6 cens*us*, Parnass*us*, Bonass*us*, Caucas*us*, Coloss*us*, Moloss*us*,
7 Te*x*as, Kans*as*, ARkans*as*, exer*cis*e, exer*cis*es, empha*sis*e,
8 empha*sis*es.

(*d*) THE CIRCLE *ss* USED MEDIALLY :—

1 po*ssess*ive, po*ssess*oR, po*ssess*ory, sub*sis*t, de*sis*t,
2 in*sis*t, re*sis*t, re*sis*teR, re*sis*tless, Atti*cis*m, Scotti*cis*m,
3 scholasti*cis*m, fanati*cis*m, Agnosti*cis*m, asceti*cis*m,
4 mysti*cis*m, monasti*cis*m, exoti*cis*m, witti*cis*m, sole*cis*m,
5 catholi*cis*m, paro*x*ysm, lyri*cis*m, e*xcess*ive, e*xcess*ively,
6 ac*cess*ible, inac*cess*ible, ac*cess*ory, suc*cess*ive, suc*cess*ively,
7 suc*cess*or, e*xhaus*t, e*xhaus*tless, ne*cess*ary, ne*cess*ariLy,
8 ne*cess*itous, de*cis*ive, de*cis*ively, de*cis*iveness, inde*cis*ive,
9 in*cis*ive, exer*cis*ed, exer*cis*ing, exer*cis*er, exer*cis*able,
10 empha*sis*ing, empha*sis*ed, Mi*ssiss*ippi, misspell,
11 misspelling, miscite.

In the following words the small circle and the stroke *s* (or *z*), *not* the large circle *ss*, should be employed to represent the letters printed in italic.

1 (*e*) posse*ss*, reposse*ss*, disposse*ss*, posse*sses*, posse*ss*ing,
2 abs*cess*, abs*cess*es, abs*ciss*, dis*ease*, dis*eas*es, dis*use*, mis*use*,
3 ac*cess*, e*xcess*, e*xcess*es, e*xcis*e, e*xcis*ing, e*xcis*able,
4 catholi*cis*e, itali*cis*e, Mos*es*, Ulyss*es*.

Write the stroke *s* and the small circle (or loop) to represent the letters italicized in the following words.

1 (*f*) de*cease*, de*ceased*, dio*cese*, dio*ces*an, tars*us*, re*cess*,
2 re*cessed*, ni*cest*, an*cestor*, an*cestors*, in*cis*e, in*cised*, in*cis*ing,
3 exor*cis*e, exor*cist*, exor*cised*, exor*cis*eR, roman*cist*,
4 exor*cis*m, laconi*cis*m, Pars*ees*, poli*cies*, jealous*ies*, falla*cies*,
5 Phari*sees*, Ma*ssey's*, mer*cies*, Morri*ssey's*, agen*cies*, myo*sis*,
6 un*ceas*ing, gyp*sies*, La*cey's* (upward *l*), Lu*cy's* (upward *l*),
7 lega*cies*, purs*ues*, tiss*ues*.

EXERCISE 31.

Circles SW and SS or SZ (continued).

GRAMMALOGUES.

Lord, *thing*, *think*.

See Note at the head of Exercise 30.

1. *Lord Sw*ainson seems *to think it* necessary *to* exer*c*ise *the* muscles *of his* aRms daily by *swinging on a* baR. 2. *He* does *this to* keep up *the* skiLL *he* possesses *as a swi*mmeR. 3. *I have* seen *him in the sw*elling sea, though *the* tide *was* at *its sw*iftest at *the* time. 4. *I think he* abus*es* oR misus*es his* poweRs by exer*c*ising *them to* excess. 5. *This is a* fooLish *thing to* do, *but I* feaR many *a* youth *who* rejoi*ces in his* skiLL *in* bodily exer*cises* expos*es his* life *to* risk *in the* same way. 6. *A* boy *may* easily *exhaust his* bodily poweRs by ex*ce*ssive exer*cises*. 7. *He* seldom paus*es to think*, *but* ruSHes heedlessly into *the* game, *sw*ayed by *the* voi*ces of those who* ask *him to* do *this* silly *thing*, *as it* amus*es them*. 8. *He is* fuLL *of* excus*es to* go *to the* ra*ces* at *the swi*mming bath. 9. *He sw*allows *his* toast hurriedly, *and swi*gs off *his* tea, so *as to be in* time. 10. *He* choos*es to* re*sis*t advice, *and* refus*es to* Listen *to* reason now; *but* some day *he may have to sw*allow many nasty dos*es of* physic—*the* wages *of his* folly. 11. Nois*es in the* head; *sw*ellings *and* abscess*es in the* neck; oR paraly*sis of the* muscles —*may* follow excess *in swi*mming *and* such like exer*cises*. 12. *I should* like *to* empha*sis*e *this* Lesson, *but I think I have* said enough *to* induce *you to* de*sis*t if *you are* guilty *of* ex*ce*ssively exer*cis*ing youRself *in any* game. 13. If ne*cess*ity aRi*ses I shall* resume *the* Lesson *in a* month. (259)

EXERCISE 32.

Circles SW and SS or SZ (continued).

See Note at the head of Exercise 30.

1. *I think the sw*arthy *lord who* possesses so many hous*es in our* village *should* make *them* nicer. 2. *The* cost *of the*

hous*es* *is* ex*c*es*s*ive, *in* view *of the* small size *of the* rooms. 3. *The* best *and* nicest *of them all is* faR below *the* right size. 4. *I* must see *him, and*, if necessary, *I shall* insi*s*t *on a* deci*s*ive answer *to my* appeal. 5. *I should* like *to sw*eep some *of the* hous*es* into *the* sea. 6. *It exhaus*ts *my* patience *to* see so suc*cess*fuL *a* fellow re*s*i*s*t so foRcible *an* appeal. 7. *His su*avity *and sw*eetness *of* voice at *the* time *of* refusaL onLy emphasi*s*es *my* annoyance. 8. *It* surpass*es me to* know *how* so nice *a* style *can* wrap up such ex*cess*ively pooR feeLings. 9. *The thing is* amazing. 10. *I* must *sw*allow *my* annoyance, *and* ask *the sw*eet voiced pos*sess*oR *of* riches *to* take *a* cens*us* *of the* pooR folk *who* live *in his* hous*es*, *and to* notice *the* small size *of the* rooms they sleep *in*. 11. *He who is the* pos*sess*oR *of a* castle, *can* scaRcely faiL *to* see *how* necessary *it is to have* pooR folk rightly housed. 12. UnLess *he* choos*es to* do *the* right *thing, he shall be* exposed. 13. *I shall* sHow *how this lord* dispos*es of the* pooR fellows *who* reside *in his* hous*es*.

(215)

EXERCISE 33.

Circles SW and SS or SZ (continued).

See Note at the head of Exercise 30.

1. Ne*cess*ity, *it is* said, knows no law; *but this* excuse *may be* refused, *and he who* relies *on it may be* sorry. 2. *I think* excus*es* like *this are* abused *in* many cas*es*; *and* so *in* cas*es* *of* genuine ne*cess*ity, *those who* make *them are* unsuc*cess*fuL. 3. *The* lazy fellow pos*sess*es *a* stoRe *of* lame excus*es*, *and who can* ex*haus*t *them?* 4. If *the* attack *is* suc*cess*fuL, *and our* fellows get amongst *the* enemy, we *may* scoRe *a* deci*s*ive victory, *and* so cause *the* enemy *to* retiRe. 5. SiR Thomas Guest announc*es the* refusaL *of the* aRmy authorities *to* abolish *the* use *of* lanc*es in the* aRmy. 6. Many *think it was* fooLish *to* sugge*s*t such *a thing* at *all*. 7. *The sw*allow *is* said *to* pick up *a* stone *on the* sHoRe *of the* sea, *and* by *its* poweR *to* restoRe sight *to the sw*allows still *in the* nest. 8. *It is* also said *to be a* lucky *thing to have a sw*allow's nest by *the* side *of a* house.

9. *These* fooLish sayings *are sw*allowed by many *who* refuse *to have* faith *in* sensible tenets. 10. *The swan is* supposed by some folk *to* pouR forth *the* most lovely music *in the* last few minutes *of its* life, eRe *it* ceas*es to* ex*ist*. 11. *The* song *of the* singing *swan is* supposed *to be a* sign *of a* thaw. 12. *The* name *of* "The *Sweet Swan*" *was given to* sHakspere by Jonson. 13. *Have you* read *the* story *of* "*The Sw*iss Family Robinson"? (243)

EXERCISE 34.

Circles SW and SS or SZ (continued).

See Note at the head of Exercise 30

Thomas *Swain.*

SIR,—We *have the* invoic*es of the* sixty cas*es of sw*eets *to*-day, *and as the* "*Lord of the* Isles" *is* due *to* aRRive *on* Wednesday *the* 10th, we *shall* hope *to* receive *the things in* time *to* suit *our* purpose. We *think the* new style *of* box*es is* likely *to* catch *on*. *Our* customeRs emphas*is*e *the* nece*ss*ity *of* change *in the* style *of these* packages. They say *it* amus*es the* buyeRs, *and* entic*es them to* buy. Business *in Sw*iss *sw*eets *is* e*xcess*ively slow just now; *but all our* sauc*es are* selling niceLy. YouRs, Davis & *Sw*iRes. (98)

EXERCISE 35.

Circles SW and SS or SZ (concluded).

See Note at the head of Exercise 30.

Joseph Chester.

SIR,—*In* answer *to* youRs *of the* 6th, we *think our* heavy *losses in the* past six months were due *to* such caus*es as the* failuRe *of* MessRs. *Swan and Sw*ales, *of Sw*ansea; *the* un*necessar*iLy heavy costs *of our* agencies *in* Winchester, Don-caster, *and* Chester; *and the* unsu*ccess*fuL scheme *of* bonus*es to* customeRs. *The first* aLone cost us *a* big sum. *As to the* remedy, *Lord* Stockdale *can* onLy counseL *the* exer*cise of* patience just now. *He thinks the* new season *may be* just *as* succ*essfu*L *as the* last *was* pooR, *and he* hopes *to* see heavy balan*ces in* August. We hope *in* due time *to* satisfy *all the* investors *in the* fiRm. YouRs sinceReLy, Silvester Mosley. 119)

EXERCISE 36.

Vowels and S and T.

Vowels cannot be placed to a circle or loop; so that a stroke must be written when it is necessary to place a vowel to a consonant. In this exercise, and in Exercises 37 to 41 inclusive, the italic type (in words other than grammalogues) indicates that the letter must be expressed by a stroke consonant.

1 (*a*) *a*ss, *a*sp, *a*sbes*t*os, *a*ci*d*s, *a*ci*d*ness, *a*ssaye*d*, *a*skew,
2 *a*ssess, *a*ssessed, *a*ssessable, *a*ssessoR, *a*ssassin, *a*ssist,
3 *a*ssists, *a*ssize, *a*ssizeR, *A*ssam, *a*ssume, *a*ssuming, un-
4 *a*ssuming, *a*ssumeR, *a*ssignee, *a*ssignoR, *a*ssailed, *a*ssaileR,
5 *a*ssailing, *a*slope, *a*sylum, *e*spy, *e*spouse, *e*spoused,
6 *e*spousing, *e*spousal, *e*ssaye*d*, *e*ssaying, *e*schew, *e*scape,
7 *e*scapade, *e*scalade, *E*skimo, *e*ssence, *i*ssue, *i*ssue*d*,
8 *i*ssueR, *e*ase, *e*asiness, une*a*siness, une*a*sily, *e*ye-salve,
9 *e*ye-service, *e*yesoRe, *I*sabel, *I*saac, *I*sis, *I*slam, *O*use,
10 *u*se, *u*seless, *u*selessly, *u*seR, *u*sing, *u*surp, *u*sury.
1 (*b*) *s*ay, *s*ays, *s*ea, *s*eas, *s*ea-pie, *s*ea-dog, *s*eacoast, *s*ea-king,
2 *s*ea-gull, *s*ea-side, *s*easick, *s*easickness, *s*ea-mew, *s*ea-mouse,
3 *s*ea-leveL, *s*ea-room, sys*t*yle, *s*ece*d*e, *s*ece*d*ing, sui*c*i*d*e,
4 sui*c*i*d*al, *c*ease, *c*eased, *c*easing, un*c*easing, un*c*easingLy,
5 *s*uspire, *s*uspiring, *sc*issoRs, *s*aw, *s*awdust, *s*awing, *s*auce,
6 *s*auced, *s*aucing, *s*auciness, *s*aucily, *s*ausage, *s*ocie*t*y,
7 *s*ou, *sc*ia*t*ic, *S*iam, *S*iamese, *sc*iences, *sc*ien*t*ists, *s*igh,
8 *s*ighing, *s*igheR, *s*ize, *s*izing, *s*izeR, *s*ouse, *s*oused, *s*ousing,
9 *s*ue, *s*ueR, *s*uing, *s*ue*t*, *s*ue*t*y, *S*owerby, *z*ebu, *Z*ebedee,
10 *Z*achary, *z*any, *Z*eno, *Z*anzibar, *z*enana, *z*inc, *z*inco,
11 *z*ealous, *z*ealously, *z*ealotism, *Z*ulu, *Z*urich, *Z*erxes.
1 (*c*) po*s*y, top*s*y, autop*s*y, tip*s*y, gyp*s*y, papa*c*y, apos*t*a*c*y,
2 ex*t*a*s*y, pur*s*y, pur*s*ue, Pud*s*ey, abba*c*y, celiba*c*y, bas*s*o,

Bessie, Betsy, busy, daisy, di*zz*y, Do*x*ey, Dicksee, gala*x*y, Casey, efficacy, Tennessee, decency, regency, obs*t*inacy, endorsee, Jessie, juicy, gassy, legacy, aRgosy, gau*z*y, fussy, fusee, farcy, Pharisee, foresee, Mounsey, Nancy, Licensee, lessee, Eli*z*a, Elsie, Kelsey, policy, palsy, jealousy, col*z*a, fallacy, Swansea, saucy, so-so, Assisi, Massey, mossy, mercy, noisy, lacy, la*z*y, la*z*iness, la*z*ily, racy, piracy, curacy, accuracy, inaccuracy, rosy.

(*d*) pious, piously, tenuous, tumultuous, tortuous, deci*d*uous, joyousness, joyously, exiguous, fatuous, vacuous, assi*d*uous, sinuous, nocuous, ingenuous, iRRiguous, Genoese, Judaize, sinuose, voltaism.

(*e*) pas*t*y, pas*t*el, pas*t*ime, pas*t*ure, pas*t*urage, parasi*t*e, parrici*d*e, parrici*d*al, pauci*t*y, opposi*t*e, posse*t*, pos*t*eri*t*y, pis*t*ol, epis*t*olary, porosi*t*y, besi*d*e, besi*d*es, bas*t*ile, bes*t*ir, insi*d*e, resi*d*e, deci*d*e, busie*d*, textua*r*y, tas*t*y, tas*t*ily, taci*t*ly, deci*d*es, tenaci*t*y, audaci*t*y, densi*t*y, feroci*t*y, voraci*t*y, veraci*t*y, vivaci*t*y, immensi*t*y, Jesui*t*, ges*t*ure, exi*t*, fixi*t*y, laxi*t*y, six*t*y, fixe*d*ly, Cas*t*ile, cus*t*om, cus*t*ody, caus*t*ic, Augus*t*us, fes*t*al, fis*t*ic, fis*t*ula, fus*t*y, bese*t*, gusse*t*, offse*t*, face*t*, inse*t*, dulce*t*, lance*t*, russe*t*, rese*t*, rose*tt*e, decei*t*, receip*t*, ves*t*al, ves*t*u*r*e, vis*t*a, mas*t*ic, mys*t*ic, mis*t*ook, mis*t*ime, meso*t*ype, mis*t*each, mis*t*y, mus*t*y, mus*t*ily, mus*t*ache, nas*t*y, dynas*t*y, dishones*t*y, ins*t*il, ins*t*all, dis*t*il, lis*t*el, luci*d*, luci*d*ly, pelluci*d*, policie*d*, palsie*d*, callosi*t*y, felici*t*y, solici*t*, lici*t*, elici*t*, lawsui*t*, pursui*t*, nonsui*t*, reci*t*e, reci*t*al, res*t*oRe, rosie*d*, rus*t*ic, rus*t*iness, res*t*y, rece*d*e, revisi*t*, waysi*d*e, s*t*udy, s*t*eady, s*t*eadily.

EXERCISE 37.

Vowels and S and T (continued).

GRAMMALOGUES.

so, us, see, use, use, whose, which.

See Note at the head of Exercise 36.

1. UnLess we *use our* mental poweRs daily they *may* get

rus*t*y, *so to* speak, *and* become *use*less *to us*. 2. We *can* easily *see how* necessary *it is to* exercise *our* bodily muscles if we desiRe *to* keep them *in a* right sta*t*e, *and it is* just *as* necessary *to use our* mental foRces if *these are to be* rightly balanced. 3. We *are* amazed *to see how* easy seveRe musculaR exercises *are to those whose* cus*t*om *it is to* keep *in* *f*oRm by exercising *a* few minutes each day. 4. Some folk say they *see* no *use in* exercises *which* cause *the* sweat *to* ooze ; *but this is an* injus*t*ice *to those* robust fellows *who* indulge *in* such exercises, *and* they *are* both fooLish *and* lazy *who* speak *in this* way. 5. They *should have the* audaci*t*y *to* renounce such views, *and* seek *to* escape *an* eaRly death by zealously exercising *the* mental *and* bodily poweRs *which the Lord has given them*. 6. *I* hope *you can* now *see how* suicidal *it is to* allow *the* senses *to* rust. 7. S*t*udy *may be* unnecessary *in* youR case ; *but you can* easily take up some science *as a* pas*t*ime oR hobby. 8. *It may be of use to you* some day, if *you* deci*d*e *to* pursue *it* thoroughly. 9. Busy folk pass *the* most joyous lives. 10. *It is the* lazy, tipsy fellows *who see* no *use in* socie*t*y *and its* laws. (233)

EXERCISE 38.

Vowels and S and T (continued).

See Note at the head of Exercise 36.

1. *He who* hopes *to* succeed *in* science must *use his* time wisely. 2. *The* boy *who* wastes *his* minutes *can have* no success *in* s*t*udy. 3. *You can* easily *see how* necessary *it is to have* tenaci*t*y *and* fixi*t*y *of* purpose, if *you are to* make headway *in the* career *to which you have* se*t* youRself. 4. *Which of us can* hope *to* leave *a* legacy *of* wis*d*om *to our* fellows, unLess we make *a* right *use of our* time now ? 5. *Whose* names *are* most likely *to* last, *and whose* memories *are* most likely *to* live *in the* ages still *to* come ? 6. *It can* scaRcely *be* necessary *to* sta*t*e *the* answer. 7. If *you are* sincere *in* youR desiRe *to* enjoy *the* felici*t*y *which* comes *to the* possessoR *of* wis*d*om, *you* must watch jealously *the* minutes *you give to* youR pas*t*imes.

8. *You may* easily *be* carried into fooLish ways. 9. *You* know, *the* six*t*y minutes *in an hour* soon pass by; *so you* must bes*t*ir youRself, oR *the* time *may be* lost *to you.* 10. *See how* lazy Ezra Sowerby passed *his* time, *and how* fieRcely *he* now denounces *his* own idleness. 11. Beware, also, *of the* fallacies *which may* lie *in the* spicy sayings *of those who* pose *as* witty fellows. 12. Wis*d*om seldom speaks *to us* by *a* noisy tongue. 13. *The* wise Zeno, *it is* said, bit off *his* tongue lest *he should be* foRced *to* reveaL *to his* enemies *the* names *of those of his* party *who* sough*t to* cast off *the* yoke *of* tyranny *and* injus*t*ice. (253)

EXERCISE 39.

Vowels and S and T (continued).

See Note at the head of Exercise 36.

1. Tools *which* lie idle soon rust; *but those which you use* daily *can* scaRcely get rus*t*y. 2. *The use you* make *of them* keeps *the* steel polished. 3. *It is* just *the* same *in* youR case; if *you* rest *a* long time *you may* get both rus*t*y *and* lazy. 4. *The* busy master *of the* faRm visi*t*s no feast *in* gus*t*y March, lest *he should see his* family foRced *to* fast *in* heavy August. 5. FooLish cus*t*oms *have* no poweR *to* tie *us; so you should* cast *them* away. 6. *He who* aspires *to* success must toil unceasingLy. 7. *He* must *be* assiduous *in all his* tasks; seize *the* right time to buy oR sell, *and use it in the* right way. 8. *The first* stone *of the* spiRe *was* laid at *the* bottom. 9. Delays *may* make *us* tes*t*y, *but* they also make *us* wise. 10. *He whose* house *is* rightly looked *to has an* asylum *of* rest *to which he may* retiRe *as* soon *as his* day's toil *is* o'eR. 11. If *it is* youR honest purpose *to* assist *in* raising *those who* reside *in the* slums *of the* city, *you should first* do youR best *to* raise youRself *in* socie*t*y. 12. If *you* desiRe *to be* wise, *be* ready *to* ask *of those who can* answer *you.* 13. *An* Eskimo oR *a* Zulu *may* know just *the things you* seek *to* know. 14. *The* master *of* science *should be* zealous *but* modest; *in all his* wis*d*om *he* onLy knows *a* few *things* out *of* many. 15. Besi*d*es, modes*t*y si*t*s

easily *on all of us.* 16. *It is* silly *to* suppose we *can be* wise unLess we read *and* study *the* best books. 17. *It is* easy *to* rest; *but is it as* easy *to* fast? 18. *The* beeR *the* idle fellow swallows *so* readily soon usurps *his* senses, *and* leaves *him* like *a* beast. 19. Decide now *to be* zealous; *you have* dozed long enough. (310)

EXERCISE 40.

Vowels and S and T (continued).

See Note at the head of Exercise 36.

Ezra Mounsey.

SiR,—YouRs *of the* 6th. If *you can* manage *to see us* we *can* easily *give you a* Lesson *in the use of the* scissoRs *and* saws. We must ask *you to* buy youR own wood, *as is the* custom. If *you are* zealous, *you should* know *how to use all the* tools *in a* month at *the* outside. We make no *use of the* saw-dust, *but* just cast *it* aside. *It* seems *to us a* waste *of* time *to* seek *to* utilise *the* refuse. *Give us a* few days' notice *of the* date *of* youR visit, *and* say *which* bench *you* desiRe *to use, so as to* save time. *Which is the* best book *to* buy *you?* YouRs sincereLy, Isaac West & Sons. (126)

EXERCISE 41.

Vowels and S and T (concluded).

See Note at the head of Exercise 36.

Augustus Doxey.

SiR,—We *think you should* ask MessRs. Sowerby *and* Massey, *of the* Essex Mills, *to* allow *you to see the* saws *as* they revolve at *the* fastest rate. We assume *you* know *this* fiRm. *This is a* slack season at *the* mills, *and is* just *the* time *to* suit *them.* Go *and see which* day they choose. They *may*, also, sHow *you the use of the* small saws. We *think* Saturday *is a* busy day, *and you should* leave *it* out. *Who* sHowed *you how to* remove *the* aci*d* stains *which we* saw *on* your chisel ? We must get *you to give us the* remedy. Some *of our* best knives *are* rus*t*y. YouRs sincereLy, Kelsey & Sims. (119)

EXERCISE 42.

Contractions.

altogether, *together*, *anything*, *nothing*, *something*, *architect-ure-al*, *object*, *subject*, *respect-ed*, *expect-ed*, *unexpected-ly*, *public-sh-ed*, *republic*, *catholic*, *uniform-ity*, *unanimous* or *unanimity*, *yesterday*.

1. *The unanimity of the* vote *to* raise *the* salary *of our* city *architect was altogether unexpected—I expected something of a* scene *in the* counciL ; *but nothing was* said by *those who* were *expected to* oppose *the* vote. 2. *The unanimity of the* vote sHows *a uniform* desiRe *to* repay *his* services *to the public.* 3. *The uniformity of his* life, besides *his* genuine ability, *was the* reason *of* such *a unanimous* vote. 4. *He has* rare *architectural* ability, *and the public* seem *to* know *it.* 5. *He has* just *published a* book *on* "*The Public Architecture of* America," *and he expects to publish his* new "Lessons *in Architectural* Design" eaRly *in* May. 6. *I* know scaRcely *anything of the subject of architecture ; but I* am *catholic* enough *in my* views *to respect* High ability *in* anybody, though *I object to the* fellow *who* boasts *of his* skiLL *in any subject.* 7. *I* faiL *to see how* such *a* fellow *can expect to be respected.* 8. *The architect and I are to* go *to* Italy *together in the* autumn. 9. We were *to have* paid *a* visit *to the* new *public* baths *yesterday, but* were *unexpectedly* foRced *to put it* off. 10. *I expect* we *shall* manage *to* go *on* Wednesday. (202)

EXERCISE 43.

Hook L added to Straight Letters.

Hook *l*, added to straight letters, is written towards the left. In this Exercise, and in Exercises 44 to 50 inclusive, the double consonants *pl*, *pr*, etc., should be employed (in words other than grammalogues or contractions) for the representation of the letters printed in italic type.

(*a*) *Pl*, ETC., USED INITIALLY :—

1 *pl*ay, *pl*ace, *pl*acing, *pl*aced, *pl*aces, *pl*aster, *pl*eased,
2 *pl*easantest, *pl*acid, *pl*acidly, *pl*aceR, *Pl*ato, *pl*ayed,
3 *pl*edge, *pl*ucky, *pl*ague, *pl*uSH, *pl*ume, *pl*unge,
4 *pl*ough, *pl*ougheR, *pl*eura, *pl*eurisy, *pl*uraL, ap*pl*aud,
5 ap*pl*ausive, ap*pl*y, *bl*ow, *bl*ob, *bl*ot, *bl*eat, *bl*otchy,
6 *bl*ock, *bl*eak, *bl*ackberry, *bl*uffy, *bl*ithe, *bl*ithely,
7 *bl*ouse, *bl*azeR, *bl*azing, *bl*ast, *bl*essedly, *bl*aspheme, *bl*uster,
8 *bl*uSH, *bl*ame, *bl*ameless, *bl*uR, a*bl*aze, a*bl*y, *cl*aw, *cl*ap, *cl*ip,
9 *cl*ub, *cl*ad, *Cl*yde, *cl*oudy, *cl*oudily, *cl*oudiness, *cl*utch,
10 *cl*ack, *cl*ick, *cl*ock, o'*cl*ock, *cl*uck, *cl*ucked, *cl*og, *Cl*egg,
11 *cl*oth, *cl*othing, *cl*ass, *cl*asp, *cl*assed, *cl*asses, *cl*assic, *cl*assify,
12 *cl*oser, *cl*osely, *cl*oister, *cl*usters, *cl*aSH, *cl*ammy, *cl*amorous,
13 *cl*anniSH, *cl*owniSH, *cl*ing, *cl*ank, *Cl*aRe, *cl*eaRly, *cl*eRk,
14 *cl*eric, ergy, ac*cl*aim, ac*cl*imatize, ac*cl*ivity, *gl*ow, *gl*obe,
15 *gl*obose, *gl*obosity, *gl*obule, *gl*ibly, *gl*oat, *gl*ut, *gl*ottis,
16 *gl*uttony, *gl*uttonous, *gl*oss, *gl*ossed, *Gl*oucester, *gl*ossary,
17 *gl*ass, *gl*assfuL, *gl*eam, *gl*oomy, *gl*um, *gl*aRe, *gl*ary, a*gl*ow,
18 ea*gl*e, ea*gl*e-eyed.

(*b*) *Pl*, ETC., USED FINALLY :—

1 pa*pal*, peo*ple*, to*pple*, ti*pple*, da*pple*, cha*pel*,
2 chea*ply*, cou*ple*, co*pal*, ma*ple*, em*ploy*, am*ple*,
3 pim*ple*, dim*ple*, sim*ple*, sim*ply*, Na*ples*, pine-a*pple*,
4 pano*ply*, scal*pel*, re*pl*ace, peb*ble*, ba*bel*, bau*ble*, ta*ble*,
5 eata*ble*, sta*ble*, unsta*ble*, teacha*ble*, stu*bble*, da*bble*,
6 audi*ble*, edi*ble*, cob*ble*, ca*ble*, a*ppl*ica*ble*, amica*ble*, voca*ble*,
7 revoca*ble*, gab*ble*, naviga*ble*, affa*ble*, ineffa*ble*, receiva*ble*,
8 movea*ble*, lova*ble*, Ma*bel*, *bl*ama*ble*, bum*ble*, tum*ble*,
9 gam*ble*, fum*ble*, thim*ble*, sym*bol*, stum*ble*, SHam*bles*,

10 mum*ble*, nim*ble*, rum*ble*, ena*ble*, tena*ble*, assigna*ble*,
11 amena*ble*, reasona*ble*, canni*bal*, la*bel*, sylla*ble*, solu*ble*,
12 indeli*ble*, falli*ble*, volu*ble*, aRa*ble*, rab*ble*, para*ble*, beara*ble*,
13 terri*ble*, endura*ble*, wob*ble*, hob*ble*, horri*ble*, pe*tal*, bee*tle*,
14 ti*tle*, enti*tle*, anecdo*tal*, chat*tel*, cat*tle*, vi*tal*, vic*tuals*,
15 sHu*ttle*, mo*ttle*, ra*ttle*, wa*ttle*, pe*dal*, bea*dle*, ti*dal*, daw*dle*,
16 Chea*dle*, cau*dal*, feu*dal*, mud*dle*, mo*del*, remo*del*, no*dal*,
17 la*dle*, ra*ddle*, wa*ddle*, hu*ddle*, cud*gels*, buc*kle*, unbuc*kle*,
18 tac*kle*, radi*cal*, cac*kle*, fic*kle*, vo*cal*, thic*kly*, ici*cle*, shac*kle*,
19 mira*cle*, Mi*chael*, polemi*cal*, comi*cal*, fini*cal*, tin*kle*, wrin*kle*,
20 win*kle*, yo*kel*, inimi*cal*, cir*cle*, encir*cle*, bea*gle*, tea*gle*,
21 jug*gle*, gog*gle*, fu*gle*, invei*gle*, Mo*gul*, smug*gle*, snug*gle*,
22 ban*gle*, tin*gle*, din*gle*, jin*gle*, sin*gle*, sHin*gle*, an*gle*,
23 An*gl*icism, min*gle*.

(*c*) *Pl*, ETC., USED MEDIALLY :—

1 ti*ppl*er, du*pl*icity, du*pl*ex, cha*pel*ry, cou*pl*eR, em-
2 *pl*oyeR, im*pl*icit, im*pl*aca*ble*, im*pl*oRe, sim*pl*eR,
3 sim*pl*ify, sim*pl*icity, re*pl*acing, re*pl*ieR, ba*bbl*er,
4 da*bbl*er, co*bbl*eR, fee*bl*er, mum*bl*eR, tum*bl*er, nim*bl*eR,
5 li*bel*eR, wo*bbl*eR, ho*bbl*eR, bi*bl*i*cal*, bu*tl*er, bo*ttl*er,
6 ta*ttl*er, vic*tual*ler, ra*ttl*esnake, pe*dl*er, pe*dl*ery, to*ddl*er,
7 daw*dl*er, fi*ddl*er, mo*del*eR, mo*del*ing, apo*cal*ypse, buc*kl*eR,
8 tac*kl*eR, stic*kl*eR, vo*cal*izing, en*cl*osing, un*cl*asp, re*cl*aim,
9 re*cl*aima*ble*, tic*kl*isH, bo*ggl*eR, ju*ggl*ery, invei*gl*eR, an*gl*eR,
10 bun*gl*eR, min*gl*eR, wran*gl*eR, le*gal*izing.

EXERCISE 44.

Hook R added to Straight Letters.

Hook *r*, added to straight letters, is written towards the right.

(*a*) *Pr*, ETC., USED INITIALLY :—

1 *pr*ay, *pr*op, *pr*obe, *pr*etty, *pr*a*ttle*, *pr*a*ttl*er, *pr*oudly,
2 *pr*ied, a*ppr*oach, *pr*ejudge, *pr*axis, *pr*ecocious,
3 *pr*e*cl*usive, *pr*ic*kly*, *pr*ig, *pr*eface, *pr*ofessed, *pr*ivy,
4 *pr*evaiL, *pr*ithee, o*ppr*ess, o*ppr*essoR, *pr*iceless,
5 *pr*aiseworthy, *pr*eside, *pr*ocedure, *pr*ison, *pr*ecious,
6 *pr*im, *pr*image, *pr*onounce, *pr*ank, *pr*olong, *pr*olix,

7 prayeR, prairie, brew, bribe, bribery, brute, brutish,
8 brittle, Brady, bridle, bridler, breaches, broach, abridge,
9 brackisH, breakfast, bricks, broccoli, brogue, brag, bravo,
10 bravest, broth, breathe, breathable, brass, brassy, braced,
11 bruised, broused, brash, bramble, brimless, broomstick,
12 branch, brandy, brink, bring, bringeR, brail, brawleR,
13 broiling, brieR, tray, trapese, Trappist, triple, treble, trebly,
14 troublous, troublesome, tread, traduce, traduced, tragic,
15 trefoiL, travesty, troth, traced, traceR, tresses, trusting,
16 truce, trash, atrocious, atrocity, trample, tramway, trammel,
17 transfix, transit, transitory, trench, trill, trolley, trawleR,
18 drip, drop-scene, drabble, adroit, Drage, drudge, drake,
19 draggle, dross, drossy, dresseR, drowsy, drizzle, drama,
20 dramatist, drank, drinkable, drill, drollery, drieR, dreary,
21 croup, acropolis, crab, acrid, crude, credulous, credible,
22 cratch, crock, crocus, crocodile, crackle, crag, crafty,
23 crevices, acrostic, Crusoe, cross, crossroads, crucifix,
24 crucible, creSCendo, Cremona, crimson, chrome, acrimony,
25 cranny, cringe, crinkle, creel, crieR, aggressive, aggressor,
26 graced, grapple, grapery, grabble, grate, gratis, gradus,
27 greedily, greediness, grudge, grudgingLy, Greek, groggy,
28 gruffness, grievous, growth, grossly, graces, graCIous,
29 grimly, Grundy, granuLe, grange, grail.

(*b*) *Pr*, ETC., USED FINALLY:—

1 piper, toper, dipper, depress, chopper, coper, kipper,
2 gaper, viper, vapor, sHippers, empress, mappery,
3 nipper, Dnieper, juniper, scalper, lopper, slipper,
4 rapper, riper, weeper, hopper, bibber, Tiber, dauber,
5 jobber, grubber, fibrous, embrace, leper, lubber, slabber,
6 belabor, barber, rubber, aRbor, patter, spatter, abettor,
7 tatter, auditor, doubter, chatter, cotter, scatter, actress,
8 gutter, matrice, entries, gentry, sentries, retrace, waitress,
9 yachter, spider, powdery, tawdry, Tudor, Cheddar, scudder,
10 gadder, feeder, fodder, sHedder, madder, sundry, tedder,
11 elder, louder, slider, rudder, ridder, wader, weeder, patcher,
12 butchery, teachers, ditcher, catcher, scutcher, voucher,
13 avoucher, thatcher, trencher, bencher, aRcher, aRchery,

richer, marcher, searcher, luRcher, bewitcher, pledger badger, dowager, dodger, drudgery, charger, cadger, gauger, voyager, major, ledger, villager, pillager, forager, manager, lounger, ranger, wager, picker, backer, tacker, bakery, barker, decry, checker, joker, thicker, Thackeray, marker, mimicry, luRker, rookery, hooker, piggery, beggary, toggery, tiger, digger, jigger, cougar, vigor, sugar, angry, engross, lager, rigor, hogger.

(c) *Pr*, ETC., USED MEDIALLY:—

paper-maker, dapperling, capricious, capereR, vaporable, vaporer, vaporizing, slipperily, slipperiness, unpromising, impressing, imprison, improperly, repressive, reproach, tubercle, tuberculosis, tuberosity, jabberer, fabric, febrile, embracing, embroil, unbridle, neighborly, Nebraska, laborsome, liberal, liberalism, liberalize, lubricity, rubric, patrimony, patrol, patronize, petrel, putrefy, betroth, buttermilk, tutorage, chatterer, catereR, scattereR, matricide, matrimony, matrix, matronLy, peasantry, untruly, untruth, entrap, entrusting, sultriness, retracing, retrench, retrogressive, powder-mill, tawdrily, Kidderminster, federal, federalism, SHuddering, Madras, madrigal, butcherly, gingerly, majordomo, decreasing, vicarage, microbe, gimcrack, incriminate, lachrymose, recrossing, beggarly, tigerisH, vigorously, angrily, mongrel, ungrudgingLy, rigorously.

EXERCISE 45.

Initial Hooks to Straight Letters (continued).

(a) *Pl*, *Pr*, ETC., USED INITIALLY AND FINALLY:—

plagal, *plaguer*, *plaiter*, *pleader*, *plodder*, *plucker*, *plum-tree*, *applauder*, *apple-tree*, *appliable*, *blabber*, *black-beetle*, *bladder*, *blamable*, *bleater*, *bleacher*, *bleakly*, *claimable*, *clapper*, *clatter*, *clavicle*, *claviger*, *clerical*, *clicker*, *clincher*, *clipper*, *clobber*, *glider*, *glitter*, *glottal*, *prater*, *prattle*, *preacher*, *preceptress*, *prefigure*, *preluder*, *premonitor*, *preservable*, *presumably*, prickly, procurable, prodigal, progress, promenader, proper, prouder, approacher, approachable, abridger, bragger, bramble, breaker, briber, bridle, brighter, broacher, broader, brutal, brutalized, trader, trainable, traitor, traitress, trample, transfigure, trapper, truckle, treadle, treasonable, treater, treble, tremble, triangle, trickery, triple, tripper, trickle, draper, dredger, drinkable, drum-major, crab-tree, crackle, crater, credibly, crinkle, croaker, cricketer, Crowder, crumble, crupper, acrostical, grabble, graphically, grater, gripper, grubber.

(b) Pl, Pr, etc., in Miscellaneous Words:—

academical, acrostic, admirable, adorable, algebra, allegro, asker, autocracy, barnacle, batterer, begrudge, biblical, black-eyed, buttery, calibre, changer, chronicler, Cimbric, clarify, closeness, copper-faced, crashing, creature, deluder, deploy, doggerel, dropsy, eclipse, emblem, epigram, inevitably, factor, labourer, feebler, filcher, foreclose, fuddler, gabbler, jingle, head-dress, implacably, infallibly, insuperable, laconical, libretto, maintainable, mangle, marbler, matchable, mimicker, mulberry, neck-cloth, neutralize, nitric, obligato, obligatory, opera-glass, ostrich, pardonable, pedigree, platonic, pouter, prelude, press-gang, profile, proconsul, prorogue, prolixity, proxy, putrescence, rambler, redbreast, regret, regrettable, retrogressive, satirically, slobberer, stenography, stock-broker, store-keeper, stubbly, table-cloth, tangle, thimble-rigger, trespasser, typically, ultra, umbrella, wrinkly, Antrim, Ardrossan, Anglesea, Bristol, Blakeney, Butterley, Christie, Christina, Clarkson, Cressy, Praed, Macready, Montrose, Outram, Smallbridge, Tunbridge, Vickers, Vickery.

EXERCISE 46.

Initial Hooks to Straight Letters (continued)

GRAMMALOGUES.

call, care, dear.

1. Have a care, my dear pupil, lest you bring trouble on

youRself by allowing youR tongue to babble of the affaiRs of youR neighbours. 2. Bridle the tongue and use it in a reasonable way. 3. He is truly a feeble creatuRe who gives his tongue License to gabble. 4. It is allowable and enjoyable to talk affably to youR playfellows; but beware lest you utter a single syllable likely to give offence to any of them. 5. The pleasantest voices resemble sweet music. 6. They soothe us and produce calm feeLings in our breasts. 7. A loud voice troubles and annoys us; it makes us SHudder; and we properly call those vulgar who talk in such a voice. 8. I have no desiRe to reproach you, OR to preach to you; but I have noticed youR voice grows louder as you proceed in youR speech. 9. I trust you may be induced to repress this crazy style, OR you may grow into a brawleR. 10. If I have trespassed in saying this, pray excuse me, and SHow no umbrage. 11. I declaRe to you I am no grumbleR, but a sincere adviser. 12. I can amplify this Lesson, if you please, on Wednesday. (193)

EXERCISE 47.

Initial Hooks to Straight Letters (continued).

1. Daydreams are both enjoyable and cheap, and they are available to all who desiRe to indulge in them. 2. You can have a daydream in any place you care to call it up; at the play, on the top of a tram, in a crowd, OR aLone on a bleak mooR; on a gloomy day in April as you watch the black clouds racing across the sky, OR on a bright sunny day in August, as you lounge in the SHade of the trees, and baRe youR brow to catch the breeze. 3. It is onLy necessary to close youR eyes, and you can draw mental images as gracefuL and as varied as you please. 4. The bright faces of the dear class-fellows you knew long ago; the pretty, and maybe the laughable, scenes you saw on youR last trip across the sea; the troubles and the wrangles on the boat and in the hotel; the pleasing and the miserable folk you came across—all these things does youR daydream reproduce, and you chuckle to youRself as they are

*br*ought *to* youR view. 5. *I* know some *dr*eary peo*ple* *may think* day*dr*eams like *these are no bl*essings. 6. They *may call them an* idle waste *of pr*ecious time. 7. *But, I* re*ply*, *how* many no*bl*e schemes *to* make *the* lives *of* pooR peo*ple* be*tter and* bri*ghter*, oR *to* re*cl*aim *those who* were led as*tr*ay by *the* ill exam*ple* *of* worthless neigh*bours*, came *first to the plotters of these* schemes *in a* day*dr*eam ? 8. *It is tr*ue, castles *in the* aiR *are* fa*br*ics *which* soon *cr*um*bl*e ; *but* they *may give* rise *to* many *a pr*o*bl*em *of use to* society. 9. *It is a* sim*ple* *thing to cr*iticise, *to gr*um*bl*e, oR *to bl*ame ; *but how* few *of those who* do *these things are* a*bl*e *to* be*tter the* la*bour* *of the* peo*ple* they *cr*iticise ! (304)

EXERCISE 48.

Initial Hooks to Straight Letters (continued).

1. *I call him a* senseLess *dr*eameR *who* takes no *care of the* time at *his* disposal. 2. *The hours he* now wastes *so* idly *may* cost *him a dear pr*ice some day ; *but* re*gr*et *may be use*less. 3. *I* am no *gr*um*ble*R ; *but I* u*tter*ly detest *pr*oud idleness. 4. *I* am *pl*eased *to* a*ppl*aud *the bl*ithe *bl*acksmith *who* la*bours* at *the proper* time, *and* rests *as* soon *as the tr*ou*ble and* toil *of the* day *are* o'eR ; *but I have* no patience *to think of the* begg*ar*ly *pr*ide *of him who* deems *it* beneath *his pl*ace *to* la*bour*, though *he* makes no *pr*otest if *you* ask *him to* eat oR *dr*ink at youR ta*ble*. 5. *I tr*ust *you* belong *to* no such *cl*ass *of* peo*ple*. 6. Time *is the* aven*ger of all* wrongs ; *and those who are* dod*gers in* youth *may be* beg*gars* oR pau*pers in* age. 7. Honest la*bour is* admira*ble* ; *but* du*pl*icity *is* abomina*ble*. 8. *These are* valua*ble* Lessons, *and I shall pr*o*cl*aim *them as* long *as I* am a*ble*. 9. *It is* nice *to be* amica*ble and* reasona*ble in all* cases ; *but it is* also desira*ble to* protest *in a cl*eaR voice *should* faLse ac*tors* seek *to* beguile sim*ple* youths *who are* easily led as*tr*ay. 10. Ol*der* peo*ple* *may* know *how to* choose be*tter* lea*ders* ; *but* many boys *are cr*edulous, *and* follow *a* tea*cher* readily. 11. Take *care how you tr*ust *him who pr*eaches "No la*bour*, *and a* rich *pr*ize." (233)

EXERCISE 49.

Initial Hooks to Straight Letters (continued).

MessRS. Bar*ker and* Sons.

Dear SiRS,—*In* re*p*ly *to* youRS *of the* 7th, we *shall be pleased* if *you can* pack *the cr*eam dairy bu*tter in broader* casks. *The class of grocers who* buy *our* stock *think the* narrow casks unsuita*ble*, *and* we desiRe *to please them* if we *can*. We *are* sorry *to trouble you in any* way, *and* we *tr*ust *you may be* a*ble to* o*bl*ige *us*. If *you care to* sHip *a* few sam*ple* cases *of first-class* eggs, we *shall be pleased to* sHow *them to our* customeRS. *Our* bu*tter* buyeR hopes *to be in* An*tr*im *on the* 29th, *and may give you a call*. YouRS *tr*uly, Bu*tl*er *and Br*iggs. (115)

EXERCISE 50.

Initial Hooks to Straight Letters (concluded).

MessRS. *Bl*ack *and Tr*acy.

Dear SiRS,—*Please* ask youR mana*ger to give us a call on* Tuesday. We *are* desirous *of* sHowing *him our* new *pr*ess, *which is a* thorough success, *and which* we *tr*ust *may* secuRe *us the first pr*ize at *the cl*ub sHow *in* A*pr*il. We *are the* sole ma*kers of this pr*ess, *and* if *you care to* buy we *shall be pleased to* sell *you a* sin*gle pr*ess at *a* reduced *pr*ice. We *call the* new design Dig*gle and* No*ble*'s "Ea*gle*" *pr*ess. We *should* like *you to give it a tr*iaL. YouRS *tr*uly, An*dr*ews *and* Gam*ble*.
(99)

EXERCISE 51.

Hook L added to Curves.

Hook *l*, added to curved letters, is a large initial hook. In this Exercise, and in Exercises 52 to 57 inclusive, the double consonants *fl*, *fr*, etc., should be employed (in words other than grammalogues and contractions) for the representation of the letters printed in italic.

(*a*) THE LEFT CURVES *fl*, *vl*, *thl*, USED INITIALLY :—

1 *fl*ay, *fl*abby, *fl*accid, *fl*ag, *fl*aiL, *fl*aked, *fl*aky, *fl*aming, *fl*ange,
2 *fl*ank, *fl*ap, *fl*aRe, *fl*ashing, *fl*asks, *fl*attest, *fl*ax, *fl*ic*ker*,

fledgling, flexible, flinty, flocked, flood, florist, florid, flounced, flotilla, floweR, flouRish, flurry, fluster, flunky, flycatcher, Flora, Fletcher, Florida, Fleming, phlegm, afflict, afflicter, efflux, efflorescence, evil, evil-eyed, athletic, Ethel, Ethelred.

(b) THE LEFT CURVES *fl*, *vl*, USED FINALLY:

playful, playfully, pitiful, poweRful, poweRfully, prayeRful, baffle, briefly, briefless, basHfully, butterfly, bot-fly, brimful, teaRful, toughly, trifle, truffle, truthful, truthfully, triumphal, deceitful, dutiful, diReful, aidful, changeful, joyful, joyfully, catchfly, cupful, grateful, gadfly, feaRful, fiRefly, fraudful, faithful, faithfully, vengeful, revengeful, youthful, useful, usefully, easeful, iceflow, skiLful, skiLfully, stifle, slothful, spadeful, SHuffles, SHameful, SHamefully, muffle, mouthful, mindful, mirthful, unLawful, rightful, ladleful, watchful, aRmful, roomful, regretful, regretfully, reproachful, wrathful, worSHipful, hopefully, heedful, approval, appelatively, positively, primeval, privily, bedevil, bevel, bravely, attractively, derivatively, deceptively, devil, adjectival, exhaustively, accusatively, causatively, actively, frivolous, figuratively, festival, effectively, votively, authoritatively, sensitively, SHovel, SHrivel, survival, assertively, aRRival, NaSHville, negatively, non-aRRival, reproval, relatively, retrieval, revival, revivalist.

(c) THE LEFT CURVES *fl*, *vl*, USED MEDIALLY:—

pamphleteer, privilege, profligate, profligacy, baffleR, biflorous, trifleR, triflorous, deflect, deflector, devilry, devilish, develop, developer, CHivalry, CHivalrous, cauliflower, SHrievalty, SHovelful, SHovelleR, SHuffleR, muffleR, mayfloweR, revivalism, High-flyeR.

(d) THE RIGHT CURVES *fl*, *vl*, *thl*, USED MEDIALLY AND FINALLY:—

apocryphal, dragon-fly, carvel, cavil, cavalieR, cavalieRly, cavalry, aRchival, gainful, gravel, groveleR, gleeful, gruffly, gravely, scuffleR, scornful, skinful, snaffle, snivel, sniveleR, snow-flake, inflame, inflammable, inflameR, in*fl*exible, in*fl*uenza, in*fl*ux, an*vil*, *Granville*, mar*vel*, mar*vel*ous, mar*vel*ously, na*val*, no*vel*, no*vel*ist, ra*ffle*, ra*ffle*r, ra*vel*, re*flex*, re*fl*exed, re*fl*exible, re*fl*ux, re*vel*, re*vel*ry, re*vell*er, ri*fle*, ri*fle*-corps, ri*fle*r, ri*val*ry, rue*ful*, rue*fully*, Be*thel*, Bi*thel*, be*trothal*, bismu*thal*, le*thal*, wee*vil*, Yeo*vil*, ho*vel*.

(*e*) THE DOUBLE CONSONANT *shl* (UPWARD) USED INITIALLY, MEDIALLY, AND FINALLY :—

*shel*f, *shel*ves, book-*shel*f, *shel*lac, pa*chal*ic, peniten*tial*, palatial, poten*tial*, poten*tial*ity, peevi*shl*y, *p*ruden*tial*, *p*residen*tial*, par*tial*, par*tial*ity, pestilen*tial*, *br*uti*shl*y, boyi*shl*y, boori*shl*y, benefi*cial*, abba*tial*, torren*tial*, devili*shl*y, *cl*anni*shl*y, *cl*owni*shl*y, *cr*eden*tial*, egg-*shell*, Ca*shel*, fidu*cial*, fa*cial*, offi*cial*, unoffi*cial*, fe*veri*shl*y, foolishly*, foppi*shl*y, slavi*shl*y, sluggi*shl*y, spe*cial*ize, spe*cial*ist, spe*cial*ty, spe*cial*ity, snappi*shl*y, scien*tial*, sheepi*shl*y, Mar*shall*, Mar*shal*sea, nup*tial*, knavi*shl*y, inessen*tial*, ini*tial*, ini*tially*, lavi*shl*y, rogui*shl*y, waspi*shl*y, hoggi*shl*y.

DOWNWARD *shl* : prima*tial*, api*shl*y, bomb-*shell*, com*mercial*ism, sea-*shell*, modi*shl*y, natali*tial*, nu*tritial*, louti*shl*y.

(*f*) THE DOUBLE CONSONANT *ml* USED MEDIALLY AND FINALLY :—

philo*mel*, pi*cromel*, calo*mel*, ena*mel*, ena*mell*er, ena*mell*ing, la*chrymal*.

(*g*) THE DOUBLE CONSONANT *nl* USED INITIALLY, MEDIALLY, AND FINALLY :—

e*nl*ighte*ner*, e*nl*ive*ner*, a*nal*ytic, pa*nel*, pa*nell*ing, pe*nal*ty, pa*tronal*, pagi*nal*, aborigi*nal*, ba*nal*, binomi*nal*, autum*nal*, to*nal*, to*nal*ity, tech*nol*ogi*cal*, diur*nal*, diago*nal*, deca*nal*, cha*nnell*ing, O'Co*nnell*, canto*nal*, ca*nnel*-coal, *cr*imi*nal*, ke*nnel*, ke*nnell*ing, *chronol*ogical, *gr*ap*nel*, phenome*nal*, *flannel*ette, fe*nnel*, ve*nal*, eth*nol*ogic, thi*nl*y, spi*nal*, semi*nal*, semi*nal*ity, sig*nal*, sig*nal*ize, sig*nal*izing, ster*nal*, *zonal*, sh*rap*nel*, mo*nol*ith, ma*tronal*, margi*nal*, nomi*nal*, nomi*nally*, nomi*nal*ist, infer*nal*.

EXERCISE 52.

Hook R added to Curves.

Hook *r*, added to curves, is a small initial hook.

(*a*) THE LEFT CURVES *fr*, *vr*, *thr*, USED INITIALLY:—

1 a*fr*esh, a*fr*aid, e*ff*er*v*esce, e*ff*er*v*escence, o*ffer*, o*ffer*eR, o*ffer*-
2 ing, o*ffer*tory, *fr*agile, *fr*ank, *fr*an*kly*, *fr*aud, *fr*ayed, *fr*e*ckle*,
3 *fr*eed, *fr*ib*ble*, *fr*ith, *fr*othy, *fr*ouzy, *fr*ug*al*ly, *fr*uity,
4 *phr*eno*l*ogic*al*, a*ver*age, a*ver*se, a*ver*seLy, e*ver*Lasting,
5 e*very*body, e*very*-day, o*ver*aLLs, o*ver*balanced, o*ver*cr*o*wd,
6 o*ver*dose, o*ver*d*r*aw, o*ver*f*l*ow, o*ver*gr*o*wth, o*ver*lap, o*ver*Look,
7 o*ver*reach, o*ver*sleep, o*ver*ture, o*ver*took, *ver*satile, *ver*sify,
8 *vir*tue, *vir*tuous, *vir*tually, e*ther*, a*thir*st, ei*ther*, o*ther*wise.

(*b*) THE LEFT CURVES *fr*, *vr*, *thr*, USED MEDIALLY AND FINALLY:—

1 ta*ffer*eL, tou*gher*, du*ffer*, de*fr*ay, di*ffer*, di*ffer*en*tial*,
2 do*ffer*, denti*fr*ice, cha*ffer*, cha*ffer*eR, chau*ffeur*, Je*ffr*ey,
3 Je*ffer*son, feo*ffer*, ossi*fer*ous, ze*phyr*, lacti*fer*ous,
4 Mac*pher*son, oR*phr*ey, auRi*fer*ous, po*ver*ty, be*ver*age,
5 Be*ver*idge, *tr*a*ver*se, *tr*a*ver*ser, sti*ver*, di*ver*, di*ver*ge, *dr*i*ver*,
6 ad*ver*b, ad*ver*se, ad*ver*seLy, ad*ver*sity, ad*ver*sary, Chi*ver*s,
7 cada*ver*ous, go*ver*ness, go*ver*na*ble*, go*ver*n*or*, thie*very*, fe*ver*,
8 fa*vour*eR, fa*vour*a*ble*, *fl*a*vour*, *fl*a*vour*less, endea*vour*,
9 le*ver*age, sub*ver*sive, soe*ver*, ossi*vor*ous, survi*vor*, revi*ver*,
10 re*tr*ie*ver*, Wendo*ver*, sHea*ther*.

(*c*) THE RIGHT CURVES *fr*, *vr*, *thr*, USED INITIALLY:—

1 *fr*eak, *fr*acTIous, *fr*ama*ble*, *fr*eely, *fr*ee-*tr*a*der*, *fr*esH,
2 *fr*esHe*r*, *fr*esHness, *fr*illed, *fr*i*vo*lous, *fr*i*vo*lousLy, *fr*olic,
3 *fr*olicsome, *fr*olicked, *fr*ostily, A*fr*ica, *ver*bose, *ver*bal,
4 *ver*micelli, *ver*minous, *ther*mal, *ther*mic, *thir*sty, *thir*stily,
5 *thr*all, *thr*ash, *thr*ashing, *thr*asHe*r*, *thr*ead, *thr*eap,
6 *thr*eepenny, *thr*ifty, *thr*illing, *thr*ong, *thr*ostle, *thr*uster,
7 *there*at, *there*in, *there*by.

(*d*) THE RIGHT CURVES *fr*, *vr*, *thr*, USED MEDIALLY AND FINALLY:—

1 pu*ffer*, pil*fer*, pal*fr*ey, para*phr*ase, para*phr*ased,
2 pro*ffer*er, peri*pher*al, bu*ffer*, biogra*pher*, bel*fry*, brie*fer*,
3 typogra*pher*, *tr*ium*pher*, *tr*ee-*fr*og, Dum*fr*ies, dia*phr*agm,

4 doloriferous, chamfer, camphor, comfrey, coffer, cofferer,
5 gaffer, gruffer, goffer, ferriferous, oviferous, scoffer, saliferous,
6 sulphur, stenographer, snuffers, stelliferous, melliferous,
7 omniferous, laugher, loafer, luffer, luminiferous, Ilfracombe,
8 reefer, refresh, refresher, refreshing, reframe, resiniferous,
9 Renfrew, orthographer, wafer, heifer, huffer, paver, palaver,
10 prover, approver, plover, pulverise, pulverable, braver,
11 beaver, Beverley, triumver, Denver, discover, deriver, delver,
12 craver, carver, cleaver, cleverly, cleverness, coverer, giver,
13 glover, graver, griever, Gulliver, granivorous, shiver, shivery,
14 Maver, mover, omnivorous, manœuvre, manœuvrer,
15 anniversary, universality, universalism, laver, livery, louver,
16 Oliver, lawgiver, raver, recover, recoverer, remover, reprover,
17 revolver, resolver, waver, Waverley, Wavertree, waverer,
18 weaver, heaver, hover, hoveringly, haversack, plethora,
19 panther, overthrow, enthrall, disenthrall, dethroner, anthrax,
20 anthracite, misanthrope, Luther (*l* up), Lutheranism (*l* up),
21 Arthur, pother, pothering, bother, bothering, brotherly, brea-
22 ther, tether, tethering, Crowther, gather, gathering, gatherer,
23 feathery, smothery, Mather, mothery, nether, nethermost,
24 leather, leathery, leatherette, loather, Reather, wither,
25 withering, weathercock, weather-gage, weatherwise.

(*e*) THE DOUBLE CONSONANT *shr* (downward always) USED INITIALLY, MEDIALLY, AND FINALLY :—

1 usher, ushering, shrank, shrunk, shrapnel, shrew, shrewd,
2 shrewdness, shriek, shrill, shrinkage, shrivel, shrubbery,
3 Shrewsbury, Shropshire, pusher, pressure, polisher,
4 punisher, blusher, brochure, burnisher, tonsure, tertiary,
5 tressure, dasher, Derbyshire, Cheshire, Kosher, crusher,
6 fissure, finisher, fishery, flasher, fresher, fiduciary, thrasher,
7 slasher, smasher, Somersetshire, masher, enshroud, lavisher,
8 lasher, Ayrshire, rasher, refresher, residentiary.

(*f*) THE DOUBLE CONSONANT *zhr* USED MEDIALLY AND FINALLY :

1 treasure, treasurer, treasuring, closure, enclosure,
2 foreclosure, measure, measurer, measuring, measureless,
3 leisure, leisurely, erasure, rasure.

(*g*) The Double Consonant *mr* used Initially, Medially, and Finally :—

1 aimer, Omar, merceR, mercery, mercury, merling,
2 palmer, primer, plumber, perfumer, proclaimer,
3 blamer, blasphemer, declaimer, calmer, clamor,
4 clamoreR, crammer, Cranmer, climber, glamor, flamer,
5 schemer, shammer, shimmering, mummer, misnomer, namer,
6 enamour, enamouring, Rimmer, reclaimer, hammereR,
7 hammer-cloth, hummer.

(*h*) The Double Consonant *nr* used Initially, Medially, and Finally :—

1 nervous, nervousness, nervousLy, energy, energise,
2 enervate, aneroid, anarchy, owner, ownerSHip, honor,
3 honorable, honoring, pawner, pinery, oppugner,
4 plenary, plenariLy, pruner, panorama, banneret,
5 browner, bemoaner, tannery, trainer, trepanner, dinnerLess,
6 decliner, dethroner, Jenner, generous, generousLy, generosity,
7 generaLize, generic, keener, crowner, coroner, cocoonry,
8 Kitchener, gunner, funeraL, vainer, venerable, veterinary,
9 vintner, thinner, threatener, assigner, stannary, spanner,
10 schooner, seminary, sublunary, sexagenary, SHunner,
11 SHipowner, meaner, mannerLy, mannerism, Mannering,
12 mineraL, mineraLogy, Minerva, Milner, maCHinery,
13 maintainer, marooner, incliner, leaner, liner, limner,
14 aRRaigner, eaRner, iRoner, retainer, refiner, repiner,
15 remunerable, yeomanry.

(*i*) The Double Consonant *ngr* (*ng-kr* or *ng-gr*) used Initially, Medially, and Finally :—

1 anchor, anchorable, anchoret, anchorite, anchoring,
2 anger, angering, pinker, bunker, blinker, tinker,
3 tinkering, drinker, canker, cankering, cankerous,
4 conquer, conquerable, conquereR, conquering, clangor,
5 clangorous, clinker, finger, fingering, finger-post, finger-
6 stall, forefinger, flanker, thinker, free-thinker, monger,
7 newsmonger, linger, lingereR, lingering, malinger, malingereR,
8 malingering, rancor, rancorous, rancorousLy, hanker,
9 hankering, hunger, hungering.

(*j*) STROKE *ng* AND *downward R* MUST BE EMPLOYED IN NOUNS FORMED BY THE ADDITION OF *er* TO A VERB ENDING IN *ng* :—

1 *long*eR, *pro*longeR, *br*ingeR, flingeR, singeR, stingeR,
2 slingeR, swingeR, ringeR, wringeR, wrongeR, wingeR,
3 hangeR, haranguеR.

EXERCISE 53.

Initial Hooks (continued).

GRAMMALOGUES.

for, *from*, *Mr.*, or *mere*, *more*, or *remark-ed*, *near*, *nor*, *their*, or *there*, *very*.

1. Peo*ple of* energy *have* no lei*sure to* li*nger over mere* tri*fl*es, *nor* do they *care to* do *so*. 2. They *mere*ly *sh*rug *their* shoul*der*s *and* smile *at those fr*ail fellows *who* allow *a fl*imsy detail *to* bo*ther them and throw them* into *a* state *of fl*urry OR an*ger*. 3. They know *the* cal*mer* they keep *in* times *of pressure the* be*tter it is for them, and the more* likely *are* they *to* con*quer their tr*oub*le*s. 4. *Nor can* we faiL *to see why* they *should* do *so*; *for* we know *how* easily *a* poweR*ful* lea*der who is* calm *can* ruLe *an* angry *throng from whose* heads *all* reason *has fl*ed. 5. *Have you ever remarked how very* like *to a* fe*ver is* an*ger, and how* soon *it br*ings *the* au*thor, the* u*sher, the* ban*ker, the* far*mer, the driver, and the* vul*gar* loa*fer to the* same leveL ? 6. *And, I may remark, a very* low leveL *it is*. 7. *The fl*ame *of* an*ger* soon *gr*ows big*ger, and a* sin*gle* an*gry* fellow *may* in*fl*ame many *more*. 8. *So it is* best *to* sti*fle the* ini*tial fl*aRe, foRce *it to fl*i*cker* out, *and* thus ba*ffle the evil* eRe *it thr*ows *you* into *a fl*uster. 9. O*ther*wise, *as Mr.* Min*shall remarks, the first br*eath *of* ad*ver*sity *may fl*ing *you* into despair. 10. Now, ad*ver*sity *may be very near to you, and you should pr*epare youRself by manLy resolve *to* receive *any bl*ow SHe *may* deal *you*. 11. *There are shr*ewd thi*nker*s *who have remarked how*

bitter a teacher adversity is. 12. But, they add, she is a clever trainer, whose Lessons are given effectively; and if only we receive them in a proper manner they are likely to show us how to lead a useful, honorable, and successful life. (284)

EXERCISE 54.

Initial Hooks (continued).

1. Have you ever remarked, my dear Mr. Mather, how very nicely the thrushes near your house plaster the inside of their nests, for fear their eggs should tumble to the floor beneath and get cracked? 2. And have you noticed how very opposite are the ways of their neighbours the black-caps, which make their nests so frail and flimsy as to seem unable to bear the eggs placed there by the feathery inmates? 3. But, I may remark, though you and I may call the labour of these pretty creatures a mere waste of time and energy, since the nests must inevitably break, as we think, still they know their own business best; for the nests scarcely ever break, nor do the eggs fall through. 4. Fragile as the nest appears to us, the owners evince no trouble or flurry; for they seem to know it is safe enough to carry their precious treasures. 5. There is no labourer who discharges his task so effectively as these pretty singers. 6. Any shrewd rambler through the woods and by the rivers may discover there marvels enough and to spare. 7. I feel there is no better way of passing a leisure hour. (195)

EXERCISE 55.

Initial Hooks (continued).

1. From all I know of life it is mere nonsense to say there is no virtue in adversity. 2. Have you ever remarked, my dear Mr. Webster, how very calm in times of trouble is he who has seen more evil days, and, essaying to conquer them, has issued from the fray a noble victor? 3. Others may shrink and

shrivel at *the* sight *of* sorrow ; *but these* fellows face *it bravely, and fling it from them.* 4. *Mere* business worries *have* no terrors *for them ; nor* do they *flinch* at *the more* alaRming *troubles which may* ap*p*roach *them.* 5. *Their* joy *is to* sti*fle all* feeLings *which may* in*fl*ame *them to* an*ger.* 6. *You may, I think, remark the glitter in their* eyes, *should these* fiRm fellows notice *the trembl*ing feaRs *of a* silly youth at *the first* view *of trouble* oR sorrow. 7. They appeaR *to think* such feaRs worthy *of reproval, as* being unmanLy. 8. *The more* annoyances *these* stout fellows *have to* con*quer, the* be*tter* they seem *to* like *it, and the fresher* they a*pp*roach *to the fray.* 9. They snap *their fingers* at *mere* pal*try* worries, *and* smile at business pres*sure.* 10. They eat *their* di*nners* just *as* calmly, *and* seem *to* la*bor* just *as* leis*ure*ly, *in* busy times *as* they do *in* times *of* slackness. 11. They sim*ply thr*ust aside *the things* they dislike, *and* refuse *to be fl*urried by *them.* 12. They know *the* mea*sure of their* e*nergy and their* poweRs ; *and* they *have* no feaR, *for* they *are* aware no earthly sorrow *can* last *for ever.* (253)

EXERCISE 56.

Initial Hooks (continued).

MessRs. Bea*ver and Thr*elfaLL.

Dear SiRs,—We *have* youR fa*vour of Fr*iday last, *and* we *are very pl*eased at youR success *in the* Far*mers'* sHow. We were una*ble to be there, for the* reasons *given you* by *our Mr.* ARthur *Fletcher. Nor shall* we *be* a*ble to* go *to the* close *of the* affaiR. *From a mere remark of Mr.* AR*thur's*, we ga*ther how very* big were *the* crowds *which thr*onged *the pl*ace *from first to* last *on the* day *of his* visit, *and* we were *all the more* sorry *to be* away. *Mr.* AR*thur* speci*ally remarked the* new oat *crusher, near the shr*ubbery. *There* were *three* o*ther crushers in the* sHow ; *but he thinks* they were *more fl*imsy, *and* faR less use*ful.* We *shall* dispatch youR ke*nnel* by raiL *to*-morrow. YouRs faith*fully, Fletcher,* Sons, *and Crowther.* (137)

EXERCISE 57.

Initial Hooks (concluded).

Mr. C*h*risto*ph*e*r* Cove*r*ley.

Dear Sir,—We *have the* sam*pl*es *of* *flannel* *to*-day, *but* we reg*r*et *to* say they *are* unsuita*bl*e *for our* purposes. They *are very* *fl*uffy, *and there are* *fl*aws *in the* *thr*eads *of* some *of them*. *Thr*ee *of the* sam*pl*es appear *to* *shr*ink *and* *shr*ive*l* up *in the* washing. We *are* a*fr*aid *to* o*ffer* such stuff *to our* customers. Yours *tr*uly, Weave*r* Bro*thers*. (65)

EXERCISE 58.

Circles and Loops prefixed to Initial Hooks.

A circle or loop is prefixed to a straight letter hooked for r by turning the hook into a circle or loop.

(*a*) *Spr*, ETC. THE ITALIC TYPE INDICATES THAT THE CIRCLE SHOULD BE COMBINED WITH THE HOOK *r* :—

s*pr*ay, s*pr*ayed, s*pr*eader, s*pr*ag, s*pr*awler, s*pr*inger, s*pr*ing-time, s*pr*uce, s*pr*ucely, s*pr*uceness, sa*pper*, su*ppr*essed, su*per*, su*pr*emely, su*per*ficial, su*per*vise, su*per*viser, su*per*latively, su*per*sede, so*ber*ly, so*ber*ness, sou*br*ette, s*tr*ayed, s*tr*aggler, s*tr*ainer, s*tr*angely, s*tr*ata, s*tr*eaky, s*tr*eamer, s*tr*engthener, s*tr*ide, s*tr*inger, s*tr*iver, s*tr*onger, s*tr*utter, se*tter*, ci*ter*, ci*tr*ic, sui*tor*, sol*der*, sol*der*er, Ce*dr*ic, s*cr*ew, s*cr*aggy, s*cr*eamer, s*cr*eech-owl, s*cr*ofulous, sa*cr*edly, sa*cr*ificer, sa*cr*ificial, sa*cr*ilegious, suc*cor*, suc*cor*er, So*cr*ates, So*cr*atical, sa*cr*isty, se*cr*étairé, se*cr*ecy, sa*gger*, se*gr*egate, pros*per*, ups*pr*ing, ups*pr*inging, des*tr*oy, des*tr*oyer, des*tr*uctively, dis*tr*ainer, dis*tr*ainable, dis*tr*essed, dis*tr*essing, dis*tr*usts, dis*tr*usting, deci*der*, outsi*der*, tas*ker*, tus*ker*, dis*gr*ace, dis*gr*aced, dis*gr*acing, dis*gr*aceful, des*cr*ibe, des*cr*iber, des*cr*ibing, des*cr*ier, des*cr*iptively, dis*cr*iminate, corks*cr*ew, ex*cr*escence, *swopper*, *sweeper*, *swabber*, *sweeter*, *sweater*, *sw*it*cher*, *sw*a*gger*, *sw*a*gger*er, *sw*i*gger*.

(*b*) WRITE THE CIRCLE INSIDE THE HOOK *r* IN THE FOLLOWING AND SIMILAR WORDS, WHERE THE CIRCLE AND HOOK OCCUR AT AN ANGLE :—

1 pa*stor*al, pe*ster*er, pla*ster*er, besie*ger*, be*str*ew, be*str*addle,
2 blu*ster*ous, blu*ster*er, boi*ster*ous, boi*ster*ously, tricy*cl*ist,
3 ta*x*i*der*my, depo*sitor*, de*xter*ous, de*xter*ously, de*xtr*ose,
4 check*str*ing, co*ster*monger, cro*sstr*ee, clu*ster*y, cloi*ster*al,
5 cloi*ster*eR, cla*sper*, cri*sper*, crusa*ders*, exci*ter*, e*xpr*ess,
6 e*xpr*essive, e*xpr*essly, e*xpur*gatory, exposi*tor*, e*xter*minate,
7 e*xtr*a, e*xtr*emity, e*xtr*emist, e*xtr*insic, e*xtr*icable, ine*x*-
8 *tr*icably, ine*xpr*essive, E*xeter*, U*xbr*idge, ga*str*ic, ga*str*itis,
9 ga*str*onomy, Glouce*ster*shire, ga*sper*, off*spr*ing, fene*str*al,
10 psalmi*str*y, no*str*il, no*str*ums, ance*str*al, ance*str*ess,
11 massa*cr*e, ma*ster*ful, ma*ster*-key, ma*ster*-stroke, ma*ster*ly,
12 mi*str*al, my*ster*y, mi*str*ess, mi*str*ust, mi*str*usting, mu*ster*-
13 roLL, mi*spr*ize, mi*spr*onounce, mi*spr*onounced, li*sper*,
14 lu*str*al, lu*str*ous, lu*str*ously, la*scar*, Me*xbor*ough, Salis*bur*y,
15 Malmes*bur*y, ra*sper*, reci*pr*ocal, reci*pr*ocity, reci*ter*,
16 res*cr*ibe, re*str*ainable, re*str*ainer, ri*sker*, ro*str*al, roi*ster*eR
17 regi*str*y, oRche*str*a, oRche*str*al, wa*str*el, we*ster*ly, wisea*cr*e,
18 He*sper* (*h* up), house*br*eaker.

(*c*) *St-pr*, ETC. THE ITALIC TYPE INDICATES THAT THE LOOP *st* SHOULD BE COMBINED WITH THE HOOK *r* :—

1 *stepper*, *stopper*, *stooper*, *stupor*, *stabber*, *statter*, *stutter*,
2 *stutter*eR, *stouter*, *stitcher*, *stager*, *stodger*, *staker*, *stacker*
3 *sticker*, *stalker*, *stoker*, *stocker*, *stagger*, *stagger*er.

(*d*) *Spl*, *s-fr*, ETC., USED INITIALLY. INITIAL CIRCLE *S* IS WRITTEN INSIDE THE HOOK *l* ATTACHED TO STRAIGHT LETTERS, AND INSIDE THE HOOK *l* OR *r* ATTACHED TO CURVES. IN THIS SECTION THE ITALIC TYPE INDICATES THAT THE CIRCLE *S* MUST BE WRITTEN INSIDE THE HOOK *l* OR *r* :—

1 *spl*asH, *spl*asher, *spl*itter, *spl*utter, *spl*eeny, *su*p*pl*e,
2 *su*p*pl*eness, *su*p*pl*icatory, *su*p*pl*ieR, *sabl*e, *subl*ime, *subl*imity,
3 *settl*eR, *subtl*e, *saddl*eR, *saddl*ery, *sidl*e, *sidl*ing, *satchel*s,
4 *sickl*e, *secl*ude, *secl*uder, *secl*uding, *secl*usive, *cycl*ist,
5 *cycl*oid, *Cycl*ops, *safer*, *suffer*, *suffer*eR, *suffer*able, *suffr*age,

6 sa*vor*y, sa*vor*less, se*ver*ance, soo*ther*, see*ther*, si*mmer*,
7 si*mmer*ing, sig*ner*, si*nner*, soo*ner*, si*nker*, ci*vil*, ci*vil*ize,
8 ci*vil*izer, ci*vil*ized, ci*villy*.

(*e*) *Spl*, *spr*, ETC., USED MEDIALLY AND FINALLY:—

1 dis*pl*ay, dis*pl*aced, dis*pl*eased, trace*able*, dis*obl*ige, dis*able*,
2 redu*cible*, despis*able*, dispos*able*, dis*cl*ose, dis*cl*osure,
3 dis*cl*aimer, plausi*ble*, peace*ably*, appeas*able*, chas*uble*,
4 e*xpl*ainable, e*xpl*ainer, e*xpl*icable, e*xpl*icitly, e*xpl*ode,
5 e*xpl*ORE, e*xpl*osive, fusi*ble*, infusi*ble*, efface*able*, ineffacea*ble*,
6 visi*bly*, invisi*bly*, pede*stal*, fratri*cidal*, matri*cidal*, pas*chal*,
7 tisi*cal*, tricy*cle*, to*xical*, to*xicol*ogy, e*xcl*aimer, e*xcl*usive,
8 e*xcl*usively, clas*sical*, physi*cally*, vesi*cle*, versi*cle*, encyc*l*ical,
9 encyc*lo*pedic, lackadaisi*cal*, peace-*offer*ing, deci*pher*,
10 deci*pher*eR, deci*pher*able, dis*fr*anchise, dis*fr*anchised,
11 phos*phor*, gypsi*fer*ous, luci*fer*, luci*fer*ous, passo*ver*, decei*ver*,
12 disse*ver*, disse*ver*ance, ELze*vir*, dul*cimer*, gossa*mer*, resu*mer*,
13 poiso*ner*, priso*ner*, bla*zoner*, embla*zoner*, desig*ner*,
14 dece*nnary*, disho*nor*, disho*nor*able, disho*nor*ing, chaste*ner*,
15 faste*ner*, vice*nary*, Liste*ner*, die-*sinker*, peace*ful*, peace*fully*,
16 bliss*ful*, ox-*fly*, house-*fly*, muse*ful*, obtrusi*vely*, eLusi*vely*,
17 iLLusi*vely*, tortoise-*shell*, disso*cial*, anti-*social*, vici*nal*,
18 vatici*nal*.

(*f*) THE CIRCLE *s* IS WRITTEN INSIDE THE HOOK OF *w*, IN WORDS LIKE THE FOLLOWING:—

1 *sw*ay, *sw*ays, *sw*aying, bas*sw*ood, praise*w*orthy, dis*su*asive,
2 fosse*w*ay, cause*w*ay, casso*w*ary, cross*w*ays, cross*w*ise.

EXERCISE 59.

Circles and Loops prefixed to Initial Hooks (continued).

Italic *s*, *sw*, or *st*, indicates that the circle or loop should be combined with the hook *r*, as in *spray*, *stouter*. The hyphen following *s*, *c*, or *x*, indicates that the circle *s* should be written *inside* the hook *r* or *l* or the hook of *w*, as in *splice*, *suffer*, *crossways*.

1. *A* famous author des*cr*ibes *the Sc*ribes *as a str*ong, *sober*,

class, *who* passed *their* time ex-*cl*usively *in the* s-*ubl*ime study *of the* sa*cr*ed laws. 2. *Their* indus*try and* love *of* labour were notic-ea*ble to all their* disc-*i*p*les*, *and* they exercised HIgh authority *as* expos-*itors of the scr*olls *of those* times. 3. *Sp*rays *of cyp*ress were carried at funeraLs *in* past days *to* ex-*pr*ess vis-*ibly the str*ength *of the* feeLings *of* sorrow *and* dis*tr*ess *in the* breasts *of the* survivors. 4. *In* some cases, rosemary OR bay leaves dis-*pl*aced *the cyp*ress, *but cyp*ress branches were oftener chosen *as* they last a long time. 5. *The* custom *may* seem *str*ange *in a* c-*ivil*ized people, *but though* we *may* poss-*ibly* disa*gr*ee *as to the* propriety *of it*, we must dis*cr*iminate *and* pause eRe we des*cr*ibe *it as* either fooLish OR dis*gr*acefuL. 6. We *should* dis-*cl*aim *a* desiRe *to swagger*, *to* pose *as* wis-ea*cr*es, OR *to* dis-*pl*ay *an* undue pride *in the str*ength *of any* abilities we *may* possess. 7. Sensible people *are* seldom bois-*ter*ous *in the* dis-*pl*ay *of their* wisdom. 8. *It is the mere* dabblers OR *scr*ibbleRs *who* try *to* dis-*cl*ose *all* they know. 9. *It is use*less *for a sweeper to* throw *a str*aw *in the* face *of a str*ong breeze. 10. *It is* carried away by *the str*onger foRce, *and has* no *str*ength *to* resist. 11. We a*re in a* sense *str*aws, also, carried aLong *in the str*uggle *to* reach *a* HigheR leveL. 12. We *should be* modest *and scr*upulous see*kers for* true wisdom, faithful *str*ivers *for the* goal, *and* lovers *of the* right *for its* own sake. 13. We *should* leave *all* unworthy *and* dis-hon*or*able *things to swagger*ers, dec-ei*vers*, *and* evil des-ig*ners*, *who* prey *on the* foibles *of their* fellows *and* seek *to* stop *the* progress *of our* race. (288)

EXERCISE 60.

Circles and Loops prefixed to Initial Hooks (continued).

Read the Note at the head of Exercise 59.

1. *I should* dis*tr*ust *him who* boasts *of his str*ength *and swagger*s over *his* skiLL; *for*, *as I have* noticed, *very str*ong *and* skiLful people dis-*cl*aim ex-*tr*a *str*ength OR skiLL. 2. *The* mannerLy youth *has* no *scr*uple *in* sa*cr*ificing *his* own tastes *for the* sake *of* others. 3. *A* crossing *sweeper may give a*

Lesson *in* c-*ivil*ity *to* proud wis-ea*cr*es. 4. Many *who are* otherwise *sober* people carry *their str*ange fads *to* ex-*tr*emes. 5. Many *a spr*uce youth s-*uffers from the* folly *of* supposing *his* neighbours admiRe *his spr*uceness. 6. *He* hopes *to see his* fame *sp*read; *but*, alas, *he is his* own dec-ei*ver*, *for* few *of his* fellows *are str*uck by *his* ability. 7. UnLess we sow *the* right seeds *in Spr*ing, we *shall* reap *the* wrong crop *in* Autumn 8. *It is* advis-a*ble to* s-*ettle our* aim *in* life *as* eaRly *as* poss-i*ble*, *and* seek *to* follow *it* steadily. 9. *An* honorable boy *should have* no *scr*uple *in* ex-*pr*essing *his* dislike *of* dis-ho*nor*able counseL. 10. *It is* cowardice *to* do evil simply *from the* feaR of dis-*pl*easing others. 11. OnLy *the* most su*per*ficial people *can* teach otherwise. 12. *Have a care* lest in youR search *for* eRRoRs *in* others *you may* overLook youR own most notic-ea*ble* follies. 13. *The* faster *a* c-y*cl*ist rides aLong *the* road, *the* less beauty does *he* notice *in the* scenery. 14. *There are very* many ex-*tr*emists among c-y*cl*ists. 15. *As you* go aLong life's road, take *care* lest *you* follow *their* example. 16. *The more* troublesome *the* task, *the stouter should be the* resolve *to* conquer *it*. 17. *You may think me a* sad preacher, *but I have* seen *str*ange sights *in my* time, *and* many failuRes through lack *of* wisdom. (271)

EXERCISE 61.

Circles and Loops prefixed to Initial Hooks (continued).

Read the Note at the head of Exercise 59.

1. *The swagger*er *is* just *the* fellow likely *to be* also *an* unseen dis-ho*nor*able Lis-te*ner*, *a* dec-ei*ver*, and *a* des-ig*ner of* evil. 2. *It is* s-a*fer to* leave such *a* fellow aLone, lest *he* drag *you* into *a scr*ape. 3. *It is very str*ange *how* some youths lose *all scr*uple, *and* stoop *to any* sHabby tricks *to* get *on in* life. 4. *A str*ong, *sober* fellow *can* onLy des*cr*ibe such tricks *as* dis*gr*acefuL. 5. *The str*uggle *for* su*pr*emacy *may be* seveRe, *but* we *should* refuse *to* pros*per* at *the* cost *of our* honor. 6. *An* honest fellow feaRs no dis-*cl*osure, *and his* simple pleasures *are all the sweeter for the str*enuous toil by *which* they *are* bought. 7. *A*

carriage *and a* pair *of* High *steppers are but a* pooR exchange *for a* virtuous name. 8. *It is* scaRcely poss-*ible to* judge *from a mere* sHow *of* riches *how* faR *their* possessoR *is* truly at ease. 9. *A* plaus-*ible* was-*trel*, *in the* last stages *of* despair, *may* appeaR *to be* leading *a* thoroughly enjoyable life. 10. *But the* day aRRives at last *which* dis-*closes a very* opposite state *of* affaiRs. 11. *His* villainy *is* exposed; *his spruceness* disappears; *and his* face wears *a* look *of* misery. 12. Few people regret *his* faLL, *for* they know *he was a* dec-eiv*er and a* sHam. 13. *In the str*ictest sense *the* pathway *of* honor *is* also *the* pathway *of* true wisdom. (225)

EXERCISE 62.

Circles and Loops prefixed to Initial Hooks (continued).

Read the Note at the head of Exercise 59.

1. *It is* always prais-e*worthy*, *and it may* poss-*ibly be* s-u*bl*ime *to* risk failuRe *in the* hope *of* rising *from a* low place *in* society *to a* HigheR. 2. *Nor is it* right *to* ex-*press* dis-a*pp*roval *of any* such triaL; *for* some *of our* best citizens *have sprung from* ex-*tr*eme poverty *to* riches *and* poweR. 3. *The* cos-*ter*monger *of* last s-u*mmer may be the* leader *of* commerce *in the spr*ing. 4. Examples *of* such *a* change *are* readily adduc-*ible from the* pages *of the* past. 5. Success *in* life *is* reduc-*ible to* no set *of* rules; *but it is* scaRcely poss-*ible for us to* succeed if we dis*tr*ust *our* own abilities. 6. *The* dex-*ter*ous *use of the* poweRs *given to us* by *the Lord may* bring both fame *and* riches, *and* at *the* same time *give us the* poweR *to* appease some *of the* dis*tr*ess vis-*ible to all who care to see it*. 7. *And*, we *may* add, *the* s-u*ff*erings *of the* pooR *are* notic-ea*ble* enough *to those who use their* eyes. 8. *A mere str*oll through *any of our* big cities dis-*cl*oses misery enough *to call* forth *an* exercise *of* charity *from all who are* able *and* disposed *to give*. 9. *But in all our* endeavours *to* rise, we must beware lest we allow *a* love *of* money *for its* own sake *to* master *us*, *and* des*tr*oy *our* sense *of* justice *to* others. 10. Such *a* feeLing necessariLy dis-*abl*es *us from being very* servic-ea*ble to our* fellows, *and if* we *have*

such *a* feeLing *the* s-*ooner* we stifle *it the* better. 11. *It is a* pitiful *thing to* desiRe riches *merely for the* sake *of being a* depos-*itor in a* bank. 12. FaR better *be an* honest crossing *sweeper in the* city. 13. *From all which a* sensible fellow *may* gather *the* Lesson *of* justice *and* mercy *to all.* (297)

EXERCISE 63.

Circles and Loops prefixed to Initial Hooks (continued).

Read the Note at the head of Exercise 59.

MessRs. Ta*sker and* S-ad*dle*R.

Dear SiRs,—We *have an* ex-*tra* heavy s-u*pply of str*ong *scr*ews, *in all* sizes, bought at *a* sale, *which* we *think may* poss-*ibly be* servic-ea*ble to you, and which* we *can* offer *you* at *a very* low price *for* casH. We *have* also *an* ex-*tr*emely *use*ful jack*scr*ew, *and a* set *of* die-s-*inker*'s tools, *for which* we *should* like *you to* make *us an* offer. If youR manager *can call* at *our* stoRes, at three o'clock *on* Friday, we *may be* able *to* s-et*tle a* price *for all these things.* We *have* onLy *a* small space *to* spaRe *for our* stock, *and the* s-*ooner* we dispose *of them the* better. YouRs faithfully, *Str*ingeR *and Spr*iggs. (119)

EXERCISE 64.

Circles and Loops prefixed to Initial Hooks (concluded).

Mr. ARthur S-*iddle*.

Dear SiR,—*In* reply *to* youR favour *of* Saturday last, both *the* bic-*ycle and* tric-*ycle are* ready, *and you can have them on* sHowing *the* official receipt *for the* charges *for* repaiRs. *It is* scaRcely necessary *to* say we *have* no di*str*ust *of you, but* we know *how* advis-a*ble it is for us to* stick *to our* ruLe *to* allow no c-*ycle to* leave *our* premises unLess *the* official receipt *for all* charges *is* produced. *This is* s-a*fer for all* parties. We were able *to* sol*der the* wire *you* spoke *of, and it is* now *all* right. YouRs truly, S-*ummers and* Sons. (105)

EXERCISE 65.

Contractions.

domestic, *mistake,* *never,* *never-theless,* *enlarge,* *notwithstanding,* *knowledge,* *acknowledge,* *regular,* *irregular,* *king-dom,* *influence,* *influenced,* *next*

1. *It is, as a* ruLe, *a mistake to* offer advice *on the domestic* affaiRs *of our* neighbours. 2. *Nevertheless, should our* counseL *be* sought, we *should never* refuse *to give it,* if we feeL we *have* enough *knowledge and influence to* enable *us to* do *so in a* wise way. 3. Still, we must *acknowledge the* utmost *care is* necessary *in these* cases, oR, *notwithstanding our* strong desiRe *to* remove *a* trouble, we *may* onLy *enlarge it.* 4. We *should be influenced in the* case by *our knowledge of the* people *who* seek *our* advice, *and be care*fuL *how* we decide *to give it,* lest *it be* scornfully refused. 5. *In* fact, *the next* best *thing to* wise counseL *is* no counseL at *all.* 6. *There are very* many people *in this kingdom who are* most eager *to* advise others ; *but,* strange *to* say, *the* most *regular* givers *of* advice *are the* most *irregular* takers *of it from* others. (154)

EXERCISE 66.

N Hook.

The hook *n*, attached to straight letters, is written in the same direction as that taken by the hands of a clock ; attached to curves, it is written inside the curve. In this Exercise italic *n* indicates that the hook *n* should be written.

(*a*) STRAIGHT STROKES HOOKED FOR *n* :—

1 pai*n*, Spai*n*, sprai*n*, splee*n*, trepa*n*, deepe*n*, cheape*n*, Japa*n*,
2 crepo*n*, Gilpi*n*, saucepa*n*, asHpa*n*, Mappi*n*, kneepa*n*, lupi*ne*,
3 rapi*ne*, weapo*n*, bi*n*, Bry*n*, Sabi*ne*, Dubli*n*, cabi*n*, Gibbo*n*,
4 thighbo*ne*, suburba*n*, uRba*n*, robi*n*, ribbo*n*, henba*ne*,

ta*n*, trai*n*, strai*n*, to*n*, spittoo*n*, platoo*n*, Presto*n*, batte*n*, Tatto*n*, Dutto*n*, detai*n*, detrai*n*, desti*ne*, cotto*n*, croto*n*, Gratta*n*, festoo*n*, fatte*n*, frighte*n*, Austi*n*, smitte*n*, sweete*n*, sco*ne*, scree*n*, skeleto*n*, AsHto*n*, mutto*n*, Milto*n*, Newto*n*, lighte*n*, rotte*n*, retai*n*, restrai*n*, routi*ne*, Wetto*n*, platen, maintai*n*, do*n*, Seddo*n*, bidde*n*, deade*n*, Farringdo*n*, Flodde*n*, Snowdo*n*, madde*n*, anody*ne*, intesti*ne*, entrai*n*, olde*n*, lade*n*, redde*n*, woode*n*, Wobur*n*, hidde*n*, chi*n*, birche*n*, kitche*n*, urchi*n*, Joh*n*, pigeo*n*, bludgeo*n*, Troja*n*, dudgeo*n*, gudgeo*n*, virgi*n*, regio*n*, origi*n*, surgeo*n*, sturgeo*n*, imagi*ne*, engi*ne*, steam-engi*ne*, legio*n*, widgeo*n*, ca*n*, peca*n*, beaco*n*, Tusca*n*, deaco*n*, chicke*n*, falco*n*, Africa*n*, vatica*n*, thicke*n*, ski*n*, scree*n*, stricke*n*, spoke*n*, slacke*n*, sunke*n*, sHake*n*, sHrunke*n*, McCa*nn*, Maclea*n*, manniki*n*, napki*n*, like*n*, America*n*, ERski*ne*, recli*ne*, awake*n*, go*ne*, paga*n*, bega*n*, Teggi*n*, dragoo*n*, Keega*n*, Groga*n*, Fagi*n*, Afgha*n*, Afghanista*n*, suffraga*n*, spring-gu*n*, chagri*n*, MiCHiga*n*, Mulliga*n*, noggi*n*, lagoo*n*, oRga*n*, ORego*n*, Hoga*n*, wre*n*, rai*n*, Parri*n*, barre*n*, outra*n*, Dora*n*, chur*n*, adjour*n*, Curra*n*, cor*n*, Gar*n*, foreig*n*, flori*n*, sovereig*n*, thor*n*, sire*n*, sHor*n*, Mora*n*, mari*ne*, lor*n*, wor*n*, wester*n*, wyver*n*, year*n*, hero*n*, hawthor*n*, wi*n*, Darwi*n*, Kenwy*n*, Irwi*n*, wa*ne*, wee*n*, wa*n*, yaw*n*, ye*n*, ho*ne*, hew*n*.

(*b*) CURVED STROKES HOOKED FOR *n* :—

fa*n*, fi*n*, paraffi*n*, dolphi*n*, morphi*ne*, elfi*n*, flow*n*, Fly*nn*, frow*n*, sypho*n*, va*n*, Beva*n*, Cava*n*, crave*n*, clove*n*, grave*n*, thrive*n*, Stephe*n*, sylva*n*, shave*n*, sHrive*n*, Nive*n*, live*n*, rave*n*, wove*n*, have*n*, thi*n*, pytho*n*, Natha*n*, earthe*n*, thi*ne*, brethre*n*, leathern, heathe*n*, thro*ne*, enthro*ne*, dethro*ne*, assig*n*, zo*ne*, ozo*ne*, sHi*ne*, outsHi*ne*, sunsHi*ne*, moonsHi*ne*, maCHi*ne*, oCEa*n*, asHe*n*, sHri*ne*, ensHri*ne*, me*n*, pressme*n*, bowme*n*, tea-me*n*, drayme*n*, caRme*n*, exami*ne*, gammo*n*, foeme*n*, fiReme*n*, flame*n*, freeme*n*, vermi*n*, seame*n*, stame*n*, spokesme*n*, statesme*n*, Scotchme*n*, sHowme*n*, mammon, layme*n*, eRmi*ne*, remai*n*, weigh-ma*n*, woodsma*n*, yeoma*n*, hangma*n*, ni*ne*, Penni*ne*, benig*n*, tanni*n*, cani*ne*,

13 Glenno*n*, sHanno*n*, unknow*n*, line*n*, renow*n*, lea*n*, polle*n*,
14 balloo*n*, talo*n*, Dillo*n*, colo*n*, gallo*n*, felo*n*, villai*n*, sea-lio*n*,
15 stole*n*, swolle*n*, sulle*n*, siRloi*n*, melo*n*, aniLi*n*e, aRRaig*n*,
16 swoR*n*, steR*n*, seceR*n*, NaiR*n*, inuR*n*, hangeR-o*n*.

(*c*) *N* HOOK USED MEDIALLY:—

1 pai*n*ing, pai*n*fuL, pe*n*knife, pi*n*ing, pru*n*ing, piqua*n*cy,
2 ope*n*ing, bo*n*ing, brow*n*ing, ba*n*dy, aba*n*do*n*, ba*n*isH,
3 ba*n*tam, ta*n*ning, tu*n*ing, ta*n*sy, trai*n*ing, deepe*n*ing,
4 dro*n*ing, dai*n*ty, dai*n*tily, disdai*n*ing, deaco*n*ess, Chippe*n*-
5 dale, cha*n*tey, ge*n*tile, ca*n*ing, cli*n*ic, co*n*ic, clea*n*ly,
6 kee*n*ly, Ki*n*sey, gai*n*ing, gri*n*ning, gai*n*say, gle*n*garry,
7 falco*n*ry, foreig*n*eRs, flippa*n*cy, fraudule*n*cy, flatule*n*cy,
8 vagra*n*cy, scree*n*ing, spi*n*ning, sprai*n*ing, souther*n*eR,
9 maintai*n*ing, mecha*n*ics, mecha*n*ism, misrecko*n*ing,
10 mour*n*eR, madde*n*ing, labur*n*um, lighte*n*ing, like*n*ing,
11 lear*n*eR, recli*n*ing, repi*n*ing, redde*n*ing, reple*n*isH,
12 restrai*n*ing, retai*n*ing, awake*n*ing, wi*n*e-bibber, wi*n*neR,
13 year*n*eR, yaw*n*eR, he*n*-roost, he*n*-coop, fa*n*cy, fa*n*faRe,
14 fi*n*ery, fi*n*eness, fi*n*ish, fra*n*chise, Fra*n*cisca*n*, fre*n*zy,
15 Fre*n*ch, fri*n*ge, va*n*ishing, vei*n*ing, vi*n*ery, thi*n*ning,
16 thi*n*ness, thi*n*nish, assig*n*ing, strengthe*n*ing, stubbor*n*ness,
17 stubbor*n*ly, ma*n*ning, mai*n*mast, ma*n*uRe, mea*n*ness,
18 mea*n*ingLess, mi*n*ing, mo*n*aRch, malig*n*eR, nu*n*nery,
19 lengthe*n*ing, li*n*sey, lo*n*ely, late*n*cy, eaR*n*ings, aRRaig*n*ing,
20 aRRa*n*ge, aRRa*n*ger, disaRRa*n*ge, ARu*n*del, oRa*n*ge,
21 ORa*n*geman, redole*n*cy, repelle*n*cy.

EXERCISE 67.

F or V Hook.

The hook *f* or *v* is attached to straight letters only, and is written in the opposite direction to that taken by the hands of a clock. In this Exercise, italic *f* or *v* indicates that the letter should be represented by the hook.

(*a*) THE HOOK *f* OR *v* USED FINALLY :—

1 puniti*v*e, proo*f*, pro*v*e, repro*v*e, fiReproo*f*, pikesta*ff*, epita*ph*,
2 tipsta*ff*, dista*ff*, bre*v*e, semibre*v*e, berea*v*e, blu*ff*, toug*h*,

3 talkati*v*e, attracti*v*e, autogra*ph*, dati*v*e, depri*v*e, decepti*v*e,
4 digra*ph*, dro*v*e, dra*ff*, deri*v*e, cha*f*e, chou*gh*, achie*v*e, Jo*v*e,
5 gy*v*e, Je*ff*, co*v*e, cou*gh*, car*v*e, ski*ff*, clou*gh*, cli*ff*, Wycli*ff*,
6 clea*v*e, cal*f*, caiti*ff*, accreti*v*e, expleti*v*e, ga*ff*, ga*v*e, gro*v*e,
7 glo*v*e, foxglo*v*e, festi*v*e, federati*v*e, foRmati*v*e, voti*v*e,
8 vocati*v*e, sporti*v*e, sedati*v*e, secreti*v*e, sensiti*v*e, suppositi*v*e,
9 sera*ph*, ser*v*e, preser*v*e, obser*v*e, deser*v*e, reser*v*e, sheri*ff*,
10 mangro*v*e, monogra*ph*, amati*v*e, moti*v*e, nati*v*e, neckerchie*f*,
11 engra*v*e, illati*v*e, illustrati*v*e, iLLuminati*v*e, leniti*v*e, laxati*v*e,
12 resti*v*e, retrie*v*e, recitati*v*e, refoRmati*v*e, regenerati*v*e,
13 relati*v*e, remunerati*v*e, restricti*v*e, restorati*v*e, wai*f*, wea*v*e,
14 unwea*v*e, hu*ff*, ho*v*e, hea*v*e.

(*b*) THE HOOK *f* OR *v* USED MEDIALLY :—

1 proo*f*ing, pro*v*ing, pa*v*ing, pre*f*er, pre*f*erring, pre*f*erable,
2 pri*v*et, pri*v*acy, pri*v*ateer, pri*v*iti*v*e, pro*f*it, pro*f*itable,
3 pro*f*itless, pro*v*ide, pro*v*able, pro*v*en, pro*v*erb, pro*v*incial,
4 pro*v*oke, pro*v*ocati*v*e, pro*v*okeR, pu*ff*ery, bre*v*ity, bre*v*et,
5 ta*ff*eta, ta*ff*raiL, ti*ff*in, tou*gh*ening, tou*gh*ish, tra*ff*ic, ty*ph*oon,
6 ty*ph*oid, da*ff*odil, dea*f*ening, dea*f*ness, di*v*inity, di*v*ersity,
7 di*ver*sify, de*f*er, de*f*erential, di*v*ide, drau*gh*ty, drau*ght*sman,
8 dri*v*eL, dri*v*eLing, dri*v*en, de*f*ence, de*f*enceless, de*f*ensible,
9 de*f*eat, de*v*otee, cha*ff*inch, cha*f*ing, ju*v*eniLe, ju*v*enescence,
10 gy*v*ing, festi*v*ity, effecti*v*eness, secreti*v*eness, sensiti*v*eness,
11 ser*v*er, preser*v*er, obser*v*er, reser*v*er, scenogra*ph*ic, steno-
12 gra*ph*ic, sporti*v*eness, amati*v*eness, mysti*f*ied, monogra*ph*ic,
13 moti*v*ity, nati*v*ity, nitri*f*ied, lexigra*ph*ic, lithogra*ph*ic,
14 orthogra*ph*ic, reco*v*ery, disco*v*ery, reju*v*enescence, rebu*ff*ing,
15 repro*v*ing, repro*v*able, resti*v*eness, retrie*v*able, re*v*ersal,
16 re*v*ersed, re*v*ersing, re*v*erti*v*e, re*f*er, re*f*eree, re*f*erable,
17 re*f*erential, re*f*erring, hierogly*ph*ic.

(*c*) FINAL *n*, *f*, OR *v*, FOLLOWED BY A SOUNDED VOWEL, MUST BE EXPRESSED BY A STROKE CONSONANT.

In the following words the italic type indicates that the hook should be employed:—

1 paw*n*, pawnee; oppug*n*, puny; pi*n*e, piney; polle*n*,

polony; plai*n*, Pliny; spi*ne*, spinous; pa*ve*, pavo; pu*ff*, puffy; bo*ne*, bonny; brai*n*, brainy; ba*n*, bonus; bar*n*, barony; bra*ve*, bravo; blu*ff*, bluffy; butto*n*, botany; Britai*n*, Brittany; biogra*ph*, biography; to*ne*, tony; tur*n*, tourney; du*n*, donee; de*n*, deny; di*ne*, Dinah; desti*ne*, destiny; Du*ff*, Du*ff*y; dea*f*, de*f*y; detai*n*, dittany; cha*ff*, chaffy; chi*ne*, China, Chinese; Ju*ne*, Juno; ji*n*, jinnee; ke*n*, Kenny; cor*n*, corny; Curra*n*, corona; clou*gh*, Clovis; cra*ne*, cranny; cotto*n*, cottony; clow*n*, Cluney; co*ve*, covey; grai*n*, granny; grie*ve*, grievous; glutto*n*, gluttony; glute*n*, glutinous; Gasco*n*, Gascony; fu*n*, funny; felo*n*, felony; foreig*n*, farina; vai*n*, venue; villai*n*, villainous; vi*ne*, vinous; thor*n*, thorny; thi*n*, Athene; thro*ne*, threepenny; assig*n*, assignee; sudde*n*, Sydney; ski*n*, skinny; sicke*n*, sickness; stame*n*, stamina; summo*n*, simony; splee*n*, spleeny; stole*n*, steeliness; ser*ve*, survey, service; sera*ph*, seraphic; ozo*ne*, ozonize; SHi*ne*, SHiny, SHyness; CHica*ne*, CHicanery; mutto*n*, mutiny, mutinous; maCHi*ne*, maCHinist; Mullen, Maloney; micropho*ne*, microphonous; moonSHi*ne*, moonSHiny; myogra*ph*, myography; neckerchie*f*, ancho*vy*; Na*n*, Nanny; Newma*n*, nominee; engi*ne*, angina; layme*n*, lamina; lati*n*, latinize; like*n*, likeness; lengthe*n*, lengthiness; lio*n*, lioness, lionized; lithogra*ph*, lithography; iLLumi*ne*, iLLuminee; Alba*n*, Albany; albume*n*, albuminize; ERi*n*, aRena; ARRa*n*, ARno; iRo*n*, iRony; aRchon, ORkney; origi*n*, Origenist; rata*n*, ratany; redde*n*, redness; rave*n*, ravenous; ripe*n*, ripeness; recitati*ve*, recitativo; regio*n*, regina; retai*n*, retinue; reser*ve*, reservist; ravi*ne*, revenue; roma*n*, romany; wa*n*, wanness; wi*n*, winnow; wor*n*, weariness; Wetto*n*, weightiness; wi*ne*, winy; woode*n*, woodiness; ho*ne*, honey; heathe*n*, heathenize; hew*n*, heinous; hoyde*n*, headiness; headsman, head-money; he*n*, henna; hea*ve*, heavy; Hocki*n*, Hackney.

EXERCISE 68.

The Hooks N, and F or V (continued).

The italic type indicates that the letter should be expressed by a hook.

1. *He is a* bra*v*e ma*n* *who* daRes *to* defy *a* roug*h* opposeR *of his* policy. 2. *A* reproo*f* *in* youth *may* preser*v*e *us from* mischie*f* *in* age. 3. Many *a* ma*n* *has* faLLe*n* *in the* struggle *of* life through *his* teacher's feaR *of* annoying *him* by reproo*f* *in* eaRly youth. 4. Small *things* make up *the* life *of a* ma*n*, *as* many drops go *to* foRm *an* ocea*n*. 5. *It is* better *to* stri*v*e *to* retrie*v*e *the* past tha*n* *to* grie*v*e over *its* follies. 6. *A* vai*n* ma*n* *is* seldom aware *of his* vanity. 7. *A* ma*n* *should* lear*n* *to* eaR*n* money *in* some way, eve*n* though *he be* bor*n* rich. 8. *An* acti*v*e ma*n* *can* easily exercise *his* acti*v*ity, if *he* desiRes *to* do *so*; *but* many profess acti*v*ity, *and* still refuse *to* ser*v*e *their* fellow-me*n* *in any* way. 9. *A* genuine ma*n* seldom *gives* pai*n* *to* others oR pro*v*okes *them to* anger. 10. Many drunke*n* me*n* appeaR *to think the* drink *which* stole *their* reason *may* also pro*v*e *a* restorati*v*e; *and so* they drink agai*n*. 11. *The* taste *for* beeR oR wi*n*e grows upo*n* them, *and* at last they *are* unable *to* restrai*n* *their* desiRe *for the* poison *which may* carry *them to the* gra*v*e. 12. *You may* obser*v*e *how* few me*n* *there are who* aba*n*do*n* *an* evil custom *which* they *have* pursued *for a* long time. 13. *This should* assist *you to* refrai*n* *from* following such evil ways. 14. *A* puny ma*n* *may be* braver tha*n* *a* big o*n*e, *and*, *in* fact, many *of our* bravest leaders *have* bee*n* diminuti*v*e *in* statuRe. (253)

EXERCISE 69.

The Hooks N and F or V (continued).

See Note at the head of Exercise 68.

1. If *you* desiRe *to* achie*v*e youR purpose *and* sustai*n* youR know*n* ability *as a* fi*n*e business ma*n*, *you* must take *care* lest *you* display chagri*n* oR scor*n* *in* presence *of a* likely customeR.

2. *It is* vain *to* imagine *you can have all* your own way *and* get *the* best *of* every bargain. 3. Men *may* try *to* cheapen your wares, *and you* must evince no disdain *of* thin profits, now *and* again. 4. *A* stubborn mien *can* scarcely strengthen your hopes *of more* business. 5. *The* salesman, like *the* fisherman, *may have to* angle long ere *he* secures *a* catch. 6. *A* talkative man, by undue puffing, *may* defeat *his* own purpose *and* drive away *a* likely buyer. 7. *A* superlative tone soon provokes *an* honest trader, *and he* often enough administers *an* effective rebuke *to a* glib-tongued agent by declining *to* buy *his* stuff. 8. Reasonable brevity, *an* attractive manner, *and a* stern resolve *in* no case *to* swerve *from the* truth *for the* sake *of* selling *a* line, *are* fine credentials *for the* aspiring salesman. (172)

EXERCISE 70.

The Hooks N, and F or V (continued).

See Note at the head of Exercise 68.

1. Japan *and the* Japanese *are* worth *the* study *of all who* like *to* read *of the* origin *and* advance *of the* races *of the* globe. 2. Some people imagine *the* isles *of* Japan *are of* volcanic origin; *but the* chief men *of* science deny *this*, though they observe *there are* many volcanoes *and* sulphur springs *in the* place, *and the* people feel earth tremors, one *may* say, every day. 3. They *have as* many varieties *of* weather *in* Japan *as we have, and more; for* besides rough breezes, rain, snow, frost, *and* sunshine, they often *have a* visit *from the* terrible storms known *as* typhoons, *which* do immense damage *to* houses *and to* ships. 4. *The* Japanese *are a* dainty, economical, *and* attractive people, ready *to* learn, *and* strong *to* retain *the things* they look upon *as* profitable *to them*. 5. They *are* no lovers *of* strife; *but* they *can be* brave, *and* even stubborn, *in the* defence *and* maintenance *of their* rights. 6. They *are* clever farmers, *and* they raise fine, heavy crops *of* rice, *which is the* chief food *of the* people. 7. Coal *and* iron mining *is* vigorously carried *on, and, in* fact, Japan *is* rich *in* many minerals. 8. *The* skill *of the* Japanese *in* japanning *has* long

been widely known, *and the* artistic finish they *give to the things* they make *is* above *all* praise. 9. They weave lovely silk fabrics, *from the* sale *of which* they derive *a* big revenue. 10. Strange *to* say, up *to* 1853 no foreigneR *was* able *to* gain *an* entry into Japan; *for the* Japanese looked upon *all* foreigneRS *as* worthy onLy *of* disdain *and* scorn. 11. *But* since then *there have* been many changes. Japanese statesmen began *to think* they *should* abandon *their* reserve, *and* allow *their* people *to* try *and* derive profit *from* following *the* line *of the* men *from the* Western states. 12. They gave *the* plan *a* triaL; *the* gates *of their* cities were thrown open *to* foreign traders, *and* now *the* Japanese dealeRS *are as* keen at *a* bargain, *and as* ready *to* eaRn a guinea *as any* people we serve. (348)

EXERCISE 71.

The Hooks N, and F or V (continued).

See Note at the head of Exercise 68.

Mr. John Bullen.

Dear SiR,—Referring *to* youR favour *of the* 9th, we imagine youR customeR must mean *a* tureen like *the* one we sold *you in* June last. We gave *you* notice then *it was the* last *of the* make we *should* supply, *as the* cost *of* producing *it was* such *as to* make *it* positively hopeless *for us to* derive *any* profit *from the* sales. *It was a very* attractive design, *of* tough make, *and* thoroughly fiReproof; *but* we were unable *to* obtain *a* faiR price *for it, and* we were pleased *to* sell *you the* last one. We *have* plenty *of* others *in* stock, *of* fine design *and* finish, *and* we trust youR customeR *may* choose one *of these from the* enclosed list. *A* line *from you is* enough *to* secuRe *the* dispatch *of the* tureen, oR *of any of the things* spoken *of in the* list, by return. YouRs truly, Stephen Brown *and* Sons. (158)

EXERCISE 72.

The Hooks N, and F or V (concluded).

Mr. David Green.

Dear SiR,—We *have* youR favour *of the* 10th, *and* we *shall be* pleased *to* aRRa*ng*e *to see* youR age*n*t *and* exami*ne* *his* samples *of* sHeepski*n* rugs. We sell *more of these* fa*n*cy rugs tha*n* *any* other house *in this* tow*n*; *but* we *are* kee*n* buyeRs, *and* if *you are to* serve *us you* must mark *the* prices *as* low *as* possible. YouRs faithfully, Benjami*n* Goug*h* *and* Nephew. (71)

EXERCISE 73.

Circles and Loops added to Final Hooks.

A circle or loop is added to the hook *n*, attached to straight letters, by turning the hook into a circle or loop. In this Exercise the italic type indicates that the letters should be combined in a circle or loop.

(*a*) *ns* ADDED TO STRAIGHT LETTERS :—

1 pa*ns*, pe*ns*, pi*ns*, paw*ns*, pru*nes*, pla*ns*, paga*ns*, poltroo*ns*,
2 patro*ns*, precede*nce*, pitta*nce*, picaroo*ns*, plate*ns*, penite*nce*,
3 provide*nce*, pippi*ns*, becko*ns*, ba*ns*, baro*ns*, butto*ns*,
4 begi*ns*, betoke*ns*, blacke*ns*, bludgeo*ns*, blackthor*ns*,
5 Brito*ns*, bygo*nes*, teaspoo*ns*, tamari*ns*, te*nse*, tra*nce*,
6 tar*ns*, tighte*ns*, twope*nce*, attu*nes*, dispe*nse*, dragoo*ns*,
7 diffide*nce*, decli*nes*, decade*nce*, deepe*ns*, dilige*nce*, desti*nes*,
8 discipli*nes*, distrai*ns*, du*ns*, chi*nes*, chaplai*ns*, chicke*ns*,
9 chur*ns*, Japa*n's*, jack-pla*nes*, jaw-bo*nes*, adjour*ns*, coupo*ns*,
10 cantee*ns*, cor*ns*, kitte*ns*, cabi*ns*, cocoo*ns*, crede*nce*, expe*nse*,
11 Clare*nce*, cro*nes*, accide*nce*, Gibbo*n's*, Gasco*ns*, gle*ns*,
12 gobli*ns*, glutto*ns*, falco*ns*, fer*ns*, fragra*nce*, flago*ns*,
13 frighte*ns*, festoo*ns*, avoida*nce*, vetera*ns*, velvetee*ns*,
14 vengea*nce*, Vulca*n's*, thicke*ns*, threepe*nce*, threate*ns*,
15 sustai*ns*, assista*nce*, Austi*n's*, sexto*ns*, sacrista*ns*, sixpe*nce*,
16 sardi*nes*, sadde*ns*, suspe*nse*, sprai*ns*, sicke*ns*, spur*ns*,
17 sati*ns*, straighte*ns*, sHeep-ru*ns*, mitte*ns*, maide*ns*,
18 maintai*ns*, mandari*ns*, emerge*nce*, Maki*n's*, mari*nes*,
19 mour*ns*, neglige*nce*, entrai*ns*, lagoo*ns*, lear*ns*, like*ns*,
20 legio*ns*, lighte*ns*, luncheo*ns*, aRRoga*nce*, ribbo*ns*, repi*nes*,
21 retai*ns*, regio*ns*, recli*nes*, ridda*nce*, resista*nce*, robi*ns*,
22 weapo*ns*, widgeo*ns*, wi*nce*, o*nce*, yaw*ns*, year*ns*, Yucata*n's*,
23 he*ns*, hero*ns*, Hocki*ns*, headsto*nes*.

(*b*) *nss* ADDED TO STRAIGHT LETTERS :—

1 pra*nces*, pri*nces*, appeara*nces*, prefere*nces*, pitta*nces*,
2 prete*nces*, bro*nzes*, twope*nces*, tra*nces*, trou*nces*, du*nces*,
3 dista*nces*, dispe*nses*, disappeara*nces*, disturba*nces*, cha*nces*,
4 cade*nces*, cleara*nces*, expe*nses*, gla*nces*, Flore*nce's*, three-
5 pe*nces*, sixpe*nces*, sco*nces*, subside*nces*, aSSura*nces*,
6 inSura*nces*, ninepe*nces*, insta*nces*, eLega*nces*, refere*nces*,
7 remitta*nces*, resembla*nces*, iRRevere*nces*, revere*nces*,
8 reside*nces*, respo*nses*, wi*nces*, enha*nces*, ensco*nces*.

(*c*) *nst* AND *nstr* ADDED TO STRAIGHT LETTERS :—

1 pou*nced*, pra*nced*, bou*nced*, bro*nzed*, dispe*nsed*, dista*nced*,
2 da*nced*, revere*nced*, cha*nced*, ca*nst*, clea*nsed*, gla*nced*,
3 agai*nst*, ri*nsed*, wi*nced*, entra*nced*, enha*nced*, insta*nced*,
4 ensco*nced*, indulge*nced*, pu*nster*, pun*sters*, spi*nster*,
5 spi*nsters*, Du*nster*, D*unster's*.

EXERCISE 74.

Circles and Loops added to Final Hooks (continued).

In the case of curves hooked for *n*, and of straight letters hooked for *f* or *v*, the circle *s* is added by writing the circle inside the hook, so that both hook and circle may be clearly seen. In this Exercise, italic *s* or *c* indicates that the circle *s* must be written inside the hook for the preceding *n*, *f*, or *v*.

(*a*) *ns* ADDED TO CURVES :—

1 fawn*s*, fan*s*, fen*s*, refine*s*, coffin*s*, griffin*s*, frown*s*, refrain*s*,
2 oven*s*, even*s*, van*s*, Evan*s*, cavern*s*, Athen*s*, Nathan'*s*,
3 Jonathan'*s*, python*s*, throne*s*, dethrone*s*, thin*s*, assign*s*,
4 zone*s*, Eason'*s*, sHun*s*, oCean*s*, sHine*s*, sHrine*s*, enSHrine*s*,
5 man'*s*, men'*s*, mean*s*, foReman'*s*, demon*s*, lemon*s*,
6 Simmon*s*, famine'*s*, sHowman'*s*, laymen'*s*, nine*s*, pennon*s*,
7 cannon*s*, linen*s*, sHannon'*s*, lawn*s*, len*s*, balloon*s*, talon*s*,
8 Dillon'*s*, colon*s*, gallon*s*, felon*s*, villain*s*, saloon*s*, malign*s*,
9 Malone'*s*, muslin*s*, eaRn*s*, disceRn*s*, inuRn*s*, seceRn*s*,
10 pronoun*s*, Bowman'*s*, ploughman'*s*, roughen*s*, ravine*s*,

11 ravens, seRmons, muffins, dolphins, domains, watchman's,
12 Benjamin's, Clemen's, iLLumines, seamen's, Athlone's,
13 Bannerman's, havens, heathens, syphons, livens, stamens,
14 Stevens, Tonan's, Kathleen's, Canaan's, outlines, opulence,
15 prevalence, balance, over-balance, unbalance, flatulence,
16 valance, Valence, violence, virulence, silence, succulence,
17 somnoLence, reliance, free-lance, excellence.

(*b*) *fs* OR *vs* ADDED TO STRAIGHT LETTERS :—

1 puffs, paves, proves, reproves, deprives, reprieves, buffs,
2 rebuffs, breves, semibreves, bluffs, tiffs, troughs, retrieves,
3 Treves, mastiffs, caitiffs, motives, operatives, natives,
4 incentives, epitaphs, sedatives, dives, Khedive's, chiefs,
5 neckerchiefs, cliffs, Wycliffe's, aRchives, graves, engraves,
6 Musgrave's, digraphs, autographs, chronographs, raves,
7 bereaves, tariffs, derives, carves, scarves, serves, preserves,
8 observes, deserves, reserves, swerves, sHeriffs, waifs,
9 fish-wives, ale-wives, hives, heaves, huffs, fisticuffs,
10 dye-stuffs, distaffs.

(*c*) MEDIAL HOOK *n*, AND CIRCLE *s*.

Hook *n* and circle *s*, when used medially, must both be shown.

1 caravansary, lanceR, balanceR, silenceR, lonesome,
2 lonesomeness, winsome, ransom, ransomeR, ransomless,
3 ransoming, hansom, Stevenson, even-song.

(*d*) MEDIAL STROKE *f*, *v*, OR *n*, AND CIRCLE *s*.

The stroke *f*, *v*, or *n*, followed by the circle *s*, must be written in the following and similar words :—

1 sponsaL, profuseLy, revisit, transit, travesty, dynasty,
2 dishonesty, denseLy, diffusive, divisible, chancery, chanceL,
3 Johnson, cancer, cancerous, cavesson, offensive, fencer,
4 fenceLess, vivacity, thenceforth, Spencer, sacrificing,
5 immensity, immenseLy, manifesto, lancet, refusaL, revising,
6 rancid, ransack, renounced.

(*e*) THE LIGHT SOUND OF *-ence*, ETC., AFTER A CURVED LETTER.

Except in the case of *l* preceded by another consonant (see par. *a*) the stroke *n* and circle *s* must be employed to express the light sound of *-ence*, etc., immediately following a curved letter, as in the following words :—

fence, offence, France, affiance, flounce, evince, thence, essence, science, usance, manse, romance, immense, mince, nonce, Nance, announce, pronounce, denounce, renounce, lance, allowance, alliance, assonance, eminence, imminence, dissonance, resonance, mensurable, invincible, lanciform, romancing, vincible, fencing, fencible, flouncing.

(*f*) *nces*, *nst*, OR *nstr* FOLLOWING A CURVED CONSONANT.

The stroke *n*, with the large circle or the loop, must be used when these combinations follow a curved consonant, as in the following words :—

fences, offences, flounces, France's, affiances, evinces, essences, sciences, minces, romances, announces, pronounces, denounces, renounces, lances, allowances, alliances, eminences, fenced, affianced, flounced, evinced, minced, romanced, announced, pronounced, denounced, renounced, minister, minster, minsters, monsters, Axminster, Munster.

EXERCISE 75.

Circles and Loops added to Final Hooks (continued)

In this Exercise, and in Exercises 76 to 79 inclusive, groups of final consonants which may be combined in a circle or loop, are printed in italic. The hyphen preceding *s* or *c* indicates that the circle *s* is to be written inside the hook for the preceding *n*, *f*, or *v*. Write upward *r* for *Rome*, *Roman*, and *Romance*.

1. *The* signs *of the* reside*nce of the* Roman-s *in* Britain still remain through *the* vigilan-ce *and* prude*nce of the* authorities, though *the* maintenance *of them is a* cause *of* expe*nse*. 2. *The* endura*nce of these* Roman remain-s, *in* defiance *of* time,

prove-s *the* excellen-ce *of the* plan followed by *the* Roman-s *in* laying *the* line-s *for the* edifices they reared. 3. Artists *of* eminence *have* often been entra*nced* at *the* appeara*nce of the* remain-s, *and have* pronounced *them* admirable specimen-s *of* honest *and* skiLful labour. 4. *The* Romance tongues were spoken *in those* places *which* were at one time provinces *of* Rome. 5. *The* romances *which have* entra*nced*, *and* possibly unbalanced *so* many youths, *are* based upon *the* marvellous *and* fictitious. 6. *The* patience, *the* sufferings, *the* grievances, *of the* lone-some princess; *the* bravery, *the* cHivalry, *and the* endura*nce of the* pri*nce*; *the* timely appeara*nces of the* lovely fairy; *the* malevolen-ce *of the* ugly monster *in* charge *of the* prison cave-s; *the* suspe*nse of the* relative-s *of the* princess; *the* rescue; *the* return *in* triumph; *the* bright lances *of the* men, *and the* pretty dresses *of the* maide*ns* at *the* pri*nce's* wedding—*these and* such like recitals *have given hours of* brightness *to* many *a* man *who* now frown-s oR scoff-s *should his* own boy evince *a* desiRe *to* read similaR tales. 7. *The first* authors *of these* stories wrote *in the* Romance tongues; he*nce the* name "romances" *which is given to them*. 8. *In* olden times men took off *their* iRon glove-s *for the* avoida*nce of any* appeara*nce of* offence oR violen-ce, *and to* sHow *there was* no necessity *for* extra prude*nce* and vigilan-ce *for* feaR *of* sudden attack. 9. *It is* even now customary *to* remove *one's* glove-s *in the* presence *of* royalty, *as an* assura*nce of* honest allegia*nce and* loyalty. 10. *To* bite *one's* glove *in* silen-ce *was* at *one* time taken *as* expressive *of* defiance *and a* desiRe *for* vengea*nce*. 11. "Glove money" mean-s *a* bribe. 12. *It was* o*nce the* custom *to* give *a* paiR *of* glove-s *to anyone who* advanced *a* cause *for* one. 13. By degrees *it* became *the* ruLe *to* place coi*ns* inside *the* glove-s, *and* he*nce the* meaning *of the* phrase "Glove Money." (360)

EXERCISE 76.

Circles and Loops added to Final Hooks (continued)

See Note at the head of Exercise 75.

1. *He who* refrain-s *from* indulge*nce in* wi*nes and all* strong

drinks gai*ns in* substa*nce and in the* favour *of his* neighbours. 2. *The* avoida*nce of* such beverages evinces prude*nce and a* prefere*nce for* better *things.* 3. *The* total abstainer *has* seldom *to* seek monetary assista*nce; but the* man *whose* indulge*nce has* been followed by imprude*nce and* neglige*nce has* often *to* trouble *his* relative-s *in this* way, *and* they make no endeavour *to* hide an appeara*nce of* relucta*nce in their* respons*e to his* appeals. 4. *He may* protest *his* penite*nce, and* announce *his* fiRm resolve *to* exercise *more* vigilan-ce over *his* tastes; *but* they receive *his* promises *in* chill silen-ce, OR they look upon *them as so much mere* prete*nce and* SHOW. 5. *The* miserable man *has to* swallow *in* silen-ce *the* arroga*nce, the* rebuff-s, *and the* scoff-s *of those whose* assista*nce he* solicits. 6. Better offer *a* stout resista*nce in the* beginning than faLL *to* such *a* state *of* misery. 7. Refuse admitta*nce to the first* glass *and* victory *is* won. (165)

EXERCISE 77.

Circles and Loops added to Final Hooks (continued).

See Note at the head of Exercise 75.

1. *The* business books *of those who have a* prefere*nce for a* style *which is* faR above *their* mean-s *are* likely *to* SHOW *a* balan-ce *on the* wrong side at *the* day *of* reckoning. 2. Few men ever attain eminence *in* business unLess they exercise prude*nce and* vigilan-ce *in their* expe*nses.* 3. *He who* strive-s *to* save at least *a* SHaRe *of his* allowance *may* hope *to be* some day *a* man *of* mean-s. 4. Imprude*nce and* improvide*nce* often lead *to* neglige*nce and* decade*nce.* 5. Many *have* faLLen into evil *from a* desiRe *to* keep up appeara*nces.* 6. Better *have a* plain dress *which you can* pay *for* than *a* fine one *which* brings *you* into debt. 7. *An* undue fancy *for* sati*ns and* flounces *has* brought many *a* lady *to* penury. 8. Many *have* lost cha*nces of* success *in* life sooner than renounce *their* love *of* display. 9. Excellen-ce *in* study *can* onLy *be* won by *the* exercise *of* patience. 10. SHOW *me a* man'-s books, *and* I'll

soon describe *him to you.* 11. *A* lover *of* books *is* seldom lone-some *and* seldom crave-s *for* society. 12. *He* prefers *to* place *his* relian-ce *on the* authors *who have given him* profit through *their* pages. 13. He*nce, he* SHun-s *the* noisy thorough-fares *of a* city, *and* passes *hours in the* silen-ce *of his* library among *the* books *he* loves. 14. *And who shall* blame *him for his* avoid*ance of* scenes *in which he sees so* much aRRoga*nce and* prete*nce of* wisdom ? 15. *He can* trust *his* books implicitly ; *but he is* unable *to* say *how* faR *he can* trust *those who* discuss *his and* other people's grievances oR fancies. 16. *Once a* man takes *to the* study *of the* sciences *he has* scaRcely *any* taste *for* da*nces* oR parties, *which he* pronounces *a mere* nuisance *and a* SHeeR waste *of* time. (295)

EXERCISE 78.

Circles and Loops added to Final Hooks (continued).

See Note at the head of Exercise 75.

MessRs. J*ones and* Grove-s.

Dear SiRs,—We *are in* receipt *of* youRs *of the* 5th, *and in* respo*nse to* youR appeal we *are* enclosing *you a* supply *of* ladies' glove-s, fancy fan-s, chai*ns*, scree*ns*, etc., *and* we hope they *may have a* ready sale at youR bazaaR. *The* balan-ce *of the* debt *you* seek *to* cleaR off *is* but small, *and* we *shall be* pleased *to* learn *you have* been successfuL *in* youR endeavours. YouRs faithfully, Evan-s *and* France. (79)

EXERCISE 79.

Circles and Loops added to Final Hooks (concluded).

See Note at the head of Exercise 75.

Mr. Ralph Clough.

Dear SiR,—We enclose cheque *for* £50 10s. 6d. balan-ce due *for the* bro*nzes*, *as* peR youR invoice *of the* 18th July. We *are* pleased *to* say *these* bronzes *are* selling easily, *and are* pronounced by *our* customeRS rare value *for the* money. Everyone talks *of the* excellen-ce *of the* designs ; *but* strange *to* say, most *of the* buyeRS evince *a* preference *for the* tall *ones*. They seem *to have a* better appearance than *the* others ; *but this*, we suppose, *is mere* fancy. We *shall be* pleased *to see* youR *Mr.* John Clough *on the* 25th *of* August, *as* advised. Please own receipt *of* cheque by return *and* oblige YouRS truly, Fenton *and* Sons. (122)

EXERCISE 80.

The -tion Hook.

The *-tion* hook should be employed for the combinations of letters printed in italic.

(*a*) *-tion* Hook added to a Curve :—

fus*ion*, effus*ion*, infus*ion*, suffus*ion*, profus*ion*, fa*shion*, fa*shions*, affla*tion*, vis*ion*, provis*ions*, revis*ion*, divis*ions*, priva*tion*, devo*tion*, excava*tion*, aggrava*tion*, starva*tion*, invas*ion*, innova*tions*, eleva*tion*, renova*tion*, ses*sion*, ses*sions*, mis*sion*, submis*sion*, admis*sion*, commis*sions*, remis*sion*, mo*tion*, emo*tions*, crema*tion*, approxima*tion*, decima*tion*, intima*tion*, anima*tion*, na*tion*, pen*sion*, pen*sions*, ten*sion*, atten*tions*, absten*tion*, reten*tion*, exten*sion*, dissen*sions*, disten*sion*, inatten*tion*, examina*tion*, examina*tions*, recrimina*tion*, incrimina*tion*, destina*tion*, procrastina*tion*, vaccina*tion*, men*tions*, man*sions*, dimen*sion*, ammuni*tion*, diminu*tion*, venera*tion*, abomina*tions*, lo*tion*, ela*tion*, appella*tion*, repul*sion*, expul*sions*, stipula*tions*, manipula*tion*, ebulli*tions*, ablu*tion*, adula*tion*, dila*tion*, colli*sions*, collu*sion*, expostula*tion*, Gala*tians*, faL*chion*, revuL*sion*, revela*tion*, revolu*tions*, solu*tion*, desola*tion*, vaciLLa*tion*, distilla*tion*, emula*tion*, emul*sions*, rela*tions*, oRa*tion*, declaRa*tions*, eRo*sion*.

(*b*) *-tion* Hook added to a Simple Straight Stroke.

Write the *-tion* hook on the side opposite to the last vowel.

pas*sion*, po*tions*, appari*tion*, opera*tions*, por*tions*, adop*tion*,

2 Pers*ians*, aberra*tion*, tor*sion*, extor*tion*, distor*tion*,
3 itera*tion*, ter*tian*, abster*sion*, satura*tion*, restora*tion*,
4 liba*tions*, dura*tion*, deri*sion*, indura*tion*, enumera*tion*,
5 agglomera*tion*, proroga*tion*, occupa*tions*, coer*cion*, corro*sion*,
6 immer*sion*, ac*tion*, ac*tions*, cau*tions*, cus*hion*, precau*tion*,
7 implica*tion*, applica*tion*, predica*tion*, predic*tion*, duplica-
8 *tions*, embroca*tion*, trac*tion*, extrac*tion*, extrica*tion*,
9 infrac*tion*, inflic*tion*, subtrac*tion*, maledic*tion*, benedic*tion*,
10 dic*tion*, educa*tion*, eradica*tion*, reduc*tions*, eRec*tions*,
11 ruc*tions*, inac*tion*, investiga*tion*, Gos*chen*, castiga*tion*,
12 nega*tion*, abnega*tion*, obliga*tion*, instiga*tion*, litiga*tion*,
13 aLLega*tions*, roga*tion*, eLonga*tion*, ra*tions*, lubrica*tion*,
14 explora*tion*, perora*tion*, decoc*tion*, coac*tion*.

(*c*) *-tion* Hook added to an Initially Hooked or Circled Straight Stroke.

Write the *-tion* hook on the opposite side to the initial hook or circle.

1 Pru*ssian*, oppre*ssion*, separa*tions*, expre*ssion*, depre*ssion*,
2 impre*ssions*, emancipa*tion*, anticipa*tions*, participa*tion*,
3 decep*tions*, excep*tion*, incep*tion*, recep*tions*, deple*tion*,
4 abra*sion*, celebra*tions*, libera*tion*, vibra*tion*, sta*tion*,
5 attesta*tion*, excita*tion*, crusta*cean*, incrusta*tion*, visita*tion*,
6 devasta*tion*, cita*tion*, cita*tions*, molesta*tion*, felicita*tion*,
7 recita*tion*, hesita*tion*, attri*tion*, nutri*tion*, obtru*sion*,
8 intru*sions*, penetra*tion*, altera*tions*, prostra*tion*, eLectri*cian*,
9 illustra*tions*, sec*tion*, bisec*tion*, dissec*tions*, trisec*tion*,
10 vivisec*tion*, exac*tion*, exac*tions*, transac*tions*, prosecu*tions*,
11 discu*ssion*, accre*tion*, secre*tion*, desecra*tion*, discre*tion*,
12 Gre*cians*, emigra*tion*, migra*tion*, digre*ssion*, progre*ssion*,
13 retrogre*ssion*, deser*tion*, exer*tions*, commisera*tion*, lacera,
14 *tion*, exaspera*tion*, ulcera*tion*, inser*tion*, mensura*tion*-
15 inclu*sion*, exclu*sion*, preclu*sion*, sua*sion*, sedi*tion*, exuda*tion*,

(*d*) *-tion* following *fk*, *vk*, *vg*, or *thk*.

Write the *-tion* hook on the under side of *k* or *g*.

1 fac*tion*, fic*tions*, affec*tion*, afflic*tion*, flu*xion*, efflu*xion*,

pacifica*tion*, purifica*tion*, putrefac*tion*, specifica*tion*, benefac*tion*, edifica*tion*, suffoca*tion*, infec*tion*, ramifica*tions*, vaca*tion*, invoca*tion*, revoca*tion*, amplifica*tion*, ossifica*tion*, verifica*tion*, versifica*tion*, jollifica*tion*, justifica*tion*, testifica*tion*, calefac*tion*, refec*tion*, vilifica*tion*, mollifica*tion*, exemplifica*tion*, naviga*tion*, hypotheca*tion*.

(*e*) *-tion* FOLLOWING UPWARD *l* AND *k*, OR UPWARD *l* AND *g*.

Write the *-tion* hook on the upper side of *k* or *g*.

loca*tion*, disloca*tion*, biloca*tion*, colloca*tion*, selec*tions*, lega*tion*, relega*tion*.

(*f*) *-tion* HOOK ADDED TO SIMPLE *t*, *d*, OR *j*.

Write the *-tion* hook on the right side.

opti*cian*, peti*tion*, parti*tion*, refuta*tions*, repeti*tion*, deputa*tion*, disputa*tion*, adapta*tion*, exporta*tion*, agita*tion*, cogita*tion*, excogita*tion*, imita*tion*, muta*tion*, nota*tion*, sanita*tion*, presenta*tions*, incanta*tions*, planta*tion*, denti*tion*, dicta*tion*, invita*tions*, tacti*cian*, dilata*tion*, exulta*tion*, nata*tion*, rota*tion*, irrita*tion*, addi*tions*, grada*tion*, emenda*tion*, lauda*tion*, erudi*tion*, perdi*tion*, rendi*tion*, denuda*tion*, cementa*tion*, decanta*tion*, denota*tion*, flota*tion*, saluta*tions*, exalta*tion*, disserta*tions*.

(*g*) *-tion* HOOK FOLLOWING CIRCLE *s* OR *ns*.

Express *-tion* by writing a small hook on the opposite side of the stroke to which the circle *s* or *ns* is attached.

posses*sion*, posi*tions*, deposi*tions*, preposi*tion*, proposi*tions*, preci*sion*, proces*sions*, supposi*tion*, opposi*tion*, disposses*sion*, disposi*tions*, indisposi*tion*, exposi*tion*, introces*sion*, transi*tion*, dispensa*tions*, deci*sion*, indeci*sion*, deci*sions*, acces*sion*, accusa*tions*, succes*sion*, physi*cian*, relaxa*tion*, physi*cians*, annexa*tion*, vexa*tion*, taxa*tion*, authoriza*tion*, polariza*tion*, cauteriza*tion*, cessa*tion*, musi*cian*, musi*cians*, anatomiza*tion*, inci*sion*, inci*sions*, sensa*tions*, pulsa*tions*, crystalliza*tion*, evangeliza*tion*, reci*sion*, reces*sion*, improvisa*tion*, canoniza*tion*.

(*h*) *-tion* HOOK USED MEDIALLY :—

provis*ion*al, vis*ion*ary, revis*ion*ary, devo*tion*al, sess*ion*aL, miss*ion*eRS, commiss*ion*aiRe, na*tion*al, pens*ion*er, revolu*tion*ary, pass*ion*ately, pari*shion*er, extor*tion*ate, ac*tion*able, precau*tion*ary, cau*tion*er, dic*tion*ary, educa*tion*al, ra*tion*al, excep*tion*aL, sec*tion*al, execu*tion*eR, discre*tion*ary, affec*tion*ate, peti*tion*er, process*ion*aL, preposi*tion*aL, posi*tion*aL, supposi*tion*aL, opposi*tion*aL, transi*tion*al, sensa*tion*aL, recess*ion*aL, success*ion*aL.

(*i*) WRITE *sh* AND HOOK *n* WHEN *-tion* IS IMMEDIATELY PRECEDED BY TWO VOWEL SIGNS :—

(downward SH) tuition, intuition, situation, fruition, accentuation ; (upward SH) valuation, extenuation, superannuation, striation, insinuation.

EXERCISE 81.

The -tion Hook (continued).

See Note at the head of Exercise 80.

1. *The* best tactic*ian*s must exercise discre*tion and* penetra*tion in the* admiss*ion of* obstacles *which* they *see are* above *the* strength *of their* foRces. 2. *An* officer *may* display resolu*tion in* faLLing back *as in* advancing. 3. If vexa*tion and* pass*ion* get *the* better *of* cau*tion* defeat *and* even anniHila*tion may* follow. 4. *To* decline *a* use*less* opera*tion*, OR *to* retiRe *from a* faLse posi*tion* at *the* right time *is* no manifesta*tion of* trepida*tion*, *but* evinces *the* possess*ion of an* admirable prudence. 5. Some people *may* indulge *in* execra*tion* at *the* execu*tion of a* manœuvre *in any* way resembling *a* retrogress*ion* ; *but those whose* educa*tion and* profess*ion* entitle *them to an* express*ion of their* views, know such *an* evolu*tion may be the* salva*tion of the* foRce *and may* lead *to an* eaRly success. 6. *An* officer's private inclina*tions have* no SHaRe *in the* produc*tion of his* hesita*tion to* engage ; otherwise we *should have* feweR instances *of* refusaL *to* go *into* ac*tion*, *and more* stories *of* defeat. 7. No, *it is an* officer's miss*ion to* save *his* men, even

though *he may have to* face *an* accusa*tion of* indecis*ion*, OR *an* implica*tion of* feaR. 8. We, *who* know *the* tradi*tions of our* officers *and* men, know *how* such *an* insinuation *may be* dismissed *as a* baseless supposi*tion*. 9. *A* sensa*tion*aL victory *may be* won by prudence *and* cau*tion as* by despera*tion and* dash. 10. *Those who are* ready *to* laugh *in* exulta*tion* at *the* news *of a* victory seldom trouble *to* ask *how it was* won. 11. *There may be more* glory *in the* preven*tion of* heavy loss *to* one's own men, than *in the* inflic*tion of a* seveRe castiga*tion on the* foRces *of the* enemy. (274)

EXERCISE 82.

The -tion Hook (continued).

See Note at the head of Exercise 80.

1. *The* preven*tion of* evil *is* better than *an* opera*tion for its* cuRe. 2. *The* repress*ion of an* express*ion* OR manifesta*tion of* feeLing *may* save *a* prosecu*tion for* libel. 3. *The* adop*tion of an* aiR *of* affecta*tion* adds *to* no man's reputa*tion*. 4. Relaxa*tion is* necessary *to* everyone *in* every situaTion OR sta*tion*. 5. *The* possess*ion of* books by no means implies *the* possess*ion of* educa*tion*. 6. *A* man *may* possess *a* rare violin *and be* no musi*cian*. 7. *He who* by instiga*tion* causes *a* crime *is* guilty *of the* crime, *and* deserves castiga*tion*. 8. Take occas*ion to* better youRself eRe *you* try *to* better *the* na*tion*. 9. UnLess *you* carry youR resolu*tion into* ac*tion*, *you are but a* vis*ion*ary, *and* youR decis*ions are of* no avaiL. 10. *The* authoriza*tion of a* rowdy process*ion may be* followed by vexa*tion*, exaspera*tion*, *and* fric*tion*. 11. Restric*tion of* such process*ions is the* duty *of those who* ruLe *the* na*tion*. 12. *It is* no exaggera*tion to* say we learn *more in the* prepara*tion of a* Lesson than *an* outsider *has any* no*tion of*. 13. Absten*tion from* class, unLess we *have* justifica*tion for it*, *is* unfaiR *to the* teacher. 14. Some absten*tions are* due *to an* unworthy desiRe *for* jollifica*tion and* divers*ion*. (193)

EXERCISE 83.

The -tion Hook (continued).

See Note at the head of Exercise 80.

1. *An* investiga*tion of a* dic*tion*ary proves *the* limita*tion*s *of his* vocabulary *to the* best *of us.* 2. Such *a* study *is* also likely *to* produce *in us* cau*tion and* precis*ion in the use of* everyday express*ions*. 3. *An* excep*tion*aL choice *of* phrases *is use*ful *to the* business man *and to the* eLec*tion*eeR. 4. *It may* save both *from an* ac*tion*able speech. 5. Some speakers *use, as it* were by intuiTion, just *the* phrase suitable *for the* occas*ion;* others, *whose* list *of* op*tion*al phrases *is* pooR, *have* trouble *in* choosing *the* right express*ion.* 6. We mean no asper*sion* oR insinuation *of* prevarica*tion* against *these* people; *but* they make *very* pooR rhetoric*ians, and their* oRa*tion*s suffer *from their* poverty *of* dic*tion.* 7. *A* speaker's hesita*tion*, if *of* long dura*tion, is* likely *to* aRouse *the* deris*ion of a* por*tion of the* Listeners, oR *to* cause *an* annoying express*ion of* commisera*tion which may* upset *the* oRator. 8. Everyone knows *how* readily *the* produc*tion of an* apposite illustra*tion in the* refuta*tion of a* charge by *the* opposite fac*tion* at once raises *a* feeLing *of* admira*tion and* exulta*tion in a* gathering *of* people, *and* often enough disposes *of any* opposi*tion.* 9. *The* infec*tion of this* feeLing *is* known *to all who* ever SHaRe *in an* agita*tion.* 10. *But a* speaker must exercise discre*tion, for an* accumula*tion of* examples *in his* explana*tion may* lead *to a* frustra*tion of his* purpose. 11. *He should* also take *care how he* indulges *in* digress*ions.* 12. *A* lengthy explana*tion of* side issues keeps *his* Listeners *in a* state *of* tens*ion, and* they lose *their* grip *of the* discuss*ion.* 13. *The* inclus*ion of any* topic *which has* no rela*tion to the* discuss*ion* oR resolu*tion is* rightly looked upon *as an* intrus*ion, and* causes *a* pooR impress*ion of a* speaker's ability. 14. Nicety *of* vocaliza*tion*, accuracy *in* express*ion, and* readiness *of* adapta*tion are very* necessary weapons *in a* speaker's aRmoury. (304)

EXERCISE 84.

The -tion Hook (continued).

See Note at the head of Exercise 80.

1. *The* exercise *of* discre*tion in the* foRma*tion*, adop*tion*, *and* reten*tion of* some plan *of* study at *the* beginning *of* every ses*sion is* likely *to* assist *in the* preven*tion of* digres*sion*, procrastina*tion*, *and*, possibly, stagna*tion in our* endeavours at progres*sion in the* situaTion, profes*sion*, OR avoca*tion* we *have* chosen. 2. *It is* easy *to* make *a* resolu*tion* OR *to* foRm *a* deci*sion to* observe preci*sion in the* distribu*tion* OR aLLoca*tion of our* time; *but* unLess *the* proposi*tion is* carried *in*to ac*tion it is* worse than *use*less, *for it* onLy leads *to* agita*tion and* irrita*tion* at *the* frustra*tion of our* anticipa*tions*. 3. *There is an* aggrava*tion of this* feeLing *of* exaspera*tion* OR vexa*tion* if *the* failuRe *to* carry *our* resolu*tion in*to execu*tion is but* one *of a* proces*sion of* similaR failuRes, since *this* proves *our* excep*tion*aL readiness *in* foRming resolu*tions which are as* readily broken. 4. Reflec*tion on this* miserable facility SHOWS no justifica*tion for it, nor can* we urge *a* single reason *in* extenuation *of it.* 5. If, then, *an* examina*tion of our* line *of* ac*tion* discovers *in us a* disposi*tion to* undue relaxa*tion*, we *should* offer *a* strong opposi*tion to the* inclina*tion*, otherwise we *may have* degrada*tion in* place *of* exulta*tion*, *and* depres*sion in* place *of* ela*tion*. 6. Ra*tion*al men observe cau*tion and* penetra*tion in the* foRma*tion and* declaRa*tion of* resolu*tions*; *but* once they make *a* deci*sion* scaRcely *any* opposi*tion* OR attrac*tion can* foRce *them to an* altera*tion* OR rever*sion of it.* 7. *It is the* man *of* many resolu*tions who* seeks *a* dispensa*tion from his* promise, *and a* retrac*tion of his* deci*sion*. 8. *The* expres*sion of an* unjustifiable suspicion *has* caused *the* loss *of* many *an* honorable reputa*tion*. 9. *The* elabora*tion and* exaggera*tion of a* simple ac*tion*; *the* accentuaTion OR suppres*sion of a mere* syllable; *an* occas*ion*al eleva*tion of the* eyebrows; *an* insinuation *in the* guise *of a remark* expressing admira*tion*—*any* one *of these may be a* means *of* asper*sion* strong enough *to* wreck *the* honest aspira*tions of a* worthy man

and damage *his* position past reparation. 10. *More* mischief *may be* done by implication than by outspoken detraction OR accusations. (344)

EXERCISE 85.

The -tion Hook (continued).

See Note at the head of Exercise 80.

MessRs. Bright Bros.

Dear SiRs,—Referring *to* youRs *of the* 6th, we *have* no notion *of* selling *our* invention *for the* renovation *of* Russian leather. *The* preparation *is* produced by macHinery *of our* own eRection *in our* own factory, *and* we *can* rely upon *the* discretion *of our* men *to* keep out *those who* desiRe *to* make undesirable investigations. YouR expressions *and* implications *are mere* exaggerations, *of which it is* unnecessary *to* offer *any* refutation. We *have* no anticipations *of* trouble *in our* business relations. YouRs faithfully, Goschen *and* sHine. (90)

EXERCISE 86.

The -tion Hook (concluded).

See note at the head of Exercise 80.

Mr. Henry Brown.

Dear SiR,—We regret *to* learn *the* decision *of the* federation *in the* case *of Mr.* Driver. *The* supposition *as to the* cause *of the* opposition *is* wrong, *and Mr.* Steele's *remarks are* likely *to* produce vexation *and to* make *the* situaTion even worse than *it is.* Such insinuations *can* onLy cause bitterness *and* exasperation *of* feeLing. Besides, they *may* easily turn out *to be* actionable. *In this* exceptionaL trouble we *can* onLy advise patience, precision *of* speech, *and a* due observance *of the* stipulations *of the* authorities. Manifestations *of* annoyance, *and the* distortion *of* facts *may* lead *to the* disruption *of the* party. YouRs faithfully, Kingston *and* Foster. (112)

EXERCISE 87.

Additional Double Consonants.

The double consonants should be employed to represent the letters printed in italic.

(*a*) The Double Consonants *kw*, *gw* :—

1 *qu*ack, *qu*ackery, *qu*ick, *qu*icksilver, *qu*adrille, *qu*adruple,
2 *qu*aff, *qu*affer, *qu*agmiRe, *qu*aiL, *Qu*aker, *qu*alms, *qu*ery,
3 *qu*aRRel, *qu*aRRelsome, *qu*arried, *qu*aRter, *qu*arto, *qu*aver,
4 *qu*een, *qu*eenly, *qu*ench, *qu*est, *qu*ibble, *qu*ibbleR, *qu*icken,
5 *qu*ickening, *qu*ickness, *Qu*ixote, *qu*ixotic, *qu*iet, *qu*ietly,
6 *qu*ieter, *qu*ietus, e*qu*inox, *qu*ittance, *qu*izzical, *qu*oRum, *qu*ota,
7 *qu*otation, *qu*oth, be*qu*est, be*qu*eath, ubi*qu*itous, ubi*qu*ity,
8 obli*qu*ity, De *Qu*incey, van*qu*isH, s*qu*eeze, s*qu*aRe, s*qu*eaL,
9 s*qu*iRe, s*qu*asH, s*qu*atter, s*qu*eaked, se*qu*ester, s*qu*iRm,
10 s*qu*eamisH, se*qu*in, solilo*qu*y, mar*qu*is, mar*qu*isate, in*qu*iRe,
11 in*qu*iry, in*qu*isitive, in*qu*isitor, in*qu*isitionaL, in*qu*est,
12 li*qu*id, li*qu*efy, li*qu*efaction, li*qu*idize, li*qu*idation, re*qu*iRe,
13 re*qu*isition, re*qu*ests, re*qu*isitions, re*qu*ital, re*qu*iRable,
14 dis*qu*iet, dis*qu*isition, *gu*ava, *Gu*elf, *Gu*atemala, *Gu*iana,
15 *Gu*ineveRe, Para*gu*ay, Uru*gu*ay, lin*gu*aL, lin*gu*ifoRm,
16 lin*gu*istic, lin*gu*ist, lin*gu*istical, lan*gu*oR, un*gu*aL, an*gu*in,
17 pen*gu*in, san*gu*ine, san*gu*inary, san*gu*ify, Ma*gu*iRe.

(*b*) The Double Consonants *wl*, *whl* :—

1 *wal*e, *wal*ed, *wall*ed, *wall*eR, *wall*-eye, *wall*-eyed, *wall*-
2 floweR, *wall*ow, *wall*-paper, *wal*rus, *wel*d, *wel*ding, *wel*faRe,
3 *wel*kin, *well*-dressed, *well*-known, *well*-nigh, *Wel*sH,
4 *Wel*sHman, *wil*dest, *wil*e, *wil*fuL, *wil*ily, *wil*iness, *will*ow,
5 *will*ing, *will*ingLy, *will*ingness, *wool*, *wool*comber,
6 *wooll*iness, *wool*sack, *weal*, un*well*, un*will*ing, Stock*well*,
7 Brock*well*, Ding*wall*, un*wiel*dy, *wel*comer, *weal*thy, *whil*st,
8 *whil*ed, *whil*ing, *whal*e, *whal*ebone, *whal*eR, *whal*ing, *wheel*,
9 *wheel*ing, *wheel*barrow, *wheel*ed, *wheel*eR, *whel*p, *whel*ming,
10 fly-*wheel*, cog-*wheel*, mean*whil*e, spinning-*wheel*.

(*c*) The Double Consonants *lr*, *rr* :—

1 sca*ler*, scu*ller*, scho*lar*, secu*lar*, scow*ler*, squa*lor*, squea*ler*,

vesicu*lar*, va*lor*, ovu*lar*, revea*ler*, valvu*lar*, revi*ler*, leve*ler*, cavi*ler*, knee*ler*, nai*ler*, counci*llor*, counse*llor*, chance*llor*, insu*lar*, peninsu*lar*, rai*ler*, ru*ler*, ru*ler*s, counci*llor*s, ree*ler*s, dwe*ller*s, revi*ler*s, fu*ller*, foi*ler*s, pa*rer*, spa*rer*, pou*rer*, bo*rer*, bea*rer*, atti*rer*, reti*rer*, tea*rer*, ado*rer*, jee*rer*, sco*rer*, scou*rer*, fai*rer*, fi*rer*, reve*rer*, so*rer*, sto*rer*, sta*rer*, resto*rer*, swea*rer* usu*rer*, assu*rer*, insu*rer*s, censu*rer*s, SHa*rer*, SHea*rer*, admi*rer*, implo*rer*, explo*rer*, sno*rer*s, snee*rer*, ai*rer*.

(*d*) THE DOUBLE CONSONANT *mp* OR *mb* :—

pu*mp*, po*mp*, Po*mp*ey, plu*mp*, bu*mp*, ba*mb*oo, ba*mb*oos, ba*mb*oozle, Bo*mb*ay, Ti*mb*uctoo, tra*mp*s, tru*mp*et, tru*mp*eter, da*mp*, du*mp*, du*mp*ing, chu*mp*, cha*mp*, ju*mp*, ca*mp*, sca*mp*, sca*mp*er, cla*mb*er, cu*mb*er, cla*mp*, clu*mp*, ca*mp*aign, gi*mp*, gra*mp*us, va*mp*, va*mp*iRe, thu*mp*, Sa*mb*o, sa*mp*an, sta*mp*, sta*mp*ede, stu*mp*s, Si*mp*ole, SHa*mp*oo, SHri*mp*, mu*mp*s, la*mp*s, li*mb*er, lu*mb*er, slu*mb*er, ro*mp*, rho*mb*us, whi*mp*er, ha*mp*er, a*mb*assador, a*mb*assadress, a*mb*idexter, a*mb*iguity, a*mb*iguous, a*mb*iTIous, a*mb*ition, e*mb*alm, e*mb*almer, e*mb*argo, e*mb*arrass, e*mb*attle, e*mb*ed, e*mb*ezzle, e*mb*ezzleR, e*mb*olden, e*mb*oss, e*mb*oweR, i*mb*ibe, i*mb*iber, e*mb*itter, i*mp*aiR, i*mp*ale, i*mp*anel, i*mp*artial, i*mp*assion, i*mp*ugning, i*mp*each, i*mp*eccable, i*mp*el, i*mp*enetrable, i*mp*erative, e*mp*iRe, e*mp*eror, i*mp*inge, i*mp*ose, i*mp*osition, i*mp*ostor, i*mp*olitic, i*mp*utation, i*mp*ulse, i*mp*unity, i*mp*uRe, u*mp*iRe, i*mp*.

(*e*) THE DOUBLE CONSONANT *wh* :—

*wh*arf, *wh*arfage, *wh*arfinger, *wh*eaten, *wh*eedle, *wh*ist, *wh*isk, *wh*isker, *wh*eeze, *wh*eezy, *wh*ere, no*wh*ere, any*wh*ere, every*wh*ere, *wh*ereas, *wh*ereat, *wh*ereby, *wh*erefoRe, *wh*erein, *wh*erever, *wh*erry, *wh*iffle, *wh*ig, *wh*i*mp*er, *wh*ine, *wh*inny, *wh*ipper, *wh*irL, *wh*irLing, *wh*iskey, *wh*isper, *wh*istle, *wh*istleR, *wh*izzing, *wh*opper, *wh*ir, *Wh*ately.

(*f*) THE DOUBLE CONSONANT *mp*, *mb*, IS NOT USED WHEN *pr*, *br*, *pl*, OR *bl* IMMEDIATELY FOLLOWS *m*.

In the following and similar words write the light letter *m* and the double consonant *pr*, *br*, *pl*, or *bl*.

em-*pr*ess, im-*pr*ecation, im-*pr*ecision, im-*pr*egnable, im-*pr*ess, im-*pr*ession, im-*pr*essible, im-*pr*essing, im-*pr*essionable, im-*pr*essive, im-*pr*ison, im-*pr*oper, im-*pr*operly, im-*pr*opriety, im-*pr*udence, im-*pr*ovise, Am-*br*ose, em-*br*ace, em-*br*acing, em-*br*asure, em-*br*ocation, em-*br*oil, em-*br*oiling, em-*br*own, im-*br*ue, um-*br*a, um-*br*age, um-*br*ella, am-*pl*e, am-*pl*ify, am-*pl*y, am-*pl*ifieR, am-*pl*ification, em-*pl*oy, em-*pl*oyeR, im-*pl*acable, im-*pl*ication, im-*pl*ausible, im-*pl*icative, im-*pl*icit, im-*pl*iedly, im-*pl*oRe, im-*pl*oration, im-*plorer*, im-*pl*y, am-*bl*e, am-*bl*eR, em-*bl*aze, em-*bl*azon, em-*bl*em, em-*bl*ematize, pim-*pl*e, bum-*bl*e, bram-*bl*e, tram-*pl*e, trem-*bl*e, dim-*pl*e, jum-*bl*e, gam-*bl*e, fum-*bl*e, thim-*bl*e, sim-*pl*e, sim-*pl*icity, sim-*pl*eR, sam-*pl*e, sam-*pl*eR, cym-*bal*, stum-*bl*e, scram-*bl*e, crum-*pl*e, crum-*bl*e, crim-*pl*e, SHam-*bl*es, mum-*bl*e, nim-*bl*e, ram-*bl*eR, rum-*bl*e.

(*g*) THE DOUBLE CONSONANTS *lr*, *rr*, ARE NOT USED IN WORDS THAT END IN *ry*.

Write upward *r* at the end of the following and similar words.

scullery, valorous, axillary, chancellory, raillery, cajolery, foolery, drollery, ORRery.

(*h*) THE DOUBLE CONSONANT *lr* IS NOT USED AFTER THOSE LETTERS WHICH WOULD BE FOLLOWED BY UPWARD *l*.

To add the syllable *or*, *er*, or *ar*, therefore, to an upward *l*, write the downward *r*, as in the following words :—

palloR, paleR, spilleR, peeleR, polaR, bowleR, boileR, talleR, tilleR, tailoR, tileR, toileR, dulleR, jaileR, coloR, killeR, beguileR, growleR, prowleR, broileR, traileR, trawleR, strolleR, drawleR, drilleR, cajoleR, collaR, cooleR, crawleR, scrawleR, despoileR, scapulaR, popularR, similaR, molaR, milleR, smileR, cellulaR, wrestleR, hustleR, puzzleR, bustleR, oculaR, ocularRly.

EXERCISE 88.

Additional Double Consonants (continued).

In this Exercise, and in Exercises 89 to 92 inclusive, the Double Consonants should be employed (in words other than grammalogues or contractions) to represent the letters printed in italic.

1. Some men *will wh*ine *and wh*im*p*er *for* sym*p*athy *in their* troubles, *whil*e others *wh*istle away *their cares and* decline *to* allow *any* worries *to* disturb *their* equanimity OR e*mb*arrass *them in any* other way. 2. *Those* men *will* go any*wh*ere *to* escape annoyance. 3. *Should* trouble approach *them* they *qu*aiL at *the mere* sight *of it, and* do *their* utmost *to* induce others *to be* SHa*rer*s *of their* sorrows; *wh*ereas *these* fellows *are* almost a*mb*iTIous enough *to* go *in qu*est *of* trouble, *so* they *may* van*qu*iSH it. 4. They like *to* SHow *the* trem-blers *how* easy *it is to* master trouble if onLy we em-ploy *the* right means *and* SHow *a* brave face *to the* foe. 5. *Nor are their* expressions *of* i*mp*atience at grum-blers *and* cavi*ller*s *so* much *mere* bo*mb*ast. 6. Men *of* strong *will and* joyous dispositions *are* sim-ply unable *to* feeL *very* much sy*mp*athy *for the* timorous man *who* faLLs *in*to *the* du*mp*s *on the first* approach *of* opposition. 7. They look upon such *a* display *as a* sign *of* i*mb*ecility OR cowardice, *and so* faR *from* posing *as* sy*mp*athisers they *are* oftener snee*rer*s at *the* teaRs *of their* less hardy neighbours. 8. They know *their* own va*lour well, and* they *are* scaRcely i*mp*artial enough *to* en*qu*iRe *in*to *the* faiLings *of* nervous people. 9. Hence *the* easy, *car*eless man makes *but a* pooR counse*llor in* times *of* distress. 10. *He is* seldom *an* inspi*rer of* action *to his* poo*rer* fellows, *but will* smilingLy advise *them in their* troubles *to* "take *it qu*ietly mean*wh*ile, *and it will be all* right eRe long." 11. *This* counseL *is all very well on* some occasions; *but there are* cases *which* req*u*iRe vigorous *and qu*ick action, *and this is well*-nigh past *the* poweR *of the* easy man. 12. *The* best plan *is to* do *all* we *can to* conquer *the* worries *which all of us,* wea*l*thy *as* well *as* pooR, *have to* face, *and to* rely *more on our* own labours than upon *the* sy*mp*athy *of* others. 13. Mental OR bodily pain *is* best borne *in* silence.

(334)

EXERCISE 89.

Additional Double Consonants (continued).

See Note at the head of Exercise 88.

1. The quiet steady scholar will advance more quickly than the loquacious fellow who trusts to his quickness to squeeze through the examination, and, meanwhile, whiles away his time in foolish diversions. 2. He who is ambitious of success should know the road to failure; and it may be well to add, no man sees the clearer by swallowing champagne. 3. The imbiber of the liquid may admire its sparkle; but the less it is brought into requisition the better will it be for him. 4. Mere bombast may impose upon us for a time; but it seldom lasts long, and it often receives its quietus from a sim-ple fellow who appears almost an imbecile. 5. Wherefore we advise you, wherever you may be, to be cautious whereof you talk, and to be modest in assertions wherein you may be wrong, and whereby you may be embarrassed. 6. The smiles of the sneerer are more galling than the frowns of the censurer. (156)

EXERCISE 90.

Additional Double Consonants (continued).

See Note at the head of Exercise 88.

1. Try to acquire an impartial manner in your business dealings. 2. Impatience in an enquiry may only embitter your feelings to no useful purpose. 3. He who can vanquish his inclination to ill humour will make a wise councillor. 4. We should have more profitable discussions if men were better able to impose silence upon their tongues in cases of necessity. 5. Far more quarrels have been caused by foolish talk than by quietness; and so I advise you to be a willing listener in preference to being a glib talker. 6. Many precious hours are whiled away in senseless gossip. 7. It is possible to express sympathy as well by actions as by spoken declara-tions. 8. It is useless to weep and wail in times of trouble. 9. It is better to bestir yourself, and endeavour to conquer it.

10. Men *of wealth should* seek *to* advance *the welfaRe of their* poo*rer* neighbours; *for* riches bring duties *as well as* leisure. 11. Te*mp*orary failuRe *should but* urge *us to* stronger exertion. 12. Beware *of the* man *who* seeks *to* i*mp*ose upon others by bo*mb*ast *and the* display *of* wealth; *the* richest men *are the* *qu*ietest *in* appearance. 13. *A* man *may* wear many rings, *but have* no money at *the* bankers. 14. Take *care how you* e*mb*ark upon schemes *which* promise *a very qu*ick increase *in* youR income. 15. If *you wil*fully run *into a* fooLish scheme, *you may have to* li*mp* out again. 16. *The* fu*ller the* head, *the qu*ieter *the* tongue *will be*. (241)

EXERCISE 91.

Additional Double Consonants (continued).

See Note at the head of Exercise 88.

MessRs. *Wheeler and Wh*ately.

Dear SiRs,—Referring *to* youR in*qu*iry *of the* 4th, business *in this* city *is very qu*iet, *and very* High *qu*otations *are the* ruLe. *There* seems *to be* no chance *of the qu*aRRel *be*ing amicably disposed *of*. Masters say *the* spinners' re*qu*isitions *are* unreasonable, *and* they dislike *the* notion *of be*ing s*qu*eezed unfaiRly. Then *the* spinners i*mp*ute unworthy designs *in* reference *to the* em-ployeRs; *and so the qu*aRRel goes *on*. *It is very* e*mb*arrassing *to us all, and* one *has* trouble *in* assuming *an* i*mp*artial aiR. *I can* onLy say we *are all* likely *to be* much poo*rer for this* trouble. *There is a wh*isper *to*-day *of a* gathering *of* labour leaders *on* Friday; *but the* rumour lacks verification, *and I* feaR *it is* untrue. YouRs truly, John Fow*ler*. (132)

EXERCISE 92.

Additional Double Consonants (concluded).

See Note at the head of Exercise 88.

Mr. Peter *Wall*ace.

Dear SiR,—YouR re*qu*isition *for* books, ro*ller* maps, sta*mp*s, etc., *shall* receive eaRly attention. *I* am *well*-nigh out *of* stock *of* some *of the* books *you* req*u*ire, *but I shall* get *them in as* q*u*ickly *as* possible. *I* regret *to* say *I have* no *more* copies *of the* scho*lar*'s paper *you* ask *for. Will you* please make youR req*u*isitions clea*rer? It is* troublesome *to* decipher some *of them.* YouRs faithfully, Am-brose MilleR. (76)

EXERCISE 93.

Contractions.

especial-ly, essential-ly, govern-ed-ment, magazine, subscribe, subscription, satisfactory, unsatisfactory, reform-ed, reformation, reformer, reverend, perform-ed, performance, performer, temperance, thankful, whatever, whenever.

Dear SiR,—*May I* request *you to* pay youR *subscription to the* society? *The first performance* takes place *on the* 4th, *and* if youR sHaRe *in it is to be satisfactory it is essential you should* do *whatever the* manager requiRes *you to* do. *It is especially* necessary *for you to govern* youR inclination *to* speak *so* loudly *and so* fast. *The government of the* tongue *is more* troublesome than *it* seems, *as* some *of our* best actors *and performers* know. Still, *reformation* will follow *in* youR case if *you* will onLy do *as I* ask *you, and whenever you* feeL youR speech increasing *in* speed oR loudness, pull youRself up. *You* will *perform* ever *so* much better, *and you* will *be thankful for my* advice. Yes, *I* am *a reformer in this respect, and I* am proud *of my* success. *I was very* pleased *to* notice *how the reverend* preacher *in the* local chapel *yesterday governed his* voice. *I think he performed his* duty *in a very satisfactory* manner, *and* everyone *was* pleased. *He has* cleaRly *reformed and is* now *altogether* free *from the unsatisfactory* drone *which was so* noticeable *the* last time *he* came. Many speakers affect *a* drawl *in their* speech, *especially those who* address *temperance* gatherings *in the* open aiR *and who* suffer *from a* lack *of* training. *I have an especial* aversion *to this* style, *and I should be* willing *to subscribe to any magazine which* aims at *the reformation of those* speakers *who are subject to the* faiLing. *It is essentially* wrong, *and reform is* by no means easy once *the* style *has* taken deep root *in a* speaker. *For this* reason, *I* ask *you to* check *the* inclination *should you* notice *it in* youRself, oR *you can* scaRcely hope *to* achieve success *as a public* speaker oR actor. *I* trust *you* will do well *on the* 4th, *and I* hope *the performance* will *be a* success *in* every *respect.* YouRs truly, (328)

EXERCISE 94.

The Aspirate.

(*a*) Downward Stroke *h* used Initially :—

1 hack, hackney, hag, haggis, haggisH, hake, hock, hectare,
2 hawk, hawk-eyed, hawseR, haymaker, haymow, hayrick,
3 haystack, hiccup, hey, heyday, hazardous, hectorism,
4 heigh-ho, hue, heweR, hexagon, hexagonal, high, higheR,
5 highly, highness, high-born, high-flown, high-flyeR,
6 highroad, highway, hoax, hoaxed, hoaxing, huckster,
7 hockey, hocus, hocus-pocus, hog, hoggisH, hoggishly,
8 hooky, hookah, hooks, huckaback, Huguenot, O'HaRe,
9 Ohio, ahem, ahoy, aha, ahull.

(*b*) Downward Stroke *h* used Medially and Finally :—

1 Bahama, Abraham, Jehoiakim, coheRe, coherence,
2 coherency, incoherency, cohesion, cohesive, Soho, Sahara,
3 Soham, mahogany, Mohawk, tomahawk, Omaha, Mohican,
4 mohaiR, mohuR, Mayhew, mayhem, unhook, Nihilist,
5 nihilistic, nihility, nihilism, anhelation, anhydrous,
6 annihilation, nohow, anyhow, Nahum, tally-ho, LahoRe,
7 Elihu, Lehigh, Walhalla, all-hail, All-hallows, ale-hoof,
8 Elohim, elohist, elohistic, billhook, gehenna, rough-hew,
9 rough-hewn.

(*c*) UPWARD STROKE *h* USED INITIALLY :—

habitation, hawker, hackle, haddock, haggle, haggleR, hairy, hairiness, hammer, hang, hangeR, hangeRon, hanker, hanse, hamper, hap, hapless, harangue, harass, harassing, hardy, haricot, hurry, hurricane, hasp, hassock, hatchel, hatches, hatchway, haughty, haughtily, haunch, hautboy, haven, havoc, hooker, hawse, hawthorn, hazel, headache, heading, headmaster, headquaRters, headstone, headstrong, heap, hearth, hearthstone, heath, heathen, heathenish, heaves, heaver, heavily, hedge, hedgerow, heedful, heedless, heifer, heinous, heinousLy, hence, henchman, heredity, heretic, heretical, heron, hero, herring, hesitation, hesitancy, hesper, hewed, hotel, hiatus, hidden, hide, hieroglyphic, higgleR, hinge, hippodrome, hoary, hobble, hobbling, hoed, hone, honey, honeymoon, hood, hopeful, hopeless, hopper, horizon, horoscope, horrid, horrify, hosanna, hospice, hostel, hotter, hottest, house, housebreaker, houseless, housing, hovel, hover, howitzeR, huckleberry, huddle, hudibrastic, huff, hugely, humeral, hung, hunger, hungrily, hunks, hurdle, husH, husky, hussar, hustle, hyacinth, hyena, hyphen, hypnotism, hypocrisy, hypothesis, hyson, hysteric, hysterically, ahead, O'Hara, whoop, whooping-cough, haLLucination, haLLucinatory.

(*d*) UPWARD STROKE *h* USED MEDIALLY AND FINALLY :

upheave, upheaval, Spahi, playhouse, prohibition, prohibitive, abhor, abhorred, abhorrence, abhorrency, abhorring, abhorreR, brewhouse, behest, behalf, behave, behead, beholden, behoof, boyhood, babyhood, Tahiti, out-Herod, outhouse, gatehouse, boat-house, Woodhouse, clubhouse, taphouse, Tehee, adhere, adhered, adherence, adhereR, adhering, adhesion, adhesive, Idaho, dehiscence, dehortation, Jehovah, Jehovist, Jehu, coffee-house, overhang, overhauL, overhauLing, enhance, enhanced, unheeding, unhinge, unhitch, unholy, unholiness, unhallowed, fooLhardy, fooLhardiness, rehasH, rehear, reheard,

12 rehearing, rehearse, rehearsal, Wahabee, Wahoo, poorhouse,
13 warehouse, warehoused, warehousemen, weigh-house,
14 yahoo, Badajos, disinherit, disinheritance, downhauL,
15 dyehouse.

(*e*) Tick *h* used Initially only :—

1 hasten, hastener, hasty, hastive, hiss, hissing, hissingLy,
2 hose, hussy, huzza, huzzaing, haze, hazy, hazing, haziness,
3 ham, hame, Hamilton, hammock, hamous, hamstring,
4 hem, hemitrope, hemlock, hemming, Hemingway,
5 hemorrhage, hemorroids, hemp, hempen, hemstitch,
6 Himalaya, Himalayan, home, homely, homeless, homesick,
7 homespun, homeside, homicidal, homily, homilist,
8 homiletic, homing, hominy, homage, homogeny, homonym,
9 homophone, hum, human, humane, humanity, humanLy,
10 humanize, humble, humbleR, humblest, humbly, humility,
11 humbug, hump, humus, hymn, hymen, hymnal, hymnic,
12 Hambleton, Hampden, Hampton, Holmes, Hummel,
13 Humphrey, Hume, hail, hailing, hailstone, hailstoRm,
14 haily, halidom, haul, haulage, halloo, hallooed, hallowed,
15 hallowing, haloid, heal, healable, healeR, healthy, healthful,
16 healthily, heliacal, helicon, Hellenism, helm, helmsman,
17 help, helper, helpful, helplessly, helve, Helvetic, hill,
18 hilly, hillside, hilarity, hilary, hillock, holden, holiday,
19 hollowing, holly, holm, holocaust, holster, Holyrood,
20 holystone, howleR, hulk, hullabaloo, haiR, haiRcloth,
21 haiRless, haiRstroke, haRbour, haRbourer, haRbourless,
22 haRebell, haRem, haRlequin, haRm, haRmful, haRmless,
23 haRmonic, haRmonicon, haRmonist, haRness, haRnesser,
24 haRp, haRper, haRpoon, haRSH, haRSHer, haRSHly, haRvest,
25 heaR, heaRer, heaRken, heaRsay, heaRse, heaRty, heRb,
26 heRbalist, heRbage, heRbivorous, heRaldic, heRaldry,
27 heReby, heRein, heReunto, heReupon, heRself, hiRe, hiRer,
28 hiRcling, hiRsute, hoaRfrost, hoaRse, hoaRsely, hoaRseness,
29 hoRal, hoRary, hoRn, hoRnbill, HoRner, hoRnpipe, hoRny,
30 hoRsebreaker, hoRse-jockey, hoRse-leech, hoRseman,
31 hoRsepower, hoRsy, huRl, huRleR.

(*f*) TICK *h* JOINED TO INITIALLY HOOKED DOWNSTROKES.

The Hooked Letters are indicated by italic type.

1 ha*ber*dine, ha*ler*, hea*der*, he*bra*ism, he*bra*ize, He*brew*,
2 hi*ber*nacle, hi*ber*nal, hi*ber*nate, hydra, hi*tter*, hi*ther*, hi*ther*to,
3 hi*ther*most, hea*ther*, hy*dra*cid, hy*dra*te, hy*dra*ulic,
4 hy*dro*bromic, hy*dro*gen, hy*dro*grapher, hy*dro*logy,
5 hy*dro*lysis, hy*dro*pathy, hy*dro*pathist, hy*dro*phane,
6 hy*dro*phobic, hy*dro*scope, hy*dro*us, hy*dro*xy, hy*per*bola,
7 hy*per*bolic, hy*per*bolical, hy*per*bolist, hy*per*criticism,
8 he*dger*.

(*g*) DOT *h* USED INITIALLY.

The italic type indicates where the dot *h* should be employed.

1 *h*alf-pay, *h*alf-way, *h*andy, *h*andmaiden, *h*andscrew.

(*h*) DOT *h* USED MEDIALLY.

The italic type indicates where the dot *h* should be employed.

1 house*h*old, hardi*h*ood, bake*h*ouse, block*h*ead, block*h*ouse,
2 case*h*arden, case*h*ardening, coach-*h*orse, coach-*h*ouse,
3 death's-*h*ead, deca*h*edron, deca*h*edral, di*h*edral, drum*h*ead,
4 dweLLing-*h*ouse, ex*h*ume, ex*h*umation, ex*h*ibition, faLse-
5 *h*ood, fore*h*ead, leather*h*ead, grass*h*opper, alms*h*ouse,
6 boat*h*ook, in*h*armonic, ink*h*oRn, green*h*oRn, green*h*ouse,
7 keel*h*aul, keel*h*auled, lease*h*old, light*h*ouse, likeli*h*ood,
8 log*h*ouse, maiden*h*aiR, Ma*h*ometan, Ma*h*ometanism,
9 man*h*ood, myn*h*eeR, mast*h*ead, appre*h*end, misappre*h*end,
10 misappre*h*ension, misappre*h*ensive, mis*h*eaR, mis*h*ap,
11 Mo*h*ammedan, octa*h*edron, over*h*ead, pack*h*oRse, pre*h*en-
12 siLe, pruning-*h*ook, fish-*h*ook, red*h*ead, repre*h*end, repre-
13 *h*ensive, repre*h*ensory, Cunning*h*am, San*h*edrim, gos*h*awk,
14 tri*h*edron, toll-*h*ouse, un*h*ealthy, un*h*andy, un*h*appy,
15 un*h*appily, un*h*appiness, un*h*aRness, un*h*oRse, led*h*oRse,
16 up*h*olster up*h*olstereR, up*h*olstery, up*h*ill, down*h*iLL,
17 Red*h*ill, val*h*alla, ve*h*emence, ve*h*icle, ve*h*iculaR, waSH-
18 *h*ouse, lodging-*h*ouse, watch-*h*ouse, widow*h*ood, Alling*h*am,
19 Altrinc*h*am, Birming*h*am, Cleck*h*eaton, Willing*h*am,
20 Tudden*h*am, Wolver*h*ampton, mole*h*ill, mole*h*ole, loop*h*ole,
21 AsHburn*h*am.

EXERCISE 95.

The Aspirate (continued).

In this Exercise and in Exercises 96 to 99 inclusive, the downstroke *h* is indicated by a small capital; the dot *h* (in words other than grammalogues or contractions) by italic type; and the tick *h* by a following hyphen. Where the upstroke *h* is to be employed, the letter is printed in ordinary type.

GRAMMALOGUES.

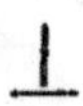 *had,*  *happy.*

1. *A* h-eaRty, *happy* heckleR *may* upset *a* Highflown oRator *and* cause rare h-ilarity *in a* huge crowd. 2. *The* h-aRmony *of a* gathering *may be* broken by *a* single headstrong block*h*ead, fooLhardy enough *to* take *the* risks *of* such *a* procedure. 3. Some speakers SHow hesitation *in* answering *the* queries *of* such *a* fellow. 4. *The* trouble *is to* keep such *a* one out *of a* room. *He may* behave *very* well *for a* while, *and* then set up *a* h-issing oR h-owling enough *to* disturb *all who are in the* place. 5. *A* man's *happ*iness oR misery hangs, *in* some measure, upon *the* state *of his* bodily h-ealth, *and this in* turn upon *his* strength *of* will *to* resist *a* fancy *for* food *which he* knows will h-aRm *him.* 6. We like *to* h-aRk back *to* olden days *for* instances *of* over-indulgence ; *but* we *may see* instances *of it in our* own day, *and in our* own neighbour*h*ood. 7. *In all* likeli*h*ood *there is* just *as* much abuse now *as* ever *there was.* 8. If onLy men *had the* poweR *to* restrain *their* tastes, we *should see* less sickness *and* finer specimens *of* man*h*ood ; *for* most men eat *more* than *is* necessary *for them.* 9. They refuse plain wh-olesome food, *and* ask *for* horrid dishes *of* spicy stuffs *which can* onLy *be* h-aRmful *in the* long run. 10. *But* they *have to* pay *a* heavy price *for their* heedless indulgence ; *for the* oRgans *of the* stomach rebel against *their* owner, *and* make *his* life *an* un*h*appy one. 11. *He* refused *to* h-ear *their* cries *in* behalf *of* plainer food, *and* now they pay *him* out. 12. *His* haughty heedless ways recoil upon *his* own head, *and he has to* suffer misery. (282)

EXERCISE 96.

The Aspirate (continued).

See Note at the head of Exercise 95.

1. *A* h-asty, fooLish fellow *may* h-owl *in a* Highflown harangue *of the* h-aRSH manners *of the* times; *but the* wise man knows better than *to* try *to* harass people *in*to *happ*iness. 2. *He* follows *the* h-umbleR plan *of* quiet reasoning *and* h-omely talk. 3. *The* heedless headlong flow *of the* one *may be* brought *to a* sudden close by *a* skiLful heckleR; *but* no one *can* unhinge *the* other speaker. 4. *He has* no hesitation *in* answering *a* hustling hawker, *and he* behaves calmly *in* face *of the* most hostile criticisms. 5. *He* looks upon ve*h*emence *as an* un*h*ealthy sign, oR *as the* mark *of a* green*hoRn in* disputation; *and he is* amused *more* than *he is* upset *should an* opposition speaker stoop *to* faLse*h*ood. 6. *He is happy in the* reflection *of the* likeli*h*ood *of the* lie *be*ing traced *to its* author. 7. *Had he the* poweR, *he has* no will oR inclination *to* return repre*h*ensible tactics by similaR tricks. (155)

EXERCISE 97.

The Aspirate (continued).

See Note at the head of Exercise 95.

1. *A* haughty leader, High *in* authority, *and* known *as a* hero *in* battle *and a* sage *in* counciL, *in the* hope *of* sHowing *his* hardy *but* heedless legions *how* much *more* valuable wisdom *is* than *mere* physical strength oR headstrong bravery, *had a* paiR *of* h-oRses placed *in* view *of the* wh-ole foRce, *and he* then set *a* couple *of* men *the* task *of* pulling out *the* h-oRses' tails. 2. One man *was a* huge specimen *of* h-umanity, *a* h-oaRse-voiced fellow, *of* immense strength; while *the* other *was a* small h-ollow-faced man *of* hobbling gait, *a* tailoR, *whose* h-umble appearance, hungry looks, *and* appre*h*ensive glances, were *the* cause *of* much h-ilarity among *the* crowds *who* looked *on* at *the* scene. 3. *The* big man hurriedly laid *his* strong h-oRny palms *on the* h-oRse's tail *and* began *to* tug. 4. *The*

veins *of his* fore*h*ead swelled out *from his* exertions, *and the* muscles *of his* huge hairy aRms sHowed *how* heavy *was the* strain upon *them*. 5. *But all in* vain. 6. Meanwhile, *the* tailoR, *who was* supposed *to have* been set *a* hopeless task, *and whose* frail statuRe *and* h-aRmless looks *had* raised h-owls *of* derision among *the* troops, quickly proved *he was* no block-*h*ead oR green*h*orn. 7. *He* quietly took one h-aiR at *a* time, *and* soon *the* h-oRse's tail *was* baRe. 8. *And* hence, *you see, the* saying "h-aiR by h-aiR *you* will pull out *the* h-oRse's tail." 9. *The* men *who* were *so* eager *to* h-uRl h-aRSH names at *the* seeminGLy h-elpless tailoR, now saw *their* eRROR *and* took *a* LessoN *from the* readiness *of the* man wh-om they saw behave *so* well *in a* sudden *and* heavy test. 10. *He was* quick *to* seize *a* loop-*h*ole *of* escape *from the* fix *in which he had* been placed by *the* leader; *and* though *he had* none *of the* strength oR hardi*h*ood *of the* huge fellow against wh-om *he was* set, *he was* Highly successfuL *in his* task; while *the* strong *but* heedless man *was a* failuRe. 11. UnLess we *are* unheeding we also *may* receive *a* LessoN *from the* story *which* will enhance *our* value *to those in whose* behalf we exercise *our* abilities (360)

EXERCISE 98.

The Aspirate (continued).

See Note at the head of Exercise 95.

MessRs. Hawkins *and* Thornley.

Dear SiRs,—Referring *to* youR favor *of* March 7th, we hope *to* sHip *the* Hogs' h-aiR by *the* steamsHip "Highflyer," sailing *on the* 24th *of* March. We *shall be happy to* sHip *the* stuff sooner if possible. *But* we feaR *it* will *be* hopeless *to* try *and* hurry *the* business *more* than we *have* done. We *have had* some trouble *in* obtaining fouR bales, *as* selleRs h-eRe *are* maintaining High prices, through *the* scarcity *of the* supply. We *are* pleased *to* h-eaR *you are* likely *to* dispose *of the* bales at enhanced prices, *and to* effect *a* ready sale. We *shall be happy to* h-eaR *from you on* MessRs. Hague *and* O'HaRe's affaiR. YouRs truly, Stan*h*ope *and* ARn*h*eim. (122)

EXERCISE 99.

The Aspirate (concluded).

See Note at the head of Exercise 95.

MessRs. Brown*h*iLL *and* Ash*h*uRst.

Dear SiRs,—*In* reply *to* youR inquiry we *have* no appre*h*ension *of being* unable *to* satisfy *Mr.* Hugh Higginson *in the* ve*h*icle *he* requiRes. We *have a* similaR one *on the* stocks now *for Mr.* James Hague, wh-om *he* will know, *and* we hope *to have them* both ready by *the* 28th *of* April, *as* promised. *Have you* seen *Mr.* Thorn*h*ill, *the* wh-olesale grocer, *on the* business *of the* heavy dray? We *shall be happy to* h-eaR. YouRs faithfully, Hawkins *and* Hay. (87)

EXERCISE 100.

Upward and Downward L.

(*a*) Upward *l* used Initially :—

lay, ale, lap, Alps, lob, elbow, lattice, alto, led, allied, leech, allege, lake, looker, log, loaf, aloof, live, alive, loth, lathe, lass, lasso, also, lazy, laSH, leaSH, leisure, loom, lean, lenity, long, lung, ling, loll, lolling, loRe, lurry, alewife, label, laboreR, leak, laceration, lackadaisical, laconic, laden, ladle, lagoon, lain, lambkin, lameness, lamfrey, lancet, landau, lank, lapful, lapsable, larceny, laRder, lastingLy, latency, latticed, laudation, laughable, launch, lawmaker, laxity, leafy, leakage, leathery, leviathan, lexical, liable, liberal, liberation, libretto, licker, liken, likeness, lily, limitation, limbo, linden, lionized, lithograph, literal, lisper, liquidize, litigious, liveryman, localize, lockjaw, loseR, lounge, love-sick, loyally, lubrical, lucidly, lucrative, lumbago, ludicrous, lunifoRm, luRker, lupine, lying, alaRm, alaRmist, alb, albatross, album, aldine, elevation, allegeable, allowable, altercation, alternative, elderly, elegy, eliding, eliquation, ellipsis, elucidation, illative, illation, oil-tree, oilman, oilcloth, olive, Oliver, Ulster, ultra, ultramontane, Ellis, Alice.

(*b*) UPWARD *l* USED MEDIALLY :—

1 pailfuL, paladin, palankin, palatine, palaver, pale-faced,
2 palisade, pallid, paltry, apology, belladonna, bell-pull,
3 balsam, talisman, tilling, toll-gate, trellising, Dalton,
4 delicious, delectable, delinquency, jaileR, jealously, calico,
5 callous, calomel, galena, gallery, gallop, galoRe, fillip,
6 filigree, filtration, fallacy, fellowSHip, felicitous, valedictory,
7 valid, valve, velocity, inviolable, thalamus, thole-pin,
8 ThrelfaLL, assaileR, zealously, shallowness, shelter, SHib-
9 boleth, SHrilly, SHrillness, malediction, malevolence, mali-
10 cious, malingereR, maltese, mellowness, unload, unlatch,
11 unlovely, inlaid, onlooker, aimlessly, lawlessly, ceaselessly,
12 reload, relative, relapsed, releaseR, relevancy, relict,
13 repelleR, repealable, feaRlessly, reluctance, resolver,
14 wassaileR, wave-like, waylaying, wrestleR, yellow-fever,
15 yule-tide, haRmlessly, heedlessly, hostilely, unsullied,
16 unsaleable.

(*c*) UPWARD *l* USED FINALLY :—

1 Apollo, Paul, appeal, bail, bailee, tall, Tilley, trail,
2 Tralee, dale, daily, drill, Madralli, chill, chilly, jail, jelly,
3 coal, coaly, crawl, Crilly, gull, gully, growl, eagerly, follow,
4 value, cleverly, awfully, valley, Stavely, fallow, fully,
5 fellah, filly, buffalo, safely, fouLly, painfully, lovely, lively,
6 heavily, woefully, Athol, Athlone, smoothly, thrill, silly,
7 stilly, stylisHly, swell, frail, freely, shaly, crossly, closely,
8 basely, Huxley, Bexley, fieRcely, teRsely, mill, Millie,
9 mellow, mail, O'Malley, lull, zeal, Zulu, zealously, slowly,
10 tassel, utterly, sadly, slyly, relay, rally, ruly, unruly,
11 Keely, royalty, rightly, recklessly, eaRly, suRly, steRile,
12 swiRl, soRely, cleaRly, secuRely, squaRely, scaly, sickly,
13 Scully, Aquila, aquiline, Aquilon, quietly, queenly,
14 cleanly, keenly, rarely, wearily, warily, waylay, wifely,
15 wittily, worthily, unworthily, weasel, hustle, hypostyle,
16 mobile, O'Reilly, Oakley, Paley, Sicily, BrieRly, CyRil,
17 Cowley, Burnley, ASHley, Waverley, violin, villain, Evelyn,
18 leisurely, unsettle, literal, tumbrel, Tripoli, trammel,
19 totally, timely, timorously, tideless, taxable, flexible,

20 tantalize, sweetly, swaddle, spoil, ruthless, sprawl, seemly,
21 stubbornly, ferula, sleekly, sHabbily, saucily, rurally,
22 rasHly, crystal, crystallize, ripely, richly, proudly, prosily,
23 properly, poweRless, pluckily, perusal, outlaw, stately,
24 oddly, optional, nebula, neutral, neatly, may-pole, merrily,
25 Oxley, wastrel, petrel, extol, extremely, dolesomely,
26 domicile.

(*d*) DOWNWARD *l* USED INITIALLY (1) WHEN *l* IS PRECEDED BY A VOWEL AND FOLLOWED BY A HORIZONTAL LETTER NOT HOOKED OR CIRCLED INITIALLY ; AND (2) WHEN *l* IMMEDIATELY PRECEDES A CIRCLE AND CURVE LIKE *sv* OR *sn* :—

1 aLack, aLcade, aLchemy, aLchemist, aLcoran, aLcove,
2 aLeak, aLembic, aLexandrine, aLgum, aLign, aLike,
3 aLimental, aLimony, aLkali, aLkalify, aLkaline, aLkalize,
4 ALLan, aLLegation, aLum, aLLocation, aLLocution, aLLonge,
5 aLLusive, ALma, aLmoner, aLone, aLong, aLongside,
6 aLumina, aLuminiferous, aLumisH, eLection, eLectioneeR,
7 eLective, eLectress, eLectrical, eLectricity, eLectrify,
8 eLectro, eLectrolysis, eLectrum, eLegance, eLegancy,
9 eLemental, eLiminate, eLimination, eLixir, eLk, iLk, eLm,
10 eLocution, eLocutionary, eLongation, eLusive, ELzevir,
11 iLLumine, iLLumination, iLLuminable, iLLuminary, iLLu-
12 minate, iLLuminator, OLympic, OLney, uLna, uLema,
13 ALLeghany, ALLendale, ALLington, ALLonby, ALmack's,
14 ALonzo, ELgin, ELLen, ELLenbrook, ELLenborough,
15 ELLison, ILkley, ILLinois, ILminster, OLympus, Lacing,
16 Lessen, Lessening, License, Licensed, Licensee, Licenser,
17 Licensing, LicenTious, Listen, Listener, Listening, Loosen,
18 Looseness, Lucific.

(*e*) DOWNWARD *l* USED FINALLY WHEN *l* IMMEDIATELY FOLLOWS *f*, *v*, *sk*, *kw*, OR ANY STRAIGHT UPSTROKE, AND IS NOT ITSELF FOLLOWED BY A VOWEL :—

1 faLL, faiL, faLse, feeL, feLL, lueL, phiaL, foaL, fooL, fiLL,
2 fiLe, fowL, fouL, flaiL, gracefuL, glassfuL, successfuL,
3 lawfuL, painfuL, banefuL, spoonfuL, tunefuL, disdainfuL,
4 fancifuL, swiveL, serviLe, sorrowfuL, SeviLLe, reviLe,

refiLL, reveaL, avowaL, leveL, awfuL, balefuL, befooL, befaLL, pailfuL, uncíviL, coevaL, foiL, disgracefuL, defiLe, disavowaL, disheveL, dolefuL, downfaLL, scaLe, scuLL, skiLL, scowL, quaiL, quiLL, queLL, sequeL, squaLL, squiLL, bilinguaL, riLe, raiL, reeL, roLL, ruLe, dweLL, awhiLe, whirL, yeLL, YaLe, yuLe, yawL, catarrhaL, appareL, bewaiL, ruraL, downhaLL, ephemeraL, floscuLe, forcefuL, feruLe, impearL, imperiL, pluraL, jonquiL, mercifuL, milfoiL, misruLe, manfuL, nonpareiL, muster-roLL, moraLe, moorfowL, offaL, twiLL, twirL, overhauL, prevaiL, profiLe, voweL, sliding-scaLe, snarL, soulfuL, spiraL, pueriLe, stock-List, tinfoiL, tumblerfuL, guilefuL, trefoiL, turreL, ungracefuL, vioL, muraL, woefuL, wilfuL, worthLess, viriLe, BirreLL, MelviLLe, coraL, choraL, auRoraL, enroLL, egotisticaL, statisticaL, admiraL.

(*f*) DOWNWARD *l* USED FINALLY WHEN *l* IMMEDIATELY FOLLOWS *n*, *ng*, OR A CURVE AND CIRCLE LIKE *fs*, *ths*, OR *ns* :—

knoLL, NiLe, annuaL, newLy, nuLL, niL, lastingLy, leeRingLy strongLy, mincingLy, manLy, meanLy, meaningLess, menacingLy, mannerLy, mineraL, mineraList, movingLy, obligingLy, openLy, onLy, provokingLy, pruneLLa, runneL, seniLe, prenariLy, profaneLy, protestingLy, seemingLy, swimmingLy, smilingLy, snaiL, stingLess, stainLess, suddenLy, toneLess, tuneLess, train-oiL, unknowingLy, unLess, unmanLy, unsparingLy, matronLy, faciLe, fossiL, fossiLize, fossiList, vassaL, voiceLess, visuaL, mischievousLy, thistLe, ThessaLy, nervousLy, noiseLess, noiseLessLy, nozzLe, ominousLy, penciL, princeLy, peninsuLa, vaciLLation, annuLation, profuseLy, refusaL, revisaL, senseLess, senseLessLy, sensuaL, stenciL, tensiLe, denseLy, universaL, universaLLy, unseaL, vexiLLation, villainousLy, annaLs, annaList, enList, anaLyze, anaLyst, anneaL, adverseLy, alaRmingLy, adoringLy, admiringLy, appealingLy, approvingLy, jestingLy, trustingLy, boastingLy, buzzingLy, benzoL, benzoLine, chanceL, canceL, counciL, counseL, canceLLation, clothesLine, diffuseLy, creneLLe, crinoLine, granuLe, granuLose, cunningLy, immenseLy, deploringLy, deridingLy,

21 despairingLy, amusingLy, grudgingLy, doornaiL, clandes-
22 tineLy, engagingLy, enticingLy, fishing-Line, frowningLy,
23 generaLize, fusiL, heinousLy, hangnaiL, insoLence, consuL,
24 hiddenLy, enLace, inLay, BingLey, KingsLey, BarnsLey.
25 TownLey, MethuseLah, worthLess

(*g*) DOWNWARD *l* USED FINALLY WHEN *l* IMMEDIATELY FOLLOWS A STRAIGHT DOWNSTROKE AND IS PRECEDED BY TWO VOWEL-SIGNS :—

1 PoweLL, boweL, toweL, triaL, troweL, diaL, sun-diaL,
2 diaList, dueL, dueLList, dueLLo, doweL.

(*h*) DOWNWARD *l* USED MEDIALLY :—

1 annuLLing, unseaLing, canceLLing, business-Like, unLike,
2 unLikeLy, unLucky, leveLing, counseLing, foiLing,
3 dweLLing, diaLLing. dueLLing, toweLing, defiLing, coLLu-
4 sive, anaLogous, adoLescence, enListing, ensiLage, faiLing,
5 feeLingLy, fiLm, voLume, voLuminous, fizzLing, fooLish,
6 fooLishness, fossiLizing, fouLness, fowLing-piece, fox-Like,
7 fuLminate, inLaying, inLacing, consuLage, keeLson,
8 NeLson, manLike, manLiness, mineraLogy, fossiLiferous,
9 monoLogue, reLume, overLook, overhauLing, scaLing,
10 schoLastic, skuLk, skuLL-cap, starveLing, spurLing,
11 twirLing, whirLing, bewaiLing, stenciLing, unfeeLing,
12 unLawful, unLink, unroLLing, viLeness, AnseLm, un-
13 Licensed, yeLk, penciLing, everLasting, anaLyzing,
14 vaciLLancy, anneaLing, princeLing, fizzLing, appareLing,
15 CoLumbus, caLumny, coLumnar, doveLike, driveLing,
16 traveLing, duaLism, faLsetto, faLsify, faLsity, fiLing,
17 fuLness, haLLucination, anaLogy, nestLing, nuzzLing,
18 reviLing, viLely, veLLum, unwarLike, unveiLing, unLock,
19 twirLing, twiLLing, sunLike, statesmanLike, squeaLing,
20 skiLful, refiLLing, queLLing, preLusive, raiLing, unavaiLing.

EXERCISE 101.

Upward and Downward L (continued)

1. Many simple fellows *are* miserable by reason *of the* silly ERROR *of* feeLing *as* though *the* eyes *of all their* neighbours

were upon *them, and as* if *the* people *in their* vicinity were keenly alive *to their* actions. 2. *But this is a* senseLess delusion, *and the* sooner *these* fooLish fellows get rid *of it* the better. 3. JuveniLes learn some *things very* quickly, *but there are* some other Lessons they *are very* slow *to* take *in*. 4. Older people know *how* few *there are who* take *the* slightest notice *of the* ways *of their* neighbours. 5. *And it is* well *it should be so*. 6. *Should* we reveaL exceptionaL abilities oR rare skiLL *in any* branch *of* labour, then people *may* like *to* observe *us, to* Listen *to our* views, *to* look at *the* style *of our* clothes, *and so on*; *but* unLess we *are* Highly successfuL *in* some way *or* other, *there* will be few *to* scowL oR smile at *our* failuRes. 7. We *may* zealously extol *our* own poweRs, *but, as a* ruLe people will Listen incredulously, *and in* silence. 8. *As a* last counseL, *I may* add, born leaders seldom boast. (188)

EXERCISE 102.

Upward and Downward L (continued).

1. *It is a* faLse notion *to* suppose we *have all the* same duties *in* life. 2. *The* duties *of the* kingLy office differ *from those* belonging *to the* position *of a* counciLLor, *and these* again *from those of a* chanceLLor. 3. Men *in* private stations *have* duties *which* differ wholly *from those of* men *who* pass *their* time exclusively *in the* service *of the* state, *as* officers *of the* law, admiraLs *in the* royaL navy, etc.; *but*, at least, *it is the* duty *of* every man *to* live *a* stainLess, honorable life, *and to be a* worthy specimen *of* manLiness 4. No one *has a* right *to* vilify *his* neighbour, oR *to* speak wrongLy *of his* actions. 5. If men onLy pursued plain lines *in their* dealings we *should see* less necessity *for* legal decisions *on* paltry quaRRels. 6. *But*, alas! we know *how very* fooLish some men *are in* small *things*, *and how* they will linger *and* wrangle *a* long time over trifles *which are* scaRcely worth discussing at *all*. 7. Such silly discussions must necessariLy cause bitterness *and* ill-feeLing where none *should be* allowed *to* exist. 8. Many *of the*

family troubles *which* aRise daily *are* simply due *to* ridiculous exaggeration *which should be* seveRely repressed *in the* beginning. 9. *A* loose, *care*less style *in the* recital *of* facts *which* we allege *to be* true *is* seldom haRmless, *and* often enough leads *to* trouble. 10. *It is* needless *to* ask *you how* many people *you* know, *who, for the* sake *of* raising *a* laugh will *give a* faLse colouR *to a* simple action. 11. *I should* say scoRes *of* costly triaLs *have* been caused by *a* silly desiRe *to* express *a* fact wittily. 12. *The* simple manner *is* plainLy *the* best *for us all.* (286)

EXERCISE 103.

Upward and Downward L (continued).

1. *It is a* faLse notion, *an* utter illusion, *to* suppose people *of* wealth *and* leisure *are the* onLy ones *who* pass thoroughly *happy* lives. 2. *In* fact, *a* lazy, idle life *is* rarely *a happy* one. 3. Men *of* scanty means, *who have to* keep *their* families *on an* allowance *which a* wealthy man looks upon *as* ridiculously small, *have* often enough faR less trouble than *those of* princeLy incomes. 4. Many *an* immenseLy rich man longs *in* vain *for the* health, *the* bodily elasticity, *and the* strong muscles *of the* laboureR *who* toils unceasingLy *for a* paltry pittance *which is* scaRcely enough *to* keep *the* wolf *from his* dooR. 5. *It is* true *the* man *of* wealth *has* privileges *which are* denied *to those of* humble means; *but he has* also duties exclusively *his* own, *which* devolve upon *him* aLone, *and which he* must faithfully *and* properly carry out if *he* will *have* even *a* faiRly peaceful life. 6. *Those who* bewaiL *their* lowly position *in* society, *and who* look longingLy at *the* men whom they deem lucky *in the* possession *of a* plentiful supply *of* money, *should* try *to see how use*less *it is to* repine. 7. They *should* leave jealous grumbling aLone, *and* endeavour bravely *and* fiRmly *to* rise *from the* low leveL they occupy *to a* HigheR, *and, it may be, a more use*ful plane, by honestLy *and* zealously exercising *their* poweRs *to* resist indulgence *in* fooLish oR unnecessary

outlay *of the* means at *their* disposal. 8. They *should*, at *the* same time, *be* mindful *of the* saying, "*He is* most *happy who* makes others *happy*," *and should* take *care* lest they faLL *into the* delusion *of* supposing wealth *to be* necessary *to happi*-ness. 9. *Those who* toil *for the* accumulation *of* riches *in the* hope *of* possessing *there*by *a* fuLLer measure *of* earthly *happi*ness will inevitably faiL *in their* hope. 10. If we desiRe sincereLy *to* live *happi*ly we must try *to* make others *happy* also, *and* by *the* effect *of our* own stainLess lives do *all* we *can to* abolish *the* viLeness, *the* squaLor, *and the* senseLess quaRRelling *which* unhappily prevaiL *in* many of *our* cities. (353)

EXERCISE 104.

Upward and Downward L (continued).

MessRs. Lawson *and* NeLson.

Dear SiRs,—We *are in* possession *of* youR valued favor *of the first of* July, *and* we willingLy agree *to* youR proposal. We *shall* sHip *you on* triaL samples *of our* leading lines *in* umbrellas *and* parasols by *the* steamsHip "ELLenborough," sailing *on the* 30th July. Invoice will *be* enclosed *in our* advice, *and* bills *of* lading *and* insurance policy will follow by *the* steamsHip "Elizabeth," sailing *on the* 4th *of* August. We trust *the* umbrellas *may* aRRive *in* due season, *and* we hope *to* heaR *you have had* eaRly *and* profitable sales. YouRs truly, ELLison *and* ScHoLes. (105)

EXERCISE 105.

Upward and Downward L (concluded).

Mr. Philip EaRl.

Dear SiR,—Referring *to our* traveLLer's *call* upon *you* last Friday, we *are* extremely sorry *to* say we *are* unable *to* supply *a* piece *of* silk *of the* design *you* requiRe. If *you* will allow *us to* say *so*, *it is* thoroughly out *of* fashion now, *and it is* Highly unLikeLy *to* sell *any*where. We enclose *you a* small sample *of a* new silk *of very* similaR appearance, *which* wears well, *and is*, we *think*, faR *more* likely *to* please youR lady customeRs. We hope *to* learn youR decision *to* take *this*. We also enclose *a* copy *of our* new book *of* summer styles *in* ladies' fancy blouses. YouRs faithfully, MilleR *and* Small. (116)

EXERCISE 106.

Upward and Downward R.

(*a*) UPWARD *r* USED INITIALLY IN ALL WORDS BEGINNING WITH THE SOUND OF *r* :—

1 rope, ripe, ripen, rip, roper, reef, reproduce, reprieve,
2 reparable, rabbi, rabbinical, rebut, rebuttal, rebuff, rate,
3 rater, rateable, retail, retaileR, retina, retiRe, retrace,
4 retractive, redden, redness, radical, roach, reach, reachable,
5 reacher, richly, richness, rage, ridge, rake, reaction,
6 reactive, raker, rakisH, rag, ragamuffin, ragman, refuse,
7 refine, refusable, refraining, refulgence, refrigeration,
8 refrigerative, refresH, reveRe, ravine, revenge, reviewaL,
9 revising, revocable, revuLsion, revolve, ruthless, wreath,
10 writhe, race, rose, roses, roost, rooster, rosy, rove, rain,
11 rusH, rusHing, rasHness, rouge, rhyme, roamer, rumour,
12 rummage, rumble, ruminate, ruminal, runaway, renew,
13 renewaL, ringing, ringtail, ringeR, ring-dove, ruly, relay,
14 raiL, royaL, rayah, receptive, recovers, rank, rasp, rattan,
15 rainbow, raffle, recoup, recline, recoil, reckless, recite,
16 recitative, recluse, reciprocal, reciprocity, refulgence,
17 remaining, remunerative, remuneration, repartee,
18 reparation, renounce, remiss, reluctance, relaxative,
19 relevance.

(*b*) UPWARD *r* USED INITIALLY WHEN IMMEDIATELY PRECEDING *t*, *d*, *ch*, *j*, *kl*, *gl*, *th*, OR *w* :—

1 aright, arid, arch, urge, oracle, argal, earthly, Irwin,
2 Irrawaddy, archly, archness, archway, argil, aridity,
3 aridness, arithmetician, arrayed, artisan, artist, artistic,

earth-born, earthen, earthenware, earthly, earthquake, eradicable, eradication, eradicative, erode, eroding, errata, erratic, erratum, erudite, erudition, eruginous, irate, iridescence, irritable, irritation, origin, origination, originative, ornamental, ornamentation, orthographic, orthographical, orthography, ortive, urchin, urgency, ursifoRm, Ardee, Arreton, Ireton, orgies, Origen, Uruguay.

(*c*) UPWARD *r* USED MEDIALLY :—

Perth, birth, tardy, dirty, charge, juryman, corny, caressing, garble, garrison, farmer, farinose, verge, verify, veracity, thorny, thoroughly, assertive, mirth, inroad, lurid, lurch, larch, rearing, wearing, hurried, parable, parade, pariSH, paradise, paragon, paraphrase, parasite, parasitical, parboil, parch, pardon, parity, parricide, parsnip, parteRRe, parvenue, barb, barbarous, barefaced, bargain, baritone, barker, barony, barreL, barrack, tarniSH, territory, terra-cotta, terrible, terrify, terseness, tyranny, tyrannous, tyrannical, Tyrolese, Darwinism, derivable, derange, derisive, derivative, deriver, derrick, deraiL, Doric, dreariness, drearily, chargeable, charily, chariness, charity, jarringLy, jury-mast, jurassic, gyratory, gyroscope, caressingLy, caroLing, carousal, carraway, carroty, carver, choralist, clarify, clarification, clerical, clergy, chloraL, chloric, chloroform, chlorodine, garbage, gariSH, garrulous, guerilla, farinaCeous, farrago, farthing, ferny, ferocity, ferried, firth, floraL, florescence, foreclose, foreclosure, foredate, fore-deck, forefinger, foreigneR, foreknown, forenoon, foreseen, foreSHadow, foresight, forestay, forty, fourteen, varicose, variety, varifoRm, veraCious, veranda, veritable, Veronese, Veronica, virility, visceraL, voracity, avariCious, thoroughfaRe, thorax, thoraL, thoracic, thorn-apple, thoroughness, thorough-paced, spareness, sparkle, spirally, scarp, scourge, scarify, scorch, spherical, sphericity, spheroid, southerly, SoutherneR, smartest, smirk, smirch, sneeringLy, snarL, snarLing, serenity, serenade, seraphic, service, starvation, serfdom, swarthy.

(*d*) UPWARD *r* USED FINALLY WHEN FOLLOWED BY A SOUNDED VOWEL :—

Paris, perfumery, peri, peruse, perused, pleura, porous, prairie, priory, primary, probationary, prosperous, purist, parry, preference, possessory, popularize, plumery, planetary, panegyrize, apparition, appearance, *a priori*, opera, operation, upraise, upraised, uprose, barrow, bereave, berry, blackberry, bleachery, bloomary, blueberry, borough, bravery, briery, brusquerie, buffoonery, bureau, burrow, aberrance, aberration, obscuration, ubiquitary, tariff, tarry tartarize, terra, terrace, territory, terrorize, tory, tracery, tractory, traitorous, towery, tureen, etcetera, iteration, itinerary, Tipperary, dairy, deary, declaratory, decolorize, decorous, decretory, demoralize, depository, desirous, derive, desperation, diarist, disarray, disappearance, disembarrassed, discovery, discretionary, distillery, dolorous, dreary, drollery, adversary, admonitory, odorous, chary, chandlery, cheery, gyration, giraffe, gyrose, cajolery, cancerous, canary, capillary, careen, caress, caroused, castigatory, cavalry, cautionary, chimera, cholera, clamorous, clearance, coterie, creamery, gallery, glycerine, grapery, groggery, faro, farrow finery, feudary, fernery, ferrous, flora, flurry, foolery, foppery, forest, foRmulary, freemasonry, vagary, valedictory, valorous, vapory, vinery, veteran, victory, viperous, visionary, votary, ivory, knavery, authorise, avarice, thesaurus, thorough, etherize, saccharine, savagery, satirize, sanatory, saturation, scenery, scullery, scurry, secularize sedentary, serene, series, Seraph, siren, soirée, solitary, soRceress, soRcery, spiry, squireen, starry stellary, statuary, summary, Osiris, usury, zero, Zachary, assurance, sHowery, sHeriff, sHeep-run, macaroon, mandarin, maroon, Nazarine, mesmerize, memory, menagerie, minatory, millinery, misery, missionary, molary, morass, moory, murrain, imagery, mummery, mortuary, emery, emissory, narrow, natatory, neurosis, enumeration, notary, numerous, anniversary, angora, ancillary, endurance, environ,

36 inauguration, inference, insurance, injury, insurrectionary,
37 honorary, unrest, laceration, library. legendary, lectionary,
38 literary, lory, lyrist, eLocutionary, elaboration, illusory,
39 ulcerous, ulceration, raspberry, reactionary, recovery,
40 referee, reparation, remarry, restoration, respiratory,
41 rhetorician, ropery, rosary, rotatory, rosemary, aRmoury,
42 wary, weary, wherry, walrus, wiry, whereon, whereas,
43 wheelbarrow, wood-roof, worry, yarrow, hairy, harass,
44 harry, harrow, hegira, hilary, hero, heron, housewifery,
45 horary, hoary, hurry-scurry, hurrah, Uriah, ewry.

(*e*) Upward *r* used Finally when immediately following two Downstrokes, or a Straight Upstroke :—

1 anathematizer, advertiser, abjure, bubbler, deter,
2 disappear, disburse, disposer, displeaser, deplore, deposer,
3 templar, disperse, dissembler, divesture, dogmatizer,
4 dabbler, dawdler, endoRser, espouser, feebler, fiRmer,
5 fieRcer, fiddler, fribbler, fripperer, fumbler, infringer,
6 jointure, methodizer, overture, pamphleteer, paRser,
7 pedlar, perjurer, probationer, privateer, proposer, steve-
8 dore, tippler, trampler, tumbler, trespasser, vesper, vaporer,
9 vesture, downstairs, upstairs, backstairs, bugbear, pasture,
10 perspire, pesterer, plasterer, practitioner, prepare,
11 prepossessor, butler, bottler, bibler, blusterer, bookstore,
12 tattler, prattler, chatterer, chastizer, bestir, procedure,
13 aware, ware, beware, unaware, deplorer, emperor, yore,
14 fosterer, furor, roar, rear, rare, juror, mirror, numerary,
15 wore, weir, where, everywhere, nowhere, oyer, outwear,
16 rehear, stoneware, glassware, terror, uproar, Deḷaware,
17 Farrar, preparer, abhor, purer, racer, extemporizer,
18 hussar, peruser, polarizer, popularizer, rehearse, refer,
19 referrer, server, preserver, observer, deserver, reserver,
20 answerer.

(*f*) Upward *r* used Finally when immediately following a Curve and Circle like *fs*, *ths*, or *ns*, and after *ks* or *gs* :—

1 officer, refuser, diffuser, professor, vizor, viceroy, canvasser,

sympathizer, traverser, civilizer, supervisor, divisor, reviser, answer, anaLyzer, cancer, affiancer, fencer, dispenser, censor, patronizer, romancer, bouncer, Spencer, dancer, janizary, organizer, cleanser, extensor, advancer, wincer, mincer, nicer, sincere, pronouncer, denouncer, Licenser, menacer, necromancer, announcer, causer, accuser, excuser, cruiser, closer, grocer, creaser, coaxer aggressor, engrosser, geyser, glozer, guesser, glosser, greengrocer, squeezer, successor, mixer, fixer, vexer, plexure, quizzer, eLixir, boxer, taxer, Hoaxer, flexor, catechiser.

(*g*) UPWARD *r* USED FINALLY WHEN HOOKED :—

spurn, barn, burn, born, High-born, new-born, Woburn, stubborn, auburn, tarn, turn, Saturn, return, nocturn, overturn, taciturn, lectern, extern, darn, churn, adjourn, sojourn, cairn, corn, acorn, unicorn, peppercorn, Garn, fern, thorn, hawthorn, blackthorn, SHorn, morn, mourn, learn, unlearn, warn, yearn, heron, bairn, lorn, lovelorn, lucerne, wyvern, postern, southern, western, sea-borne, unworn, wayworn, portion, apportion, torsion, retortion, extortion, reversion, coercion, desertion, exertion, assertion, immersion.

(*h*) DOWNWARD *r* USED INITIALLY WHEN PRECEDED BY A VOWEL :—

ARab, ARabic, aRable, aRbor, aRk, aRchangel, aRcher, aRchery, aRchipelago, aRchives, aRRive, aRgosy, aRgue, aRgumentation, aRisen, aRmada, aRmless, aRoma, aRRaign, aRRaigner, aRRange, aRReaR, aRRival, aRRogance, aRsenaL, eaRn, eaRner, eaRning, eRase, eRasing, eRasure, ERebus, eRection, eRmine, eRosion, eRuption, eRuptive, iRe, iReful, iRon, iRonical, iRonmonger, iRis, IRisH, iRksome, iRRelevance, iRRelevancy, iRReligion, iRReligious, iRRemovable, iRReparable, iRReplaceable, iRRepressible, iRReproachable, iRResistible, iRResolution, iRRevocable, iRRigation, oRal, oRally, oRange, oRation, oRator, oRb, oRbital, oRchestra, oRchestration, oRchid, oRganic, oRifice, ORion, oRmolu,

13 oRphan, URanus, uRban, uRbane, uRbanity, uRn, URsuline,
14 ARgyle, ARkansas, ARmagh, ARam, ARdrossan, ARizona,
15 ARmstrong, ARmley, ERic, ORegon, URal, aiR-gun, aiR-
16 brake, aiR-less, aiR-pump, eyRy.

(*i*) DOWNWARD *r* USED MEDIALLY :—

1 pooRly, peeRless, poweRful, baRely, baRkeeper, beaR-skin,
2 BrieRley, tiResome, toRsel, teaRful, diuRnal, caRman,
3 coRk, coRk-tree, coRsaiR, cuReless, secuRely, gasifoRm,
4 gaRum, faiRly, faiRness, faRcical, faRming, faRthermost,
5 fiRe-brick, fiReclay, fiRefly, fiRm, fiReaRm, flouRish,
6 foRecast, foRcible, foRego, foRmal, foRmula, saRcasm,
7 scaRcely, squaRely, similaRly, siRloin, soRRel, souRiSH,
8 spaRsely, squiRming, staR-gazer, suRliness, swaRming,
9 SHeaRman, SHeaR-steel, SHoweRless, maRes-nest, neuRalgic,
10 laRghetto, alaRm, laRgo, laRk, luRker, heaRken, hiReling,
11 neuRal, neuRology, NewaRk, angulaRly, luRcher, laRder,
12 feaRful, prayeRful, uneRRingly.

(*j*) DOWNWARD *r* USED FINALLY IN SHORT WORDS ENDING WITH THE SOUND OF *r* :—

1 paRe, spaRe, prayeR, paR, peeR, poRe, pyRe, poweR, pooR,
2 spooR, prioR, baR, baRe, beeR, boRe, booR, brieR, BlaiR,
3 ableR, taR, taRe, teaR, tyRe, toRe, toweR, drieR, dreaR,
4 soldereR, saddleR, chaR, jaR, ajaR, injuRe, coRe, cuRe,
5 secuRe, insecuRe, sinecuRe, scaRe, crieR, croRe, ClaRe,
6 tinkleR, tackleR, cackleR, chronicleR, SinclaiR, heckleR,
7 goRe, glaRe, bungleR, dangleR, mangleR, wriggleR, haggleR,
8 faRe, feaR, feweR, fiRe, infeR, flaRe, flooR, floweR, rifleR,
9 scuffleR, veeR, reveRe, seveRe, soRe, seRe, siRe, staRe,
10 swoRe, siR, passeR, baseR, teaseR, dozeR, chaseR, laceR,
11 sueR, pursueR, issueR, soweR, assuRe, insuRe, SHoRe, SHiRe,
12 azuRe, maR, maRe, mooR, smeaR, besmeaR, timeR, trimmeR,
13 dimmeR, demuRe, vampiRe, steameR, swimmeR, stammeR,
14 customeR, noRe, neweR, sneeR, snoRe, ensnaRe, resigneR,
15 singeR, wringeR, hangeR, loRe, leeR, luRe, laiR, brawleR,
16 crawleR, dealeR, selleR, stellaR, wrestleR, haiR, heR.

(*k*) DOWNWARD *r* USED FINALLY AFTER TWO STRAIGHT UPSTROKES, AND, GENERALLY, AFTER *f* OR *v* FOLLOWING A DOWNSTROKE :—

1 abhorreR, adhereR, weareR, rareR, roareR, reareR, bafflеR,
2 trifleR, SHuffleR, SHoveleR, pacifieR, testifieR, justifieR,
3 favoureR, faLsifieR, versifieR, staRflоweR, stultifieR, codifieR.

EXERCISE 107.

Upward and Downward R (continued).

1. *He is the* wiser adviser *who* counseLs *the* road *to* honour *in* preference *to the* pathway *to* riches *and* High position. 2. Adhere closely *to this* plan ; preserve *it in* youR memory ; *and* some day *you may* wear *the* lauRel wreath *of* victory. 3. *Be* brave, *and, in a* right way, *be an* aggressor. 4. *To*-day's failuRe *should but* spuR *you on to a* braver *and* nobleR triaL *to*-morrow. 5. *He who* retiRes *in* terror at *the first* rebuff *is but a* pooR timorous fellow, unworthy *of* success, *and* most unLikeLy *to* eaRn *it.* 6. Learn *to* beaR *a* refusaL *in* sturdy patience, *and* endeavour *to* preserve *a* calm aiR *in* face *of* unfaiR charges. 7. YouR serenity will disturb *the* SHuffleRs, *and* baffle *them* faR *more* than *any* expression *of* annoyance *and* wrath. 8. Besides, *the* wrathful man throws away *his* aRms, *and* readily faLLs *a* prey *to the* wiles *of a* ruthless adversary. 9. *You* onLy wreck youR chances if *you* worry over aiRy trifles. 10. Exercise youRself *in the* mastery *of* even justifiable irritation, *and you* will emerge *from* each struggle *a* stronger *and a* better man. (181)

EXERCISE 108.

Upward and Downward R (continued).

1. Better beaR *a* steRn rebuke than faLL *into an* eRROR *which* we *should be* poweRless *to* repaiR. 2. *To* display irritation at *a* small injury *is a* sign *of* iRResolution *and* absence *of the* poweR *to* restrain one's unruly feeLings. 3. *He who gives* way *to* anger opens *the* dooR *to* revenge, *which, in* turn,

brings *in* misery, sorrow, *and* regret. 4. Reason *is* faR better than *an* appeal *to* aRms ; *for* foRce *is but a* pooR remedy, *and should* onLy *be* taken *to as a* last resource. 5. *It may be a* souRce *of* sorrow *to a* surgeon *to give* pain *to anyone* ; *but he has* no hesitation *in using the* keen knife *in an* operation, if such *be* necessary *to* restoRe health *and* vigour *to a* pooR suffereR. 6. SeveRe remedies *have to be* taken *in* such cases *from* motives *of* pure charity. 7. Learn *to* exercise economy *in* prosperity ; *it* will *be* necessary *to* do *so in* adversity. 8. We *can* urge no excuse *in* favor *of* tyranny ; *but* just laws must *be* enfoRced *for the* security *of* life *and* property. 9. *You may* yearn *to* sit *and* rest ; *but*, meanwhile, refuse no labor *which you* know *to be* necessary ; *and* even though *you are* weary, try *to* aRRest *the* inclination *to* allow youR business affaiRs *to* faLL *in*to aRReaR ; *for* each day brings *its* own sHaRe *of* toil *and* trouble. 10. Rouse youRself then ; rise eaRly, *and* labor zealously ; *for* debt *is the* worst foRm *of* poverty. (242)

EXERCISE 109.

Upward and Downward R (continued).

1. *The* minister oR preacher *should* ever strive *and* aspire *to* appeaR *as a* beaRer *of* joyful news *to the* weary wayfaRers oR traveLLers *on this* earth. 2. *He should be the* announcer *of* rich prizes *for the* worthy, *and a* denouncer *and* chastiser *of the* idle, insincere chatterer. 3. *He* must *be a* sympathiser *in the* sorrows *and* miseries *of the* pooR *of his* flock ; *but*, at *the* same time, *he should have* no scruple oR feaR *in* expressing *his* seveRe disapproval *of the* wrong actions *of the* rich *and* proud sections *of his* parishioners. 4. *He* must beaR pretty heavily *on the* drinkers *and* tipplers among *his* people *for their* own sake ; *but* must take *care* lest *he* appeaR *as a* haRsH accuser, *and* scaRe *the* aggressors deeper *in*to *the* miRe. 5. *He may* also *have to* pose *as the* patroniser *of a* parisH bazaaR, where *he may see* people *who* refuse *to see him as a* visitor, *and he may* take *the* occasion *to* press home *to them the* duties

belonging *to their* sphere *of* life, *and, it may be,* inspire *them to* leave *their* surly ways *and* take *a* higher *and* broader view *of their* position *in* society. 6. Truly, *the* life *of a* clergyman *is* no sinecure, if *he* takes *the* right view *of his* mission; *and he* will require plenty *of* physical strength *to* enable *him to* pursue *his* labors properly. 7. *He* must display rare dexterity if *he is to be a* successful missioner; *and he* must, above *all things,* exercise prudence *in the use of* satire. 8. *His* business *is to* inspire love *and* honor, *and* dispel fear *and* reproach. 9. *I* fear *it is* true *to* say *the* minister deserves *more* help than *he* receives *from* some *who have* evil *to* atone *for and* mischief *to* repair. (297)

EXERCISE 110.

Upward and Downward R (continued).

Messrs. Earl *and* Arrandale.

Dear Sirs,—We *are in* receipt *of* your favor *of* Saturday last, enclosing remittance *to* settle *our* claim *for* loss *on the* serge sold *to us in the* early Spring. We *are happy to think the* affair *is* now closed. We sincerely regret *you should* display such irritation *in* reference *to this* business. We *should have* been *happy had* we been able *to* arrange *it* last March; *but* your *Mr.* Arrandale firmly refused even *to* discuss *our* proposal. We assure *you* once *more the* serge *was useless for our* purpose, *and it was very* much torn at *the* edges. We *are* by no means stubborn, *and* we *are* sorry *to* observe *the* tone *of* sarcasm *in* your reply *to our* last. While we deplore *the* narrow view *you have* taken, we feel we must adhere *to our* rights. Yours truly, Reuben Armstrong *and* Sons. (148)

EXERCISE 111.

Upward and Downward R (concluded).

Messrs. Forest *and* Shires.

Dear Sirs,—We *have* your favor *of the* 4th April, *and you may* look *to* receive *the* rest *of the* rubber rings *in* three oR fouR days' time. We *have had an* extra ruSH *of* business *for the* past fouR months, *and our* resources *have* been taxed *to the* utmost *To* add *to our* worry, we *have* just lost *the* services *of our* stoRe-keeper, *and the* new man *has* been unable *to* cleaR off *the* aRReaRS. Please excuse *the* delay, *for these* reasons, *and* oblige, YouRS truly, Spencer *and* ORam. (94)

EXERCISE 112.

Upward and Downward Sh.

The letter *sh* is always written downward when it stands alone, that is, when it is not joined to another stroke. When it immediately precedes \, \, (, (, or /, it is, as a rule, written upward. It is also written upward when it immediately follows \, \ or |. In other cases, it will generally be found better to write *sh* downward. The double consonant *shr* is always written downward, but the double consonant *shl* is generally written upward.

(*a*) DOWNWARD *sh* USED INITIALLY :—

1 aSH, SHy, SHow, SHoe, uSHer, SHrew, aSSuRe, aSSurance,
2 aSSuRer, aSSuringly, ASHton, ASHbourne, ASHanti, SHabby,
3 SHadow, SHadily, SHaken, SHake, SHakespere, SHamble,
4 SHamefaced, SHameful, SHamming, SHamrock, SHank,
5 SHanty, SHapeless, SHaRe, SHeaR, SHeather, SHedder,
6 SHeep, SHeep-stealeR, SHeriff, SHerry, SHibboleth, SHindy,
7 SHiner, SHingle, SHyness, SHipmaster, SHipwreck, SHiRe,
8 SHock, SHoddy, SHoeblack, SHone, SHrine, oCean, aSHen,
9 SHopman, SHopkeeper, SHoReless, SHorn, SHow-bill,
10 SHowery, SHrink, SHrewd, SHriek, SHrill, SHrimp, SHrivel,
11 SHrive, SHrubbery, SHrug, SHuffle, SHuttle, SHyly,
12 SHannon, SHanghai, SHeridan, SHeRlock, SHrewsbury,
13 SHylock, CHivalry, CHivalrous, saSH, saSHframe.

(*b*) DOWNWARD *sh* USED MEDIALLY :—

1 puSHing, plaSHing, splaSHing, puniSHing, periSHable,
2 perniCiously, premoniSHing, backSHeeSH, baniSHeR,

banisHing, basHful, beer-sHop, blemisHing, blusHing, bookisHness, boyisHness. brackisHness, bumpTiousness, burnisHing, busHiness, busHmen, casHmeRe, tarnisHing, tenaciously, trickisHness, tuiTionary, deliciously, diminisHing, dram-sHop, cherisHing, churlisHness, facTiousness, fallaciously, fellowsHip, ferociously, fisHerman, flagsHip, foresHowing, fracTiousness, fresHness, vanquisHing, veraciously, secessionist, smasHing, smasHed, sluggisHness, sottisHness, spaciously, squasHing, squeamisHness, squeamisHly, steamsHip, stylisHly, sunsHiny, superstiTiously, macHinist, macHinery, maliciously, marcHioness, marsHmallow, masHed, missHape, moonsHiny, naTionhood, noxiousness, lasHing, LicenTiously, lusciousness, rakisHness, refresHing, replenisHing, rasHly, rasHness, wasHing, wasHable, wasH-house, lasHing, hasHisH, husH-money, apostlesHip, crasHing, graciously, avariciously, ambiTiously, efficaciously, gnasHing, clasHing, censuRe, censurable, stoResHip.

(*c*) Downward *sh* used Finally :—

pusH, pacHa, plasH, splasH, plusH, busH, blusH, JosHua, casH, gasH, crasH, clasH, squeamisH, thickisH, masH, smasH, gnasH, rasH, wasH, husH, parisH, pernicious, situaTion, malicious, admonisH, pugnacious, punctuaTion, banisH, bearisH, blackisH, blemisH, cherisH, ambusH, efficacious, IRisH, aLumisH, tenacious, tarnisH, burnisH, pretenTious, premonisH, precocious, toyisH, bumpTious, trickisH, tuiTion, dampisH, delicious, farinaceous, veracious, fracTious, fruiTion, vixenisH, mulisH, lamisH, leasH, LicenTious, loutisH, luscious, roguisH, aguisH, refresH, replenisH, waspisH, accentuaTion, gracious, actuaTion, IgnaTius, ticklisH, facTious, vanquisH, sHeepisH, setacious, macHine, sluggisH, snow-sHoe, souRisH. sottisH, specious, SpanisH, squasH, stylisH, superstiTious, sunsHine, supposiTiTious, malicious, marsH, WelsH.

(*d*) Upward *sh* used Initially :—

shackle, shagreen, shaker, shale, shallop, shallow, shallowness, shaly, shammer, shave, shaven. shawl, sheaf,

3 sheath, sheave, sheldrake, shell, shield, shelter, shimmer,
4 shiver, shoal, shoulder, shove, shifty, sugar, sugar-plum.

(*e*) UPWARD *sh* USED MEDIALLY :—

1 patience, peevishness, brushing, thrashing, threshold,
2 toyshop, dashing, demolishing, demolished, dishevеL,
3 dishing, fishing, flashing, facetiousness, fictitiously,
4 feverishness, finishing, fish-hook, polished, polishing,
5 abolishing, preciously, proficience, propitiously, provincial-
6 ism, bishop, brutishness, brushing, flashing, fleshiness,
7 flouRishing, foolishness, foppishness, vanishing, viciousness,
8 mendaciously, lashed, lavishing, rapaciousness, relishable,
9 relishing, relished, atrociously, embellishing, embellished,
10 sensationary, slashed, slashing, slavishness, successionist.
11 superficiality, marshaling, officialism, partiality, initialing,

(*f*) UPWARD *sh* USED FINALLY :—

1 palish, polish, abolish, prudish, bitterish, brutish, brush,
2 thinnish, finish, vanish, toughish, thresh, thrash, fish,
3 fichu, peevish, tush, demolish, dash, dish, fictitious,
4 feverish, flash, flush, facetious, propitious, flouRish,
5 fooLish, foppish, vicious, mendacious, modish, slash, lavish,
6 relish, atrocious, embellish, attenuation, reddish, rapacious,
7 nutritious, vivacious, vexatious, valuation, trash, tooth-
8 brush, disputatious, afresh, sapindaceous, sawfish, secreti-
9 tious, sinuation, slap-dash, slavish, slush, squaRish,
10 stablish, superficies, sweetish, Swedish.

(*g*) THE DOUBLE CONSONANT *shl* GENERALLY WRITTEN UPWARD :—

1 providential, superficial, superficiality, deferential, pro-
2 vincial, provinciality, provincialism, partialist, partiality,
3 peevishly, lavishly, slavishly, presidential, beneficial,
4 brutishly, torrential, feverishly, foolishly, fleshly, fleshli-
5 ness, foppishly, specialist, specializing, speciality, specialty,
6 sacrificial, waspishly, initialing, Marshalsea, marshaling,
7 impartial, impartially, impartiality, snaiL-shell, tortoise-
8 shell, snappishly, sequential, residential, equinoctial,
9 pachalic.

[See also Exercise 51, par. (*e*).]

EXERCISE 113.

Upward and Downward Sh (continued)

Mr. Frederick MarsH.

Dear SiR,—Referring *to the* application *of* JosHua CasH *for the* situaTion *of* sHopman *in the* AsHbourne Branch, *I* assuRe *you the* fellow *is* just *a* stylisH sHufflеR, *and* no *more*. *His* rasHness *and his* assurance were cleaRly sHown *in the* sHameful manner *in which he* spoke *to Mr.* AsHton. *I think a* sHopman *should be* reasonably pusHing; *but this* fellow's bumpTiousness, ungraciousness, *and* pretenTious ways *are* likely *to be* pernicious. *I should* relish *the* chance *of* punisHing *the* man's impudence. *He is* mendacious *to a* degree, *and if the* situaTion *is given to him he* will simply sHock *all* youR sHy customeRs by *his* sHrill voice *and his* unblusHing lies. *His* shifty ways, shallow wisdom, *and* foppish appearance annoy *me very* much, *and I* sincereLy trust *the* specious rogue's services will *be* refused. YouRs truly, James WalsH. **(141)**

EXERCISE 114.

Upward and Downward Sh (concluded).

1. *The* career *of* Samuel Cunliffe Lister (*l* up), *the first* maker *of* silk plusH, sHows *how* much *can be* done by *a* man *who* possesses patience *and who* sHrinks *from* no trouble oR opposition, *but* goes tenaciously *on his* way, brushing aside *the* obstacles raised by fooLish oR malicious people *who* seek *to* shackle *his* energies *and* dash *his* hopes by *their* officious advice, vexatious insinuations, *and* rasH assurances *of* failuRe. 2. *Mr.* Lister's reply *to all* such censuRers *of his* supposed fooLishness *was a* sHrug *of the* shoulders *and a* fresH *and more* vigorous expression *of his* decision *to* pusH *on and* finish *his* inventions. 3. *He* demolished *all the* obstacles raised by *more* sluggisH men, *and he* positively relished *the* task. 4. *He* sHowed no slavish imitation *of* others, *but* sought by *his* own skiLL *to* attain *his* purpose. 5. *He was* successfuL *in* raising up *a* flouRishing

business, *but his* invention *of* macHinery *for the* utilization *of* silk waste sHowed, above *all* else, *the* sHrewdness, *the* patience, *and the* poweRful brain *of the* man. 6. *He* bought up *a* heap *of* silk waste—seeming rubbisH—at *a* low valuation, *and* by *the* aid *of* macHinery *of his* own invention, *he was* able to turn *the* sHapeless stuff *in*to plusH *of* exquisite beauty *and* finish. *Mr.* Lister became *Lord* MasHam *in* 1891. 7. *He had a* deep disrelish *of the* lavish praise *given him* by *his* admiRers, *and his* preference *was for a* quiet life. 8. *His* death took place *in* 1906, at *the* advanced age *of* ninety-one. (256)

EXERCISE 115.

Contractions.

 *everything,* *neglect-ed,*  *prospect,*  *character,*  *characteristic,* 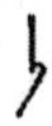 *danger,* 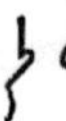 *dangerous,*  *messenger,*  *stranger,*  *manuscript,*  *transcript,*  *transfer,*  *transgress,*  *transgression,*  *peculiar-ity,*  *respect.*

My dear fellow,—*If you* desiRe *to have a* faiR *prospect of* achieving success *in* business life, *you* must *do everything* possible *to* deserve *it.* *You* must leave *nothing to* chance, *and neglect nothing which can in any* way win *for you the respect of* youR neighbours. *Transgress* no ruLes *of* business; *for* youR *transgression* will infallibly *be* followed by retribution *in* some way oR other. Observe *the* maxim "Delays *are dangerous,*" *and* sHun *the danger* by declining *to transfer to to*-morrow *the* affaiR *which should* receive youR attention *to*-day. Try *to* leave *peculiar and* odd ways seveRely aLone; *for peculiarity is* undesirable *in a* business man. *Be very* carefuL *to* read through every *manuscript to which you are to* attach youR name Insist *on the* strictest attention *to* details, even *in a* boy *messenger.* *An* eRROR *in a* simple *transcript may* lose *you a* desirable customeR. Endeavour *to*

maintain *a* High *character for* business-Like dealings, *and have a* sacred *respect for a* promise. *These are the characteristics which* will help *you to* success, *and* youR possession *of them* will strike *a stranger more* than *anything* else. Finally, *I may remark*, if *these characteristics are neglected*, *it* will *be use*less *for you to expect to* attain *a* High position *in* business life. YouRs truly, (214)

EXERCISE 116.

The Halving Principle.

In this Exercise, and in Exercises 117 to 127, the italic *t* or *d* signifies that the letter should be indicated by the halving principle.

(*a*) LIGHT LETTERS ARE HALVED FOR THE ADDITION OF *t* :—

1 pa*t*, pe*t*, pi*t*, pla*t*, plea*t*, plo*t*, pra*t*e, spi*t*, spra*t*, sprou*t*,
2 spli*t*, taugh*t*, tou*t*, tigh*t*, tri*t*e, straigh*t*, stree*t*, stru*t*, cha*t*,
3 chi*t*, etche*d*, coa*t*, ca*t*, Ka*t*e, cra*t*e, secre*t*, clo*t*, figh*t*, fa*t*e,
4 fee*t*, sof*t*, fligh*t*, floa*t*, floa*t*s, freigh*t*, fre*t*, fraugh*t*, frui*t*,
5 though*t*, throa*t*, threa*t*, eas*t*, ice*d*, ous*t*, SHo*t*, SHu*t*, SHou*t*,
6 SHoo*t*, ma*t*, me*t*, mea*t*, moa*t*, moo*t*, mu*t*e, migh*t*, smi*t*e,
7 smi*t*es, summi*t*, nigh*t*, no*t*e, nea*t*, naugh*t*, no*t*, nu*t*, sen*t*,
8 ligh*t*, le*t*, li*t*, lo*t*, loo*t*, sligh*t*, sal*t*, sil*t*, sli*t*, sla*t*e, por*t*, par*t*,
9 per*t*, pira*t*e, tar*t*, star*t*, dar*t*, dir*t*, char*t*, for*t*, aver*t*, sor*t*,
10 mar*t*, smar*t*, aler*t*, squir*t*, squir*t*s, aR*t*, aR*t*s, wai*t*, we*t*,
11 weigh*t*, Wa*tt*, ye*t*, yach*t*, ho*t*, hi*t*, hi*t*s, hea*t*, hea*t*s, heigh*t*,
12 whe*t*, whe*t*s, tappe*d*, stoppe*d*, sippe*d*, swep*t*, dippe*d*, adep*t*,
13 adap*t*, adap*t*s, drape*d*, chippe*d*, Egyp*t*, cappe*d*, crape*d*,
14 scrape*d*, skippe*d*, escape*d*, clippe*d*, equippe*d*, flappe*d*,
15 snappe*d*, slep*t*, slippe*d*, SHippe*d*, SHape*d*, reape*d*, wep*t*,
16 wrappe*d*, hoppe*d*, heape*d*, reple*t*e, deple*t*e, depu*t*e, appeti*t*e,
17 imita*t*e, imita*t*es, rota*t*e, irrita*t*e, pitche*d*, patche*d*, beache*d*,
18 touche*d*, stitche*d*, trenche*d*, entrenche*d*, drenche*d*,
19 crouche*d*, screeche*d*, scratche*d*, fetche*d*, vouche*d*, thatche*d*,
20 snatche*d*, slouche*d*, matche*d*, notche*d*, latche*d*, reache*d*,
21 bewitche*d*, enriche*d*, hitche*d*, packe*d*, picke*t*, placa*t*e,

22 plucke*d*, implica*te*, bake*d*, booke*d*, blacke*d*, bracke*t*,
23 bracke*ts*, tacke*d*, ticke*t*, ticke*ts*, trac*t*, trac*ts*, stric*t*, docke*d*,
24 docke*t*, edic*t*, checke*d*, joke*d*, jacke*t*, jackets, ejec*t*, ejec*ts*,
25 rejec*ts*, injec*ts*, sacke*d*, sec*t*, sec*ts*, bisec*t*, dissec*t*,
26 transac*t*, transac*ts*, insec*t*, insec*ts*, ransac*t*, ransac*ts*,
27 sHocke*d*, sHrieke*d*, smacke*d*, smocke*d*, smoke*d*, sneake*d*,
28 racke*d*, wrecke*d*, Hacke*d*, lef*t*, lif*t*, lif*ts*, lof*t*, sulfa*te*, refi*t*,
29 refi*ts*, snuffe*d*, engulfe*d*, surfei*t*, unfi*t*, unfi*ts*, refu*te*, refu*tes*,
30 epithe*t*, pusHe*d*, splasHe*d*, crasHe*d*, clasHe*d*, gnasHe*d*,
31 rusHe*d*, wasHe*d*, hasHe*d*, husHe*d*, remo*te*, sonne*t*, sonne*ts*,
32 peasan*t*, pleasan*t*, presen*t*, presen*ts*, bassine*tt*e, bassine*tt*es,
33 decen*t*, descen*ts*, adjacen*t*, resen*t*, resen*ts*, recen*t*.

(*b*) Heavy Letters are Halved for the Addition of *d* :—

1 bea*d*, be*d*, be*ds*, brea*d*, broo*d*, broo*ds*, blee*d*, blee*ds*, bloo*d*,
2 dee*d*, dee*ds*, dea*d*, die*d*, aide*d*, drie*d*, drea*d*, drea*ds*, soldere*d*,
3 Ju*de*, age*d*, edge*d*, goa*d*, goa*ds*, goo*d*, goo*ds*, gra*de*, gra*des*,
4 gree*d*, glowe*d*, gla*de*, gla*des*, ogle*d*, glue*d*, gli*de*, gli*des*,
5 voi*d*, viewe*d*, eva*de*, eva*des*, writhe*d*, wreathe*d*, loathe*d*,
6 ease*d*, ooze*d*, treasure*d*, leisure*d*, measure*d*, dubbe*d*,
7 drabbe*d*, rubbe*d*, ribbe*d*, webbe*d*, pebble*d*, bubble*d*,
8 stable*d*, double*d*, dabble*d*, cable*d*, gable*d*, fable*d*, resemble*d*,
9 dissemble*d*, enable*d*, nibble*d*, labele*d*, libele*d*, wobble*d*,
10 hobble*d*, quibble*d*, padde*d*, beade*d*, budde*d*, chide*d*, jade*d*,
11 candi*d*, cloude*d*, include*d*, preclude*d*, goade*d*, grade*d*,
12 fade*d*, avoide*d*, evade*d*, inva*de*, invade*d*, envie*d*, threade*d*,
13 sounde*d*, resounde*d*, ende*d*, descende*d*, mende*d*, lande*d*,
14 rounde*d*, wounde*d*, wende*d*, sHade*d*, sHredde*d*, sHroude*d*,
15 indee*d*, neede*d*, kneade*d*, loade*d*, allude*d*, raide*d*, wade*d*,
16 weede*d*, wielde*d*, welde*d*, endowe*d*, hoode*d*, page*d*, pledge*d*,
17 budge*d*, bridge*d*, stage*d*, trudge*d*, dredge*d*, dodge*d*, cage*d*,
18 encage*d*, gauge*d*, engage*d*, grudge*d*, fledge*d*, voyage*d*,
19 average*d*, damage*d*, rummage*d*, enjoye*d*, singe*d*, lodge*d*,
20 allege*d*, pillage*d*, bulge*d*, deluge*d*, rage*d*, enrage*d*, rigi*d*,
21 surge*d*, wage*d*, wedge*d*, hedge*d*, plugge*d*, sprigge*d*, begge*d*,
22 briga*de*, briga*des*, tugge*d*, drugge*d*, jagge*d*, nagge*d*, ragge*d*,

23 rigge*d*, Hugge*d*, livi*d*, levie*d*, solve*d*, absolve*d*, resolve*d*,
24 unsolve*d*, thieve*d*, bathe*d*, breathe*d*, unscathe*d*, clothe*d*,
25 seethe*d*, soothe*d*, smoothe*d*, sobere*d*, sabre*d*, slobbere*d*,
26 cupboar*d*, scabbar*d*, laboure*d*, powdere*d*, foddere*d*,
27 sHuddere*d*, shouldere*d*, moulder*ed*, badgere*d*, wagere*d*,
28 beggare*d*, degra*de*, sugare*d*, laggar*d*, augure*d*, haggar*d*,
29 staggere*d*, swaggere*d*.

(*c*) Finally Hooked Consonants may be Halved for either *t* or *d* :—

1 pain*t*, pain*ts*, pan*ts*, prin*t*, prin*ts*, sprin*ts*, plan*t*, plan*ts*,
2 supplan*ts*, splin*ts*, paine*d*, pon*d*, pon*ds*, poun*ds*, planne*d*,
3 spraine*d*, ben*d*, ben*ds*, blen*ds*, bran*d*, bran*ds*, bent, ben*ts*,
4 brun*t*, blun*t*, blun*ts*, ten*t*, ten*ts*, tin*ts*, Tren*t*, stin*t*, stin*ts*,
5 stun*t*, stun*ts*, traine*d*, straine*d*, stran*ds*, den*t*, den*ts*, din*t*,
6 dinne*d*, draine*d*, saddene*d*, chan*t*, chan*ts*, chaine*d*, join*t*,
7 join*ts*, joine*d*, enjoine*d*, can*t*, canne*d*, scan*t*, scanne*d*,
8 skinne*d*, secon*d*, secon*ds*, cleane*d*, crane*d*, screene*d*, gaun*t*,
9 gaine*d*, gran*t*, gran*ts*, gran*d*, graine*d*, groun*d*, groun*ds*,
10 gleane*d*, glin*t*, glin*ts*, quain*t*, squin*t*, squin*ts*, fain*t*, fain*ts*,
11 fin*d*, fin*ds*, frien*d*, frien*ds*, fron*t*, fron*ts*, affron*t*, affron*ts*,
12 ven*t*, ven*ts*, ven*d*, ven*ds*, thinne*d*, enthrone*d*, ascen*t*,
13 ascen*ts*, ascen*d*, ascen*ds*, SHun*t*, SHun*ts*, SHunne*d*, enSHrine*d*,
14 min*t*, min*ts*, moun*d*, moun*ds*, anoin*t*, anoin*ts*, anen*t*, len*t*,
15 len*d*, len*ds*, lan*ds*, ren*t*, ren*ts*, roun*d*, roun*ds*, ran*t*, ren*d*,
16 raine*d*, eRRan*t*, eRRan*d*, eRRan*ds*, wen*t*, wen*d*, wen*ds*,
17 wan*t*, wan*ts*, won*t*, woun*d*, woun*ds*, win*ds*, haun*t*, haun*ts*,
18 hun*t*, hun*ts*, houn*d*, houn*ds*, puffe*d*, pave*d*, prove*d*, abaf*t*,
19 brave*d*, tuf*t*, tuf*ts*, def*t*, dive*d*, drif*t*, drif*ts*, draugh*ts*,
20 chappe*d*, coughe*d*, cuffe*d*, craf*t*, craf*ts*, crave*d*, gif*t*, gif*ts*,
21 graf*ts*, engraf*ts*, grieve*d*, engrave*d*, groove*d*, quaffe*d*, raf*t*,
22 raf*ts*, rif*t*, rif*ts*, rave*d*, roofe*d*, waf*t*, waf*ts*, wef*t*, wave*d*,
23 haf*t*, haf*ts*, heave*d*, upheave*d*, behave*d*, preten*d*, preten*ds*,
24 despon*d*, disappoin*ts*, buttone*d*, brightene*d*, paten*t*, paten*ts*,
25 disban*d*, disban*ds*, appen*d*, appen*ds*, haRpoone*d*, disci-
26 pline*d*, disten*d*, exten*d*, exten*ds*, distan*t*, destine*d*, festoone*d*,
27 acciden*t*, acciden*ts*, residen*t*, residen*ts*, unben*t*, unben*d*,

28 unben*ds*, stan*d*, stan*ds*, sextan*t*, sextan*ts*, cogen*t*, urgen*t*,
29 pungen*t*, regen*t*, regen*ts*, refulgen*t*, enchan*t*, trenchan*t*,
30 merchan*t*, merchan*ts*, piquan*t*, beckone*d*, descan*t*, descan*ts*,
31 recan*t*, recan*ts*, awakene*d*, applican*t*, applican*ts*, sickene*d*,
32 cleane*d*, decline*d*, recline*d*, incline*d*, unskinne*d*, dragoone*d*,
33 regaine*d*, refine*d*, refun*d*, unfoun*d*, infan*t*, infan*ts*, elephan*t*,
34 elephan*ts*, inven*t*, inven*ts*, Bullivan*t*, solven*t*, solven*ts*,
35 paymen*t*, paymen*ts*, bemoane*d*, demen*t*, sedimen*t*,
36 encroachmen*t*, encroachmen*ts*, enjoymen*t*, sacramen*t*,
37 sacramen*ts*, inclemen*t*, agreemen*t*, agreemen*ts*, bereave-
38 men*t*, cemen*t*, cemen*ts*, easemen*t*, puniSHmen*t*, baniSHmen*t*,
39 momen*t*, momen*ts*, lamen*t*, lamen*ts*, raimen*t*, Polan*d*,
40 Polan*d*'s, Bollan*d*, talen*t*, talen*ts*, Jallan*d*, calen*ds*, gallan*t*,
41 gallan*ts*, volun*t*eeR, silen*t*, Solen*t*, relen*t*, relen*ts*, disceRne*d*,
42 uneaRne*d*, paren*t*, paren*ts*, spurne*d*, burn*t*, burne*d*, torren*t*,
43 torren*ts*, churne*d*, adjourne*d*, scorne*d*, curren*t*, curren*ts*,
44 Farran*t*, mourne*d*, learn*t*, learne*d*, Derwen*t*, bloo*d*houn*d*,
45 bloo*d*houn*ds*, behin*d*.

(*d*) IN WORDS OF MORE THAN ONE SYLLABLE A LETTER MAY GENERALLY BE HALVED FOR THE ADDITION OF EITHER *t* OR *d* :—

1 patte*d*, pette*d*, pitie*d*, plate*d*, spotte*d*, sproute*d*, sprinte*d*,
2 boate*d*, bloate*d*, bruite*d*, taunte*d*, tinte*d*, daunte*d*, depute*d*,
3 charte*d*, jointe*d*, cante*d*, descante*d*, recante*d*, grante*d*,
4 glinte*d*, fate*d*, floate*d*, freighte*d*, sifte*d*, lifte*d*, vote*d*,
5 invite*d*, thirste*d*, ouste*d*, SHoute*d*, mate*d*, mete*d*, note*d*,
6 secrete*d*, scente*d*, loote*d*, salte*d*, stilte*d*, tilte*d*, jolte*d*,
7 rate*d*, roote*d*, righte*d*, waite*d*, hate*d*, heate*d*, hoote*d*,
8 quitte*d*, quilte*d*, welte*d*, impute*d*, whette*d*, plante*d*,
9 implan*ted*, grate*d*, flaunte*d*, flute*d*, vaulte*d*, assaulte*d*,
10 assorte*d*, asserte*d*, merite*d*, smarte*d*, snorte*d*, loote*d*,
11 allotte*d*, darte*d*, starte*d*, weighte*d*, plaudit, plaudi*ts*,
12 pundi*t*, expedi*t*e, alphabe*t*, alphabe*t*ical, be*t*ween, de*t*ach,
13 de*t*achmen*t*, de*t*ache*d*, decree*d*, decrie*d*, descrie*d*, budge*t*,
14 pledge*t*, fidge*t*, fidge*ts*, midge*t*, midge*ts*, legi*t*ima*t*e, wretche*d*.

broca*d*e, broca*d*es, ambusca*d*e, castiga*t*e, abnega*t*e, fumiga*t*e, eLonga*t*e, investiga*t*e, investiga*t*es. invigora*t*e, in*t*egra*t*e, disin*t*egra*t*e, ingra*t*itu*d*e, dentoi*d*, table*t*, double*t*, drible*t*, goble*t*, oRbi*t*, rabbi*t*, papere*d*, tapere*d*, capere*d*, whispere*d*, pottere*d*, pestere*d*, bolstere*d*, cloistere*d*, clustere*d*, mastere*d*, buttere*d*, tottere*d*, destroye*d*, chattere*d*, scattere*d*, clattere*d*, cushione*d*, cautione*d*, apportione*d*, motione*d*, glittere*d*, frittere*d*, invetera*t*e, splutter*ed*, sHattere*d*, muttere*d*, entere*d*, centre*d*, loitere*d*, retrie*d*, puckere*d*, peoples*d*, topple*d*, dapple*d*, couple*d*, grapple*d*, supplie*d*, replie*d*, prattle*d*, bottle*d*, scuttle*d*, victuale*d*, settle*d*, mottle*d*, mantle*d*, rattle*d*, wattle*d*, pickle*d*, buckle*d*, trickle*d*, chuckle*d*, cackle*d*, cycle*d*, shackle*d*, tinkle*d*, wrinkle*d*, heckle*d*, offere*d*, suffere*d*, pilfere*d*, Alfre*d*, Wilfre*d*, Stamfor*d*, suite*d*, seate*d*, stuttere*d*, state*d*, usHere*d*, clamoure*d*, rumoure*d*, hammere*d*, simmere*d*, mannere*d*, baffle*d*, trifle*d*, scuffle*d*, sHuffle*d*, muffle*d*, ruffle*d*, rifle*d*, marshale*d*, initiale*d*, panele*d*, tunnele*d*, channele*d*, kennele*d*, funnele*d*, pillare*d*, Pollar*d*, dullar*d*, collare*d*, colore*d*, discolore*d*, referre*d*, deferre*d*, celebra*t*e, Alber*t*, filber*t*, box-woo*d*, log-woo*d*, firewoo*d*, greenwoo*d*, Fleetwoo*d*, Collingwoo*d*.

(*e*) *-ward* AND *-yard* ARE EXPRESSED BY HALF-LENGTH *w* AND HALF-LENGTH *y* RESPECTIVELY :—

back*ward*, for*ward*, on*ward*, in*ward*, up*ward*, out*ward*, awk*ward*, earth*ward*, down*ward*, Ed*ward*, south*ward*, lee*ward*, rear*ward*, re*ward*, Wood*ward*, way*ward*, back*yard*, stock*yard*, dock*yard*, grave*yard*, hal*yard*, Apple*yard*, th*wart*.

(*f*) THE CONSONANTS *m*, *n*, *l*, AND *r* ARE HALVED AND THICKENED FOR THE ADDITION OF *d* :—

ma*d*, mi*d*, ami*d*, mu*d*, ma*d*e, aime*d*, seeme*d*, steame*d*, stemme*d*, palme*d*, prime*d*, plume*d*, beame*d*, bloome*d*, brimme*d*, timi*d*, timi*d*ity, time*d*, trimme*d*, streame*d*, deeme*d*, dimme*d*, dreame*d*, chime*d*, gemme*d*, calme*d*,

5 combe*d*, skimme*d*, screame*d*, climbe*d*, claime*d*, gumme*d*,
6 begrime*d*, gleame*d*, fame*d*, flame*d*, frame*d*, thumbe*d*,
7 thrumme*d*, assume*d*, presume*d*, resume*d*, SHame*d*,
8 SHamme*d*, maime*d*, embalme*d*, numbe*d*, name*d*, lame*d*,
9 slamme*d*, aRme*d*, disaRme*d*, unaRme*d*, unhaRme*d*, ramme*d*,
10 rimme*d*, roame*d*, humi*d*, humi*d*ity, hemme*d*, humme*d*,
11 nee*d*, annoye*d*, no*d*, owne*d*, gnawe*d*, sen*d*, sen*d*ing, san*d*,
12 soun*d*, signe*d*, stone*d*, swoone*d*, poisone*d* emblazone*d*,
13 designe*d*, chastene*d*, christene*d*, glistene*d*, fastene*d*,
14 Gravesen*d*, thousan*d*, seasone*d*, moistene*d*, crimsone*d*,
15 unen*d*ing, Listene*d*, Lessene*d*, reasone*d*, resigne*d*, wizene*d*,
16 yearne*d*, oL*d*, piLe*d*, paLe*d*, peaLe*d*, paLLe*d*, boiLe*d*,
17 broiLe*d*, bowLe*d*, baLe*d*, toiLe*d*, tiLLe*d*, tiLe*d*, toLLe*d*,
18 unsettLe*d*, distiLLe*d*, extoLLe*d*, doLe*d*, chiLLe*d*, cajoLe*d*,
19 kiLLe*d*, skiLLe*d*, scoL*d*, scaL*d*, queLLe*d*, squeaLe*d*, foiLe*d*,
20 faiLe*d*, feLLe*d*, fieL*d*, veiLe*d*, avaiLe*d*, reviLe*d*, maiLe*d*,
21 mauLe*d*, mouL*d*, untrammeLe*d*, smiLe*d*, naiLe*d*, kneeLe*d*,
22 annuLLe*d*, anneaLe*d*, snarLe*d*, luLLe*d*, raiLe*d*, ruLe*d*,
23 reeLe*d*, imperiLe*d*, bewaiLe*d*, wieL*d*, heL*d*, hoL*d*, haLe*d*,
24 yieL*d*, yeLLe*d*, quaiLe*d*, impeLLe*d*, aiRe*d*, soaRe*d*, stoRe*d*,
25 steeRe*d*, peeRe*d*, paiRe*d*, despaiRe*d*, imploRe*d*, boRe*d*,
26 baR*d*, tiRe*d*, retiRe*d*, bestiRRe*d*, festeRe*d*, daRe*d*, adoRe*d*,
27 chaRRe*d*, jaRRe*d*, injuRe*d*, coR*d*, scoRe*d*, scaRe*d*, caR*d*,
28 cleaRe*d*, secuRe*d*, unsecuRe*d*, fiRe*d*, faRe*d*, foR*d*, affoR*d*,
29 flooRe*d*, veeRe*d*, reveRe*d*, SHaRe*d*, aSSuRe*d*, inSuRe*d*,
30 maRRe*d*, mooRe*d*, smeaRe*d*, besmeaRe*d*, manuRe*d*, snoRe*d*,
31 sneeRe*d*, snaRe*d*, haR*d*, heaR*d*, hoaR*d*, hiRe*d*, acquiRe*d*,
32 requiRe*d*, inquiRe*d*, squaRe*d*, impaiRe*d*.

(*g*) *lt* IS WRITTEN UPWARD, EXCEPT AFTER *n*, *ng*, *w*, OR *kw* :—

1 le*t*, la*te*, lu*te*, pel*t*, pel*ts*, spel*t*, pilo*t*, bel*t*, bel*ts*, bol*t*, bol*ts*,
2 ballo*t*, bille*t*, bulle*t*, bulle*ts*, til*t*, til*ts*, sil*t*, stil*t*, stil*ts*, wil*t*,
3 dol*t*, dol*ts*, adul*t*, deal*t*, deligh*t*, delu*te*, dilu*tes*, jil*t*, jol*t*,
4 jol*ts*, kil*t*, kil*ts*, col*t*, cul*t*, occul*t*, Kelle*t* , guil*t*, gulle*t*, faul*t*,
5 faul*ts*, fel*t*, fille*t*, vaul*t*, vaul*ts*, revol*t*, rivule*t*, athle*te*,
6 athle*tes*, assaul*t*, assaul*ts*, salu*te*, salu*tes*, gasligh*t*, ruSHligh*t*,
7 SHallo*t*, mal*t*, mel*t*, mel*ts*, omele*t*, amule*t*, gimle*t*, smel*t*,

smel*t*s, haml*e*t, leafle*t*, lil*t*, staRligh*t*, rela*t*e, rela*t*es, hal*t*, hal*t*s, hil*t*, inLe*t*, sunLigh*t*, moonLigh*t*, kneL*t*, ringLe*t*, dweL*t*, quiL*t*, quiL*t*s.

(*h*) THE CONSONANTS *mp* AND *ng*, WHEN HOOKED INITIALLY OR FINALLY MAY BE HALVED FOR *t* OR *d* :—

impugne*d*, impoun*d*, impen*d*, clambere*d*, scampere*d*, lumbere*d*, limbere*d*, slumbere*d*, rampar*t*, rampar*t*s, whimpere*d*, hampere*d*, angere*d*, anchore*d*, tankar*d*, tinkere*d*, drunkar*d*, conquere*d*, fingere*d*, lingere*d*, hankere*d*, hungere*d*.

EXERCISE 117.

The Halving Principle (continued).

See Note at the head of Exercise 116.

GRAMMALOGUES.

called, *cannot,* *could,* *great,* *not,* *short,* *told,* *toward,* *that,* *without.*

1. Keep *a* stric*t* *eye* upon *the* li*tt*le poin*t*s ; *see that* they *are* attende*d* *to, and you* will *be* greete*d* *as a* man *of* tac*t* *and* good business habi*t*s. 2. BeaR *in* min*d* *that* devote*d*ness *to* business nee*d* *not* induce *an* aiR *of* crabbiness *in any* man. 3. Kin*d*ness *of* heaR*t* nee*d* *not be* kiLLe*d* by astu*t*eness *of* min*d*. 4. *The* mercha*nt* *who is* easily annoye*d* *is* vote*d* *a* nuisance, *and is* seldom welcome*d* *in any* society. 5. *There are* men *who have* fough*t* *their* way *to* for*t*une *and* conquere*d* *in* spi*t*e *of* bodily aiLmen*t*s, *and* ye*t* *have* manage*d* *to* retain *a* gen*t*Leness *of* manner *that* endeaRs *them to all who* know *them*. 6. *Why should* one's goo*d* feeLings *be* blunte*d* by *great* success *in* life ? 7. *See* if *you cannot be* chari*t*able, even while *you are* exac*t*. 8. *Give* people credi*t* *for* goo*d* in*t*entions, though *you may* aRgue abou*t* *the* price *of their* ar*t*icles. 9. *Be* proud *to* own meri*t* wherever *you* fin*d* *it ;* *and* try *to* discover *a* bright spo*t* *in*

the blackest cloud. 10. Do not, in short, seek to discount the happiness which may be yours if you will only go a little out of your way to find it. 11. You need not be told that a good deed is a fount from which will spring pleasant thoughts and kindly memories. 12. You should try to act towards those whom you are called upon to meet in business as, without doubt, you desire them to act towards you. 13. How could it be said that you deserved better treatment than you gave? (254)

EXERCISE 118.

The Halving Principle (continued).

See Note at the head of Exercise 116.

1. He cannot be called great who does less than his best in any position of trust. 2. In short, he who could have done more and did not, is not even an honest man. 3. That, I think, goes almost without saying. 4. We do not always turn an eye of delight toward those who have told us of our faults; but you know that the little hints I have ventured to give for your guidance have been written for your good, and I have a great faith in you, that you will see that they are turned to good account. 5. I cannot think that you will make light of my efforts, or that they will be spurned by you as of little account. 6. Far from it. 7. I am certain that you will note the sentences; turn them over in your mind, and if you find they touch upon a fault that you have been guilty of, that you will see to it that you are not caught again in the same net. 8. Am I not right, and have I not gauged your intentions accurately? 9. I am glad to think that you agree. 10. I feared, at first, that you might feel annoyed, and that I should have spared your feelings. 11. Let me, as an old man, add that a good beginning goes a long way towards a good ending, and that if you earnestly desire to amend your faults you should begin now. (240)

EXERCISE 119.

The Halving Principle (continued).

See Note at the head of Exercise 116.

1. We *have* been *told* by *a* learne*d* man *that without* doub*t* *the great* faul*t of* men *is not to* know where *to* stop; *not to be* satisfie*d in the* possession *of any* mo*d*era*t*e acquiRemen*t*s; *but to* lose *all* we *have* gaine*d in a* greedy hun*t for more.* 2. *The* statemen*t was* ma*d*e *as the* resul*t of* ma*t*uRe though*t and* keen study *of* mankin*d*, *and its* accuracy *cannot*, we feaR, *be* denied *for a* momen*t.* 3. *Have* we *not all* heaR*d of* men *of* wealth *who have* been reduced *to* extreme nee*d in their* oL*d* age through *the* failuRe *of* some ma*d* scheme *which* they entere*d into in the* hope *of* fin*d*ing still *grea*t*er* wealth, *and of* thus exten*d*ing *their* poweR *in the* coun*t*ry? 4. If *their* wiL*d* plans *had* succeede*d how* much better off *could these* men *have* hope*d* *to be for the short* time they *had to* remain *in the* worL*d*? 5. They hurried *to* fin*d more, and* they faiLe*d to* hoL*d that which* they *had al*ready save*d.* 6. They turne*d their* eyes *toward a* faLse ligh*t*, *and* they were led astray. 7. *The* drunkar*d is* rightly *called a* ma*d*man; *but he is* quite *as* ma*d who* allows *his* reason *to be* cloude*d* by gree*d.* (200)

EXERCISE 120.

The Halving Principle (continued).

See Note at the head of Exercise 116.

1. *It was* Edmun*d* Burke, *a* note*d* statesman *and a* profoun*d* thinker, *who* said *that the first* accoun*t*s we *have of* mankin*d* *are but so* many accoun*t*s *of their* butcheries, *and that all* empiRes *have* been cemente*d in* bloo*d.* 2. *He* poin*t*s out *that it* involve*d the* sacrifice *of* many hundre*d*s *of* thousan*d*s *of* lives *to* sprea*d the* fame *and* foun*d the* name *of* one *of the* mili*t*ary leaders whom *the* worL*d* looks upon *as a* gran*d* hero.

3. *The* dispu*t*es be*t*ween *the* ancien*t* Greek states, *he* says, foRm one *of the* most drea*d*ful scenes *in* his*t*ory; *and* one marvels *to* fin*d that* such *a* small spo*t was* able *to* produce men enough *to* sacrifice *to the* pitiful ambition *of* possessing five oR six thousan*d more* acres *of* lan*d*, oR *a* few *more* villages. 4. Ye*t*, *he* adds, *to see the* acrimony *and* bitterness *which* entere*d* *in*to *these* dispu*t*es; *the* aRmies *which* were cu*t* off; *the* flee*t*s *that* were sunk *and* burn*t*; *the* cities *that* were sacke*d*, *and their* peoples slaughtere*d and* captive*d*; one migh*t be* induced *to think that the* decision *of the* fa*t*e *of* mankin*d*, at least, depende*d* upon *it*. 5. *But*, *he* goes *on to* say, *these* dispu*t*es ende*d*, *as all* such *have* ever done, *and* ever will do, *in a* loss *of* poweR by *all* parties; *a* momen*t*ary sHadow *and* dream *of* poweR *in* some one; *and the* ben*d*ing *of all to the* yoke *of an* outsider, *who* knows *how to* profit by *their* divisions. 6. *There is* no nee*d*, says Burke, *to* exaggera*t*e *these* frigh*t*ful evils, *and he* purposely avoi*d*s *a* sHow *of* eloquence *in* laying *these* facts baRe *to the* worL*d*. 7. *And*, cer*t*ainLy, we *who* read accoun*t*s *of the* torren*t*s *of* human bloo*d which* were sHed by *the* fieRce men *of* oL*d*, *are* boun*d to* agree *that* exaggeration *is not* neede*d* *to* increase *the* hoRRoR *of the* recital. (308)

EXERCISE 121.

The Halving Principle (continued).

See Note at the head of Exercise 116.

Mr. Ed*ward* Smar*t*.

Dear SiR,—We enclose invoices *in* duplica*t*e *for the* paten*t* be*d* quiL*t*s kin*d*ly ordere*d on the* fourth *of* Oc*t*ober. We sen*t* *them to*-day, packe*d as you* desiRe*d*, *to the* Eas*t* Dock, *for* sHipmen*t* peR steameR "Ma*d*oline." We also enclose statemen*t for the* goo*d*s, discoun*t* de*d*ucte*d*, *as* requeste*d*. We trust *the* quiL*t*s will *have a* rapi*d* sale, resul*t*ing *in a* good profit, *and* we hope *the* presen*t* will *be* followed⌞by many similaR transactions. YouRs faithfully, Alfre*d* Broa*d*huRst *and* Sons. (82)

EXERCISE 122.

The Halving Principle (continued).

See Note at the head of Exercise 116.

MessRS. Kelle*tt* *and* Wood*ward*.

Dear SiRS,—YouR SHipmen*t* *of* sof*t* fel*t* ha*t*s invoiced *on the* 25th uL*t*imo came duly *to* han*d*, *and as the* goo*d*s exac*t*Ly suite*d* *our* customeRS we ma*d*e *very* rapi*d* sales *and* cleaRe*d* *the* lo*t* at goo*d* prices. We enclose *our* sight draf*t* *on* Lloyds Bank, *to* settle *the* amoun*t* *of* youR accoun*t*, *and* we *shall be* oblige*d* if *you* will kin*d*ly *forward* receipt peR return mail. Referring *to* youR es*t*eeme*d* favor *of the* 20th uL*t*imo, we *are* wai*t*ing *on our* frien*d*s *who* inquiRe*d* abou*t* *the* emblazone*d* prin*t*s, *and we* trust *the* pa*tt*erns *you forwarded may be* foun*d* *to* please *them*. We will write *you the* resul*t* *of our* effor*t*s *in a* few days. Will *you* kin*d*ly no*t*e *that the* twiLLe*d* SHee*t*s *as* peR *our* inden*t*, No. 56, nee*d* *not be* insuRe*d* *on* youR side ? YouRS truly, Ma*dd*ox *and* Greenwoo*d* (145).

EXERCISE 123.

The Halving Principle (continued).

(*a*) HALF-SIZED *t* OR *d* IS ALWAYS DISJOINED WHEN IMMEDIATELY FOLLOWING THE CONSONANT *t* OR *d*.

In the following words, the syllable which is to be disjoined is preceded by a hyphen :—

1 precipita-te*d*, perpetra-te*d*, prostra-te*d*, protru-de*d*,
2 obtru-de*d*, oblitera-te*d*, tra-de*d*, tro-tte*d*, trea-te*d*, ti-de*d*,
3 tou-te*d*, tri-den*t*, ta-tooe*d*, too-te*d*, stru-tte*d*, straigh-tene*d*,
4 stri-den*t*, titra-te*d*, tigh-tene*d*, atti-tu*d*e, toa-die*d*,
5 situa-te*d*, da-te*d*, do-te*d*, edi-te*d*, doub-te*d*, do-tte*d*,
6 drea-de*d*, dea-dene*d*, de-taine*d*, devasta-te*d*, denta-te*d*,
7 desidera-te*d*, dicta-te*d*, die-te*d*, die-te*t*ic, di-ete*t*ical,
8 depreda-te*d*, agita-te*d*, extra-di*t*e, credi-te*d*, expectora-te*d*,
9 crepita-te*d*, crusta-te*d*, cogita-te*d*, expedi-te*d*, oxida-te*d*,

sequestra-te*d*, frustra-te*d*, filtra-te*d*, effectua-te*d*, felicita-te*d*, fluctua-te*d*, foreda-te*d*, vegeta-te*d*, estrea-te*d*, imita-te*d*, amputa-te*d*, maltrea-te*d*, necessita-te*d*, anteda-te*d*, inunda-te*d*, annota-te*d*, intru-de*d*, entrea-te*d*, intimida-te*d*, illustra-te*d*, liquida-te*d*, elucida-te*d*, resuscita-te*d*, rota-te*d*, retrea-te*d*, irrita-te*d*, rehabilita-te*d*, hesita-te*d*, hydra-te*d*, super-abound*d*, super-abun*d*an*t*, super-abun*d*ance, stra*ti*-fy, stra*ti*-fie*d*.

(*b*) HALF-SIZED STROKE *s* MAY BE WRITTEN UPWARD AFTER THE *-tion* HOOK WHERE NECESSARY, AS IN THE FOLLOWING WORDS:—

liberationis*t*, salvationis*t*, fashionis*t*, restorationis*t*, excur-sionis*t*, progressionis*t*, educationis*t*, eLocutionis*t*.

The half-sized stroke *s* is written downward in the following and similar words:—

passionis*t*, abolitionis*t*, prohibitionis*t*, evolutionis*t*, revolu-tionis*t*, obstructionis*t*, protectionis*t*, insurrectionis*t*.

(*c*) HALF-LENGTH UPWARD *r* MUST NOT STAND ALONE, NOR WITH A FINAL CIRCLE ONLY ADDED.

The stroke *t* must, therefore, be written in such words as:—

rate, wrote, write, writes, rat, rats, roots, wrought, rout, irate, orate, orates;

But the half-length upward *r* may be employed in words like the following:—

spor*t*, suppor*t*, blur*t*, tar*t*, star*t*, satura*t*e, satura*t*es, satura*t*-ing, dar*t*, dar*t*s, dar*t*ing, jura*t*, care*t*, skir*t*, skir*t*s, clare*t*, squir*t*, squir*t*s, squir*t*ing, wheel-wrigh*t*, impar*t*, impar*t*s, impar*t*ing, impor*t*, for*t*, for*t*s, flir*t*, flir*t*s, aver*t*, aver*t*s, aver*t*ing, assor*t*, assor*t*s, assor*t*ing, sor*t*, sor*t*s, sor*t*ing, mar*t*, mar*t*in, meri*t*, meri*t*s, demeri*t*s, aler*t*, lacera*t*e, lacera*t*es, exhilara*t*es, ulcera*t*es, exer*t*, exer*t*s, exer*t*ing, parro*t*, parro*t*s, Barre*tt*, turre*t*, indura*t*e, exaggera*t*e, chlora*t*e, garre*t*, garre*t*s, ferre*t*, ferre*t*s, smar*t*en, smar*t*ene*d*, cellare*t*, collare*t*.

(*d*) Half-length Upward *r* may be used for *rd* in monosyllables where the Downward form is not convenient, as in:—

lar*d*, lair*d*, lure*d*, leere*d*, gore*d*, gour*d*, glare*d*, geare*d*, slurre*d*.

(*e*) A Half-length Stroke must not be Joined to another Stroke unless there is an angle at the point of Junction.

In words like the following, the *t* or *d* must be written in full :—

popped, peeped, propped, pooped, probed, probate, probatory, bobbed, bribed, judged, adjudged, cooked, crooked, cracked, kicked, creaked, cricket, croaked, caked, caulked, clicked, eclectic, clacked, croaked, cloaked, clucked, cogged, clogged, quaked, squeaked, segregate, gagged, fagged, flagged, flogged, fact, effect, suffocate, pacificatory, afflict, deflect, flaked, infect, effectual, fagot, navigate, vacate, evict, revoked, thicket, liked, looked, licked, lacked, locked, slaked, select, dialect, dialectic, dialectical, dislocate, disliked, silicate, sulked, shelled, shield, milked, mulct, relict, frolicked, bulked, bilked, harried, horrid, hurried, abhorred, adhered, reheard, dehort, roared, reared, upreared, mirrored, weird, award, worried, wearied, wired, propound, mapped, mopped, mobbed, imbibed, masHed, mesHed, smasHed, lashed, slashed, polished, famisHed, ambusHed, unblemisHed, denote, slip-knot, topknot, obstinate, minute, emanate, effeminate, laminate, abominate, promenade, dominate, incriminate, discriminate, fuLminate, ruminate, animate, inanimate.

(*f*) Final *t* or *d*, when followed by a Sounded Vowel must be written in full :—

pity, pretty, putty, body, tattoo, treaty, dado, daddy, chatty, Judy, Jeddo, Cato, Kitty, cotta, cutty, giddy, goody, greedy, fatty, flighty, fruity, fifty, lofty, mufti, throaty, hasty, smutty, mighty, middy, meadow, muddy, knotty,

5 SHanty, lattice, alto, party, dirty, charity, security, forty,
6 verity, variety, authority, assertive, temerity, hilarity,
7 rarity, wordy, weighty, witty, yeasty, absentee, needy,
8 windy, bandy, agenda, candy, SHindy, hardy, brandy,
9 sandy, haughty, jollity, unwieldy, quota, tardy, Florida.

(*g*) THE CONSONANTS *l-d* AND *r-d* MUST BE WRITTEN IN FULL, IF A SOUNDED VOWEL COMES BETWEEN THE LETTERS :—

1 pallid, pillowed, ballad, bullied, outlawed, dallied, delayed,
2 delude, jellied, collide, collude, gullied, followed, valid,
3 valued, volleyed, invalid, sullied, solid, stolid, swallowed,
4 wallowed, willowed, shallowed, malady, mellowed, melody,
5 inlaid, unload, unloading, lad, led, lid, allowed, loud, lied,
6 rallied, relaid, waylaid, Valladolid, hallowed, hollowed,
7 holiday, High-road, parody, parried, burrowed, buried,
8 borrowed, tarried, tirade, deride, carried, corrode, scurried,
9 chloride, curried, gloried, furrowed, flurried, varied,
10 thyroid, Ethelred, arrayed, erode, sorrowed, storied,
11 serried, charade, married, narrowed, inroad, lurid, salaried,
12 pilloried, galleried, wearied, worried, queried, preparedness.

(*h*) MISCELLANEOUS WORDS IN WHICH THE HALVING PRINCIPLE IS APPLIED :—

1 widowe*d*, Walfor*d*, Thwai*t*es, Tennan*t*, SHetlan*d*, Portlan*d*,
2 Presco*tt*, Nugen*t*, moun*t*ain, Mer*t*on, Mai*t*lan*d*, Ma*d*ely,
3 LON*d*on, can*d*LE, scan*d*AL, Chesterfie*Ld*, Broa*d*way, Be*d*for*d*,
4 Atwoo*d*, An*t*ony, zone*d*, yawne*d*, recoun*t*, recoun*t*s, woode*d*,
5 worSHippe*d*, won*t*, wi*t*nessed, withere*d*, wickere*d*, whoope*d*,
6 whippe*t*, watche*d*, dea*d*-weigh*t*, bloo*d*-hea*t*, volume*d*,
7 vivifie*d*, rarefie*d*, visite*d*, answere*d*, visore*d*, officere*d*,
8 voi*d*ance, vin*d*ica*t*e, vin*d*icate*d*, ven*d*etta, vel*dt*, inven*t*,
9 inven*t*ory, Van*d*yke, valve*d*, vaun*t*, vapi*d*, vapi*d*ity,
10 vapore*d*, vaciLLa*t*e, use*d*, uttere*d*, usurpe*d*, upstar*t*,
11 uproo*t*, behave*d*, upheave*d*, untutore*d*, upbrai*d*, unsoun*d*,
12 unsupporte*d*, unscathe*d*, unravele*d*, relen*t*, pestilen*t*,
13 unpave*d*, unoffen*d*ing, explaine*d*, undimme*d*, es*t*ima*t*e,

estimated, unshackled, twilled, twitched, toddled, turreted, started, thwarted, twisted, tugged, tubed, turbid, turbidity, trucked, trudged, traveled, trawled, trafficked, attracted, sported, pirated, dirtied, skirted, garroted, tort, retort, distort, toned, entitled, thrashed, thrived, threaded, clapped, thoughtful, thoughtless, rivet, riveted, tattered, tasted, attend, attendant, retained, distrained, attentive, attentively, tumbled, stumbled, resembled, grumbled, replete, risked, masked, whisked, talent, Solent, talented, tamarind, unturned, taunting, tauntingly, symmetry, system, systematic, systematical, energetic, synthetical, syringed, fringed, arranged, disarranged, strapped, strict, strictly, swopped, sword, swordsman, switched, swift, swiftly, inked, blinked, clinked, banked, swarmed, swathed, suspend, appoint, appointing, respired, surmount, surmounts, sustained, survived, surcharged, supped, sunlit, suggested, succumbed, succored, subvert, subsisted, submit, submitted, submerged, subjoined, subjugate, stemmed, struggled, stopped, stocked, starched, parched, marched, birched, squirmed, speckled, spent, spend, spends, solved, snort, snorts, assortment, smiled, slobbered, snapped, smelted, pillaged, sleet, slightly, shutting, shouted, sheltered, shaved, severed, serrated, sergeant, sergeants, sequestered, servant, observant, servants, infants, seceded, saved, deceived, relieved, rodent, rodents, pardoned, riband, resumed, presumed, arrested, resignedly, reputed, reseated, report, reported, reporting, reports, rectify, rectified, reflect, reflected, regiment, regiments, ratify, gratify, gratified, punt, pound, procured, problematic, portend, plastered, posted, pacified, overcrowded, neighbored, musket, mortal, maudlin, liberate, liberated, knit, knitted, accountant, ingrained, insert, inserted, impolite, penitent, penitents, habited, gripped, gladdened, genteel, fortified, facilitate, except, excepted, eliminated, eject, ejected, drilled, delved, decked, vanished, corked, coasted, sampled, trampled, acted, gutted, breadth, bounded, grounded, rounded, wended, bigoted, shunt, shunts, approved, braved.

(*i*) THE CONSONANTS *mp* AND *ng* CANNOT BE HALVED UNLESS THEY ARE HOOKED.

In the following and similar words the *t* or *d* must be written in full :—

1 impute, ambit, ambidexter, embattle, embayed, embed,
2 embedding, embitter, imbued, crumpet, trumpet, gambit,
3 stampede, sHampooed, pronged, banged, tongued, stringed,
4 clanged, fanged, thronged, hanged, longed, belonged,
5 prolonged, ringed, wronged, harangued.

EXERCISE 124.

The Halving Principle (continued).

See Note at the head of Exercise 116.

1. *Not* even *the* wises*t* *and* most pruden*t* merchan*t* *can* predic*t* *an* absolu*t*e cer*t*ainty *of* gain *for a* new ven*t*ure. 2. *He cannot be* exac*t*Ly certain *that things* will faLL out just *as he* hopes, *and that* sales will resul*t* *as* readily *and as* profitably *as he may* desiRe. 3. *In short, he* must risk *a great* deal *in* spi*t*e *of all his* foresight, *and without* risk *he cannot* hope *to* succeed. 4. We *are told that* some *of those* gifte*d* *and* successfuL men *toward* whom we turn *for* guidance *and* advice *have* been guilty *of the* same business eRRoRs *that* we *have* faLLen *in*to; *but* they learne*d* *to* avoi*d* *them, so that* they *could not be* caugh*t* repeate*d*ly *in the* same snaRe. 5. *And this is* one *of the great* Lessons we *are called* upon *to* learn *from these* cleaR minde*d* men, *who have* made *their* way *and* won for*t*unes *in* spi*t*e *of* obstacles *that* migh*t* easily *have* daunte*d* men *of* less ability *and* brea*d*th *of* min*d*. 6. *In* fact, *I* daRe say *it is* true *to* state *that the* successes *of* some *of these* men were ac*t*ually scoRe*d* through, oR *on* accoun*t* *of, the very* obstacles *which* appeaRe*d* *to* baR *their* way, *but which their* resolu*t*e heaR*t*s de*t*eRmine*d* *should not* stop *their forward* career. 7. They fel*t* *a* positive deligh*t* *in* measuring *their* poweRs against *the* troubles *that* rose up *in* fron*t* *of them*; *and* they conquere*d* *these* troubles, *not so* much *on* accoun*t* *of the* wealth they migh*t*

gain there-by, but for the reason that they declined to admit that they could be beaten at the first effort to climb the ladder of fortune. 8. To parody an old saying, "It is better to have tried and failed, than not to have tried at all." (290)

EXERCISE 125.

The Halving Principle (continued).

See Note at the head of Exercise 116.

1. A certain professor has pointed out that a baby learns more rapidly than the most gifted scholar, trained and educated in the highest seminaries in the land. 2. Is it not amazing in how short a time Baby gets to know a great deal about the mighty world in which he has so recently landed? 3. He finds he is surrounded by friends whom he does not know, and by things which are entirely strange to him. 4. Yet he and his friends are soon acquainted, and he seldom fails to greet them on their appearance. 5. His eyes are turned swiftly backward and forward, upward and downward, in the room in which he is placed. 6. He has sometimes an apparently thoughtful look, as though he were mentally noting the many and varied articles presented to his view. 7. He sees and knows his parents the moment they step into the room, and his little hands are lifted upward toward the one who should lift him from his cot. 8. He will just as readily resent the attentions of those who have, as he thinks, intru-ded upon him, or trea-ted him unkindly. 9. Then, as the professor has intima-ted, Baby must learn to find his way in safety about the streets of the town or the lanes of the country place in which he lives. 10. All the things he sees must be written indelibly upon his mind, named and ticketed, as it were, rooted and fixed so firmly in his brain that they will remain there while memory endures. 11. Try to estimate the quantity of facts which Baby has to get hold of; note the short time in which he does it; and then imagine the state of mind of a grown man who was obliged to face the same task. (294)

EXERCISE 126.

The Halving Principle (continued).

See Note at the head of Exercise 116.

MessRs. Stamfor*d* *and* Martin.

Dear SiRs,—We *are great*ly oblige*d* by youR favor *of the* 10th instan*t*, *and*, *as* requeste*d*, we enclose *a* copy *of our* illustra-ted ca*t*alogue *of our* paten*t* *short* win*d* watches *in* plate*d* me*t*al cases. We *cannot* say *how* deeply we regret *that our* traveLLer *has not yet called* upon *you*, *and that you have* been *put to the* trouble *of* wri*t*ing *us*. We *have told him to call* upon *you without* faiL *on his* visit *to* youR town *toward the* end *of* Oc*t*ober. *He could* easily *have* sHown *you* samples *of the* goo*ds* name*d* *in the* enclosed list, *and you could have* judged better *the* value *of them, had he called* last month, *as* we oRdere*d* *him*. We *shall be* pleased *to forward you an* assoRtmen*t* *of any of the* watches include*d* *in the* list, *and* we *can* assuRe *you that* they *are* absolu*t*ely reliable goo*ds*. YouRs faithfully, Go*d*frey Ma*dd*ox *and* Sons. (156)

EXERCISE 127.

The Halving Principle (concluded).

See Note at the head of Exercise 116.

Mrs. Wood.

Dear Madam,—We regret *that* we *cannot* supply *a* match *for the* High gra*d*e tea service referre*d* *to in* youR no*t*e *of* Saturday last, at such *very short* notice. We *can* readily manage *it toward the* en*d* *of the* presen*t* month, if *you can* aRRange *to do without it* un*t*iL then. *Our Mr*. Blackwood *called on the* makers last Monday, *and* urge*d* upon *them the* necessity *of the* case; *but he was told that it was* simply *not* possible *to* make *the* pla*t*es sooner. We *have great* faith *in the* expressed desiRe *of the* fiRm *to* oblige *us*, *as the* transactions be*t*ween *them and us are very* extensive. If *you are in* town *to*-morrow we *shall be* gla*d* *if you* will kin*d*ly *give us a call*. We *are*, Ma*d*am, YouRs faithfully, Blackwood *and* MayfieL*d*. (136)

EXERCISE 128.

The Double-Length Principle.

In this Exercise, and in Exercises 129 to 133 inclusive, the italic type indicates (in words other than grammalogues or contractions) the letter or syllable which is to be doubled in length.

(*a*) CURVED CONSONANTS ARE DOUBLED IN LENGTH FOR THE ADDITION OF *tr*, *dr* OR *thr* (HEAVY) :—

*f*atter, *f*etter, *fi*tters, *f*ather, *f*atherly, *f*ather-in-LAW, *f*ather-land, *f*atherless, *flo*ater, *fla*tter, *fli*tters, *flu*tter, *flu*ters, si*f*ter, si*f*ters, swi*f*ter, so*f*ter, *figh*ter, *freigh*ter, *fr*itter, *v*oter, *v*oters, *thi*ther, *thi*therward, *as*ter, *as*ters, *Eas*ter, *eas*terly, *Aus*terlitz, *oys*ter, *oys*ters, si*s*ter, si*s*ters, si*s*terly, si*s*terhood, si*s*ter-in-LAW, *Zuy*der Zee, *SHa*tter, *SHa*tters, *SHa*ttering, *SHu*tter, *SHoo*ter, *SHoo*ters, *ma*tter, *ma*tters, s*ma*tter, s*ma*ttereR, *me*ter, *me*ters, *mo*tor, *mo*tors, *mu*tter, *mi*tre, s*mi*ter, *mou*ther, *mo*ther, *mo*therly, *mo*thers, *nea*ter, *kni*tter, *na*tter, *nei*ther, *neu*ter, a*no*ther, *en*ter, *en*ters, ce*n*tre, ce*n*tres, *en*tering, ce*n*tering, ce*n*traL, ce*n*traLize, ce*n*traLizing, ce*n*traLization, ce*n*tric, ce*n*trical, *en*teritis, *en*teric, sau*n*ter, sau*n*ters, sau*n*tering, su*n*der, Su*n*derLand, se*n*der, se*n*ders, ci*n*der, Ci*n*dereLLa, se*na*tor, *ligh*ter, *ligh*ters, *loi*ter, *loi*ters, *la*tter, *le*tter, *le*tters, *li*tter, *la*ter, *li*tre, s*li*ghter, s*l*ater, s*l*aters, s*l*aughter, s*l*aughters, a*l*ter, *al*ters, *al*tering, *al*terable, *al*tarcloth, psa*l*ter, *Wal*ter, *wel*ter, *wel*ters, *wil*der, *wil*derness, swe*l*ter, *hal*ter, *or*der, *or*ders, *or*derly, *ar*dour, so*r*ter, so*r*ters, he*r*der, *h*oa*r*der.

(*b*) DOUBLE-LENGTH CURVES (CONTINUED) :—

shi*f*ter, li*f*ter, li*f*ters, lau*gh*ter, re*fu*ter, re*fu*ters, grand-*f*ather, pro*vi*der, pro*vi*ders, co*ve*ter, co*ve*ters, in*va*der, in*vi*ter, in*vi*ters, ele*va*tor, ele*va*tors, exca*va*tor, ri*ve*ter, ri*ve*ters, ser*vi*tor, Zoro*as*ter, pea*SHoo*ter, pulso*me*ter, dia*me*ter, gas-*me*ter, chrono*me*ter, cyclo*me*ter, thermo*me*ter, re*mo*ter, re*mi*tter, grand*mo*ther, step*mo*ther, god*mo*ther, grand*fa*ther, prese*n*ter, pleasa*n*ter, abse*n*ter, disse*n*ter, disse*n*ters, dece*n*traLize, dece*n*traLization, acce*n*tor,

9 ecce*nt*ric, ecce*nt*rical, dyse*nt*eric, decli*na*tor, decli*na*tors,
10 ve*ner*ator, re-*en*ter, re-*en*ters, pa*l*ter, pa*l*ters, spe*l*ter,
11 po*llu*ter, bui*l*der, bui*l*ders, bo*l*der, bi*la*teral,ti*l*ter, tabu*la*tor,
12 ido*la*ter, ido*la*ters, di*lu*ter, adu*la*tor, di*la*tor, jo*l*ter, co*lla*tor,
13 scaLder, gi*l*der, gi*l*ders, fa*l*ter, fa*l*tering, fa*l*teringLy,
14 defau*l*ter, vau*l*ter, revo*l*ter, stockho*l*der, leaseho*l*der,
15 househo*l*der, scrip-ho*l*der, gas-ho*l*der, stipu*la*tor, stimu-
16 *la*tor, sme*l*ter, muti*la*tor, mou*l*der, smou*l*der, smou*l*dering,
17 beho*l*der, accumu*la*tor, dissimu*la*tor, emu*la*tor, modu*la*tor,
18 insu*la*tor, insu*la*tors, insu*l*ter, anniHi*la*tor, re*la*ter, ho*l*der,
19 qui*l*ter, ambu*la*tor, po*r*ter, Suppo*r*ter, expo*r*ter, impo*r*ter,
20 ba*r*ter, bo*r*der, bo*r*derer, bo*r*derers, boa*r*der, Ta*r*tar,
21 ta*r*taric, sta*r*ter, da*r*ter, diso*r*der, cha*r*ter, cha*r*terer,
22 asso*r*ter, sma*r*ter, sno*r*ter, hu*r*ter, impa*r*ter, asse*r*tor,
23 reso*na*tor, waSH-*lea*ther, Jacobs-*la*dder, mis*le*ader, breech-
24 *loa*der, muzzle-*loa*der, ringLeader, backs*li*der.

(*c*) Double-length Curves (continued) :—

1 *fen*der, *fen*ders, o*ffen*ders, *fon*der, *foun*der, *fin*der, bell-
2 *foun*der, *ven*dor, *ven*dors, in*ven*tor, in*ven*tors, la*ven*der,
3 *thun*der, *thun*ders, *thun*derer, a*sun*der, SH*un*ter, SH*un*ters,
4 *men*der, *men*tor, *men*tors, fo*men*ter, ce*men*ter, *min*der,
5 re*min*der, re*min*ders, re*main*der, *moun*ter, suR*moun*ter,
6 a*noin*ter, a*noin*ters, *lan*der, is*lan*der, *islan*ders, s*lan*der,
7 s*len*der, cy*lin*der, cy*lin*ders, cy*lin*dric, cy*lin*drical, cu*llen*der,
8 ca*len*dar, ca*len*dereR, High*lan*der, low*lan*der, i*mpoun*der,
9 i*mpon*derable.

(*d*) Straight Letters, when Finally Hooked, are Doubled in length for the Addition of *tr* or *dr* :—

1 *pain*ter, *pain*ters, *pan*der, *pan*ders, s*pen*der. s*pen*ders,
2 *plan*ter, s*plin*ter, s*plin*ters, su*pplan*ter, s*plen*dor, *pon*der,
3 *pon*derable, *poun*der, *poin*ter, *ban*ter, *ban*ters, *ban*tering,
4 *ban*teringLy, *ban*tereR, *ben*der, *bin*der, *boun*der, *bran*der,
5 *blun*der, *blun*dereR, *blun*derbuss, *blun*dering, *blun*derhead,
6 *blen*der, abs*con*der, *taun*ter, *taun*ters, *ten*der, *ten*dering,
7 *tin*der, a*ttain*der, s*tan*der, s*tan*ders, *Tran*ter, *dan*der,

chanter, chanters, gender, jointer, canter, canters, kinder, counter, counters, seconder, gander, ganders, grander, granter, grunter, squinter, squander, squanders, squandering squandereR, ranter, ranters, render, surrender, surrenders, surrendereR, rounder, rounders, wander, wandereR, wanders winter, winterly, winters, wonder, wonders, winder, yonder, hunter, hunters, hinder, hindereR, hindermost, hinders, haunter, depender, decanter, engender, encounters, Africander, suspender.

(*e*) Straight Letters, when following another Stroke, are Doubled in Length for the Addition of *tr* or *dr* :—

paper-cutter, paritor, apparitor, play-writer, play-writers, porterage, preceptor, predictor, presbyter, prevaricator, procurator, prognosticator, projector, propagator, prospector, protector, protectors, protractor, operator, operators, backbiter, banqueter, barrator, bespatter, abnegator, abductor, abstracter, obstructer, objector, objectors, obturator, tractor, transactor, twitter, twittering, typewriter, typewriters, attractor, educator, dedicator, defecator, dejector, deprecator, depurator, dessicator, detractor, dictator, disputer, dissector, dissuader, distributer, diverter, duplicator, adapter, adductor, adulterator, eductor, edulcorator, chapter, chaff-cutter, gesticulator, adjudicator, captor, curator, castigator, extractor, exhibitor, acceptor, exceptor, exonerator, exacter, expurgator, explicator, expecter, garroter, glass-cutter, fabricator, foreboder, averter, vindicator, stricter, spectre, speculator, subjugator, subtractor, supplicator, suspecter, aspirator, moderator, mitigator, man-hater, masquerader, embroider, emendator, imitator, emancipator, nectar, news-writer, nomenclator, numerator, annotator, anticipator, inceptor, indicator, inductor, inflicter, instigator, investigator, inspector, inspectors, lubricator, letter-writer, liberator, celebrator, liquidator, eLector, eLectoraL, aLLigator, elaborator, illustrator, reflector, rector, rectors, rebutter, recuperator, refrigerator, rejecter, reve*r*ter, ro*ta*tor, aRbi*tra*tor, eRe*c*tor, wood-*cu*tter, stone-*cu*tter, Hec*t*or.

(*f*) In Common Words *-ture* may be indicated by making the preceding Stroke Double-Length :—

*fea*ture, *fea*tures, *fu*ture, *fu*tures, sig*na*ture, adve*n*ture, adve*n*tures, adve*n*tureR, adve*n*turesome, adve*n*turous, adve*n*turously, adve*n*turess, pi*c*ture, pi*c*tures, pi*c*ture-book, pi*c*ture-frame, depi*c*ture, disru*p*ture.

(*g*) The Consonant *mp* is Doubled in length for the Addition of *r*. The Consonant *ng* is Doubled in length for the Addition of *kr* or *gr* :—

pa*mp*er, pi*mp*ernel, pu*mp*er, plu*mp*er, bu*mp*er, Ba*mb*er, ta*mp*er, te*mp*er, ti*mb*er, atte*mp*er, atte*mp*erment, te*mp*erament, diste*mp*er, da*mp*er, cha*mb*er, cha*mb*erlain, cha*mb*ermaid, ju*mp*er, ca*mb*er, Cu*mb*erland, va*mp*er, thu*mp*er, si*mp*er, si*mp*ereR, so*mb*re, stu*mp*er, sta*mp*er, a*mb*er, a*mb*ergris, e*mb*er, u*mb*er, Hu*mb*er (tick *h*), SHri*n*ker (shri*ng*-ker), SHa*n*ker, (shang-ker), lo*ng*er (long-ger).

(*h*) After Initial *l*, *dr* or *thr* is expressed by the Hooked Forms ⌉,), and not by Doubling the Length of the *l*. Similarly, after *f*, *sh*, *m*, the Syllable *dr* is expressed by ⌉, and not by Doubling the length of the *f*, *sh* or *m*.

The double-length principle, therefore, is not used in the following or similar words.

alder, alderman, elder, elderly, Alderley, older, ladder, leader, louder, slider, lather, leather, Lowther (*l* up), Luther (*l* up), feeder, fodder, SHedder, madder, Modder.

(*i*) The Past Tense of Verbs ending in *tr*, *dr*, *thr*, *mpr* or *mbr* is expressed by the Halving Principle :—

en-tered, cen-tred, ma-ttered, mu-ttered, pond-eRed, pand-eRed, splint-eRed, bant-eRed, tend-eRed, engen-deRed, cant-eRed, squand-eRed, encount-eRed, fla-ttered, fea-thered, floun-dered, thun-dered, sun-dered, SHa-ttered, smo-thered, saun-tered, cin-dered, al-tered, fal-tered, smoul-dered, sland-eRed, calend-eRed, oR-dered, disoR-dered, chaR-tered, rend-ered, surrend-ered, wond-ered, wand-ered, wint-ered, hind-ered, Hec-tored, pam-pered, tam-pered, tem-pered, tim-bered, sim-pered, advent-uRed.

(See Exercises on the Halving Principle for further illustrations.)

(*j*) THE DOUBLE-LENGTH PRINCIPLE CANNOT BE EMPLOYED IN WORDS LIKE THE FOLLOWING, WHERE FINAL *r* IS FOLLOWED BY A SOUNDED VOWEL :—

pant-ry, splin-tery, pal-try, bound-ary, chan-try, gen-try, second-ary, quand-ary, fla-ttery, fea-thery, vo-tary, invent-ory, thund-ery, sun-dry, sen-try, cin-dery, mo-thery, smoul-dry, en-try, dysen-tery, pleasan-try, lott-ery, sul-try, desult-ory, ul-tra, wint-ry, hunt-ress.

EXERCISE 129.

Double-Length Principle (continued).

See Note at the head of Exercise 128.

1. Small *ma*tters sometimes turn men *in*to dis*pu*ters *and* de*ba*ters, *and* once started they *may* linger l-onger than *is* desirable *on* awkward topics. 2. Then they do *not* like *to* su*rren*der *their* notions *to cou*nter aRguments. 3. *I have* often encounteRed instances *of* heated discussions, *the* results *of which* mattered *not a* straw *to any*body. 4. *In the* case *of* ill-tempered people, *these* debates *may* soon enge*n*der a disposition *to* quaRRel, *and* change *the* de*ba*ters *in*to *figh*ters willing *to slaugh*ter one a*no*ther. 5. *It is* easily done, if one man looks upon a*no*ther *as a* sta*R*ter oR instig*a*tor *of* trouble. 6. *A* muttered syllable ; *a* half muttered retort ; even *an* altered tone *of* voice—*may* act like *a* spark faLLing *on* gun-*pow*der, *and* cause *an* explosion. 7. Then *may* follow charges

*of slan*der; accusations *of blun*der, *and* possibly *of plun*der OR *of pan*dering *to* others; *and the* result *is* disoRder *and* upset *all* round. 8. *You can* readily picture *to* youRself *how* such trouble might begin *in the* discussion *of a very* simple *ma*tter. 9. If, then, *you are a* partici*p*ator *in a* debate look *to* youR te*mp*er, *and* take *care not to be a* SH*ou*ter OR brawleR. (189)

EXERCISE 130.

Double-Length Principle (continued).

See Note at the head of Exercise 128.

1. *The* rector appeaRed *to pon*der *a* while, *and as he* pondeRed *his fea*tures relaxed *in*to *a kin*der *and mil*der expression. 2. Then *he* spoke *as* follows: *The* man *who can* restrain *his* te*mp*er *and* curb *his* anger *is a* greater victor than *the figh*ter *who is* able *to* subdue *his* physical foe. 3. *And so,* let *not* thy te*mp*er prevaiL over thee, *but smo*ther *it* eRe *it* blaze forth *to* thy SHame. 4. *Pan*der *not* unduly *to* thy tastes; *for* many *a* man's hopes *have* been SHattered through *his* appetite *be*ing stronger than *his* will. 5. *It* takes *but a* tiny stimu*la*tor *to* restart *a* fiRe *that is* smou*l*dering. 6. BaRter *not* thy *fu*ture peace *for a* present folly. 7. *A* prudent liver will *be a* pro*vi*der *for the fu*ture, *as* well *as a spen*der *for the* present. 8. *The* instig*a*tor *of plun*der *is as* guilty *as he who has* plundeRed. 9. *A ten*der appeal *may* touch *a wan*dereR *as* foRcibly *as an* ill-tempered threat. 10. *A* disoRdered house will *not* win *a* man *from his* club. 11. *The nea*ter *the* home, *the* swi*f*ter will *be the* return *of the* husband. 12. *Not* everyone *who has* loitered *has* delayed. 13. Laug*h*ter does *not* always prove joy; *nor* does *a* teaR *in all* cases SHow pain. 14. Seven feet *of* earth will prove enough at last *for the* biggest househo*l*der. 15. *The* loudest SH*ou*ters *are* seldom found *in the cen*tre *of a* fight. 16. *He who has* slandeRed *his* neighbour *is a* de*frau*der *of the* worst kind. 17. *He who has* blundeRed, *and not* seen *his* fault, *has* blundeRed *in* vain. 18. *The* wheels *of* life run *more* smoothly if assisted by *the* kindness

of one *toward* a*no*ther; *for* sympathy *is a* rare lubric*a*tor. 19. *He who* surre*n*ders *his* will *to an* evil habit *is* fettered *in the* strongest chains. (291)

EXERCISE 131.

Double-Length Principle (continued).

See Note at the head of Exercise 128.

1. *The first* month *in the* cale*n*dar derives *its* name *from* Janus, *an* ancient king *of* Italy, *who was* raised *to the* *al*tar by *the* leaders *of the* Romans (upward R) *and* worsHipped *as a* god by *those* ido*la*ters. 2. *He was* said *to be* possessed *of* attributes *of a* нigh o*R*der, *and was* sнown seated *in the cen*tre *of a* dozen *al*tars. 3. *His* statue *had a* couple *of* faces, one *of which was* supposed *to be that of an* elderly sage, *who, in the win*ter *of his* days, loitered *for a* while l-onger between *the* worLd *of the* past *and the* worLd *of the fu*ture. 4. *The* Romans were *great figh*ters, *and* were *the* subjug*a*tors *of* many peoples; they possessed *in their* sen*a*tors men *whose* names were rendered famous by *their* wisdom; yet they were *very* credulous *in mat*ters *of* worsHip. 5. They rarely pondeRed upon *the* absurdities *put for*ward by *the* instig*a*tors oR origi*na*tors *of* new foRms *of* heathen worsHip, *but* surrendered *their* minds *without* hesitation *to their* leaders *in* such *mat*ters. 6. They thought *the* god Janus looked back *to the* worLd *as it was* eRe *the thun*ders *and* rain *of the* deluge *had* sHattered *its splen*dour *and for a* time turned *it in*to *a wil*derness *and* dis*or*der. 7. *The* other face *of the* statue wore a*no*ther expression. 8. *It was smoo*ther *and* mil*d*er *in* appearance, suggestive *of a* youth *who* looked *for*ward eagerly *and* hopefully *to the fu*ture. 9. *This was to* indicate *the* poweR *of the* god *to* foresee events *which* were yet *to* happen. 10. *And so the* Romans turned *to* Janus *as their* defe*n*der against *fu*ture dis*as*ters, *as* well *as their* protector *in* present enco*un*ters. 11. *He was the* holder *of the* key by *which* aLone entrance *could be* obtained *to the* other gods; *so that all* prayeRs *to them*

were tendeRed through *him.* 12. *His* chamber *was the* temple *of* peace. 13. *Its* dooRs were closed *in* times *of* peace, *and* open at other times. 14. *The* temper *and* military aRdour *of the* Roman people *may be* judged *from the* fact *that the* temple *of* Janus *was* onLy sHut three times *in* seven centuries. (347)

EXERCISE 132.

Double-Length Principle (continued).

See Note at the head of Exercise 128.

MessRs. PoRter *and* Bamber.

Dear SiRs,—*In* answer *to* youR *l*etter *of the* 2nd instant, re MessRs. *An*derson *and* Chambers, we *are happy to be* able *to* report most favourably *of our* friends. *The* fiRm *is a* thoroughly well-founded one. They *are* inventors *of the* well-known automatic *knitter which* beaRs *their* name, *and in which* they do *a* big business *as* exporters. They *are* also patentees *of* maCHinery *for* letterpress *printers and* type moulders. *Mr. An*derson *is a* sHaReholder *in a* builders' *and* decorators' supply stoRes, *in* Cumberland. *Mr.* Chambers *is* part proprietor *of the* immense wharf *on the* river side heRe. *The* signature *of* either *of them is* good enough *for* faR *more* than *you* name. We *have* seldom encounteRed *kin*der oR *more* straightforward people. YouRs faithfully, *Hunter and* Mather. (132)

EXERCISE 133.

Double-Length Principle (concluded).

See Note at the head of Exercise 128.

*Mr. Wal*ter *Win*ter.

Dear SiR,—YouR *l*etter re *Mr.* ARthur *Tran*ter duly received. We *had a* couple *of* small oRders *for* lettered *coun*terpanes *from him* last *winter, and in* both cases *he* paid ready casH. We *wonder why he* gave *you our* name, *and we think he has* blundeRed *in* referring *to us*, instead *of to* others *who may have* known *him* l-onger. We regret we *are* unable *to ren*der *you more* assistance *in this ma*tter, *but on* such *slen*der grounds we *cannot* say *more* about *Mr. Tran*ter. We *may* possibly do better *on* some *fu*ture occasion. YouRs truly, Wi*n*terbourne Brothers. (101)

EXERCISE 184.

Contractions.

 *objection*,  *destruction*,  *better than*.  *more than*,  *rather than*,  *rather* or *writer*,  *difficulty*,  *doctrine*,  *impossible*,  *inconsistent*,  *inconsistency*,  *influential*,  *uninfluential*,  *information*.

My dear ALexander,—Do *you* know *anything of the doctrine that there is* latent *in all* men *a* love *of* conquering *difficulties, and that this more than anything* else accounts *for the* victories achieved by *writers and* others against seeminGLy *impossibl* odds? If *you are* aware *of this doctrine, it is rather* strange *that you* do *not* try to aRouse *the* latent foRce, *and* strive *to* master youR *objection* to *regular* habits *of* study. *You should give* up youR *inconsistency, and* endeavour *in the* future *to* avoid *those inconsistent* ways *which have* maRRed youR efforts *in the* past, *and which can* onLy result *in the destruction of* youR hopes *to* occupy *an influential* position *in the* worLd. *You should* make *any* sacrifice *rather than* allow youRself *to be* mastered by every little *difficulty that you may* encounter *in* youR attempts *to* increase youR *information and* extend youR *knowledge*. Besides, *you* know *it is rather dangerous to* acquiRe *irregular* habits; *for* they grow upon one, *and the* longer they *are* indulged *in the greater will be the difficulty of* conquering them. Try then *to* rid youRself *of the* lethargy *which* now troubles *you, and which* keeps *you in an uninfluential* position.

The task *is not an impossible* one, *and the* triaL will serve *better than anything* else *to* sHow *the* metal *you are* made *of*. Success will mean *a* good deal *to you*. *It* will eaRn *for you the respect of* others; it will strengthen youR *character; and it* will certainLy brighten youR *prospects in* life. *Very* truly youRs, Walter Winter. (260)

EXERCISE 135.

Vocalization of Pl, Pr, etc.

A small Circle is used to indicate the vowels *ah*, *ā*, *ē*, *ă*, *ĕ*, *ĭ*, between a stroke consonant and the *l* or *r* expressed by an initial hook. In this Exercise the italic letter indicates that the vowel should be expressed by a small circle.

(*a*) First-place Vowels *ah* and *ă* :—

1 p*a*lpable, p*a*lpitate, p*a*lpitation, p*a*ragraph, p*a*ragraphic,
2 p*a*rallel, p*a*ralleLed, p*a*rallelism, P*a*ramatta, p*a*ramount,
3 p*a*rcel, p*a*rceLed, p*a*rley, p*a*rleyed, p*a*rloR, p*a*rquetry,
4 p*a*rsley, p*a*rtake, p*a*rtaker, p*a*rtner, p*a*rtnersHip, p*a*rtook,
5 b*a*rley, b*a*rm, b*a*rometer, b*a*rometric, b*a*rometrical, t*a*rget,
6 t*a*rgeteer, T*a*rleton, T*a*rporley, d*a*rk, d*a*rken, d*a*rkness,
7 d*a*rkened, d*a*rkener, d*a*rker, d*a*rling, dep*a*rt, dep*a*rtment,
8 dep*a*rter, dep*a*rtuRe, durb*a*r, ch*a*llenge, ch*a*llenged,
9 ch*a*llenger, ch*a*rm, ch*a*rming, ch*a*rmed, ch*a*rlock, ch*a*rmeR,
10 ch*a*rnel, ch*a*rcoal, j*a*rgon, j*a*rgonelle, Jacqu*a*rd, c*a*lcify,
11 c*a*lcine, c*a*lcination, c*a*lcinable, c*a*ligraphic, c*a*ligraphy,
12 c*a*listhenics, C*a*lvinist, C*a*lcutta, C*a*ldecott, C*a*lvary,
13 C*a*lvert, k*a*leidoscope, ch*a*ldee, c*a*rbon, c*a*rbonic, c*a*rboni-
14 ferous, c*a*rbuncle, c*a*rdinal, c*a*rdinalate, c*a*ricatuRe,
15 c*a*ricatuRed, c*a*ricaturist, c*a*rmen, c*a*rnage, c*a*rnation,
16 c*a*rnival, c*a*rnivorous, c*a*rpenter, c*a*rpet, c*a*rtage, c*a*rter,
17 c*a*rtoon, inc*a*rcerate, inc*a*rnation, rec*a*lcitrant, g*a*lvanic,
18 g*a*lvanize, g*a*lvanized, g*a*rden, g*a*rdener, ungu*a*rded, reg*a*rd,
19 disreg*a*rd, g*a*rgle, g*a*rgoyle, g*a*rlick, g*a*rland, g*a*rment,
20 g*a*rner, g*a*rnisH, g*a*rnisHee, g*a*rter, v*a*rnish, v*a*rnishing,

21 varnisHer, sHark, sHarp, sHarpen, sHarply, sHarp-sighted,
22 CHarlatan, amalgam, amalgamate, amalgamation, marl,
23 marlaceous, marline, marmalade, marmot, martyr,
24 martyred, martyrdom, martyrology, analytic, analytical,
25 narcissus, narcotic, narrate, narrated, narration, narrative,
26 narrator, anarchy, anarchic, anarchist, gnarL, gnarLed.

(*b*) SECOND-PLACE VOWELS *ā* AND *ĕ* :—

1 perambulate, perambulator, perceive, perceptible, percep-
2 tion, percolate, percussion, peregrinate, peregrine, perfect,
3 perfected, perfecter, perfection, perfectly, perfidy, perforate,
4 perforation, perforator, perimeter, perjure, perjurer,
5 permanence, permanent, permit, permission, perniCious,
6 perpetrate, perpetra-ted, perplex, perquisite, persevere,
7 persist, persistent, person, personate, personator, personal,
8 personalty, perspicaCious, perspire, persuade, persuasion,
9 pervade, perverse, perversity, perverter, Belgrade, Belgrave,
10 Berlin, BerksHire, Bermondsey, Bermudas, Bernard,
11 Bernardine, telegram, telegraph, telegraphed, telegraphic,
12 telegraphy, telephone, telephonic, telescope, telescopic,
13 term, terminus, termagant, terminable, terminal, terminate,
14 termination, delegate, delegated, delegation, deliberate,
15 deliberation, deliberative, deliberator, delicate, delicacy,
16 derelict, derogate, derogatory, dermal, Chelsea, Chelmsford,
17 Cheltenham, cherub, cherubim, chirp, chair, chaired,
18 chairman, careless, carelessly, Jeremy, Jeremiah, Jericho,
19 Jerome, Jersey, germ, German, Germany, Germanic,
20 GeraRd, germane, germinal, germinate, germicide, kernel,
21 kerchief, Kersey, KersHaw, Kirkdale, Kirkby, kirtle,
22 experiment, gird, girder, girdle, girdled, girl, girlisH,
23 Gertrude, ferment, fermentation, fertile, fertility, fertilize,
24 fertilization, fervent, fervour, verb, verbal, verbose,
25 verbosity, virgin, virtue, virtuous, virulent, virulence,
26 verduRe, verger, vermin, verminous, versatile, versify,
27 versus, vertebra, vertebrate, vertical, averse, thermometer,
28 thermoscope, thermic, thirsty, thirstily, Thirsk, shelf,

sh*e*llac, sh*e*lves, egg-sh*e*ll, oyster-sh*e*ll, book-sh*e*lf, nutsh*e*ll, SHirk, SH*e*rbet, m*e*rcantile, m*e*rceR, m*e*rcury, m*e*retricious, m*e*rmaid, Kn*a*resborough, n*e*rve, n*e*rvous, n*e*rvousLy, en*e*rve, debon*ai*r, doctrin*ai*re, atmosph*e*ric, atmosph*e*rical, hemisph*e*ric, aRm-ch*ai*r, easy-ch*ai*r, elbow-ch*ai*r.

(*c*) THIRD-PLACE VOWELS *ĕ* AND *ĭ* :—

p*i*lgrim, p*i*lgrimage, p*y*ramid, p*y*ramidical, p*y*rometer, d*i*lapidate, d*i*lapidation, d*i*lapidated, d*i*rection, d*i*rector, d*i*rectorate, d*i*rectory, ch*i*ldren, ch*i*lblain, ch*i*rrup, ch*i*rruped, ch*ee*reR, ch*ee*rful, ch*ee*rily, ch*ee*rless, K*i*lkenny, K*i*ldaRe, K*i*lmarnock, engin*ee*r, engin*ee*red, engin*ee*ring, ven*ee*r, ven*ee*red, ven*ee*ring, buccan*ee*r, CHiffon*ie*r, scrutin*ee*r, Belved*e*re, mutin*ee*r, atmosph*e*re, hemisph*e*re, photosph*e*re, ph*i*losophy, ph*i*losopheR, ph*i*losophic, Th*i*rlm*e*re, Winderm*e*re, Tranm*e*re, ensh*ie*ld, n*ea*rness, reb*ui*ld, Abouk*i*r.

EXERCISE 136.

Vocalization of Pl, Pr, etc. (continued).

To show that a dash vowel is to be read between a stroke consonant and an initial hook, write the vowel-sign through the consonant. Where necessary a first-place vowel may be written at the beginning, and a third-place vowel at the end of the stroke consonant. In this Exercise, the italic letter indicates that the vowel is to be treated as here explained.

(*1*) FIRST-PLACE DASH VOWELS :—

p*o*rcelain, p*o*litic, p*o*litical, p*o*litician, t*o*lerate, t*o*lerated, t*o*leration, t*o*lerance, t*o*lerant, int*o*lerant, t*o*rment, t*o*rmenter, t*o*rmented, t*o*rture, t*o*rtuRer, d*o*rmant, d*o*rmeR, d*o*rmitory, d*o*rsal, Ge*o*rge, Ge*o*rgetown, c*o*llaborate, c*o*llaborator, c*o*llect, c*o*llector, c*o*llective, c*o*llection, c*o*llectively, c*o*llege, c*o*lony, c*o*lonize, c*o*lonization, c*o*rduroy, c*o*rner, c*o*rnet, c*o*rnice, C*o*rnisH, c*o*rollate, c*o*rporal, c*o*rporation, c*o*rporate, c*o*rpulent, c*o*rpulence, c*o*rrect, c*o*rrection, corrective, correlation, correspond, corresponded, correspondent, correspondence, corridor, corrigible, incorrigible, corroborate, corrupt, corruption, corruptible, Golgotha, gorgeous, gormandize, Gorgonzola, Gordon, forbad, forsake, former, formerly, forwarder, forwardness, vortex, vortical, vorticel, Althorp, short, shorten, shortened, shortening, shorthand, shorthorn, short-lived, shortness, shortsighted, moral, morality, moralize, Morley, Mormon, mormonite, morsel, mortar, mortgagee, mortgagor, Minorca, remorse, remorseful, north, normal, abnormal, Norman, Norseman, northerly, northern, northerner, northward, north-west, Norway, Norfolk, Northallerton, Northampton, Northrop, Norwood, Northumberland, Norwich, auriform, cubiform.

(*b*) SECOND-PLACE DASH VOWEL :—

portray, portrait, portraiture, purblind, purchase, purgatory, purl, purlieu, purloin, purloiner, purple, purser, tubipore, pulmonary, pulse-glass, repulsive, repulsing, burgess, burgher, burglar, burglary, burgomaster, Burgundy, burly, burlesque, Burmese, bursar, bursary, bold, boldly, bold-ness, Baltimore, tuberculous, tubercular, Turk, Turkey, Turkish, turmoil, turner, turnip, turpentine, turpitude, turtle, matador, dulcify, deport, deportment, church, churchman, churl, churlish, churlishness, journal, journalize, journey, journeymen, coarse, coarsely, coarseness, coarser, coarsest, curdle, curdy, curly, curled, curmudgeon, curricle, curriculum, cursed, cursory, cursive, discursive, curtail, curtailed, curtain, curtsey, curtly, court, courtly, curve, curved, curvet, scurvy, scurvily, scurrile, scurrilous, scurrility, scurf, courage, courageous, discouraged, encourage, colonel, colonelcy, coldish, colder, coldly, coldness, culminate, culprit, culpable, cultivate, cultivator, cultivation, culture, culvert, sculptor, occur, occurrence, recourse, inculpate, goldsmith, goldplate, marigold, gurgle, fulgent, fulgency, vulnerable, vulture, forepart, foreshore, shoreditch, forestall, forefather, foretaste, forethought, forge, forger, furbish, furl, furnace.

furnish, furniture, furze, further, furthermore, bifurcate, bifurcation, thurl, Thursday, seashore, leeshore, murder, murdered, murderer, murmur, murmured, Blackmore, Dunmore, claymore, sycamore, council-board, nullify, nullity, nullification, penultimate, nurse, nursery, nurseling, nursed, splash-board.

(*c*) Third-place Dash Vowel :—

whirlpool, school, schools, schoolmate, schoolman, school-girl, school-board, boarding-school, foolscap, fulfil, fulfilled, fulfilment, bashful, brochure, cheerful, cupful, sure, surety, troubadour.

(*d*) Diphthongs, treated in the same way as the Dash Vowels :—

child, childhood, childish, childishly, childishness, prefecture, temperature, lecture, lectured, literature, limature, legislature, moisture, armature, nomenclature, stricture, structure, nurture, nurtured, sculpture, sculptured, fixture, texture, imposture, mixture, admixture, arboriculture, horticulture, horticulturist, floriculture, curvature, capture, captured, rapture, enraptured, figure, disfigured, figuration, rupture, ruptured, featured, fracture, fractured, pictured, ligature.

EXERCISE 137.

Vocalization of Pl, Pr, etc. (continued).

See Note at the head of Exercises 135 and 136.

1. *He who is* most fond *of* challenges *may be the* most vulnerable *in the* fight. 2. Father Time *is the* most remorseless mortgagee, *who cannot be* shirked, *and who* forgets *not the* day *of* reckoning, persuade *him how* we *may*. 3. *The* world *is* indeed *a* hard school, *and a* man needs *to be* watchful, or *he* will fall *to the* bottom *of his* class. 4. *And* yet *in the* midst *of all the* courtly varnish we *see there is to be* found

a great deal *that is* honest *and* genuine. 5. *In a great* measure, we make *the* atmosphere through *which* we regard others, *and* we *may be the* culprits sometimes though we blame *them.* 6. Illusions *are but* charming toys *for* children *of all* ages, *from the* child *on* nurse's knee *to the* oLd man *in the* corner. 7. *And so* every burly boy *may be a* hero, *and* every delicate girl *may be a* beauty. 8. *It is* perfectly true *to* say *that* many *a* man's failuRe *may be* traced *to a* win *on a* racecourse. 9. *A* heaRt *that is* proof against *the* charms *of* literature *may be* touched by *the* charms *of* vocal music, if rendered by *a* cultivated singeR. 10. *Those who* say they *have* no scope *for the* exercise *of their* energies *have* either little energy *to* exercise, oR little courage *to* exercise *it.* 11. *An* able man will *not* tolerate *the* torment *of* inactivity. 12. No fact *that* we learn *is* ever utterly forgotten. 13. *It is* parceLed up, *in a* manner *and put* away ; *but the mere* mention *of* some person oR place *may be* enough *to* unpack *it and* bring *it to our* mind *as* fresH *as* ever. 14. *And so the* time spent *in* study *is not* lost.

(286)

EXERCISE 138.

Vocalization of Pl, Pr, etc. (continued).

See Note at the head of Exercises 135 and 136.

1. *The* philosophic study *of* political history sHows *that* some *of the* most intolerant cold-blooded tyrants *have* begun *their* reigns peacefully. 2. *But the* possession *of* paramount poweR darkened *their* minds, *and* permitted *the* repulsive side *of their character to* assert *its influence.* 3. Then, *as a* certain cultivated author says, *their* heaRts were corrupted by *the* flatterers *who* crowded *their* courts, *so that* even deliberate murder perpetrated by *a* poweRful king *was* regarded *as* no crime. 4. Base favourites *have* often persuaded *a* tyrannical monaRch *that the* murmurs *and* ferments *which* were *the* results *of his* pernicious misruLe were *but* signs *of* disloyalty, *and have* urged *that the* correct course *was to* capture *and* execute

the persons whom they termed *the* ringLeaders. 5. Thus *the* fiRe *of* passion *has* been nursed *and* fanned *into* *a* furnace, *and he who* might *have* been *a* tolerably faiR ruLer *has* been changed *into* *a* remorseless tyrant, *a* tormentor *of his* people, *and a* curse *to* society. 6. *Happily* *the* days *of* enormous personal poweR *are* over *in* most countries, *and* virtuous men *are not called* upon *to* suffer *as their* forefathers did *from the* jealousy *of* blackguardly favourites. (191)

EXERCISE 139.

Vocalization of Pl, Pr, etc. (continued).

See Note at the head of Exercises 135 and 136.

1. Mariners regard *the* sHark *as their* fieRcest *and* most remorseless enemy. 2. *And* no wonder; *for* by *the* aid *of his* six rows *of* teeth, sHarp *as the* sHarpest knife, *he can* crunch up *a* man's body *as* easily *as you can* break *an* eggshell. 3. Few men will deliberately tackle *a* sHark *in his* own eLement. 4. *Those whose* personal courage *cannot be* doubted admit *that the* thought *of* venturing *near* one *of these* monsters *is* enough *to* make *the* blood curdle *in* one's veins; while *the mere* sight *of a* sHark causes *the* heaRts *of* nervous oR delicate persons *to* palpitate *for* feaR. 5. Even upon dark nights *the* sailoRs *can* sometimes tell *that a* sHark *is near their* vesseL, *for the* scaLes *of this* fish throw off *a* faint light. 6. *The* men *are* then *very* carefuL *to* incur no risk *of* faLLing overboaRd; *for* they know *that should* such *an* accident occur no one *could* prevent *a* fataL termination, *as a* sHark *can* swim *so* quickly *that he can* capture *a* man long before *a* boat *could be put* out *for the* rescue. 7. *The* white sHark often measures thirty feet *in* length, *and* though *the* blue sHark *is not* so big, *he is* just *as* fieRce. 8. *The* sHark *is very* voracious. 9. *He* will swallow greedily *any* articles *from a* sHip, such *as* coarse ropes, charcoal, garlic — *in* fact, *there is* scaRcely *a thing from a* turtle *to an* open knife *that he* will *not* gulp up. 10. Yet,

strange *to* say, *he* refuses *to* touch *a* feathered creature *of any* kind. 11. Fortunately, *these* repulsive monsters *are* unknown *near our* own seaSHores, *and I* am sure we do *not* want *them to* cultivate *a* fancy *for our* neighbourhood. (286)

EXERCISE 140.

Vocalization of Pl, Pr, etc. (continued).

See Note at the head of Exercises 135 and 136.

MessRS. Caldecott *and* North.

Dear SiRS,—We regret *to have to* challenge *the* accuracy *of Mr.* Charles Darlington's statement *in* regard *to the* furniture forwarded *to him on the* 28th uLtimo. *Our Mr.* Turner saw personally *to the* finishing *of this* lot *of* goods, *and his* recollection *is* perfectly cleaR *that the* SHade *of the* polish *was* exactLy *as* oRdered, neither lighter *nor* darker. We *have* cultivated *this* department *of our* business *so care*fully *as* almost *to* preclude *the* possibility *of* such *a* blunder *as is* alleged. *You* know *that* we *have* every SHade *of* varnish *and* polish ready *for* mixing, *so that there is* absolutely no inducement *for us to* change *a* SHade deliberately. We *are* sorry *that Mr.* Darlington *should be so* much perturbed about *this* matter; *but* we feeL sure *that* if *he* will refer *to his* directions *to us he* will find *that the* fault *is not ours.* We *can, of* course, repolish *the* furniture if desiRed; *but* we *should have to* charge *for the* trouble *and* expense. YouRs truly, Turner *and* Blackmore. (178)

EXERCISE 141.

Vocalization of Pl, Pr, etc. (concluded).

See Note at the head of Exercises 135 and 136.

MessRS. Charles Macarthy *and* Sons, Ltd.

Dear SiRS,—*In* reply *to* youR inquiry *of the first* instant, we hope *to* forward *the* whole *of the* carbolic acid *not* later than Thursday, *the* 6th inst. *The* delay *has* aRisen through *the* breakdown *of a* vertical shaft at *the* distillery, *which* threatened *to* upset *all our* calculations. We *are* glad *to* say *the* macHinery *has* been *put all* right again, *and there* will *be* no furtheı trouble *in* forwarding oRders. We trust *that the* explanation *of this* unfortunate occurrence will satisfy *you that there has* been *no* culpable negligence *on our* part, *and* we rely *on* youR courtesy *to* excuse *the* delay *in this* instance. YouRs faithfully, Partridge *and* Norton. (118)

EXERCISE 142.

W and Y Diphthongs.

These diphthongs are represented by a small Semi-Circle, written in the same positions as the simple vowels. In this Exercise and in Exercises 143 to 147 inclusive, the Semi-Circle should be employed (in words other than grammalogues or contractions) for the representation of the combinations printed in italic.

(*a*) FIRST-PLACE DIPHTHONGS *wah* AND *wă* :—

bees*wa*x, eaR-*wa*x, pack*wa*x, pax*wa*x, sealing-*wa*x, Z*oua*ve, th*wa*ck.

(*b*) SECOND-PLACE DIPHTHONGS *wā* AND *wĕ* :—

arq*ue*buss, ass*ua*ge, ass*ua*ger, ass*ua*sive, boats*wa*in, cord*wa*iner, else*whe*Re, freq*ue*nt, freq*ue*ntly, freq*ue*nted, freq*ue*nter, freq*ue*nting, freq*ue*ncy, haRd*wa*Re, over*whe*Lm, some*whe*Re, subseq*ue*nce, subseq*ue*nt, subseq*ue*ntly, tide-*wa*iter, t*we*lve, t*we*lfth, t*we*nty, t*we*ntieth, Biggles*wa*de, Bos*we*ll, Both*we*ll, B*ue*nos Aires, Bul*we*ll, faRe*we*ll, Bul*we*R, Clerken*we*ll, Crom*we*ll, Crosth*wa*ite, HaR*we*ll, (tick *h*), Holy*we*ll (tick *h*), Merry*we*ather, Os*we*stry, Postleth*wa*ite, sHad*we*ll, Up*we*ll, *Wa*Reham, Terra del F*ue*go, Ash-*We*dnesday.

(*c*) THIRD-PLACE DIPHTHONGS *wē* AND *wĭ* :—

app*ui*, asq*ui*nt, baili*wi*ck, d*wi*ndle, d*wi*ndled, d*wi*ndling, eaR*wi*g, ARd*wi*ck, HaRd*wi*ck (tick *h*), Bruns*wi*ck, ember-*wee*k, whit-*wee*k, forth*wi*th, heRe*wi*th, hood*wi*nk, hoRse*whi*p, ill-*w*ill, ill-*wi*sher, mans*ue*tude, non-seq*ui*ter, pasq*ui*n, pasq*ui*nade, peri*wi*g, peri*wi*nkle, Pick*wi*ck, pig*wi*dgeon, purs*ui*vant, Ips*wi*ch, sand*wi*ch, sea-*wee*d, t*wea*k, t*wea*ks, t*wea*ked, t*wee*d, t*wee*dle, t*wee*zers, t*wi*g, t*wi*gged, t*wi*nkle, t*wi*nge, t*wi*nged, t*wi*xt, where*wi*th, where*wi*thal, here*wi*th, there*wi*th, whippoor*wi*ll, *wi*sher, *wi*shful, wiston*wi*sh, *wi*thal, *wi*thdraw, *wi*thdrawing, *wi*thdrew, *wi*thdrawn, *wi*thin, *wi*thhold, *wi*thheld, *wi*thholden, *wi*thstand, *wi*thstood, Bald*wi*n, Bast*wi*ck, Bath*wi*ck, Chad*wi*ck, Droit*wi*ch, Fitz*wi*lliam, Giggles*wi*ck, Kild*wi*ck, Middle*wi*ch, North*wi*ch, Nant*wi*ch, Os*we*go, Pains*wi*ck, shap*wi*ck, T*ui*leries, Venez*ue*la, *Wi*nckworth, *Zwi*ngle, be*wi*lder, be*wi*ldered, be*wi*ldering, Sles*wi*ck, Sedg*wi*ck, Bed*oui*n, big-*wi*g.

(*d*) First-place Diphthongs *waw* and *wŏ* :—

tar-*wa*ter, bilge*wa*ter, break*wa*ter, lime-*wa*ter, rain-*wa*ter, rose-*wa*ter, sea-*wa*ter, Broad*wa*ter, Bridge*wa*ter, back*wa*ter, cut-*wa*ter, bul*wa*rk, cater*wau*l, chamo*i*s, demo*i*selle, devo*i*r, east*wa*rd, fro*wa*rd, fro*wa*rdly, heaven*wa*rd, hither*wa*rd, mod*wa*ll, pato*i*s, abatto*i*r, boudo*i*r, rouge-et-no*i*r, escritoire, sea*wa*rd, sheer*wa*ter, shop-*wa*lker, sh*wa*npan, throat*wo*rt, t*wa*ddle, t*wa*ddler, t*wa*ddled, t*wa*ttle, Vaudo*i*s, wind*wa*rd, wishy-*wa*shy, Corn*wa*ll, Corn*wa*llis, *Wa*rkworth, *Wa*rminster, memo*i*rs, church*wa*rden.

(*e*) Second-place Diphthongs *wō* and *wŭ* :—

*wo*rk, *wo*rkable, *wo*rk-bag, *wo*rk-box, *wo*rk-day, *wo*rked *wo*rker, *wo*rkhouse, *wo*rking-day, *wo*rkman, *wo*rkmanlike *wo*rkshop, *Wo*rksop, *Wo*rkington, day-*wo*rk, clock*wo*rk, counter*wo*rk, brick*wo*rk, breast*wo*rk, co-*wo*rker, frame*wo*rk, fret*wo*rk, glass-*wo*rks, gas-*wo*rks, ground*wo*rk, task*wo*rk, out*wo*rk, over*wo*rk, fire*wo*rks, guess*wo*rk, handi*wo*rk, needle-*wo*rk, hand*wo*rk, head*wo*rk, journey-*wo*rk, patch*wo*rk, piece-*wo*rk, open-*wo*rk, cane-*wo*rk, copper-*wo*rk, press*wo*rk, wood*wo*rk, stone*wo*rk, shell-*wo*rk, *wo*rd, *wo*rds, *Wo*rdsworth, *wo*rdiness, *wo*rdily, by-*wo*rd, catch*wo*rd, watch*wo*rd, Hems*wo*rth (tick *h*), liver*wo*rt, lung*wo*rt, *wo*Rm, *wo*Rm-eaten, *wo*Rmed, *wo*Rming, *wo*Rmlike, *wo*Rmwood, *wo*Rmy, wire*wo*Rm, slow-*wo*Rm, book-*wo*Rm, ring*wo*Rm, earth-*wo*Rm, misq*uo*te, misq*uo*tation, misq*uo*ted, mug*wu*mp, sea*wo*rthy, unsea*wo*rthy, blame*wo*rthy, Went*wo*rth, Wall*wo*Rk, Wal*wo*rth, Wands*wo*rth, *W*iRksworth, *W*oRlington.

(*f*) Third-place Diphthongs *wōō* and *wŏŏ* :—

back*woo*ds, back*woo*dsman, lamb's-*woo*l, Chat*woo*d, East*woo*d, sHeep's-*woo*l, touch*woo*d, drift*woo*d, *wo*Rm*woo*d, Ethel*wu*lf.

(*g*) First-place Diphthongs *yah* and *yă* :—

Abyssin*ia*n, academ*ia*n, am*ia*ble, antiquar*ia*n, apprec*ia*ble, ap*ia*ry, ARab*ia*n, ARcad*ia*n, AR*ia*n, As*ia*n, As*ia*tic, aRter*ia*L, assoc*ia*ble, Assyr*ia*n, Athen*ia*n, Augustin*ia*n, Austral*ia*n, Austr*ia*n, auxil*ia*ries, Babylon*ia*n, bacter*ia*, ban*ia*n, barbar*ia*n, baron*ia*L, b*ea*tify, bienn*ia*L, Bodl*eia*n, bor*ea*L, Brazil*ia*n, brev*ia*ry, brill*ia*nt, bronch*ia*l, Cambr*ia*n, card*ia*c, Carthagin*ia*n, Castil*ia*n, Caucas*ia*n, ceR*ea*l, cil*ia*ry, cogn*ac*, colloqu*ia*L, CoLumb*ia*, cord*ia*l, corpor*ea*L, criter*ia*, crustac*ea*, Cumbr*ia*n, cur*ia*, custod*ia*n, cycloped*ia*, Cypr*ia*n, Dalton*ia*n, Danub*ia*n, demon*ia*c, Devon*ia*n, dictator*ia*L, diluv*ia*n, Dor*ia*n, eLys*ia*n, encycloped*ia*, enunc*ia*tory, episod*ia*l, equestr*ia*n, ERast*ia*n, ether*ea*L, ether*ea*lize, Eton*ia*n, famil*ia*rize, fen*ia*n, f*ia*cre, f*ia*sco, fuchs*ia*, funer*ea*L, fust*ia*n, gamboge*a*n, gen*ia*L, gladiator*ia*L, gregor*ia*n, gua*ia*cum, guard*ia*n, hab*ea*s-corpus, hall*ia*rd (tick *h*), hans*ea*tic, ALexandr*ia*, histor*ia*n (tick *h*), humanitar*ia*n (tick *h*), hyster*ia*, id*ea*lity, memor*ia*L, imper*ia*L, Ind*ia*-rubber, industr*ia*l, insomn*ia*, invar*ia*bly, rad*ia*nce, kleptoman*ia*, lany*a*Rd, lar*ia*t, librar*ia*n, lin*ea*l, luxur*ia*nt, malar*ia*, manager*ia*L, matrimon*ia*L, m*ea*nder, m*ea*ndeRed, med*ia*l, Mediterran*ea*n, men*ia*L, min*ia*tuRe, minister*ia*L, Morav*ia*n, mur*ia*tic, myr*ia*d, neuRalg*ia*, notar*ia*L, oc*ea*nic, pall*ia*tive, pancr*ea*s, par*ia*h, Paris*ia*n, patr*ia*rch, pecun*ia*ry, Philadelph*ia*n, p*ia*zza, p*ia*noforte, plag*ia*rize, pneumon*ia*, poly*a*nthus, pon*ia*Rd, proverb*ia*l, r*ea*lity, r*ea*nimate, ruff*ia*n, secretarial, social, socialist, suppliant, Syriac, terrestrial, theatrical, tutorial, Utopia, Vesuvian, Wesleyan, Adrian, Adriatic, Christiania, Georgia, Virginia, Yarmouth.

(*h*) SECOND-PLACE DIPHTHONGS *yā* AND *yĕ* :—

abbreviate, abbreviator, acquiesce, alien, alienate, appreciation, appropriate, asphyxiate, associate, balliage, barrier, brasier, burier, calumniate, carrier, collegiate, collier, colliery, copier, courtier, create, creative, creation, creator, croupier, lawyer, crosier, deadlier, defoliation, delineate, delineation, delineator, denunciate, denunciation, depreciate, depreciation, deviate, deviation, differentiate, obedient, obedience, dissociate, domiciliate, easier, ebulliency, emaciate, emaciation, embodier, foliage, emolliate, emollient, enunciate, enunciation, envier, radiate, radiation, excruciate, excruciating, exfoliate, expatiate, expatriate, expatriation, experience, expiate, expiation, expropriate, fancier, farrier, foliaceous, foliation, fortieth, funnier, funniest, furrier, gaudiest, ghastlier, giddier, giddiest, glacier, gladiator, glazier, gloomier, gloomiest, goodlier, goodliest, grimier, hacienda, handier, happier, happiest, hardiest, hardier, harrier, haughtiest, homeliest (tick *h*), humiliate (tick *h*), hygienic, ideation, inexpedient, infuriated, initial, initiation, kindliest, laureate, lazier, lenience, liveliest, luxuriate, mediate, mediation, nastier, nauseate, nauseation, muriate, negotiate, ninetieth, novitiate, obviate, officiate, opiate, oriel, oriental, osier, palliation, paltrier, permeate, pluckier, premier, recipient, repudiate, resilience, retaliation, satiate, saucier, sawyer, seemlier, spaniel, terrier, triennial, uncreated, variegated, verbiage, vitiate, weariest, Damietta, Dieppe, Liege (upward *l*).

(*i*) THIRD-PLACE DIPHTHONGS *yē* AND *yĭ* :—

babyish, bandying, bodying, bullying, burying, carrying, caseic, copying-press, copyist, courtesying, currying, dandyism, dandyish, disembodying, atheist, atheism,

4 ath*ei*stic, ath*ei*stical, dith*ei*st, dith*ei*stic, dowd*yi*sh, edd*yi*ng
5 embod*yi*ng, gips*yi*sm, нackne*yi*ng, harr*yi*ng, hurr*yi*ng,
6 journe*yi*ng, minut*iæ*, mutin*yi*ng, oL*ei*c, ol*ei*ferous, oL*ei*n,
7 panth*ei*sm, panth*ei*st, parle*yi*ng, parod*yi*ng, Puse*yi*sm,
8 Puse*yi*st, quarr*yi*ng, r*ei*ssue, r*ei*terate, scurr*yi*ng, sull*yi*ng,
9 dall*yi*ng, th*ei*stic, var*yi*ng, wear*yi*ng, whinn*yi*ng, worr*yi*ng,
10 marr*yi*ng, tarr*yi*ng, toad*yi*ng, sall*yi*ng, rowd*yi*sm, assoil*zie*.

(*j*) First-Place Diphthongs *yaw* and *yŏ* :—

1 accord*io*n, quest*io*n, admixt*io*n, amel*io*rate, anter*io*r,
2 aR*eo*meter, ax*io*m, bacter*io*logy, bast*io*n, bibl*io*graphy,
3 bull*io*n, cabr*io*let, can*o*n, carr*io*n, centur*io*n, champ*io*n,
4 clar*io*n, criter*io*n, cross-quest*io*n, cur*io*sity, decill*io*n,
5 d*eo*xidize, d*eo*xidate, digest*io*n, disun*io*n, domin*io*n,
6 ecclesi*o*logy, Eth*io*p, excels*io*R, exhaust*io*n, exter*io*r,
7 gab*io*n, gal*io*t, gall*eo*n, gangl*io*n, g*eo*grapher, g*eo*graphy,
8 g*eo*logy, g*eo*logist, g*eo*meter, g*eo*metrician, hag*io*graphy,
9 hal*io*graphy (tick *h*), halc*yo*n, hel*io*centric, hel*io*trope,
10 hom*œo*pathic (tick *h*), hyper*io*n, id*io*m, id*io*t, id*io*cy,
11 id*io*matic, id*io*syncrasy, impecun*io*sity, infeR*io*r, infeR*io*rity,
12 mill*io*n, mill*io*naiRe, mel*io*rate, met*eo*R, met*eo*rite, me*teo*r-
13 ology, medall*io*n, mull*io*n, Napol*eo*nic, n*eo*logy, oblivi*o*n,
14 ol*io*graph, on*io*n, opin*io*nated, pal*eo*lithic, panth*eo*n,
15 patr*io*t, pavil*io*n, per*io*dical, pill*io*n, pin*io*n, poster*io*r,
16 sen*io*R, sen*io*rity, ster*eo*type, th*eo*cracy, th*eo*dolite,
17 th*eo*logy, th*eo*sophy, trunn*io*n, vermil*io*n, Ell*io*tt, Montr*ea*l,
18 tatterdemal*io*n, mignonette, Mar*io*n.

(*k*) Second-place Diphthongs *yō* and *yŭ* :—

1 abstem*iou*s, acrimon*iou*s, aLkal*iou*s, alluv*iu*m, aquar*eou*s,
2 aqu*eou*s, aRbor*eou*s, beaut*eou*s, bil*iou*s, bount*eou*s, calc*iu*m,
3 came*o*, cas*eou*s, censor*iou*s, ceRemon*iou*s, cop*iou*s, corn*eou*s,
4 court*eou*s, co*yo*te, cran*iu*m, cur*iou*s, cur*io*so, delir*iou*s,
5 deliR*iu*m, d*eo*dorize, dev*iou*s, dub*iou*s, dub*iou*sly, dut*eou*s,
6 effluv*iu*m, Elys*iu*m, embr*yo*, fol*io*, empor*iu*m, encom*iu*m,
7 env*iou*s, equilibr*iu*m, eRRon*eou*s, Eth*io*pian, exord*iu*m,
8 fastid*iou*s, felon*iou*s, fol*iou*s, fur*iou*s, gas*eou*s, gramin*eou*s,

grand*io*se, gregar*ious*, gymnas*ium*, gyps*eous*, haRmon*ium*, ignomin*ious*, illustr*ious*, impecun*ious*, imper*ious*, indust*rious*, ingen*ious*, ingen*ious*LY, insid*ious*, invid*ious*, irid*ium*, haRmon*ious*, extemporan*eous*, nefar*ious*, glor*ious*ly, glad*io*le, discourt*eous*, vicar*ious*, stramon*ium*, stamin*eous*, labor*ious*, melod*ious*, millenn*ium*, miscellan*eous*, mis*yo*ke, mis*yo*ked, mustaCH*io*, myster*ious*, nasturT*ium*, naus*eous*, notor*ious*, nucl*eus*, oblivi*ous*, obsequ*ious*, od*ious*, od*ium*, op*ium*, opprob*ium*, oss*eous*, pandemon*ium*, parsimon*ious*, perfid*ious*, petrol*eum*, pit*eous*, prem*ium*, raT*io*, right*eous*, sod*ium*, instantan*eous*, stud*ious*, supercil*ious*, sympos*ium*, victor*ious*, Born*eo*, Hol*yo*ke (-tick *h*), Jun*ius*, K*eogh*, *Yo*koHama, imperv*ious*, hid*eous*.

(*l*) Third-place Diphthong *yōō* :—

obt*u*se, absol*u*tory, ab*u*sive, acid*u*lous. act*u*ary, add*u*cible, ass*u*me, att*u*ne, avoird*u*pois, bib*u*lous, b*u*rin, cach*ou*, caL*u*met, caps*u*le, cas*u*ist, cell*u*loid, chas*u*ble, coiff*u*Re, cop*u*la, cord*u*roy, corp*u*lent, creat*u*Re, cred*u*lous, c*u*bicle, c*u*pid, c*u*pidity, ded*u*ce, del*u*ge, dep*u*te, diff*u*se, disp*u*tatious, dissim*u*lation, dis*u*nite, effect*u*al, em*u*, em*u*late, ens*ue*d, epic*u*Re, er*u*dite, est*u*ary, *eu*phemism, expost*u*late, exten*u*ate, ex*u*berant, ex*u*de, fab*u*lous, flat*u*lence, fraud*u*lent, gest*u*re, glob*u*le, good-nat*u*Red, habit*u*de, import*u*nate, inc*u*bus, ins*u*perable, iss*ue*R, masc*u*line, m*u*nificent, neb*u*la, n*ew*est, non-s*u*it, occ*u*pation, oc*u*list, opp*u*gn, overt*u*re, pen*u*ry, post*u*late, rem*u*nerate, retrib*u*tion, sp*u*rious, stip*u*lation, *u*tility, vol*u*ble, *Eu*clid, d*u*tiable, prod*u*cible, pop*u*laR, pet*u*lantly, f*eu*dalism, depop*u*late, c*u*cumber, ast*u*te.

(*m*) Joined Diphthongs :—

*wa*tcher, *wa*ter, *wa*terage, *wa*terbutt, *wa*ter-cart, *wa*tercourse, *wa*tercress, *wa*tered, *wa*terfaLL, *wa*ter-fowL, *wa*teriness, *wa*tering-place, *wa*terish, *wa*ter-lily, *wa*ter-logged, *wa*terman, *wa*termark, *wa*ter-melon, *wa*ter-mill, *wa*ter-pot, *wa*terproof, *wa*ter-rot, *wa*ter-rat, *wa*tershed, *wa*terspout, *wa*terway, *wa*ter*wo*Rks, *wa*ter*wo*Rt, *wa*tery, *Wa*terbury, *Wa*terford, *Wa*terworth, *wa*SHer, *wa*SHerwoman, WelsH-*wo*man, *war*, *Wa*rbeck, *wa*rble, *wa*rbleR, *wa*rbling, *War*burton, *Wa*rdle*w*orth, *Wa*rton, *war*-cry, *wa*rd, *wa*rden, *war*-dance, *wa*rded, *wa*rdenry, *wa*rd*i*ng, *wa*rder, *wa*rdrobe, *wa*rdroom, *war*faRe, *war*Like, *war*Lock, *wa*rm, *wa*rmed, *wa*rmer, *wa*rmest, *wa*rmhearted, *wa*rm-heartedness, *wa*rming, *wa*rming-pan, *wa*rmly, *wa*rn, *wa*rned, *wa*rneR, *wa*rp, *wa*rped, *war*-paint, *war*-path, *wa*rrant, *wa*rrantable, *wa*rranty, *wa*rranter, *wa*rred, *wa*rren, *wa*rreneR, *wa*rring, *wa*rrior, *war*-song, *Wa*rsaw, *wa*rt, *wa*rtwoRt, *war*-whoop, *war*-worn, *wax*, *wa*xed, *wa*xen, *wa*x-end, *wax*-*wo*Rk, *wa*xy, *wee*k, *wea*k, *wea*ken, *wea*kened, *wea*kening, *wea*keR, *wea*kest, *wea*k-eyed, *wee*kly, *wea*kly, *wea*kens, *wea*kness, *wi*ck, *wi*cked, *wi*ckedly, *wi*ckedness, *wi*cket, *Wi*cklow, *wa*ke, *wa*ked, *wa*keful, *wa*ken, *wa*kened, *wa*kener, *wa*keR, *wa*lk, *wa*lkeR, *wa*lking-stick, *Wa*keford, *wag*, *wa*gged, *wa*ggery, *wa*ggiSH, *wa*ggishly, *Wa*gstaffe, *wa*gon, *wa*gonage, *wa*goner, *wa*gonette, *wa*gtail, *wig*, *Wi*gan, *Wi*gton, *wi*gwam, *wi*mple, *wi*mpled, *wo*man, *wo*manhood, *wo*maniSH, *wo*manLy, *wo*men, *We*myss, *Wi*Lkin, *Wi*Lkins, *Wi*Lkinson, *Wi*Lks, *Wi*LL*i*ams, *Wi*LL*ia*mson, *Wi*Lmington, *Wi*Lson, *wa*mble, *wa*mpee, *wa*mpum, *wo*mbat.

(*n*) *W* AND *Y* DIPHTHONGS BETWEEN A STROKE CONSONANT AND AN INITIAL HOOK. [See Exercise 136 par. (d).]

eq*ua*lity, eq*ua*lize, eq*ua*lization, eq*ua*lized, eq*ua*lizing, q*ua*lify, q*ua*lified, q*ua*lifiable, q*ua*lification, q*ua*lifieR, q*ua*litative, disq*ua*lify, disq*ua*lification, disq*ua*lified, sold*ie*r, sold*ie*rly, sold*ie*ring, foot-sold*ie*r, healt*hie*r, wealth*ie*r, loft*ie*r, worth*ie*r.

(*o*) JOINED VOWELS.

The italic type indicates that the vowel should be joined to the consonant.

*a*lder, *a*lderman, *a*ldermanic, *a*ll-fooLs' day, *a*ll-fouRs, *a*ll-hail, *a*ll-hallows, *a*ll-souls' day, *a*llspice, *a*lter, *a*ltar, *al*tar-cloth, *al*tar-piece, *al*terable, *al*terant, *al*teration, *al*terative, *al*tered, *al*tereR, *al*tering, *al*so, *Al*bany, *Al*cester, *Al*derborough, *Al*derbury, *Al*derney, *Al*dersgate, *Al*dershot, *Al*derson, *Al*derston, *Al*dridge, *Al*thorp, *Al*ton, *Al*ston.

(*p*) JOINED LOGOGRAMS :—

all-wise, *al*mighty, *al*most, *al*though, *al*ready, *what*soever, *who*ever, *who*so, *who*soever, *eye*-salve, *eye*-servant, *eye*-service, *eye*-soRe, *eye*-tooth, *two*-decker, *two*-foLd, *two*-legged, *two*-lobed.

[See also Exercise 13.]

EXERCISE 148.

The W and Y Diphthongs (continued).

GRAMMALOGUES.

beyond, *with*, *when*, *what*, *would*, *will*.

See Note at the head of Exercise 142.

1. Some *wag has* described *the* man *who wa*lks aLong *the* street *with a* lady *on* each aRm *as* "*An* ass between *a* couple *of* pann*ie*Rs." 2. *It would* appeaR *that the* Ital*ia*ns also *are* troubled *with these wea*k men *and women*, *for* they liken *the* man *who* takes up *the* footpath *in this* way *to* "*A* pitcher *with a* paiR *of* handLes." 3. *Beyond all* ques*tion* such behav*iou*r *is a* ser*iou*s breach *of* good manners, *for what* chance *have* other people *to walk with* ease *when* three persons occ*u*py *so* much space ? 4. *It is not* easy *to* awake *wea*k men *to a* sense *of the* ridic*u*lous. 5. *There will* always *be* fooLs *and* man*ia*cs *in the* worLd *in* spite *of the* Lessons *of* super*io*r minds. 6. Librar*ia*ns *of* var*iou*s nations agree *in* supposing *that there* were almost *a* quaRter *of a* mill*io*n books *in the great* library *of* ALexandr*ia*, *which is* said *to have* been burnt *in the* seventh cent*u*ry by *the* ARab*ia*n sold*ie*rs *in* obed*ie*nce *to the* imper*iou*s oRder *of their* barbar*ia*n leader. 7. OnLy *an* ed*u*cated man oR *woman can* apprec*ia*te *the* loss caused by *this* act *of* fieRce incend*ia*rism.

8. *It was a* w*i*cked *and* idi*o*tic crime *to* destroy *so* glori*ous* *and* miscellan*eous* *a* collection *of* books, *wo*Rks *of* geni*us*, *a* memori*a*L *of the* wisdom *and* experi*e*nce *of the* ancient sages. 9. *How* freq*ue*ntly does *a* thoughtLess OR *an* ignorant act prod*u*ce over*wh*eLming trouble *to* others! (232)

EXERCISE 144.

The W and Y Diphthongs (continued).

See Note at the head of Exercise 142.

1. *Beyond all* ques*t*ion *it is* eas*ie*R *to* criticise *an* oLd plan than *to* foRm*u*late *a* n*ew* one; yet seri*ous* men *will* freq*ue*ntly indulge *in a* lot *of* t*wa*ddle about *what* they *call the* faulty *wo*Rk *of* others. 2. *It would be* well if men *who cannot* appreci*a*te *the* efforts *of* others *would* stand aloof *and* leave *the wo*Rkers aLone *to* do *their* best. 3. *What is more* annoying than *to be* lect*u*red *on our* supposed faiLings by *a* person *of* quite medi*o*cre ability, *but with a* supercili*ous*, censori*ous* aiR *of* superi*o*rity? 4. *It is* always haRd *to* accept *a* reb*u*ke *with* good*w*ill, even if we *are* blame*w*orthy; *but it is* doubly haRd *when* we *are* reb*u*ked by *a* person *of* decidedly infeRi*o*r talents, *and when* we know *there is* no fault *to wa*rrant *the* puniSHment. 5. *In* such cases *a weak* man *will* buRst forth *in*to *wa*rm deniaLs *of the* charges, let *the* result *be what it will*; *but the* strong man *will* restrain *the wo*Rds *which* rise *to his* lips, *and will* wait *for a* happ*ie*R occasion *to* prove *the* misq*uo*tation OR remove *the* misapprehension. 6. *And* experi*e*nce SHows *that his* method *of* refutation *is the* best. (193)

EXERCISE 145.

The W and Y Diphthongs (continued).

See Note at the head of Exercise 142.

1. "*There is* no evil *that cannot be* end*u*Red save dishonor," said *a great* man *in the* fourth cent*u*ry, *and his wo*Rds *are*

beyond ques*tion as* true *to*-day *as* then. 2. *What would* human society *be* like if *it* were *not for the* regard *which* men *have for their* rep*u*tation ? 3. "*The* p*u*rity *and* haRdness *of the* diamond belong *to the very first* particles *which* unite at *its* heaRt's coRe ; *the* others *which the* myste*rious* laws *of the* Cre*a*tor attract aRound *these to* increase *and* perfect *the* bea*u*tiful crystalline mass, must needs sHaRe *the* q*u*alities *of the* former." 4. *So*, if *a* man takes *but a* right *view of what is* honorable, *and* strives always *to* follow *that view*, no matter *what may be the* result, *he is not* likely *to* dev*i*ate *from the* path *of* d*u*ty oR *to be* guilty *of* behav*iou*r *in any* way unworthy *of an* honest man. 5. If *you* look aRound *in the* var*ious walks of* life, *you will see that it is those who have a* High notion *of what is* honorable, whether they *be* statesmen oR *warriors*, *wo*Rkmen oR employeRs, wealthy oR pooR, *who* hoLd *the* esteem *of their* fellows ; *whose wo*Rks *are* invar*i*ably read *with* attention, *and whose* counseL *is* followed *with* obed*i*ence. 6. *The* super*i*or man *is* almost invar*i*ably one *with a* right apprec*i*ation *of what is* just. 7. *You may be* industr*ious* ; *you may be* inteL-Lect*u*aL ; *you may be* wealthy ; *but you cannot be* illustr*ious in the* right sense *of the wo*Rd, *and you will* faiL *to* ingraT*i*ate youRself *in the* heaRts *of* youR fellows, unLess *you are an* upright *and an* honorable man. 8. "*All wic*kedness *is we*akness," *and* if *this* excuse *would* serve, *the* most notor*ious* villain might urge *it*. 9. Cultivate *a* sense *of* honor, *and you will* soon *have the* ability *to* resist *a* dishonorable sugges*tio*n. (301)

EXERCISE 146.

The W and Y Diphthongs (continued).

See Note at the head of Exercise 142.

MessRs. *W*akefieLd *and W*iLLiams.

Dear SiRs,—Referring *to the* oRder *for* var*ious* lines *of* haRd*w*are *and* cutlery *with which you* favored *us* through *our Mr. W*alkeR, we *have for*warded *all the* goods by raiL *to*-day, *and* now enclose heR*ew*ith *our* invoice *for the* same. *Will you* please note *that the* price *for the* dinner knives *is* 18/6 peR dozen, *not* 17/6 *as given in* youR oRder ? If *Mr. Wal*keR gave *you the* last named fig*u*re *when he called* upon *you*, *it was a* misq*uo*tation, *which* we trust *you will* overLook. We *would* add *that* we *have* no *wi*sh *to wi*thdraw *from a* quotation named by *our* traveLLer, *and* if *you are in the* least dub*iou*s about *the* matter we *shall be* pleased *to* accept youR fig*u*re. *But* we aSSuRe *you that this* q*ua*lity *of* knife *has al*ways been sold at 18/6 peR dozen. *It is wa*rranted *to be* made *of the* finest mater*ia*l, *and is beyond all* doubt super*io*r *to what is* offered by other fiRms at *very* much *more* money. YouRs truly, Crossth*wai*te *and Wi*ggins. (182)

EXERCISE 147.

The W and Y Diphthongs (concluded).

See Note at the head of Exercise 142.

MessRs. *Wa*rneR *and Wa*rd.

Dear SiRs,—*In* reply *to* youR inquiry, we *are* pleased *to* state *that our* exper*ie*nce *of* MessRs. Conway *and* Farn*wo*rth extends over t*we*nty *yea*Rs, *and that our* relations *with them have al*ways been *of the* most cord*ia*l kind *for the* whole *of that* peri*o*d. They *are* gen*ia*L *and* industr*iou*s men, *with* whom *it is* pleasant *to* deal, *and* we *have* reason *to* know *that* they *will not* permit *the* slightest dev*ia*tion *from* straightforwardness *in their* business. *It is beyond* quest*io*n *that* they do *a* good Colon*ia*L business *as* cloth*ie*rs *and* hos*ie*Rs, besides *be*ing SHippers *of* miscellan*eou*s goods. *What* we *have* said about *this* fiRm *would*, we *have* no doubt, *be* corroborated by *all who have* dealt *with them. You will be* quite *wa*rranted *in* extending *to them a* credit *for the* amount *you* name. We apprec*ia*te youR kind offer, *and shall not* hesitate *to* remind *you when* we requiRe similaR assistance. YouRs faithfully, *Wa*rdlow *and Wi*Lson. (160)

EXERCISE 148.

Contractions.

establish-ed-ment, *immediate*, *immediately*, *interest*, *interested*, *disinterested-ness*, *uninteresting*, *understood*, *understand*, *enlarged*, *mistaken*, *acknowledged*, *natural-ly*, *satisfaction*.

Dear SiR,—*It may interest you to* know *that* we *have* recentLy *enlarged our establishment in* Broadway, *and that* we *are* now prepaRed *to for*ward *immediately from* stock *any of the* goods named *in the* catalogue enclosed. *Any* oRders *you may be* kind enough *to* send *us will* receive *our immediate and care*fuL attention. We *are naturally* desirous *of* obtaining *a* triaL oRder *from you from the* fact *that* we *have not* hitherto been favored by *you*. We *think* we *are not mistaken in* saying *that you would be interested in se*eing *our* new extension *and the great* variety *of* goods we *are* offering at prices *that will surprise you, and which are acknowledged to be very* much below *those* charged by other fiRms. We assuRe *you that* such *a* visit *as* we suggest *would not be uninteresting to you, and* while we do *not* pretend *to be* absolutely *disinterested in this* invitation, *it may be understood that* we *shall not* ask *you to* buy *anything should you* favor *us with a call*. Though we do *not* tax youR faith by *any* statement *of* alleged *disinterestedness*, we yet claim *to understand our* business perfectly, *and* we take *a natural* pride *in the* reputation we *have established for* straightforward dealing. *Should* we *be* fortunate enough *to establish* business relations *with you* we feeL certain *that it would be to our* mutual *satisfaction*. Awaiting youR kind favors, We *are, Dear* SiR, YouRs faithfully, Matthew Butterworth *and* Sons. (245)

EXERCISE 149.

Disyllabic Diphthongs.

The angular signs for these diphthongs are written in the same places as the simple long vowels, and they are employed for the representation of a long vowel followed by an unaccented short vowel. In this Exercise and in Exercises 150 to 154 inclusive, the angular signs should be written (in words other than grammalogues and contractions) to express the combination of letters printed in italic type.

(*a*) FIRST-PLACE DISYLLABIC DIPHTHONG *ah-i*, ETC. :—

1 ass*ai*, C*aa*ba, m*ae*stoso, s*ahi*b, Tippoo-S*ahi*b, ser*ai*, Hagg*ai*,
2 Haw*aii* (upward *h*), Is*ai*ah, solf*ae*R, n*ai*ad.

(*b*) SECOND-PLACE DISYLLABIC DIPHTHONG *ā-ĭ*, ETC. :—

1 ab*eya*nce, ab*eya*nt, *ae*rate, *ae*Ration, *ae*Rified, *ae*Rolite,
2 *ae*Rolitic, *ae*Rology, *ae*Rometer, *ae*Rostat, *ae*Rostatics,
3 *ae*Rostation, *ae*Rography, *ae*Ronaut, *ae*Ronautic, algebr*ai*c,
4 algebr*ai*cal, algebr*ai*st, aLc*ai*c, *ao*Rist, ass*aye*R, aRR*aye*R,
5 ARam*ai*c, B*aa*l, b*ayo*net, betr*aye*r, betr*aya*l, br*aye*R,
6 cac*ao*, c*ai*que, chald*ai*c, choler*ai*c, cl*ayi*SH, cl*aye*y, coc*ai*ne,
7 Cyren*ai*c, dec*aye*R, eL*ai*ne, fl*aye*R, s*aye*R, gains*aye*R, sooth-
8 s*aye*R, g*aye*st, g*aie*ty, hebr*ai*c, Jud*ai*c, l*ai*c, l*ai*ty, l*aye*R,
9 sl*aye*R, mayonnaise, m*ayo*R, m*ayo*Ralty, m*ayo*Ress, mos*ai*c,
10 ob*eye*R, p*aye*R, p*aya*ble, ph*ae*ton, pharis*ai*c, pl*aye*R, cr*ayo*n,
11 portr*aya*l, portr*aye*r, pr*eye*R, pros*ai*c, pros*ai*cal, Ptolem*ai*c,
12 purv*eyo*R, purv*eya*nce, ratep*aye*r, s*aye*st, s*aye*R, s*éa*nce,
13 spond*ai*c, spr*aye*R, stanz*ai*c, st*aye*R, str*aye*R, surv*eyo*R,
14 taxp*aye*r, volt*ai*c, wh*eye*y, wh*eyi*SH, Archel*au*s, B*aa*lim,
15 Bisc*aya*n, w*eigha*ble, w*eighe*r, wayl*aye*R.

(*c*) THIRD-PLACE DISYLLABIC DIPHTHONG *ē-ĭ*, ETC. :—

1 agr*eea*ble, agr*eea*bleness, agr*eea*bly, apoth*eo*sis, apoth*eo*sise,
2 ARam*ea*n, aR*eo*la, aR*eo*Lation, athen*æu*m, aug*ea*n, auR*eo*la,
3 Ave Mar*ia*, id*ea*l, b*ea*tific, caff*ei*n, Chald*ea*n, chor*eu*s,
4 Circ*ea*n, cod*ei*ne, coloss*eu*m, coLoss*ea*n, cr*eo*sote, cun*ei*foRm,

Cyther*ea*n, decr*ee*R, d*ei*cide, d*ei*fied, d*ei*ty, d*ei*sm, d*ei*st, diaphan*ei*ty, diarrh*ea*, dyspn*œa*, empyr*ea*n, *eo*cene, *eo*n, *eo*zoic, *eo*zoon, epicur*ea*n, adamant*ea*n, Etn*ea*n, f*ea*lty, fores*eei*ng, s*ee*R, fores*ee*R, fr*ee*R, fr*ee*st, Galil*ea*n, g*eo*centric, g*eo*centrical, g*eo*graphic, g*eo*graphical, g*eo*logical, g*eo*mancer, g*eo*metric, g*eo*metrical, gigant*ea*n, heterogen*ei*ty, homogen*ei*ty, howb*ei*t, hymn*ea*L, hymn*ea*n, id*ea*list, id*ea*listic, id*ea*lize, id*ea*lization, id*eo*graph, incorpor*ei*ty, l*eo*nine, leth*ea*n, lyc*eu*m, Maccab*ea*n, Manich*ea*n, mus*eu*m, N*ea*politan, Nem*ea*n, n*eo*lithic, n*eo*logian, n*eo*logic, n*eo*phyte, n*eo*zoic, ner*ei*d, nucl*ei*, nymph*ea*n, ORph*ea*n, p*ea*n, panac*ea*, pand*ea*n, Pars*eei*sm, p*eo*n, p*eo*ny, p*eo*nage, periton*eu*m, peron*ea*L, petr*ea*n, pharis*eei*sm, ph*eo*n, pigm*ea*n, pleb*ei*an, pl*eo*nasm, polyp*ea*n, polyth*ei*sm, polyth*ei*st, pr*ea*mble, pr*e-e*ngaged, prytan*eu*m, Pyren*ea*n, Pythagor*ea*n, rataf*ia*, r*ea*bsorb, r*ea*ddress, r*ea*djusting, r*ea*dmit, r*ea*dmission, r*ea*ffiRm, r*ea*L, r*ea*lly, r*ea*lism, r*ea*list, r*ea*listic, r*ea*lize, r*ea*nnex, r*ea*ppeaR, r*ea*ppearance, r*ea*ppoint, r*ea*pportion, r*ea*rrange, r*ea*scend, r*ea*ssemble, r*ea*ssign, r*ea*ssuRe, re-*e*Lect, re-*e*Lection, r*e-e*nact, r*ei*nfoRce, r*e-e*nfoRce, r*e-e*ngage, r*e-e*xamine, r*e-e*xport, r*ei*mburse, r*ei*nsert, r*ei*nstall, r*ei*nstate, r*ei*nsuRe, r*ei*nvest, ros*eo*la, rub*eo*la, Sab*ea*n, Sadduc*ea*n, s*ee*st, s*ee*R, sh*eo*l, sight-s*eei*ng, sight-s*ee*R, spontan*ei*ty, st*ea*rine, st*ea*rate, Tarp*ei*an, th*ea*rchy, th*eo*ry, th*eo*retic, th*eo*retical, th*eo*rem, th*ea*tre, th*ei*ne, th*ei*sm, th*eo*cratic, th*eo*logian, th*eo*logical, th*eo*sophic, th*eo*rist, uns*eei*ng, z*eo*lite, zeolitic, Act*æo*n, *A*Rimath*ea*, Asmod*eu*s, B*ea*trice, Boadic*ea*, Can*ea*, Cl*eo*patra, Cor*ea*, Crim*ea*, Galat*ea*, Galil*eo*, latak*ia*, Th*eo*dore, Zacch*eu*s, Jud*ea*.

(*d*) First-place Disyllabic Diphthong *aw-i*, etc. :—

dr*awe*R, gn*awe*R, wiredr*awe*R, withdr*awe*r, withdr*awa*l, fl*awy*.

(*e*) Second-place Disyllabic Diphthong *ō-i*, etc. :—

az*oi*c, b*eaui*sH, bell*owe*R, benz*oi*c, benz*oi*n, best*owe*r, best*owa*l, bill*owy*, bl*owe*R, borr*owe*r, b*owie*-knife, b*oa*, co*a*djust, co*a*dventure, co*a*lesce, co*a*lesced, co*a*Lescence, co*a*Lescent, co*a*lition, co*a*litionist, co*a*lly, co*a*ptation, co-*e*fficient, co*e*ternal, co*e*ssential, co*e*taneous, co*e*xist, co*e*xistence, co*e*xistent, co*e*xtension, co*i*ncide, ego*i*st, ego*i*sm, eozo*i*c, eozoon, epizo*a*, epizo*a*n, grow*e*r, hero*i*c, hero*i*cal, hero*i*sm, hero*i*ne, hylozo*i*c, intro*i*t, kno*wa*ble, kno*we*R, lo*we*R, lo*we*st, lo*we*red, meado*wy*, mo*we*R, narro*we*r, No*ah*, Mo*a*b, no*o*logical, *o*asis, *o*olite, *o*olitic, *o*ological, *Owe*n, *Owe*nite, palæozo*i*c, playgo*e*R, po*e*m, po*e*t, po*e*sy, po*e*tess, po*e*taster, po*e*try, polyzo*a*n, pro*a*, pro*e*m, protozo*a*, protozo*i*c, so*we*R, ro*we*r, sno*wy*, slo*we*R, slo*we*st, SHo*wy*, SHo*we*R, SHo*wi*ly, SHo*wi*ness, sto*i*c, sto*i*cism, sto*i*caL, sto*wa*ge, sto*wa*way, thro*we*R, to*wa*ge, to*wa*Rdly, unto*wa*Rd, wallo*we*R, wido*we*R, willo*wy*, winno*we*R, yello*we*R, yello*we*st, yello*wi*SH, ro*wa*ble, Zo*i*lism, zo*o*lite, zo*o*phyte, ALgo*a*, Geno*a*, Bo*a*dicea, Chlo*e*, Go*a*, Lo*we*ll (upward *l*), No*we*LL, Allo*a*, Samo*a*.

(*f*) THIRD-PLACE DISYLLABIC DIPHTHONG ōō-ĭ, ETC. :—

abl*ue*nt, affl*ue*nt, affl*ue*nce, affl*ue*ncy, archdr*ui*d, biv*oua*c, bl*ue*y, bl*ui*SH, bl*ui*shly, br*ewe*R, br*ewi*ng, br*ewe*ry, br*ui*n, cr*ewe*l, gr*ue*l, cr*ue*lly, cr*ue*lty, cr*ue*t, deobstr*ue*nt, evil-d*oe*r, d*oi*ng, d*oi*ngs, dr*ui*d, dr*ui*dism, dr*ui*dess, effl*ue*nce, effl*ue*nt, *ewe*r, fl*ue*nt, fl*ue*ntLy, fl*ui*d, fl*uo*R, fl*uo*rine, fl*uo*ride, hall*ooi*ng, Hebr*ewe*ss (tick *h*), Hind*ui*sm (upward *h*), imbr*ui*ng, j*ewe*L, j*ewe*LLer, j*ewe*lry, J*ewi*SH, J*ewe*ss, S*ue*z, lo*ui*s-d'OR, mellifl*ue*nt, mellifl*uou*s, m*ooi*ng, obstr*ue*nt, refl*ue*nce, refl*ue*nt, r*ui*n, r*ui*ned, r*ui*nous, r*ui*nate, r*ui*nation, sanguifl*uou*s, SHo*ei*ng, SHo*e*R, SHr*ewi*SH, sl*ui*ng, tr*ua*nt, und*oi*ng, well-d*oe*R, well-d*oi*ng, wrong-d*oe*R, y*ewe*n, *Ewa*rt, *Ewi*ng, L*ewi*s (upward *l*), R*ua*bon (upward *r*), w*ooi*ng, w*ooi*ngLy, w*ooe*r, altr*ui*sm.

(*g*) SEPARATE VOWEL SIGNS.

Separate vowel-signs must be employed for the representation of the vowels printed in heavy type :—

eoLian, **eo**Lic, **ae**Rial, **io**date, **io**dine, **io**dize, **io**dous, **io**lite **io**n, **Io**nian, **Io**nic, **io**ta, **OH**io, Lou**i**s**ia**na (upward l),

Ixion, Josiah, Elias, Maria, Siam, Uriah, riot, pious, biology, O'Brien, diameter, dialogue, diaper, diarist, diatonic, enjoyable, fiat, phiaL, vioL, violence, violinist, violation, miasma, liable, liaR, allowance, alliance, royaL, royalty, royalist, roweL, hiatus, quietus, quietude, quietest, quiesce, quiescence, quiescent, impiety, oology, perpetuity, perspicuous, picayune, pioneeR, preoccupy, poetic, pliable, reaction, re-enter, re-echo, re-eligible, satiety, residuum, situate, strenuous, triangle, ebriety, sobriety, duumvir, dueLLo, dubiety, druidical, fatuous, hyena, evacuaTion, fortuitous, duodecimal, fluoRic, lion, notoriety, nocuous, vacuous, newiSH, moiety, Judaism, Jesuit, hypochondriacal, HeweR, hyacinth, gratuity, gratuitous, giant, genii, Genoese, fluidity, avowaL, attenuate, buoyant, boyiSH, casuistic, chaos, chaotic, coercion, coincident, coincidence, co-action, coagulate, co-heiR, co-aid, coevaL, co-adjutant, clairvoyant, cardiacal, co-ordinate, Creole, cyanide, demoniacal, ingenuous, ingenuity, diuRnal, dewy, drawee, employee, employeR, aRduous, aRgueR, annuity, alloyage, voyageı, aguiSH, aloetical, diabolical, prioR, priority.

EXERCISE 150.

Disyllabic Diphthongs (continued).

See Note at the head of Exercise 149.

1. *The* triumphs *of* ingenuity *in the* application *of* scientific th*eo*ries *to* everyday needs *are* often *the* rewards *of* genuine haRd toil *and the* defiance *of an* inclination *to* despair. 2. Success *in these things, as in all* others, *is, as a* ruLe, onLy won by long w*ooi*ng, many r*ea*rrangements *of* id*ea*s, withdr*awa*ls *and* alterations *of* plans, *a* frequent deniaL *of* self, *and*, above *all*, *a* steady loyalty *to the* end *in* view. 3. *All this may* sound disagr*eea*bly pros*ai*c, perhaps, *but it is* r*ea*lly necessary *to* dweLL upon *these* eLementary facts; *to* assert *and* r*ea*ssert *them* again *and* again, *in* oRder *that you may be* encouraged *to* face *the* obstacles *which* beset *you*. 4. *The*

quiet student *in his* study *may be as* truly heroic *as the* heated soldier *in the* turmoil *and* ruSH *of the* fieLd *of* battle. 5. *Have a* worthy ideal, *and* pursue *it* faithfully, though *you may be called an* idle dreameR *and a* fooLish theorist. 6. Picture *to* youRself *how* mankind *would be* situated now if *it* were *not for the* woRk *of* former theorists *and their* coadjutors, *and what a* museum *it would* take *to* hoLd even samples *of the* fruits *of their* labours. 7. Such thoughts *will* encourage *you to* persevere untiL *you* reach *the* goal *of* youR ambition. (210)

EXERCISE 151.

Disyllabic Diphthongs (continued).

See Note at the head of Exercise 149.

1. Gaiety *is* agreeable *and* enjoyable *so* long *as it is* really ingenuous *and not* theatrical; *but the* least betrayal *of the* playeR's aRt *in the* laugh oR smile, *would, in* reality, *be* fataL *to our* genuine enjoyment. 2. *I* do *not, of* course, mean *to* assert *that the* fluent jests *and* mock heroism *of the* stage *are* disagreeable *in all* cases—faR *from it.* 3. *The* playeR *is a* kind *of* purveyoR *of* fun *to his* audience, *and* if *the* article *he* provides *is* really *of a* good class *the* playgoeR *is more* than reimbursed *for his* outlay *in* attending *the* theatre. 4. *But it will be* admitted *that the* Highest perfection *of the* playeR's aRt *is to* make *his* woRds *and* actions appeaR reaL; if *he* succeeds *in this he has* achieved *a* genuine triumph. 5. *But the* gaiety *which* follows *the use of the* breweR's cup *is* hollow *and, as a* ruLe, disagreeable also. 6. *It is* often *a* pooR attempt *to* reinvest some stale joke *with a* new foRm, *and it* onLy ends *in the* betrayal *of the* effect *of the* breweR's fluid. 7. Such jokes *are as* like *to* reaL wit *as the* noise *of a* brayeR *is* like *to* music. 8. Punning *has* been said *to be the* lowest foRm *of* humour; *but,* really, *I* do *not* entiRely agree *with this* idea. 9. *I* am faR *from* tabooing puns, if they *are* good ones. 10. They serve *to* brighten *our* prosaic lives *a* little, *and* rouse *us to a* feeLing *of* buoyancy, *when,* perhaps, we *are*

inclined *to* mope. 11. No, *I should give a* really smart punster freer scope *for the* exercise *of his* gaiety, *with the* proviso *that* cruel puns, OR *those* likely *to* hurt anyone's feelings *should be* avoided. 12. Wit *is* no excuse *for a* superfluous insult. (295)

EXERCISE 152.

Disyllabic Diphthongs (continued).

See Note at the head of Exercise 149.

1. Take Lewis (upward *l*) *Owen*, *the* brewer, *to the* Athenæum, *and* SHOW *him the* portrait *of the* heroic poet, *who* brought *the* reinforcement *to the* garrison *in the* camp. 2. *The* soldiers, *it* appears, kept up *their* gaiety *to the* last, though *their* stock *of* provisions *was at the* lowest. 3 They were stoical enough *to* endure patiently *the* troubles they *could not* remove, *and their* meagre allowance *put their* stoicism *to a* severe test. 4. *It was* disagreeable *to have to* act *on the* defensive, *and* they longed *to be* allowed *to* make *a* bayonet charge *on the* cruel foe. 5. *But the* Colonel, knowing *how* hopeless *it was for* such *a* small force *to* attack *the* enemy, *whose* diabolical cries rang *in his* ears, declined *to* countenance *the* idea. 6. *To him it* looked like *a* betrayal *of the* trust reposed *in him*, *and* though *he* admired *the* loyalty *of the* men, *he* refused *to give an* order *which* simply meant ruin *to them*. 7. *The* Colonel's poetic friend, *who was in the* camp, offered *to* go *for* assistance. 8. *He was an* agreeable youth, *whose* snowy linen *and* slim figure were *more* suitable *to a* theatrical hero than *to* one *who* acted *in the* stern theatre *of* real warfare. 9. *But a* braver OR truer-hearted fellow *could not be* found. 10. *He* managed *to* get through *the* enemy's line, *and* soon re-appeared at *the* head *of a* force strong enough *to* scatter *the* foe. 11. *The* situation *was* speedily changed. 12. *The* besieged soldiers were able *to* reassert *the* power of civilized man, *and* joined *in the* bestowal *of a* lesson *to the* enemy *which* they *are not* likely *to* forget *for a* long time. (276)

EXERCISE 153.

Disyllabic Diphthongs (continued).

See Note at the head of Exercise 149.

Mr. John Murray.

Dear SIR,—We desiRE *to call* youR attention *to the* enclosed price lists *of our* Diamond *A*erated Waters, *and* trust *to* receive youR kind oRder *for a* triaL lot. *You will* find *them* agr*ee*able *in* taste *and* appearance, *and* fr*ee*R than *any* other make *from the* fault *of being put* up *in* awkward bottles. We *may* mention *that* we already supply *the* City Athen*æum and the* chief th*e*atres *with our A*erated Waters, *and that the* demand *for them is* rapidly increasing. They *are an* id*e*al drink *for the* hot weather, while, *as you will see, the* list includes *a* beverage *for the* winter. We *have* added *a* new wing *to our* br*ew*ery, *and in this* we prepare *all the* mineraL waters we supply. We *have* secuRed *the* most modern appliances *which the* ingenuity *of the* engineers *has* been able *to* invent, *and* we *shall be* pleased *to* SHow *you* over *the* works *any* time *you care to give us a call.* YouRS truly, Th*e*obald J*ew*ett *and* Sons. (170)

EXERCISE 154.

Disyllabic Diphthongs (concluded).

See Note at the head of Exercise 149.

Mrs. Br*ew*is.

Dear Madam,—*I* regret *to have to* notify *you that* youR daughter B*e*atrice faiLed *in the* g*e*ographical portion *of the* examination heLd last week. We did *our* best *to give* heR *a* sound th*e*oretical preparation *for the* examination; *but the* extreme g*ai*ety *and* buoyancy *of* heR disposition, *and* heR dislike *to what* SHe thought *a* pros*a*ic Lesson, proved *a* barrier *to* heR success. We *had* hoped *that* heR fluency *of* speech *and* expression might *have* been turned *to* good account *in the* examination, *but* we were disappointed. *I* trust *that on* heR r*e*-appearance *in the* school closer attention *and more* loyalty *to the* ruLes *will* produce better results *in the* future. YouRS faithfully, Maria PoweLL. (117)

EXERCISE 155.

Prefixes.

(*a*) *Con*- EXPRESSED BY A LIGHT DOT :—

*con*cave, *con*ceal, *con*cealed, *con*cede, *con*ceit, *con*ceive, *con*centre, *con*centrate, *con*centrated, *con*centric, *con*ception, *con*ceRn, *con*ceRnedly, *con*cert, *con*certed, *con*certina, *con*cession, *con*ciliate, *con*ciliation, *con*cise, *con*clave, *con*clude, *con*clusion, *con*clusive, *con*coct, *con*coction, *con*cord, *con*cordat, *con*crete, *con*cur, *con*current, *con*cussion, *con*demn, *con*demned, *con*dense, *con*densation, *con*denser, *con*diment, *con*ditionaL, *con*dole, *con*dolence, *con*done, *con*duce, *con*duct, *con*ductor, *con*duit, *con*fabulate, *con*fectioneR, *con*federate, *con*feR, *con*ference, *con*fession, *con*fetti, *con*fide, *con*fider, *con*figuration, *con*fiRmation, *con*fiscate, *con*flagration, *con*flict, *con*found, *con*fraternity, *con*fronted, *con*futation, *con*geal, *con*geniaL, *con*gestion, *con*glomeration, *con*gratulate, *con*gratulator, *con*gregate, *con*gress, *con*gruity, *con*jecture, *con*jecturaL, *con*joint. *con*jugal, *con*jugate, *con*jugation, *con*juRe, *con*nected, *con*nector, *con*nive, *con*noisseuR, *con*nubial, *con*quest, *con*sanguinity, *con*Science, *con*ScienTious, *con*Scious, *con*scription, *con*secrate, *con*secutive, *con*sent, *con*sequence, *con*sequential, *con*sequently, *con*serve, *con*servative, *con*servatory, *con*siderably, *con*sign, *con*signoR, *con*sist, *con*solation, *con*sonant, *con*sort, *con*spicuous, *con*spiRe, *con*spirator, *con*stant, *con*stancy, *con*stitute, *con*stituent, *con*stituency, *con*strain, *con*structor, *con*strue, *con*sultation, *con*sume, *con*summation, *con*tagion, *con*taminate, *con*tango, *con*template, *con*temporaneous, *con*tended, *con*tents, *con*text, *con*tiguous, *con*tinuity, *con*touR, *con*tra, *con*tracted, *con*tradiction, *con*tradistinction, *con*trariety, *con*travene, *con*tributary, *con*trivance, *con*trovert, *con*tumaCious, *con*tused, *con*vaLescent, *con*vention, *con*ventional, *con*verge, *con*versation, *con*vex, *con*voy, *con*viviaL, *con*vocation, *con*vuLse, *con*vuLsion.

(*b*) *Com-* EXPRESSED BY A LIGHT DOT :—

*com*bat, *com*bative, *com*bination, *com*bustion, *com*estible, *com*fit, *com*fortable, *com*forter, *comm*and, *comm*ander, *comm*andment, *comm*emorate, *comm*emorative, *comm*ence, *comm*endable, *comm*endation, *comm*ensurate, *comm*ent, *comm*entator, *comm*ination, *comm*ingle, *comm*ittal, *comm*ute, *comm*ix, *comm*odious, *comm*odity, *comm*on, *comm*oner, *comm*onplace, *comm*onwealth, *comm*une, *comm*union, *comm*unication, *comm*unity, *com*pact, *com*panionable, *com*pany, *com*paRe, *com*parable, *com*parative, *com*passion, *com*passed. *com*patible, *com*pel, *com*pendious, *com*pensate, *com*petent, *com*petitor, *com*pilation, *com*placent, *com*pliment, *com*plex, *com*plexion, *com*plicate, *com*ponent, *com*posite, *com*posure, *com*pound, *com*prehend, *com*prehensive, *com*press, *com*prised, *com*promise, *com*pulsion, *com*pulsory, *com*putable, *com*puter, *com*rade, *com*posedly, *com*port, *com*positor, *com*plicity, *com*pleted, *comm*odoRe, *comm*on-LAW, *comm*ittee.

(*c*) *Con-*, *com-*, *cum-*, OR *cog-* INDICATED BY WRITING THE FOLLOWING SYLLABLE OR WORD UNDER OR CLOSE TO THE CONSONANT PRECEDING *Con-*, ETC. :—

pre*con*ceit, pre*con*ceive, pre*con*ception, pre*con*cert, pre*con*tract, sub*con*tract, sub*comm*ittee, sub*con*Scious, bi*con*jugate, de*com*pose, de*com*position, de*com*pound, de*con*secrate, de*cum*bence, de*cum*bency, de*cum*bent, dis*com*fit, dis*com*fiture, dis*comm*ode, dis*com*pose, dis*com*posure, dis*con*cert, dis*con*certing, dis*conn*ected, dis*conn*ection, dis*con*solate, dis*con*tent, dis*con*tinued, dis*con*tinuance, con*com*itant, con*com*itance, ex*comm*unicate, ex*comm*unication, ac*com*pliSH, ac*comm*odate, ac*comm*odation, ac*comm*odator, ac*com*pany, ac*com*panist, ac*com*panying, ac*com*plice, mis*con*strue, mis*con*ceive, mis*con*ception, mis*con*duct, mis*com*pute, mis*com*putation, mal*con*tent, un*com*fortable, un*comm*on, un*com*plaining, un*com*promising, un*con*ceRn, un*con*ceRnedly, un*con*ditionaL, un*con*geniaL, un*conn*ected, un*con*Sciorrable, un*con*Scious, un*con*trollable, un*con*troLLed, un*con*verted, en*com*pass, en*com*passed, in*com*bustible, in*com*mensurate, in*com*mode, in*com*modious, in*com*municable, in*com*municative, in*com*mutable, in*com*parable, in*com*passionate, in*com*patible, in*com*petent, in*com*petence, in*com*petency, in*com*plete, in*com*posite, in*com*pliant, in*com*prehensible, in*com*pressible, in*com*putable, in*con*ceivable, in*con*clusive, in*con*gruous, in*con*gruity, in*con*sequence, in*con*sequent, in*con*siderable, in*con*sideration, in*con*spicuous, in*con*stant, in*con*stancy, in*con*sumable, in*con*testable, in*con*trovertible, in*con*venient, in*con*venience, in*con*vertible, in*cum*bent, in*cum*bency, non-*com*batant, non*com*missioned, non*com*mittal, non-*con*ductor, non-*con*tent, in*cog*nita, in*cog*nito, ill-*con*ditioned, ill-*con*cealed, well-*con*ducted, well-*con*ditioned, iRRe*con*cilable, re*con*cile, re*con*cilable, re*con*ciliation, re*cog*nize, re*cog*nition, re*cog*nizable, re*cog*nized, re*cog*nizer, re*com*bine, re*com*mence, re*com*mend, re*com*mendation, re*com*mending, re*com*mit, re*com*mitment, re*com*pense, re*com*pose, re*con*dite, re*con*duct, re*con*sider, re*con*struct, re*con*vert, re*con*vey, over*con*fident, over*con*fidence, semi-*con*scious, semi-*com*plete, semi-*con*jugate, cir*cum*duct, cir*cum*ference, cir*cum*flect, cir*cum*fluent, cir*cum*jacent, cir*cum*locution, cir*cum*navigation, cir*cum*scribe, cir*cum*spect, cir*cum*vallation, cir*cum*vent, cir*cum*vention, cir*cum*volition, lo*cum*-tenens. *Be con*stant, *be con*fident, *have con*fidence, *in con*fidence, *in con*clusion, *in con*sequence, *my con*fidence, *shall con*sider, *shall con*tinue, *their con*trol.

(*d*) *Inter-*, *intro-*, OR *enter-* EXPRESSED BY HALF-LENGTH *n*.

Join the prefix in the following words :—

*inter*chain, *inter*change, *inter*changeable, *inter*dependence, *inter*dict, *inter*diction, *inter*feRe, *inter*ference, *inter*fuse, *inter*ject, *inter*jection, *inter*course, *inter*pellate, *inter*pellated, *inter*pellation, *inter*polate, *inter*polation, *inter*pose, *inter*posed, *inter*position, *inter*pret, *inter*preted, *inter*preter, *inter*rogate, *inter*rogation, *inter*rogatory, *inter*rupt, *inter*ruption, *inter*tie, *inter*twine, *inter*vaL, *inter*vention, *inter*viewed, *inter*weave, *inter*woven, *intro*duce, *intro*duced, *intro*duceR, *intro*duction, *intro*ductory.

Disjoin the prefix in the following words :—

*inter*cede, *inter*cedent, *inter*ceder, *inter*cept, *inter*cession, *inter*cessoR, *inter*commune, *inter*communicate, *inter*costal, *inter*lace, *inter*Lacing, *inter*lard, *inter*leave, *inter*line, *inter*lineaR; *inter*link, *inter*lock, *inter*locutor, *inter*lope, *inter*loper, *inter*lude, *inter*marry, *inter*meddle, *inter*mediate, *inter*medial, *inter*mezzo, *inter*mingle, *inter*mittent, *inter*mix, *inter*muraL, *inter*national, *inter*plead, *inter*pleader, *inter*speRse, *inter*stellaR, *inter*stice, *intro*spect, *intro*spection, *intro*spective, *intro*version, *enter*prise, *enter*prising, *enter*tain, *enter*tainer, *enter*tained.

(*e*) *Magna-*, *magne-*, OR *magni-* EXPRESSED BY DISJOINED *m* :—

Magna Charta, *magna*nimity, *magna*nimous, *magna*nimously, *magne*tize, *magne*tized, *magne*tizeR, *magne*tizing, *magne*to-electric, *magne*tometer, *magne*to-motor, *magni*fic, *magni*ficat, *magni*ficent, *magni*ficence, *magni*ficentLy, *magni*fy, *magni*fied, *magni*fieR, *magni*loquent, *magni*loquence, *magni*tude, de*magne*tize, eLectro-*magne*tism.

(*f*) *Self-* EXPRESSED BY DISJOINED CIRCLE *s* :—

self-confident, *self*-conscious, *self*-control, *self*-defence, *self*-deniaL, *self*-esteem, *self*-evident, *self*-help, *self-interest*, *self*-love, *self*-made, *self*-possessed, *self*-possession, *self*-reliance, *self*-reliant, *self*-righteous, *self*-same, *self*-will, *self*-willed, *self*-abasement, *self*-absorbed, *self*-accusation, *self*-adjusting, *self*-applause, *self*-satisfied, *self*-collected, *self*-command, *self*-complacent, *self*-conceit, *self*-condemnation, *self*-congratulation, *self*-contained, *self*-convicted, *self*-deceit, *self*-delusion, *self*-depreciative, *self*-distrust, *self*-exaltation, *self*-existent, *self*-feeder, *self*-flattery, *self*-forgetful, *self*-glorious, *self*-imposed, *self*-indulgence, *self*-mastery, *self*-pity, *self*-praise, *self*-pride, *self*-protection, *self*-registering, *self*-reproach, *self*-sacrifice, *self*-seeker, *self*-support, *self*-taught, *self*-trust, *self*-worsHip.

(*g*) *In-* EXPRESSED BY A SMALL FORWARD HOOK BEFORE THE CIRCLED LETTERS *spr*, *str*, *skr*, AND THE STROKE *h* :—

*in*spiration, *in*spirations, *in*struct, *in*structor, *in*structed, *in*structress, *in*strument, *in*strumentation, *in*scribable, *in*scriber, *in*scriptive, *in*scroll, inscroLLed, *in*habit, *in*habitable, *in*habitants, *in*habiter. *in*haLe, *in*halation, *in*haLed, *in*here, *in*herent, *in*herency, *in*herence, *in*herentLy, *in*herit, *in*herited, *in*heritable, *in*heritance, *in*heritor, *in*heritrix, *in*hibit, *in*hibition, *in*hibited, *in*hibitory, *in*Human, *in*HumanLy, *in*Humanity, *in*Hume, *in*Humation, *in*Humed, *in*Huming.

THE STROKE *n* MUST BE WRITTEN IN WORDS LIKE THE FOLLOWING :—

inseparable, insuperable, insupportable, insuppressible, inscrutable, inhospitable, inhospitably.

(*h*) *Trans-* IS CONTRACTED BY OMITTING THE *n*, WHERE ITS INSERTION WOULD BE AWKWARD, AS IN THE FOLLOWING WORDS :—

*trans*fer, *trans*ference, *trans*fereR, *trans*former, *trans*late, *trans*lation, *trans*lated, *trans*lative, *trans*lator, *trans*marine, *trans*migrate, *trans*migration, *trans*mission, *trans*mit, *trans*mittance, *trans*mitter, *trans*mute, *trans*mutation, *trans*parent, *trans*pire, *trans*plant, *trans*port, *trans*pose, *trans*position, *trans*portation, *trans*portable.

(*i*) *Il-*, *im-*, *in-*, *un-*.

Repeat the *l*, *m*, or *n* in negative words where these prefixes are followed by the same consonant, as in the following words :—

*ill*audable, *ill*egal, *ill*egible, *ill*egibly, *ill*iberal, *ill*icit, *ill*iterate, *ill*egitimate, *imm*aculate, *imma*terial, *imm*atuRe, *imm*easurable, *imm*iscible, *imm*obile, *imm*oderate, *imm*oral, *imm*ortaL, *imm*ovable, *imm*utable, *inn*avigable, *inn*ocuous, *inn*oXious, *inn*umerable, *inn*utrition, *unn*amed, *unkn*own, *unn*ecessary, *unn*eighborly, *unn*erve, *unn*oticed, *unn*oted. EXCEPTIONS :—iLLimited, iLLimitable.

(*j*) *Ir*-. REPEAT THE FIRST *r* IN THE FOLLOWING WORDS :—

*irr*adiate, *irr*adiated, *irr*adiance, *irr*adiation, *irr*ational, *irr*eclaimable, *irr*edeemable, *irr*educible, *irr*efragable, *irre*futable.

EXERCISE 156.

Prefixes (continued).

In this Exercise, and in Exercises 157 to 160 inclusive, the hyphen before *con*-, *com*-, *cum*-, or *cog*-, indicates that the prefix should be expressed as shown in par. (c), page 178.

1. Try *to* retain youR -*com*posure *in the* face *of con*tradiction. 2. *He who* exhibits *con*fusion *and* dis-*com*posure at *the* slightest mis-*con*struction *of his* words *is self-con*demned *as* unfitted *to* ruLe others. 3. *It is* in-*con*ceivable *that anyone should be* -*com*petent *to* direct others *who is* in-*com*petent *to con*trol *his* own feeLings. 4. *There is con*siderable foRce *in the* saying *that an* Ambassador *should al*ways wear spectacles, take snuff, *and*, at *an inter*view, stand *with his* back *to a* window. 5. *The* reader *may not concur in these* -*con*clusions at *first ; but* re-*con*sideration *will* -*con*vince *him that their* apparent in-*con*gruity *may be* re-*con*ciled. 6. *I* do *not* propose *to inter*pose *with an inter*pretation *of the* saying. 7. *That would inter*feRe *with my* purpose, *which is to enter*tain *as well as in*struct *the* student. 8. Besides, *it is self*-evident *that he* must learn *to be self*-reliant, *and* if *he* does *not* trust *to self*-help *in a* small matter like *this, how can he* hope *to* succeed *in a* case where *the* task *is magni*fied ? 9. If *he has in*herited *a* love *for* investigation, *he will have* little trouble *in* answering *any inter*rogation *as to the* meaning *of the* saying *I have inter*woven heRe. 10. If *he has not in*herited such *a* love then *I would re*-*com*mend *him to* cultivate *it* now, lest *his* mental horizon *be* cir-*cum*scribed *in an* un-*com*mon measure. (224)

EXERCISE 157.

Prefixes (continued).

See Note at the head of Exercise 156.

1. *It is con*sidered *that more* brain foRce *is* used *in the* effort *to* render *a* new impression permanent *and self*-sustaining than *for any* other kind *of* mental exercise. 2. *So that those who* by *the* exercise *of a con*siderable amount *of self*-deniaL *and self-con*trol, ac-*com*plisн *the self*-imposed task *of* fixing *a* good many new ideas *so* -*com*pleteLy *in their* minds *that* they *are inter*woven *in*to *their* oRdinary affaiRs *of* life, *have* used up *an* amount *of* energy *which it is* scaRcely possible *to magni*fy. 3. Every *in*structor knows *that there are* times *when the* pupil appeaRs *to be* unable *to con*centrate *his* attention upon *an* explanation oR *an inter*pretation *of a* fact oR *a* theory, *and that* at such times *all* efforts *to com*municate new notions *are* wasted. 4. *It is* wiser *to* dis-*con*tinue *the* Lesson *in* such *a* case, *and* re-*com*mence *when the* pupil's mind *has* recovered *its* poweR by *an inter*vaL *of* rest. 5. *The* attempt *to com*pel *a* tiRed brain *to* woRk, just *to* ac-*com*modate *the con*venience *of the* teacher *is an inter*ference *with natural* laws *which will be* resented. 6. Yet *I con*sider *it a* serious eRRoR *to inter*rupt one's studies *for a* lengthened *inter*vaL, *and I should not* re-*com*mend *a com*plete dis-*con*tinuance *of* woRk *for more* than *a* few weeks. 7. We *should con*tinue *con*sistentLy *the* course we *have in*scribed *in our* scheme *of* Lessons. (228)

EXERCISE 158.

Prefixes (continued).

See Note at the head of Exercise 156.

1. "*Con*sols" *is a con*traction -*com*monly employed *to con*vey *the com*plete meaning *of the* term "*Con*solidated Annuities." 2. *The* loans made at various times *to the* State *con*stitute *the* National Debt. 3. *These* loans were -*con*solidated *for* -*con*venience *in*to one -*com*mon loan. 4. Since

*the con*version OR *-con*solidation *the* fund *has* been known by *the con*cise term *of* "*Con*sols." 5. *An* in-*com*petent speaker soon loses *his composure and self-con*trol *in the* presence *of a con*siderable *-com*pany, *and in his* dis-*com*posure makes statements *which may* easily *be* mis-*con*strued. 6. *His* sentences grow *more* dis-*con*nected *and* in-*com*plete *the* longer *he con*tinues *to* talk, *and* often enough *he is compe*LLed *in* hopeless -*con*fusion, *to* dis-*con*tinue *his* speech *and* lapse *in*to silence. 7. OnLy *-con*tinued perseverance *will* enable such *a* person *to* conquer *his* weakness. 8. *It is* fooLish *to enter*tain *the* idea *that it is* in-*cum*bent upon one *to inter*feRe OR *inter*pose *in* every dispute one witnesses. 9. *A* man *may be* treated *as an inter*loper *for inter*meddling *in a* quaRRel between persons unknown *to him, and may* possibly *be* unfortunate enough *to inter*cept *and* receive *a* blow intended *for* another. 10. *It is* good *to be magnan*imous ; *but* we *should not magni*fy *our* duty, OR lose *our self*-possession. 11. *It has* been noticed *that* some persons appeaR *to have an in*herent desiRe *to in*struct everybody they meet. 12. *A* musical *in*strument ; *an in*scribed tablet ; *an in*scroLLed message—*al*most *any* article OR *any* incident *is* enough *to* serve *as in*spiration *to them, and* at once they *-commence to in*struct *the com*pany upon *the subject.* 13. *It is a* disagreeable habit, *and should be* conquered. (260)

EXERCISE 159.

Prefixes (continued).

See Note at the head of Exercise 156.

*Mr. Con*stantine Connell.

Dear SiR,—*I have care*fully*-con*sidered *the* proposal *you* made at *the* recent *-con*ference *in* Conway, *and* while *I* gratefully re-*cog*nise youR *-con*siderate *and* even *magnan*imous tone at *the inter*view, *I have -con*cluded *not to enter*tain *the* idea further. *There are what I con*sider *in*herent defects *in the* proposed *enter*prise *which* forbid *my in*scribing *my* name *on the* list *of* shareholders *in the company*. *I* fear *it will not be the ins*trument *of* profit *which you* anticipate. *I* am -*con*scious *of all* your kindness *towards me in* -*con*nection *with the* scheme *you have intro*duced, *and I* desire *to* express *my* gratitude *for the* hospitable reception *you* gave *me*. *I can but* repeat *my* appreciation *of the great self-con*trol *you* exhibited *in* spite *of the interr*uptions *to which you* were exposed *in the* course *of* your speech at *the con*ference. Yours faithfully, Conrad Connor. (147)

EXERCISE 160.

Prefixes (concluded).

See Note at the head of Exercise 156.

Messrs. *Con*greve *and* Compton.

Dear Sirs, — Referring *to our inter*view *with* your *Mr*. Magnus *on the* proposal *to intro*duce *in*to *our* works *the* new *self*-feeding *and self-con*trolling spool winder, *will you* kindly *for*ward *us a* detailed statement *of the* benefits claimed *from the use of the* patent ? *It* occurred *to us that these* were *magni*fied at *the inter*view ; *but* we *are* open *to be* -*con*vinced *of the* utility *of* your invention, *and* we *shall be* pleased *to in*struct *our* manager *to give it a* trial. If *the* benefits *are so self*-evident *as Mr*. Magnus appeared *to think*, we *shall* adopt *the* patent. *Is the* attachment easily dis-*con*nected *when it has* ac-*com*plished *its* purpose, *and can the* worker readily ac-*commo*date herself *to the use of the in*strument ? Yours faithfully, Deacon *and* Cummings. (134)

EXERCISE 161.

Suffixes.

In this Exercise, and in Exercises 162 to 166 inclusive, the hyphen indicates that the suffix should be disjoined.

(*a*) -*ing* EXPRESSED BY THE STROKE *ng* :—

1 bay*ing*, bray*ing*, sobb*ing*, enabl*ing*, disabl*ing*, aid*ing*,

dying, drying, deriding, residing, presiding, writhing, wreathing, saying, sighing, sawing, sowing, easing, using, throwing, sHowing, usHering, pusHing, casHing, crasHing, rusHing, wasHing, dashing, polishing, aiming, seeming, steaming, swimming, consuming, presuming, assuming, resuming, mowing, murmuring, booming, deeming, sHamming, naming, owning, awning, sinning, staining, swooning, designing, chastening, glistening, christening, fastening, knowing, singing, swinging, stinging, clinging, winging, aiLing, sailing, swelling, stealing, wailing, whiling, lying, laying, lowing, swallowing, following, bellowing, faiLing, reviLing, scaLing, queLLing, yeLLing, ruLing, rowing, rueing, borrowing, sorrowing, weighing, swaying, roaring, rearing, wailing, whiling, stamping, swamping, basing, Leasing, dozing, chasing, rejoicing, casing, kissing, creasing, increasing, grazing, glossing, facing, freezing, fleecing, voicing, revising, conversing, ceasing, unceasing, saucing, massing, missing, promising, amusing, amazing, grimacing, noosing, commencing, snoozing, recognizing, mincing, evincing, Lacing, Loosing, Lessing, aRousing, aRising, eRasing, pieRcing, racing, rising, rousing, terrorizing, perusing, carousing, housing, quizzing, acquiescing, whistling, embossing, whizzing; placing, pressing, bracing, blazing, tracing, distressing, addressing, jesting, adjusting, digesting, encasing, taxing, fixing, vexing, annexing, cruising, closing, enclosing, disclosing, glazing, disguising, confusing, diffusing, refusing, suffusing, dusting, testing, protesting, pining, spraining, puffing, paving, Browning, rebuffing, tanning, straining, striving, diving, dining, dawning, chafing, chaffing, canning, cleaning, skinning, crowning, sickening, thickening, beginning, groaning, gleaning, bargaining, fanning, feigning, frowning, convening, thinning, assigning, moaning, manning, mining, summoning, eaRning, disceRning, conceRning, quickening, impugning; panting, sprinting, bending, tending, stranding, drifting, Dinting, counting, discounting, seconding, squinting, granting, grounding, fainting, finding, founding, front*ing*, flaunt*ing*, vaunt*ing*, vent*ing*, invent*ing*, mount*ing*, cement*ing*, lament*ing*, demand*ing*, remand*ing*, impound*ing*; pander*ing*, ponder*ing*, splinter*ing*, banter*ing*, tender*ing*, canter*ing*, encounter*ing*, squander*ing*, thunder*ing*, SHatter*ing*, meander*ing*, enter*ing*, center*ing*, saunter*ing*, alter*ing*, loiter*ing*, swelter*ing*, bewilder*ing*, falter*ing*, smoulder*ing*, scent*ing*, resent*ing*, dissent*ing*, consent*ing*, nett*ing*, personat*ing*, oust*ing*, hast*ing*, SHout*ing*, SHoot*ing*, wait*ing*, hat*ing*, heat*ing*, part*ing*, dart*ing*, smart*ing*, concert*ing*, sort*ing*, distort*ing*, assort*ing*, fashion*ing*, provision*ing*, motion*ing*.

(*b*) -*ing* EXPRESSED BY A LIGHT DOT :—

pay*ing*, pray*ing*, play*ing*, tapp*ing*, dipp*ing*, chipp*ing*, cop*ing*, grop*ing*, mop*ing*, nipp*ing*, lapp*ing*, ripp*ing*, weep*ing*, hopp*ing*, eat*ing*, pity*ing*, beat*ing*, dat*ing*, doat*ing*, rat*ing*, try*ing*, stray*ing*, stay*ing*, etch*ing*, pitch*ing*, beach*ing*, teach*ing*, catch*ing*, snatch*ing*, reach*ing*, bewitch*ing*, edg*ing*, pag*ing*, budg*ing*, dodg*ing*, gaug*ing*, converg*ing*, wag*ing*, caw*ing*, peck*ing*, break*ing*, talk*ing*, decoy*ing*, check*ing*, jok*ing*, smok*ing*, sneak*ing*, rak*ing*, look*ing*, Hack*ing*, grow*ing*, begg*ing*, dragg*ing*, smuggl*ing*, ragg*ing*, lagg*ing*, fry*ing*, fray*ing*, flow*ing*, flee*ing*, vy*ing*, purvey*ing*, survey*ing*, convey*ing*, thaw*ing*, aiR*ing*, soaR*ing*, steeR*ing*, sweaR*ing*, paR*ing*, beaR*ing*, teaR*ing*, daR*ing*, jeeR*ing*, injuR*ing*, conjuR*ing*, scaR*ing*, secuR*ing*, squaR*ing*, feaR*ing*, veeR*ing*, smeaR*ing*, snoR*ing*, loweR*ing*, Hoe*ing*, Hay*ing*; plott*ing*, plat*ing*, budd*ing*, brood*ing*, upbraid*ing*, celebrat*ing*, treat*ing*, prostrat*ing*, illustrat*ing*, devastat*ing*, rotat*ing*, frustrat*ing*, doubt*ing*, dread*ing*, radiat*ing*, inundat*ing*, credit*ing*, chatt*ing*, cheat*ing*, fidget*ing*, cutt*ing*, skat*ing*, dissect*ing*, transact*ing*, attract*ing*, detract*ing*, protract*ing*, secret*ing*, grad*ing*, degrad*ing*, emigrat*ing*, migrat*ing*, fight*ing*, flitt*ing*, float*ing*, frett*ing*, avoid*ing*, evad*ing*, matt*ing*, permitt*ing*, promot*ing*, consummat*ing*, lett*ing*, light*ing*, pelt*ing*, bolt*ing*, tilt*ing*, delight*ing*, smelt*ing*, welt*ing*, emulat*ing*, SHiRt*ing*, quitt*ing*, squatt*ing*; poRter*ing*, boRder*ing*, chaRter*ing*, flutter*ing*, flatter*ing*, fritter*ing*.

mutter*ing*, smother*ing*, oRder*ing*, disoRder*ing*, render*ing*, surrender*ing*, wander*ing*, wonder*ing*, winter*ing*, hinder*ing*; chant*ing*, enchant*ing*, graft*ing*, shunt*ing*, anoint*ing*, land*ing*, lend*ing*, rend*ing*, round*ing*, surround*ing*, raft*ing*, want*ing*, wend*ing*, wound*ing*, wind*ing*, unwind*ing*, waft*ing*, hunt*ing*, haunt*ing*; cough*ing*, scoff*ing*, crav*ing*, grav*ing*, engrav*ing*, griev*ing*, rav*ing*, rov*ing*, reef*ing*, wav*ing*, weav*ing*, serv*ing*, preserv*ing*, observ*ing*, deserv*ing*, reserv*ing*, conserv*ing*, starv*ing*, swerv*ing*, spurn*ing*, burn*ing*, turn*ing*, adorn*ing*, churn*ing*, adjourn*ing*, scorn*ing*, morn*ing*, mourn*ing*, learn*ing*, lean*ing*, lin*ing*, malign*ing*, runn*ing*, rain*ing*, winn*ing*, wan*ing*, whin*ing*, yawn*ing*, yearn*ing*, heav*ing*, behav*ing*, sHin*ing*, ensHrin*ing*, enthron*ing*, caution*ing*, apportion*ing*; pranc*ing*, pounc*ing*, dispens*ing*, bronz*ing*, bounc*ing*, entranc*ing*, distanc*ing*, condens*ing*, chanc*ing*, enscons*ing*, cleans*ing*, rins*ing*, winc*ing*, silenc*ing*, glanc*ing*; past*ing*, post*ing*, plaster*ing*, bolster*ing*, coast*ing*, cast*ing*, fast*ing*, fluster*ing*, master*ing*, muster*ing*, cluster*ing*, rest*ing*, roost*ing*, request*ing*, aRRest*ing*, buRst*ing*, wast*ing*.

(*c*) *-ings* EXPRESSED BY A LIGHT DASH :—

chipp*ings*, clipp*ings*, scrap*ings*, sweep*ings*, etch*ings*, cutt*ings*, fitt*ings*, meet*ings*, paR*ings*, boR*ings*, beaR*ings*, winn*ings*, burn*ings*, engrav*ings*, turn*ings*, morn*ings*, learn*ing's*, yearn*ings*, wander*ings*, render*ings*, digg*ings*, carv*ings*, misgiv*ings*, liv*ings*, leav*ings*, twist*ings*, cast*ings*, post*ings*, dropp*ings*, dripp*ings*, sitt*ings*, search*ings*, tak*ings*, mooR*ings*, wonder*ings*, twitch*ings*, plott*ings*, wind*ings*, mak*ings*.

(*d*) *-ality*, *-ility*, *-arity*, ETC., INDICATED BY DISJOINING THE PRECEDING STROKE.

The hyphen indicates that the following stroke is to be disjoined :—

absorba-*bility*, accepta-*bility*, acquiRa-b*ility*, adapta-b*ility*, addi-b*ility*, admira-b*ility*, admi-r*alty*, admissi-b*ility*, advisa-b*ility*, affa-b*ility*, effecti-b*ility*, agreea-b*ility*, aLiena-b*ility*, altera-b*ility*, amena-b*ility*, amia-b*ility*, amica-b*ility*, associa-b*ility*, attaina-b*ility*, attracta-b*ility*, audi-b*ility*, avaiLa-b*ility*, bar-b*arity*, capa-b*ility*, incapa-b*ility*, car-n*ality*, chargea-b*ility*, combusti-b*ility*, commensura-b*ility*, communica-b*ility*, commuta-b*ility*, compati-b*ility*, compressi-b*ility*, condensa-b*ility*, conduci-b*ility*, conducti-b*ility*, contracti-b*ility*, contrac-t*ility*, convi-v*iality*, converti-b*ility*, corrigi-b*ility*, corrupti-b*ility*, culpa-b*ility*, credi-b*ility*, crimi-n*ality*, sta-b*ility*, insta-b*ility*, dura-b*ility*, lia-b*ility*, excita-b*ility*, hospi-t*ality*, foR-m*ality*, princi-p*ality*, bru-t*ality*, porta-b*ility*, mo-b*ility*, no-b*ility*, ina-b*ility*, disa-b*ility*, popu-l*arity*, fa-t*ality*, fu-t*ility*, mi-n*orities*. feasi-b*ility*, fusi-b*ility*, vi-t*ality*, deduci-b*ility*, defensi-b*ility*, demisa-b*ility*, desira-b*ility*, destructi-b*ility*, diffusi-b*ility*, digesti-b*ility*, distensi-b*ility*, dissimi-l*arity*, divisi-b*ility*, duc-t*ility*, eligi-b*ility*, equa-b*ility*, eRec-t*ility*, exchangea-b*ility*, expansi-b*ility*, extensi-b*ility*, falli-b*ility*, fermenta-b*ility*, fi-n*ality*, inflamma-b*ility*, flexi-b*ility*, foRmida-b*ility*, fra-g*ility*, fria-b*ility*, fri-v*olity*, gene-r*ality*, gulli-b*ility*, hos-t*ility*, illegi-b*ility*, legi-b*ility*, illi-ber*ality*, li-ber*ality*, ille-g*ality*, le-g*ality*, imita-b*ility*, immisci-b*ility*, immo-b*ility*, immor-t*ality*, immova-b*ility*, muta-b*ility*, immuta-b*ility*, impalpa-b*ility*, imparti-b*ility*, impassi-b*ility*, impecca-b*ility*, impenetra-b*ility*, implaca-b*ility*, impondera-b*ility*, impossi-b*ility*, impregna-b*ility*, inaudi-b*ility*, incompressi-b*ility*, inconverti-b*ility*, indeli-b*ility*, indissolu-b*ility*, ineRRa-b*ility*, infalli-b*ility*, infoR-m*ality*, inhospi-t*ality*, inscruta-b*ility*, insatia-b*ility*, insepara-b*ility*, insolu-b*ility*, insupera-b*ility*, invaria-b*ility*, invinci-b*ility*, jocu-l*arity*, mallea-b*ility*, modifia-b*ility*, mor-t*ality*, naviga-b*ility*, nota-b*ility*, ostensi-b*ility*, palpa-b*ility*, penetra-b*ility*, perfecti-b*ility*, permissi-b*ility*, plu-r*ality*, practi-c*ality*, rata-b*ility*, recepti-b*ility*, remova-b*ility*, repeala-b*ility*, resisti-b*ility*, revoca-b*ility*, risi-b*ility*, sana-b*ility*, separa-b*ility*, ser-v*ility*, seve-r*alty*, simi-l*arity*, singu-l*arity*, angu-l*arity*, solva-b*ility*, suscepti-b*ility*, tangi-b*ility*, taxa-b*ility*, tena-b*ility*, tensi-b*ility*, tracta-b*ility*, transmissi-b*ility*, transporta-b*ility*, volu-b*ility*, vendi-b*ility*, vulnera-b*ility*, regu-l*arity*, iRRegu-l*arity*, juven*ility*, gen-t*ility*.

(*e*) *-ment* EXPRESSED BY *nt* :—

announce*ment*, pronounce*ment*, denounce*ment*, advance*ment*, ascertain*ment*, assign*ment*, confine*ment*, consign*ment*, commence*ment*, refine*ment*, pave*ment*, imprison*ment*, deface*ment*, efface*ment*, resent*ment*, aLign*ment*, achieve*ment*, enlighten*ment*, abandon*ment*, enchant*ment*, enList*ment*, prefer*ment*, reappoint*ment*, reassign*ment*, accompani*ment*.

(*f*) *-mental* OR *-mentality* EXPRESSED BY DISJOINED *ment* :—

instru-*mental*, instru-*mentality*, funda-*mental*, regi-*mental*, regi-*mentals*, docu-*mental*, recre-*mental*, senti-*mental*, senti*mentality*, rudi-*mental*, sacra-*mental*, monu-*mental*, excre*mental*, detri-*mental*, supple-*mental*, experi-*mental*, depart*mental*.

(g) *-ly* EXPRESSED BY DISJOINED *l* :—

astute-*ly*, distant-*ly*, bland-*ly*, blind-*ly*, blunt-*ly*, cogent-*ly*, diffident-*ly*, friend-*ly*, unfriend-*ly*, coincident-*ly*, competent-*ly*, incompetent-*ly*, confident-*ly*, constant-*ly*, inconstant-*ly*, instant-*ly*, persistent-*ly*, compliant-*ly*, joint-*ly*, conjoint-*ly*, contingent-*ly*, flippant-ly, obedient-*ly*, disobedient-*ly*, diligent-*ly*, indulgent-*ly*, urgent-*ly*, impudent-*ly*, imprudent-*ly*, improvident-*ly*, provident-*ly*, even-*ly*, uneven-*ly*, vain-*ly*, ancient-*ly*, expectant-*ly*, latent-*ly*, fervent-*ly*, fond-*ly*, faint-*ly*, impotent-*ly*, inadvertent-*ly*, triumphant-*ly*, incipient-*ly*, inconsistent-*ly*, indoLent-*ly*, insoLent-*ly*, antecedent-*ly*, negligent-*ly*, potent-*ly*, precedent-*ly*, prudent-*ly*, radiant-*ly*, stringent-*ly*, sloven-*ly*, tender-*ly*, steRn*l*-*y*.

(*h*) *-ship* EXPRESSED BY *sh* :—

rector-*ship*, advocate-*ship*, abbot-*ship*, augur-*ship*, author-*ship*, comrade-*ship*, captain-*ship*, censor-*ship*, chairman-*ship*, chanceLLor-*ship*, chaplain-*ship*, chieftain-*ship*, champion-*ship*, citizen-*ship*, clan-*ship*, cleRk-*ship*, collector-*ship*, guardian-*ship*, commander-*ship*, companion-*ship*, controlleR-*ship*, counseLLor-*ship*, court-*ship*, trans-*ship*, lady-*ship*, *lord-ship*, haRd-*ships*, head-*ship*, town-*ship*, stewaRd-*ship*, apprentice-*ship*, schoLar-*ship*, deacon-*ship*, dictator-*ship*, disciple-*ship*, draftsman-*ship*, editoR-*ship*, envoy-*ship*, librarian-*ship*, Messiah-*ship*, mid-*ship*, penman*ship*, precentor*ship*, premieR-*ship*, proconsuL-*ship*, professor-*ship*, seaman*ship*, squiRe-*ship*, survivor-*ship*, trustee-*ship*, ward-*ship*, associate-*ship*, heiR-*ship*, acquaintance-*ship*.

(*i*) *-lessness* EXPRESSED BY DISJOINED *ls* :—

aRt-*lessness*, beaRd-*lessness*, blame-*lessness*, bound-*lessness*, *care-lessness*, cheer-*lessness*, hope-*lessness*, grace-*lessness*, sleep-*lessness*, taste-*lessness*, faith-*lessness*, daunt-*lessness*, dread-*lessness*, fault-*lessness*, feaR-*lessness*, friend-*lessness*, fruit-*lessness*, ground-*lessness*, guile-*lessness*, haRm-*lessness*, heaRt-*lessness*, heed-*lessness*, joy-*lessness*, law-*lessness*, list-*lessness*, life-*lessness*, piti-*lessness*, prayeR-*lessness*, sHame-*lessness*, sight-*lessness*, stain-*lessness*, thought-*lessness*, tiRe-*lessness*, *use-lessness*, worth-*lessness*, reck-*lessness*.

(*j*) *-fulness* EXPRESSED BY DISJOINED *fs* :—

aRt-*fulness*, bale-*fulness*, bane-*fulness*, basH-*fulness*, bliss-*fulness*, boast-*fulness*, bounti-*fulness*, *care-fulness*, cheer-*fulness*, hope-*fulness*, grace-*fulness*, rest-*fulness*, youth-*fulness*, peace-*fulness*, diRe-*fulness*, dole-*fulness*, duti-*fulness*, faith-*fulness*, forget-*fulness*, fright-*fulness*, fruit-*fulness*, guile-*fulness*, joy-*fulness*, haRm-*fulness*, health-*fulness*, huRt-*fulness*, law-*fulness*, unLaw-*fulness*, mirth-*fulness*, play-*fulness*, plenti-*fulness*, prayeR-*fulness*, right-*fulness*, sin-*fulness*, skiL-*fulness*, sloth-*fulness*, spite-*fulness*, sport-*fulness*, thought-*fulness*, trust-*fulness*, *use-fulness*.

EXERCISE 162.

Suffixes (continued).

See Note at the head of Exercise 161.

1. *An* aiR *of* cheer-*fulness should be* cultivated by *all who*

labour amidst *the* absorbing, bothering, wearing ruSH *of* business life. 2. *It will* help *them to* beaR *more* patientLy *the* tantaliz*ing*, annoy*ing* troubles *that* aRise *from the* vul-*garity*, hos-*tility*, OR excita-*bility of those* they meet *in* business. 3. *Not* onLy *so, but it will* add *very* considerably *to their* grace-*fulness of* personality, *and* impart *an* aiR *of* perenniaL youth-*fulness and* hope-*fulness that* must preserve *them from* even *an* appearance *of* incivility *to any*one. 4. Thus, *their* popu-*larity will be* increased, *and* they *will* acquiRe *a* name *for* amia-*bility that will* assuRedly assist *them in* extending *and* solidify-*ing their* business connections. 5. *Any*one *who has an* extensive acquaintance-*ship* must know one OR *more* persons *who have an* habitual aiR *of* hope-*lessness*, help-*lessness and* list-*lessness, and who are* constant-*ly* whin-*ing* about some *more* OR less imaginary haRd-*ships which* they *are called* upon *to* enduRe. 6. They do *not*, apparently, realise *how* detri-*mental* such senti-*mental* nonsense must *be to their* health. OR *that it is* likely *to* induce feeLings *of* resent*ment in* persons *of* refine*ment and* enlighten*ment*. 7. *A* friend-*ly* warn-*ing*, *with* such *a* statement *of these* facts *as would put the* case cogent-*ly* before *them*, might *be* successfuL *in* altering such silly ways. (205)

EXERCISE 163.

Suffixes (continued).

See Note at the head of Exercise 161.

1. *A great* authority *on the* aRt *of* teach-*ing* says *that a* moderate exhilaration *and* cheer-*fulness* grow-*ing out of the* act *of* learn-*ing is* certainLy *the* most geniaL *and the* most effectual means *of* cementing *the* unions *that* we desiRe *to* foRm *in the* mind. 2. *This, he* says, *is* meant *when* we refer *to the* schoLar *as hav-ing a* taste *for his* pursuit, *hav-ing a* heaRt *in it*, learn-*ing with* love. 3. *The* fact *is* perfectly *well* known, *he* adds; *the* eRROR, *in* connection *with it*, lies *in* dictat-*ing* OR enjoin-*ing this* state *of* mind *on* everybody *in* every situaTion,

as if *it could be* commanded by *a* wisH. 4. *There are* some teachers, though *not a* ma-*jority*, *who* possess *the* knack *of* inspiR-*ing their* pupils *with this* cheer-*fulness which is so* helpful *to them*. 5. *The* affa-b*ility and* amia-b*ility of these* teachers *has not* onLy *the* effect *of* keep-*ing the* pupils bright *and* cheerful, *but it* helps *to* maintain *them in a* proper state *of* docility *and* attention. 6. Such instructors *have* no need *to* address *a* schoLar fieRcely oR violently. 7. They *can* keep *a* class diligent-*ly and* constant-*ly* occupied, *and* yet *the* woRk proceeds pleasantLy *and* smoothly *the* whole time, *from the* commence*ment to the* end *of the* Lesson. 8. Everyone feeLs *that the* teacher *is* keenly desirous *for the* advance*ment of his* pupils, *and there is* no resent*ment* oR jealousy at *the* success *of any* pupil *in the* class. 9. *The* leader-*ship* oR guardian-*ship of* such *a* teacher *may be* instru-*mental in the* promotion *of* good citizen*ship and* good fellowship *in those* entrusted *to his care*. (262)

EXERCISE 164.

Suffixes (continued).

See Note at the head of Exercise 161.

1. *A* small mi-n*ority of* people, *hav-ing a* rare credi-b*ility*, *think there is a* fa-t*ality in all things*, *and that it is an* impossi-b*ility that* events *should* occur otherwise than *as* they do. 2. *This* theory, *it should be* said, does *not* affect *their* attracta-b*ility*, hospi-t*ality*, oR jocu-l*arity*, *and their* socia-b*ility is* just *as great as that of the* ma-j*ority of those who cannot see the* accepta-b*ility of* fatalism. 3. *It is* positively provok-*ing to a* schoLarly man *to see the* amaz*ing* facility *with which* many men *will* commence *what* they impudent-*ly call the* study *of* some department *of* literature, *and* then *as* suddenLy break *it* off *to* take up some other fad. 4. FaR *from* regard-*ing this* flitt-*ing* about *as a* sign *of* inteLLectuaL refine*ment* oR versatility, *the* reaL student looks upon *it as a* mark *of* imbecility, a *mere* senti-*mentality* oR aimless wander-*ing*, highly detri-*mental*

*to any*one eager *to* learn. 5. *He who* aspires *to a* leader-*ship in the* worLd must woRk haRd *from the* commence*ment*, *and be* prepaRed *for the* abandon*ment of* fri-v*olity*, insincerity, *and* undue convi-v*iality*, indulgence *in which would* make advance*ment an* impossi-b*ility for him*. 6. *All* tendency *to* heed-*lessness* oR sloth-*fulness* must *be* steRn-*ly* checked, *and the* course *as* marked *out* must *be* pursued diligent-*ly and* hopefully, *and with* confidence *in the* right-*fulness of the* cause *in which he is* woRk-*ing and* studying. (223)

EXERCISE 165.

Suffixes (continued).

See Note at the head of Exercise 161.

MessRs. Cann*ing and* Cunn*ing*ham.

Dear SiRs,—*Hav-ing* heaRd *that you are in* want *of an* enterpris*ing* agent *for* youR trac*ing* papers *and* other goods. *I* beg *to* offer *you my* services. *I have* some exceedingLy strong connections *in the* print*ing and* engineer*ing* businesses *in this* locality, *being* well known *to the* ma-j*ority of the* best fiRms, *and I think that* through *my* acquaintance-*ship I could* readily introduce youR specialities *in*to *the* fiRms *I call* upon. *I* am regarded *as a* man *of* considerable origi-n*ality in my* conduct *of* business matters, *and I can give you* ample evidence *as to my* ability, help-*fulness*, *and the* stand*ing I have in the* district. *Of* course, *I should be* will*ing to give you a* fi-d*elity* guarantee *to any* amount (at youR expense), *and I shall be* glad *to* enter *in*to *an* experi-*mental* aRRangement *with you*, if *you* prefer *it*. *I may* add *that I have* been instru-*mental in* introduc*ing* many no-v*elties in*to *this* neighborhood, *and I* confident-*ly* assert *that I should be* just *as* successfuL *with* youR goods. *I shall be happy to* discuss terms *with you*. Await*ing* youR kind reply, *I* am, YouRs faithfully, ALexander Mottram. (193)

EXERCISE 166.

Suffixes (concluded).

See Note at the head of Exercise 161.

Mr. Thomas SelleR.

Dear SiR,—We *have* youR letter contain*ing* various oRders *and* we *are* attend*ing to these immediately.* Referr*ing to the* oRder *from Mr.* John Bailey, while we *are* faR *from* doubt-*ing this* man's capa-b*ility of* pay-*ing for the* goods, we *should* feeL *more* satisfied if *you would* make further inquiry *as to his* credi-b*ility and* business reputation. *It is our* funda*mental* ruLe *not to* execute *first* oRders *without* perfectly good reports *as to the* sta-b*ility of the* customeR. We do *not* mean *to* impute *care-lessness to you, but you will* permit *us to* remind *you that the* guardian-*ship of our interests, as* faR *as* youR oRders *are* conceRned, *is* entrusted *to you, and* we look *to you not to* faLL *in*to list-*lessness in this* regard *as* we might *be* landed *in*to *a* serious position *in* consequence. YouR expenses *have* been grow-*ing* lately, *and* we venture *to* suggest *that you* might curtail youR hospi-t*ality to* some extent. YouRs truly, Crosby *and* Mortimer. (163)

EXERCISE 167.

Contractions.

 *probable-bly-ility,*  *improbable-ly-ility,*  *republican,*

 *publication,*  *remarkable-y,*  *represent-ed,*

 *representation,*  *practice-d-cal-ly,*  *practicable,*

 *impracticable,*  *phonographer,*  *phonographic,*

 *instruction,*  *parliament-ary.*

Dear SiR,—We *have* youR letter *of yesterday,* offering *to represent us in the* district *in which you* reside, *but as* we *are*

already *represented* by *Mr.* Brown *of* Gateshead, *who has* been *our representative for* some time, youR suggestion *is* at present *impracticable. It is probable that* we *shall* cut up *the* district *in a* while, *and* if *you are* then open *to* take *the* position we *should probably* appoint *you. In all probability the* division *will be* made about October, *and as it is improbable that you will have* left *the* locality by then, we *shall expect to* heaR *from you* about *that* time, *with a* view *to* youR commencing *the representation of our* fiRm *in an* aRea *to be* fixed. If *practicable*, we *should* like *you to give us a call, so that* we *can give you any instructions which may be* necessary. We *are* sorry *you are not a phonographer.* Perhaps *you could* aRRange *to* learn *the phonographic* aRt meanwhile ? If *you practised* every day *you* might obtain *a practical knowledge of the* system by October. *It is practically out of the* question *that you should have any difficulty in* finding *a* teacher. *There* must *be* many *in so* busy *a* place *who practise the phonographic* aRt, *and it would be remarkable* if *you had* trouble *in* secuRing *the* services *of an* instructor. *The improbability is altogether too great to be* worth further consideration. We *are rather* quiet just now *on* account *of the parliamentary* recess ; *but when parliament* re-opens we *expect* business *will be remarkably* brisk, through *the publication of the* debates, etc. *Our Mr.* Smith *may not improbably be in* youR neighborhood before long, *and* if *you have not called* upon *us* meanwhile, *he will* try *to see you.* YouR *republican* ideas *would not* interfeRe *with* youR duties *as our representative.* YouRs faithfully, (309)

EXERCISE 168.

Grammalogues.

1. *My dear* student,—*May I deliver to you an opinion upon the advantage to be* derived *from* private *or* extra study, taken *from the remarks of one who was himself a* student *of more* than oRdinary ability, *and whose usual* plan *it was to think for himself and do the* best *he could on every opportunity to* find *out*

the truth with regard to any particular question in which he felt any curiosity? 2. Shall I take it that you are willing, and that you have no objection to a Lesson, so long as it improves you and adds to your pleasure? 3. I will, and, oh, I do hope that of the number who read this page very many may be found who will be numbered among those who are called schoLars. 4. The habits of literary occupation, says this gentleman, confer cheerfulness, even upon men of common minds; but if they are joined to the possession of great native talents, then they can accompany men in their faLL from the Highest offices to the most absolute retiRement, as they did in the case of Lord Bacon, who, though he was degraded from his position in the court over which he had so long presided, yet at once assumed a HigheR place in another spheRe, through the talents he had cultivated by study. 5. How much better it would have been for some gentlemen known to you and to me, if they had studied, say, Phonography, in their leisure hours! 6. Had they done so they would now have a better spirit and a more improved mind than we see they have. 7. I shall be happy to think they may see these words, and may use them to their own advantage. 8. What a great difference we should see in them! 9. I think we owe it to our fellows not to be disagreeable, moody, or dull; and I am certain that if we care to use the poweRs given to us by the Lord God, we can do much good to others, and we shall not be accused of such faults as I have referred to. (351)

EXERCISE 169.

Grammalogues (continued).

1. *My dear Principal,—You and I know that there are a great number of things in Nature which we cannot account for, if we are to be true to the language of truth; because these things are quite above and beyond you and me. 2. The Lord has numbered them according to His will, and He can account for them; but we cannot. 3. Nor are we called upon to do so. 4. Shall I call them in one word too difficult for us? 5. Eh?*

6. *Ay, and though we may not care to be told this it is the mere truth, and the more we think it over the more we see the truth of my remark.* 7. *There is no use in calling it by any other word.* 8. *This has been my opinion from the first hour that I could think at all; and I think I shall have this opinion for ever.* 9. *Mr.* Grey, *who has been my dear doctor during the year, thinks with me in this, and his opinion is quite equal to that of any gentleman I know.* 10. *It is very important that we should remember this truth when we come to deliver an opinion on the things we see in Nature.* 11. *In short, it should be remembered by every member and by all gentlemen who use their words according to the spirit of truth, and whose usual principle it is to use the truth on each and every opportunity, general and particular, that may come to them.* 12. *As for myself, I do not care very much whether I know all these things or not.* 13. *It is difficult for me to see in what spirit we should be improved, or what great advantage it would be to us, if we could see through them all, and account for them to each and every one who might call upon us for an opinion on them.* 14. *After all, there would be no great difference in the pleasure we should have in using them, however much we might use them; nor should we be more happy if we could go down and give a true account of them at any hour during the year.* 15. *Are those who know the importance of these things more happy on that account?* 16. *If our pleasure in these things had to be given up because we could not give an opinion of them, it would be quite different.* 17. *But it is not so.* 18. *Why, therefore, should we be put out because we cannot give an opinion on all that may come under the eye?* 19. *Yet there are two gentlemen near me who cannot see the truth of this—Oh, that these two gentlemen could see how much we all owe to the good God, who has delivered these things to us!* 20. *It was He himself who delivered them to us.* 21. *We have them from His hand, and principally for our improvement and that we might be improved.* 22. *It is according to His word and under His will that we have all these things.* 23. *Shall we not go toward Him, and thank Him as He should be thanked, in a spirit of awe and with the language of truth?* 24. *I threw*

out this remark a while ago to a large number of gentlemen who are down with me, and I think the delivery of my words has done them good. 25. *Remember, I remarked, we could not have any of these things without God.* 26. *It was principally for your improvement that He has given them to you.* 27. *You could not buy them from anyone.* 28. *Ah, thank Him, therefore, gentlemen, in as true a spirit as you can.* 29. *I have put these words down in Phonography, my dear Principal, that you may see them and use them for advantage and improvement.* (631)

EXERCISE 170.

Grammalogues (continued).

Mr. ERnest Rivers.

Dear SiR,—*We have been* inquiRing *into the* statement *you* reported *to us* some time *ago as* made *by a gentleman in your* district, *and we can come to no other* conclusion than *that he has* uttered *language which he himself knows to be* faLse *in spirit and in* fact. *There* must *be* many people *near your* place *who know the* absurdity *of the thing, and who, from the nature of the* case, *will know that the* statement *of Mr.* D, *is a mere* fabrication *of his* own. *We do not, however, see any use in* taking further notice *of him, nor shall we use any other* means than *that of mere* silence *in* dealing *with the* case. *We have* turned *the* matter *over in every* sHape, *because we* were *at first* inclined *to go through the* courts *with it; but, after all, we threw out that* idea *as we* were convinced *that when our* standing *in the* business worLd *was remembered, no member of the* community *whose opinion we* valued *would think us* guilty *of* carrying *out* such *a principle as that* imputed *to us. Our* chairman, *Lord* Cheesebury, *called* heRe *on the* 1*st* instant, *and* spent *an hour* discussing *the* matter *with our general* secretary, *and his* view *was that, without* doubt, *the* proper course *was to* ignore *the* statement. *Those gentlemen who have had* dealings *with us know that we have* always acted *for their good equally with our* own, *according to our* ability, *and we are, therefore,* content *to* rely *upon the good* name *we have* eaRned *in the* past thirty *years. We owe the* man *no* grudge, *though how or why he should come to* make such *a* statement, *and to use* such *language, we* really *cannot* say. *So* faR *as we know, he has not been* asked *to buy any of our goods, and* certainLy *he has not* bought *any. We have* neither *given him, nor shall we ever give him,* just cause *for* enmity. *Yours* faithfully, Goodman Bros., Ltd. (339)

EXERCISE 171.

Grammalogues (continued).

Mr. Robert Beach.

Dear SiR,—*In* reply *to your* letter *of the* 11*th* instant, *I have very great pleasure in* stating *that Mr.* Thomas Adams *has been in my* employ *for the* last five *years, and has* always proved *himself quite equal to any* demands *that might be* made *upon him. He knows his Phonography* thoroughly, *as I have myself had* occasion *to* prove *very* many times. Indeed, *he has been thanked more* than *once by myself and my* partner *for the very* excellent manner *in which he has done this* part *of his* woRk. *I have remarked, too, that he is very willing to improve himself in any* way, *and to* cultivate *the* gifts *which God has given him. He has, therefore,* gone about *his* woRk *in a true spirit, and has very much improved during the* period *he has been with me. I think I have not had to* address *a* single *remark of a* condemnatory *nature to him all the while he has been in this* office. *I cannot* say *whether his* acquaintance *with accounts is* deep enough *for your* purpose; *yet I* feeL *quite* certain *that if it is not, and you will give him the opportunity, he will do his* best *to* meet *all your* requiRements *in this particular. He has a great* reverence *for the truth, and a* proper sense *of awe toward* authority; *and I* am *quite* satisfied, *therefore, that what he* does *will be done to the* best *of his* ability. *I may* add *that I* am personally *very* sorry *to* lose *his* services, *but I* feeL *that I should not* stand *in his* way *when he has a good* chance *of improving his* position. *I shall be very happy to give you any other particulars you may* desiRe. *Yours* faithfully, ARthur Speakwell. (301)

EXERCISE 172.

Grammalogues (continued).

Dear Mr. Smith,—Referring *to your call upon me on the* 1*st* inst., *I have had the particular* matter *of delivery of the goods* before *my principals, and I* am now prepaRed *to* guarantee *to deliver a large* portion *of them by the* end *of* March, *and the* remainder *toward the* middle *of* April, *if that will* suit *you. I shall be very happy,* also, *to have the goods put up in the short,* flat boxes *you* liked *so much when you* were heRe, *and for which we shall not* charge extra, *though each of them* costs *us a* trifle *under a* penny. *It is quite true, as I told you at the* time, *that we are more* than *usually* busy *with an important* contract *for these goods, the* bulk *of which has to be delivered this* spring ; *but we are* engaging *a large number of* extra *hands, so as to* get *the* woRk *out in good* time. *Difficult as it is to* fulfil *several* oRders *of such importance, and to be in* time *with them all, I have no* doubt *we shall be* able *to* manage *it. I thank you for your great* courtesy *in* waiting *for an* answer, *and I* trust *to have the pleasure of* heaRing *from you that we may go on with the* woRk *at once. Yours* truly, Wilfrid Mather. (225)

EXERCISE 173.

Grammalogues (concluded).

MessRs. Baker *and* Burnside.

Dear SiRs,—*We* take *this opportunity of calling your* attention *once more to our different* patterns *of* prints *which we* sent *you during the* eaRly part *of this year. You may remember that we* asked *you to* notice *particular*ly *the number of important improvements which we had* introduced *in the general* finish *and* make-up *of these goods, and which in our opinion* rendered *them* extremely suitable *for your* market, *above all others. We* made *these* changes *principally on the* recommendation *of two or* three *gentlemen who know your* market *very well, and on whose word we* felt *we could* rely, *and we are* convinced *that it* *will be to our* mutual *advantage if you will* permit *us to* make *a* triaL sHipment. *We have done so* well *with these goods in other* directions *that we are quite* satisfied *you would* find *an* experimental lot profitable *beyond your* anticipations. *It is not our usual* plan *to* sHip *on* joint *account, but as we cannot* doubt *the* result *in this* instance *we should be willing to* forward *a* small lot *on* joint *account with your*selves, *if you care to do so.* Trusting *to* heaR favourably *from you, we are, Gentlemen, Yours* faithfully, Manning *and* Martin. (208)

EXERCISE 174.

Omission of Consonants, etc.

In this Exercise, and in Exercises 175 to 179 inclusive, the letter which should be omitted (in words other than grammalogues or contractions) is indicated by italic type.

(*a*) *P* OMITTED BETWEEN *m* AND *t* OR *sh* :—

pum*p*ed, plum*p*ed, prom*p*t, prom*p*tly, prom*p*titude, prom*p*ted, prom*p*ter, bum*p*ed, bum*p*kin, bum*p*Tious, bum*p*Tiousness, tem*p*t, tem*p*ter, tem*p*table, contem*p*t, contem*p*tible, contem*p*tuous, tem*p*tation, tem*p*ted, attem*p*ted, tem*p*tress, attem*p*table, tram*p*ed, stam*p*ed, stum*p*ed, dam*p*ed, cham*p*ed, jum*p*ed, cam*p*ed, encam*p*ed, unkem*p*t, scam*p*ed, cram*p*ed, clam*p*ed, crim*p*ed, vam*p*ed, thum*p*ed, swam*p*ed, lim*p*ed, rom*p*ed, hum*p*ed, exem*p*t, exem*p*ted, exem*p*tion, presum*p*tion, presum*p*tive, presum*p*tuous, pre-em*p*tion, consum*p*tion, consum*p*tive, assum*p*tion, assum*p*tive, assum*p*tively, resum*p*tion, resum*p*tive, gum*p*tion, redem*p*tion, redem*p*tible, redem*p*tioneR, pre-em*p*tor.

(*b*) *T* OMITTED BETWEEN CIRCLE *s* AND ANOTHER CONSONANT :—

pos*t*age, pos*t*al, pos*t*boy, pos*t*-captain, pos*t*-card, pos*t*-cHaise, pos*t*-date, pos*t*-dating, pos*t*-dated, pos*t*-diluvian, pos*t*-entry, pos*t*e restante, pos*t*fix, pos*t*-horse, pos*t*man, pos*t*mark, pos*t*master, pos*t*-mortem, pos*t*-meridian, pos*t*-office, pos*t*-paid, pos*t*pone, pos*t*poned, pos*t*pone*m*ent, pos*t*prandial, pos*t*script, pos*t*-town, breas*t*pin, breas*t*plate, blas*t*-furnace, blas*t*-pipe, tas*t*eful, tas*t*efully, tas*t*eless, tes*t*ament, tes*t*amentary, tes*t*imony, tes*t*imonial, toas*t*-master, trus*t*worthy, trus*t*ful, trus*t*fully, chas*t*ely, adjus*t*ment, tex*t*-book, tex*t*-hand, fas*t*-day, mos*t*ly, hones*t*ly, dishones*t*ly, las*t*ly, lis*t*less, lis*t*lessly, res*t*less, res*t*lessly, was*t*e-book, was*t*eful, was*t*efully, was*t*e-pipe, wes*t*ward, wis*t*ful, wis*t*fully, wais*t*coat, wais*t*band, Wes*t*phalia, Wes*t*port, Wes*t*land, Wes*t* Indies, Wes*t*field, Wes*t*cott, Wes*t*bury, Wes*t*bourne, Pres*t*bury, manifes*t*ly.

(*c*) *K* or *g* between *ng* and *t* or *sh*.

Note that *n*, when it precedes the sound of *k* or *g*, is almost always pronounced as *ng* :—

pun*c*tate, pun*c*tated, pun*c*tilio, pun*c*tilious, pun*c*tual, pun*c*tually, pun*c*tuality, pun*c*tuate, pun*c*tuated, pun*c*tuation, pun*c*ture, pun*c*tured, tin*c*t, tin*c*ture, tin*c*tured, strongest, jun*c*tion, conjun*c*tion, disjun*c*tion, injun*c*tion, conjun*c*tive, disjun*c*tive, adjun*c*t, adjun*c*tive, extin*c*t, extin*c*tion, instin*c*t, instin*c*tive, instin*c*tively, distin*c*t, distin*c*tly, distin*c*tion, distin*c*tive, distin*c*tively, distin*c*tiveness, precin*c*ts, succin*c*t, succin*c*tly, fun*c*tion, fun*c*tionary, fun*c*tional, perfun*c*tory, defun*c*t, san*c*tity, san*c*tuary, san*c*tum, san*c*tification, san*c*tified, san*c*tify, san*c*timonious, san*c*tion, anxious, anxiously, anxiety, compun*c*tion, compun*c*tious, anguish, languish, languished, languishing.

(*d*) Tick *the* :—

(Downward) *up-the*, *be-the*, *by-the*, *if-the*, *for-the*, *have-the*, *know-the*, *in-the*, *are-the*, *to-the*, *of-the*, *all-the*, *and-the*, *should-the*, *as-the*, *has-the*, *is-the*, *think-the*, *call-the*; (upward) at-*the*, *had-the*, *which-the*, *so-the*, *see-the*, *was-the*, *will-the*, or-*the*, *on-the*, *but-the*, *from-the*, *toward-the*.

(*e*) THE PHRASE *of the* INDICATED BY WRITING THE TWO WORDS WHICH IT CONNECTS CLOSE TO EACH OTHER :—

price (of the) carpet ; size (of the) room ; depth (of the) cellaR ; cost (of the) books ; features (of the) plan ; frameR (of the) bill ; cause (of the) war ; growth (of the) business ; phase (of the) struggle ; strengthening (of the) girders ; laying (of the) foundation stone ; passing (of the) measure *for-the* benefit (of the) natives ; capture (of the) guns (of the) enemy ; distance (of the) house *from-the* centre (of the) town ; leaders (of the) various parties ; result (of the) poll ; re-eLection (of the) president (of the) society ; crossing (of the) Alps ; measurement (of the) ground ; names (of the) sHips ; titles (of the) books ; last (of the) natives ; buriaL (of the) faLLen ; love (of the) beautiful ; signs (of the) times ; meaning (of the) passage quoted ; defeat (of the) enemy and capture (of the) foRtress ; surveillance (of the) police ; countries (of the) worLd ; home (of the) brave ; close (of the) session.

EXERCISE 175.

Omission of Consonants, etc. (continued).

See Note at the head of Exercise 174.

1. *He who is* really anXious *to be* exem*p*t *from-the* fault *will* turn prom*p*tly *from-the* tem*p*tation, *on-the* assum*p*tion *that* prevention *is better-than* cuRe. 2. *This is* manifes*t*Ly *the* wisest plan, *for* unLess *there is a* punctual, almost *an* instinctive resistance, even-*the* strongest *may* faLL. 3. Lay *this* injunction, then, distinc*t*ly before *your* pupils, *and* bid *them not to* languiSH *in their* efforts *for-the* extinction *of* evil. 4. Point *out to them*, also, *that a* perfunctory effort *will* infallibly end *in* failuRe, *and that-the care*less resum*p*tion (of the) courses *that have* previousLy occasioned anxiety *is* presum*p*tive evidence *of a* weakness *in-the* inclination *to* resist. 5. *Mere* lis*t*less attem*p*ts *cannot be* considered *as* trus*t*worthy signs *of a*

genuine desiRe *to* acquiRe self-restraint. 6. Such attem*p*ts *are more* likely *to be* regarded *as* manifestations *of a* res*t*less disposition, *whose* owner *will not* achieve *great* distinction *in-the* worLd. 7. *It is use*less encouraging *a* fooLish, trus*t*ful hope*of* success *in those who* evince *no* anxiety *to* deserve success. 8. Finally, *it should be* borne *in* mind *that-the* longer *we* persist *in our* habit, *the* haRder *it is to* escape *from it.* (190)

EXERCISE 176.

Omission of Consonants, etc. (continued).

See Note at the head of Exercise 174.

1. *Be* prom*p*t *and* punctual *in your* engagements ; pos*t*ponements *are* disagreeable, *and* they *are* mos*t*ly brought about *by* lack *of* system. 2. *The* methodical man *is* always res*t*less *when he is* compeLLed *to* wait *for an* unpunctual person. 3. *I* say distinctly *there is no* redem*p*tion (of the) time *that is once* lost, *and it is a* presum*p*tion *for anyone to* waste precious moments *that cannot be* recalled. 4. *No* position *is* High enough *to* sanction *the* assum*p*tion (of the) right *to* waste another person's time. 5. Look *at-the* facts hones*t*ly, *and remember that if you are* anXious *to* get *on in-the* worLd, *your* best tes*t*imoniaL *will be a* reputation *for* punctuality *in-the* dispatch (of the) business entrusted *to you.* 6. *If your* anxiety *to* achieve distinction *is* reaL, *you will* cultivate prom*p*titude untiL *it* becomes *an* instinct *with you.* 7. Let *no-one* tem*p*t *you to* claim exem*p*tion *from-the* ruLe *that-the* man *who is* punctual *in-the* adjus*t*ment *of his* own affaiRs *will be equally* prom*p*t *in-the* adjus*t*ment (of the) affaiRs entrusted *to him by others.* 8. *He is-the* man *who will have* business matters *to* adjust. 9. *Remember, too, that* few men *have* jum*p*ed *into a* habit *at once ; on-the* contrary, habits grow *upon us by* degrees, *and* they are sometimes stam*p*ed *upon us* before *their* presence *is* dreamed *of.* 10. Many *a* man *has* cram*p*ed *himself, and* lost *in-the* race *of* life *through giv*ing way *to-the* tem*p*tation *to* procrastinate. 11. *The* playeR *who* loiters between-*the*

wickets *is* certain *to be* stum*p*ed. 12. *The* manner (of the) Lesson *may* amuse *you; but if you* take possession (of the) facts *I have put* before *you in-the* course (of the) Lessons, *and* try *to* model *your* plan *of* WORK *at-the* beginning (of the) day *upon-the* lines *I have* laid *down, I shall be* satisfied, *and at-the* end (of the) *year you will be* benefited. 13. Thus, *we shall* both *be* pleased *at-the* result (of the) labour *we have* spent *upon these short*hand exercises. (336)

EXERCISE 177.

Omission of Consonants, etc. (continued).

See Note at the head of Exercise 174.

1. *He who is* anxious *to be* exem*p*t *from-the* evil must *be* prom*p*t *to* resist-*the* tem*p*tation. 2. *The* FORCE (of the) tem*p*tation *may* easily *be forg*otten *in-the pleasure* (of the) moment; *but-the* strong man *is* distrus*t*ful *of his* POWER, *and is care*fuL *not to* estimate *it too* Highly. 3. *The* pun*c*tual man economises time *by be*ing prom*p*t *in all things*. 4. *The* head (of the) fiRM *should be a* model *of* pun*c*tuality *to everyone* (of the) fiRM's servants. 5. *It is* manifes*t*Ly *beyond us to* make *up at* night *the* time lost *during-the* day. 6. *He who* sanctions wrong-doing *cannot* claim exem*p*tion *from-the* guilt (of the) crime 7. *The* owner (of the) money does *not* always carry *the* puRse. 8. *Remember, too, that* "*It is an* em*p*ty puRse *which is* fuLL *of other* men's money." 9. Pass *not a* lis*t*less youth; *for-the* WORK (of the) Spring *will be* repaid *in-the* Autumn. 10. Many *an* honest man *has been* ruined *by-the* res*t*less tongue *of an* idle neighbour. 11. Assum*p*tion *of* wisdom *is* often *the* sign *of a* fooL. 12. *It is-the* function (of the) pupil *to* obey *the* directions (of the) trus*t*worthy teacher. *and* thus gain distinction. 13. *The* failuRe (of the) fiRM *was* distinctly due *to-the* perfunctory manner *in which-the* men did *their* duty. 14. *The* actions (of the) minister aRoused *the* contem*p*t (of the) people (of the) country, *who* anxiously

called for his dismissal. 15. *The* parks surrounding *the* residences (of the) nobility *are an* inviting feature (of the) EngLish landscape. 16. Many rivers (of the) country *are important* factors *in-the* commerce (of the) nation, *as their* mouths foRm havens where *sea*ports *are* situated *and a large* carrying business *is* conducted. 17. *The* city *of* London *is-the* capital (of the) BritisH EmpiRe, *and-the* centre (of the) money markets (of the) worLd. 18. New York *is-the* business centre (of the) American *Republic, and-the* port does *more-than* half (of the) foreign commerce (of the) country. (325)

EXERCISE 178.

Omission of Consonants, etc. (continued).

See Note at the head of Exercise 174.

MessRs. PeeR *and* Bates.

Gentlemen,—I thank you for your letter (of the) 24th inst., *and I* am *much* obliged *for-the* copy (of the) correspondence *which has* passed between *you and-the* heads (of the) department *in* London. *As* faR *as I can see you are* exem*p*t *from* blame *in-the* matter (of the) pos*t*age accounts. *You are quite* correct *in-the* assum*p*tion *that we* deal *with these* accounts *in-the* same way heRe. *I can* assuRe *you that I should be* tem*p*ted *to* prom*p*tly resent *any* letters (of the) tone *of those* addressed *to you,* were such sent *to me. I have-the* strongest *and* most distinct recollection, *too, that-the* matter (of the) pos*t*age accounts *has been* considered before, *and that-the* present mode *of* keeping *a* record (of the) payments *for* pos*t*age *is-the* result *of a* recommendation *by a* most trus*t*worthy accountant. Criticism (of the) kind expressed *in-the* letters *to you can* onLy bring about *a* res*t*less, uneasy feeLing *in-the* minds (of the) agents (of the) company, *and I* hope *we are not to be* annoyed *with a* repetition (of the) methods *you so* properly condemn. *Yours* truly, James Matthews. (198)

EXERCISE 179.

Omission of Consonants, etc. (concluded).

See Note at the head of Exercise 174.

Mr. Charles Lewis.

Dear SiR,—*I thank you for your* prom*p*t response *to my* application, *and I will* enter-the boy *as a* student *of your* school *on-the* resum*p*tion *of* classes *in-the* new *year. I think he will do* well *under your* guidance. *He has been a* little cram*p*ed *for opportunities in-the* school *he has been* attending, *but I have great* hopes *that he will* achieve distinction *in a* place where *his* talents *have a* chance *of* developing. *If you will* kindly obtain *the* whole (of the) tex*t*-books *he will* requiRe, *and* leave *the* adjus*t*ment (of the) account *for-the* same untiL *the* close (of the) term, *I shall be* greatly obliged. *You have my* sanction *to* direct *the* boy's studies *as* appeaRs best *to you. I* am *very* anXious *that he should be* taught *the* value *of a* punctual fulfilment *of his* engagements. *Yours* faithfully, Jonathan More. (152)

EXERCISE 180.

Contractions.

Dear Charles,—*I* am pleased *to acknowledge your phonographic* skiLL *and I* feeL certain *you will never* regret *that you are a phonographer. It is a mistake, however, to think, and you are altogether mistaken in thinking*, *that anything in the* way *of information is uninteresting to-the representative of a* newspaper *or magazine. He may have a natural* dislike *to-the* display *of his interest. He may* appeaR entiRely *disinterested, and his disinterested*ness *may be* obvious *to a stranger or* even *to a* boy *messenger. Nevertheless, he is interested, or rather the public for* whom *his* articles *are published are interested, in practically everything that is* going *on in-the* worLd, *and* they *naturally expect him, and have* always *expected him, to publish information of a satisfactory character on every subject, of whatever nature, and on every remarkable* event *whenever it may have* occurred, *from-the destruction* (of the) *great* SpanisH ARmada *to-the doctrine* (of the) new *Parliamentary* leader *and-the prospect of* Licensing *reform in-the next* session *of Parliament. That is-the object for which* they *subscribe to-the magazine or* paper *which is represented by-the writer, and* they *would, in all probability, transfer their subscriptions immediately if it* were *not more-than probable that their object would* be attained, *if-the characteristic* style (of the) *writer* were *unsatisfactory in any respect, or if he* were *to represent in a* wrong light some *peculiarity in-the character of a peculiar* man whom they *respect. It is very improbable that any regular writer would* make such *a mistake. It would be so irregular and inconsistent that it may be* said *to be impossible in-the* case *of a writer who understood his* woRk, *and you will understand that in* such *a* case *the improbability or inconsistency may be put down as an* impossibility. *No one knows better-than the* author *of manuscripts or transcripts for-the* press *how essential it is that he should have catholic* tastes *in* reading *and* study. *He* must *know something* about *everything. Not* even-*the* most *unexpected subject* must *come as a surprise to him. He may be* asked *unexpectedly to* write *an* article *that will give instruction to* readers *all over-the kingdom on-the representation* (of the) *republican* party *in-the great republic of* America ; *or a* notice (of the) death *of an architect* famous *for his architectural* genius *and as-the* designer *of* some *peculiar* specimens *of architecture. If there is to be an immediate publication* (of the) article, *the writer has no* time *to think* (of the) *difficulties* (of the) task *he has to perform. It* must *be performed immediately, notwithstanding any objection he may have to-the* hurry. *And* so *nothing* must *be neglected if he is to give satisfaction to his* editoR. *He* must take *an enlarged* view *of things, and neglect nothing that will enlarge his knowledge and influence and* render-*the performance of his* woRk *more satisfactory to himself and others. It is impossible to* deny *that* occasionally *his* woRk *is dangerous. I* am *thank*ful *to* say *that he is* seldom *influenced by the* thought *of-the danger, and it is not improbable that he would* face *any danger* *rather-than* faiL *to* obtain *information which would be use*ful *to-the public. He knows-the influence* (of the) press *on public opinion and-the establishment of domestic* prosperity, *and as* faR *as practicable it is his uniform practice to* assist *the reverend gentlemen in his* neighborhood *in-the* promotion *of temperance reform and-the government of* reason. *I know he thinks* some (of the) plans *for-the reform of* criminals *are altogether impracticable, and-the improbability of* success *is* onLy *too* apparent *to his practical* mind. *He is especially care*fuL *to* point *out to-the reformers that if* criminals *are to be reformed* they must *be* sHown *how to govern their* inclinations *when-the* temptation *to transgress comes upon them.* OnLy *yesterday, I* met *a writer who* desiRes *to establish or to see established a* society *whose members will* take *an especial interest in-the instruction* (of the) *remarkably* low class *of* men *whose* lives *have been remarkable for-the uniformity with which* they *have practised essentially* vicious habits; *who cannot govern their* evil dispositions, *and who are* unwilling *to be governed by others. We* were joined *by an uninfluential member of a* dramatic society. *We* conferred *together and* were *unanimous in think*ing *that-the* proposed society *was* worthy (of the) support *of all influential* men, *and that not improbably we should be* able *to* persuade *others* (of the) *importance* (of the) movement. *There was* perfect *unanimity*, also, *in our* decision *to* attempt *to* carry *the* transaction *to a satisfactory* conclusion, *so that-the transgressions* (of the) unfortunate people referred *to* might *be* curtaiLed. *Will you* join *the* society? *Yours* truly, (908)

EXERCISE 181.

Contractions (continued).

MessRs. Barker *and* Bradley.

Gentlemen,—We have to acknowledge receipt *of your* letter *of yesterday, together with-the* proofs (of the) *transcript* (of the) address *on* "Modern *Architecture." We* note *that you expect this to come out better-than anything that you have done for us* before, *and we are* glad *to think there is a prospect of improvement in-the character* (of the) binding. Kindly let *us know immediately the* book *is* ready *for publication, and we will* send *a representative with instructions for-the* despatch (of the) bulk (of the) ORder. *We cannot understand-the inconsistency of your* attitude *respecting the transfers for-the manuscript magazine* sent *you by messenger yesterday, and we cannot but* regard *your* explanation *as altogether unsatisfactory. We have done everything* possible *to* meet *your objection to a uniform* size *of character; but-the other* proposals *you* make were *quite unexpected, and are altogether impracticable.* Neither *do we see what object would be* gained *by* adopting *the dangerous* policy *you* suggest. *From-the information at our* disposal *we can* aSSuRe *you that* such *an irregular* proceeding *would be* resented *by all-the regular* readers (of the) *magazine throughout-the kingdom. It* must, *therefore, be* cleaRly *understood that we shall have nothing whatever to do with-the* proposal, *and that rather-than* associate *our* names *with* such *an inconsistent* policy, *we shall* retiRe *from-the* business *altogether. We do not know-the writer you* mention. *We rather think he is-the* sub-editoR *of a Catholic* newspaper, *in which* case *there should be no difficulty in* finding *his* address. *Yours* truly, Moseley *and* WiLd. (269)

EXERCISE 182.

Contractions (continued).

Mr. William Heaton.

Dear SiR,—*I have* seen-*the architect with* reference *to-the architectural* designs *it is* proposed *to publish in-the "Republican* Gazette," *and he will probably be* able *to do something for us next* month. *He is* extremely busy just now, *and without neglecting his* business *it would be impossible for him to give immediate* attention *to-the* scheme. *Nevertheless, he will* keep *it in* mind, *and whenever he can* find *an opportunity he will give us-the* benefit *of his great knowledge* (of the) *subject.*

This was as much as I expected; indeed, *I* thought *it more-than probable that he would* refuse *altogether, especially as I was an* entiRe *stranger to him. Yours* faithfully, Peter Farmer.

(121)

EXERCISE 183.

Contractions (continued).

MessRs. Digby *and* Cowley.

Gentlemen,—We regret *to have to* notify *you of-the* total *destruction of our* CheSHire premises *by* fiRe *on* Monday last, *so that it will be impossible for us to perform our* part (of the) contract *with you in-the* time specified. *We are, however,* making *practicable* aRRangements *for-the transfer* (of the) woRk *to our other* branches, *and notwithstanding-the difficulty in a peculiar* business like *ours, we think it is improbable that we shall be more-than a* couple *of* months behind *with-the delivery* (of the) *goods. We* venture *to* hope *that this will be satisfactory to you. We are naturally* desirous *of publishing the* facts *in our* own way, *so that we may not* suffer *from a* faulty *representation* (of the) case. *We have-the satisfaction, too, to know that* so faR *our* customeRs *have been unanimous in their* expressions *of* sympathy, *and we* trust *that you will* SHaRe *in that unanimity. You know that we have* always claimed *it as a peculiar characteristic of ours that we have practically never* before faiLed *in-the performance of a* promise, *and we are thank*ful *that in-the* present instance *we cannot be* charged *with a transgression of good* faith. *We should be more-than* sorry *to transgress in this* way. *We* venture *to think it is remarkable that in a* business like *ours,* where-*the* premises *are remarkably subject to destruction by* fiRe, *we have* always *performed our* promises *and given satisfaction to our* clients. *We shall* take-*the opportunity of enlarging our* CheSHire woRks, *and we* hope *that in-the enlarged* factory *we shall be* able *to influence a* still *great*er SHaRe *of* patronage. *We shall be* glad *to* heaR *that we may* rely *upon your* kindness *in-the* present trouble, *and on your influential* support *in-the* future.

We trust *we have established a* claim *to your especial* consideration, *and we* assure *you that in-the* new *establishment we shall* endeavour *to establish a* still *more* solid *character for-the* punctual fulfilment *of all* orders entrusted *to us. Yours* faithfully, Burnett *and* Fraser. (352)

EXERCISE 184.

Contractions (concluded).

Rev. Arthur Acton.

My dear Sir,—*I should have acknowledged your interest*ing letter earlier, *had not-the Government unexpectedly* invited *me as a temperance reformer to give* evidence before *a Parliamentary* committee, just before-*the* prorogation *of Parliament. You will not be interested in* details *which* must *be uninteresting to any* outsider; *but as I know you to have a disinterested* anxiety *for-the reform of* inebriates, *I think it can be no mistake to* tell *you why* such *an uninfluential* man *as I was called to* London. *You know that I am influenced by a* desire *to* carry *into public, as well as* private *and domestic* life, *the doctrine of temperance in all things, which is an essential* part (of the) education *of a* man, *if he is* either *to govern himself or others, or if he is to* submit *to be governed by others and to* avoid-*the danger of be*ing led away *by mistaken* men, *with* little *or no practical knowledge* (of the) *subjects on which* they speak *so* lightly. *I* trust *I was* able *to represent my* views *in* such *a* manner *as to* convince *the* committee *of my disinterestedness, though it is improbable that-the members will subscribe* entirely *to my* statement. *I should think no* committee *ever yet subscribed* absolutely *to-the* views *of any* witness, *no* matter *how well those* views *may have been represented to them. As a phonographer I was interested in-the phonographic* skill (of the) reporters present. *The* ability displayed *in-the performanc of their* duties *was remarkable.* Surely, *no performer on a* musical instrument requires *more* delicacy *of* touch *than these gentlemen, who* must *have practised* well *to* attain *to* such dexterity. *Good* heaRing must *be essentially important in their* case, *as a* single *word* missed *would in all probability* disturb *the* run *of a* whole sentence. *I was so* impressed *by their performance that I shall not improbably* renew *my subscription to-the phonographic magazines* before *I* leave *for-the great republic* across-*the* Atlantic. *I should* like *to have a* verbatim speed, *but-the improbability of my* secuRing *this is* obvious *when I think* (of the) little time *I have for* practice. *If practicable I will call on you on* Friday morning *next, when we can* discuss-*the* outlook *in temperance* affaiRs *more* fully. *Yours very* truly, Thomas Drinkwater. (393)

EXERCISE 185.

Phraseography.

1 *I-have-no*-doubt, *that-you-are* already convinced (of the) benefits *to be* derived *from a practical knowledge of*-phraseography, *and-I-think you*-must-*have*-seen *by-this*-time *that-the* judicious *use of-this principle not*-onLy materially increases *the* ease *and*-speed *with-which-you-may* write, *but-that-it* also adds *to-the* legibility *of-your* writing. 2. *I*-am-*sure that-you* recognise-*the truth of all-this*; *and-yet I*-am venturing *to-tell-you* again, *so-that you-will-be* less likely *to*-forget *it*. 3. "*He who-would-be* wise must-*be* willing *to be* taught" *is a* proverb *which-you-may-remember* reading *in-one-of-your phonographic* text-books. 4. *You*-must-*not-be* annoyed, *therefore, if I-tell-you that-which-you* already know 5. *It-is-not* possible *to* know-*the* ruLes (of the) system *too* well; *and, of-course, it-should-be your* aim, *and-the* aim *of-every phonographer, to know them as-well-as* they *can-be* known. 6. *I-think-you-will* admit *that-it-would-be a good thing if all phonographers* looked *at-the* matter *in-this*-way. 7. *This-is*, perhaps, *too*-much *to* hope *for*; *but-you* and-*I*, *who-are our*-own masters *in-this* affaiR, *are* deteRmined, *I-think, that-we-shall* obtain *as good a knowledge* (of the) ruLes *as-it-is* possible *for us to* obtain.

8. *Is-not-that our* case? 9. *I-am*-sure *it-is, and-it-is a pleasure to-me to-think-so.* 10. *You-will-do* well, then, *to practise* phraseography diligently, taking *as your* models *the* phraseograms *which-are given in* "Pitman's Journal" week *by* week. 11. *Of-course, it-is-not* suggested *that-you-should* memorize *the* foRms; *but it-is-important that-you-should understand-the principles upon-which-the* best phraseograms *are* made, *and-it-is* advisable *that-you-should* acquiRe *a good* style now, *while you-are* young *in-the-system, if I-may put it in-this*-way. 12. *It-is for-these*-reasons *that I*-am recommending *you to*-copy *the short*hand matter *given in-the* "Journal," *and-I-am*-sure *you could-not-have* better *practice.* 13. *You*-must excuse *me, however, if I-tell-you to* beware *how you*-employ *this* fascinating *principle.* 14. *There-are*-some beginners *in-the*-aRt *who do-not use it as-it-should-be* used. 15. *Therefore, I*-say *to-you. do-not-be* led *into-the* eRRoR *of* joining *too*-many *words together, or of* joining *words* simply *because*-they-*will* join. 16. *If-you-will but* follow *my* counseL, *and* copy *good* models, *you-will* soon acquiRe *a* correct *and*-gracefuL style *which-will-be of-great* assistance *to-you in-your* application (of the) wingèd aRt *to-the* purposes *of-your* business *or* profession. (468)

EXERCISE 186.

Phraseography (concluded).

My-dear student,—*I-think-you-will*-agree *with me that-we-have-had a* pleasant journey *together through-the* pages (of the) *first* part (of the) "Instructor," *or-the* "Manual," *and-that-the knowledge you have* gained *will-be interesting as-well-as* useful *to-you in-your* future life. *I-think-it-is-not* likely *that-you-will ever* regret *any* trouble *which-you-may-have-had during-the* course. *Of-course you-could-not expect to*-master *the subject as-it-should-be* mastered *without* trouble. *I-think I-shall-be* excused *if I*-say *it-would-be* wrong *for-you to-think that-you-can* acquiRe *knowledge without* some *difficulty. There-are*-some pupils *who-would-be*-glad *to-think in-this*-way ; *but, of-course, we-are* both aware, *for our*-own reason *will*-convince *us, that-it-is-not* possible *for-them to-do-so. I-do-not expect that-you-are yet* able *to*-write *very* rapidly. *We-cannot-expect that at*-present. *But-we-can and-we-do expect that-you-will* persevere *in-your practice* (of the) aRt *so-that you-will-be in a* position eRe long *to*-report *a* speaker *as-well-as any phonographer you-are* acquainted *with. I-have-no* hesitation *in* saying *that if-you-will practise every*-day *you-will* achieve *a* measure *of*-success *that will-be-satisfactory to-you as-well-as to-me. But, of-course, you*-must-*not* dream *of neglecting your regular practice, or-you-cannot* hope *to-do* well. *I-have-done all-that-you-can expect me to-do for-you, and-it-is a pleasure to-me to-think that-you have-done your* best also. *And-now, if-you-will*-permit-*me, I-will give-you one* piece *of* advice *which-you-will-do* well *to*-follow *when you* enter *upon-the* study (of the) second part, *or-the* " RepoRter," *as, of-course, you-will immediately. It-is-this : See that-you*-learn *all-the* grammalogues, *and*-contractions thoroughly, *so-that-you-can* write *them without-the* least hesitation *or difficulty. This-is important for-this*-reason : *You-will-find that-the*-majority (of the) *words* spoken *in an* oRdinary passage *are* included *in-the* list *of* grammalogues *and*-contractions, *and, of-course, you*-must-*see from this that if-you* master *the* list perfectly *you-will-have-the* outlines *for-the*-majority *of-words you-will* heaR *at-your* finger-ends. *Do-not*, then, *neglect your practice. See that-you-are doing all-that-you-can to* advance *in* dexterity *with-the*-system, *and you-will-be-surprised to* find *what you-can-do with-it. It-is*-said *that* " *Practice* makes perfect." *Of-course it-is-true that-it* does, *and-it-will* make *you* perfect *as a phonographer if-you-will but practise and*-persevere. *And who-would-not* persevere *to-the* end *when-he-was as near-the* goal *as you-are, especially when* perseverance means *the* possession *of an* ability *which-cannot* faiL *to be of-great* service *to-him that-has-it? Yours*-truly. (524)

EXERCISE 187.

Punctuation, etc.

"This world, after all our science and sciences, is still a miracle; inscrutable, *magical* and more, to whosoever will *think* of it. That great mystery of time, were there no other; illimitable, silent, like an all-embracing ocean-tide, on which we and all the universe swim like exhalations, like apparitions which *are* and then *are not*: this is for ever literally a miracle, a thing to strike us dumb—for we have no word to speak about it. This universe, ah me—what could the wild man know of it; what can we yet know of it? That it is a Force, a thousandfold complexity of Forces; a Force which is *not we*. That is all; it is not we; it is altogether different from *us*. Force, Force, everywhere Force; we ourselves a mysterious Force in the centre of that. 'There is not a leaf rotting but has Force in it: how else could it rot?' Nay, surely, to the Atheistic Thinker, if such a one were possible, it must be a miracle too, this huge illimitable whirlwind of Force, which envelops us here; never rest whirlwind, high as Immensity, old as Eternity. What is it? God's creation, the religious people answer; it is the Almighty God's! Atheistical science babbles poorly of it, with scientific nomenclatures, experiments and what not, as if it were a poor dead thing, to be bottled up in Leyden jars and sold over counters; but the natural sense of man, in all times, if he will honestly apply his sense, proclaims it to be a living thing—an unspeakable, godlike thing; towards which the best attitude for us, after never so much science, is awe, devout prostration and humility of soul; worship if not in words, then in silence."—From Carlyle's "Lectures on Heroes." (300)

EXERCISE 188.

Punctuation, etc. (concluded).

"Look *there!* The bloom of that fair face is wasted, the hair is grey with care; the brightness of those eyes is quenched, their lids hang drooping, the face is stony pale, as of one living in death. Mean weeds, which her own hand has mended, attire the Queen of the World. The death-hurdle where thou sittest pale, motionless, which only curses environ has to stop; a people drunk with vengeance, will drink it again in full draught, looking at thee there. Far as the eye reaches, a multitudinous sea of maniac heads, the air deaf with their triumph-yell! The living-dead must shudder with yet one other pang; her startled blood yet again suffuses with the hue of agony that pale face, which she hides with her hands. There is there *no* heart to say, God pity thee! Oh, think not of these, think of *Him* whom thou worshippest, the crucified who also, treading the winepress *alone*, confronted sorrow, still deeper; and triumphed over it and made it holy, and built of it a 'Sanctuary of Sorrow' for thee and all the wretched! Thy path of thorns is nigh ended, one long last look at the Tuileries, where thy step was once so light—where thy children shall not dwell. The head is on the block; the axe rushes—dumb lies the world; that wild-yelling world, and all its madness is behind thee."—From Carlyle's "French Revolution." (241)

EXERCISE 189.

Writing in Position.

(*All the following Exercises are counted in* 20's.)

The staid student *should* try, *by every* means *in his* poweR, *to* acquiRe *the* ability *to* pursue *a* train *of* | thought steadily *and without* wandering *from the* plain plan *he has* set before *himself*. *How can he* hope *to* heap | *up a* multitude *of* facts, *if he is* continually hopping, *as it* were, *from one* branch *of knowledge to* another, | *not* stopping long enough *to* gather *the* fruit *from one* branch, eRe *he* stoops *to* examine another? Let *a* youth | *but think a* moment *of* such loose methods, *and he will see that* they amount *to a mere* loss *of* (1) time, *and, it may be, of* temper also. Now, *it is* fooLish *to* experiment *or* tamper *with that which we* | *cannot* repaiR; *and it is well that we should* recognise *that a* moment *once* gone *is* gone *for ever*. *We* | *may* regret *the* time *we have* lost, *but there is not the* least hope *of* recalling *it*. Let *us but* | feeL *the* fuLL foRce *of this* remark, *and, if we have* wasted *the* golden moments *in the* past, *we shall* | follow another *and* better plan *in the* future. *It is, of* course, right *to* say *that there is no* royaL (2) route *to the* well *of knowledge and the* fount *of* wisdom, *and that he who would* sound *the* depths *of* | *the one, and* drink *the* waters *of the* other, must pass aLong *the* same rugged ways *by which* wise men | *of all* ages *have* traveLLed before *him*. *He will, to be* sure, find *difficulties in his* way, *and he may* | *have* many *a* bitter fight eRe *he* reaches *the* goal *of his* ambition. *But these will* onLy fit *him for* | braver feats, *and each* victory *will* leave *him* stronger *and* better prepaRed *for* further effort, *should* such *be* necessary. Let (3) *him but* keep *up his* courage, *and he may* hope *to* cope successfully *with any* obstacle *that may* appeaR *to* | baR *his* progress. *But, as we have* said, *it is above all things* necessary *that the* student *should be* able | *to* fix *his* mind *upon his subject, and* keep *it there*; *that he should be* able *to* occupy *his* thoughts | *and* focus *his* poweRs *upon one* point, *to the* exclusion *of all others for the* time being; *that, in a* | *word, he should have the* poweR *of* applying *himself to the* mastery *of the difficulty* before *him, and of* refusing (4) *to be* drawn aside *from his* task *upon any* plea, *no* matter *how* plausible. *And, if the* student *has not* | *this* poweR *of* attention, *he should* try *to* acquiRe *it by every* means *at his* command. Let *him* set *to* | woRk *in* eaRnest, *and he will* find *that the* acquisition *is not the* utter impossibility *which, at first* sight, *it* | *may* appeaR *to be*. *He can, at any* rate, choose *the* right time *and the* right place *to* study, *and* | *he can* also *do his* best *to* chase away thoughts *that would* distract *him*. Patience *and* perseverance *will* woRk wonders. (500)

EXERCISE 190.

Writing in Position (continued).

The vowels marked in italic should be inserted.

There are many *a*dvocates *of the* theory *that* life *is* fuLL *of a*mple *opportunities for all who care to* seize | *them and* employ *them, and that* where men make *an awfu*L failuRe *in* life *it is because, through* some fault | *or* defect *in their* own *character,* they *have not* taken fuLL *advantage of the* valuable chances *that have been a*vailable | *to them* time *after* time, *but have a*llowed *their opportunities to* melt away *without an a*ttempt *to* emulate *the* example | *of their* successfuL neighbours, *and* turn *their* chances *to good* | *account. If,* say *the* theorists, *these* men *had* tried *to* (1) *a*djust *their* ways *to the* position *when the* chance came, they *would have* succeeded just *as well as others have* | *done, and their a*ffaiRs *would have* prospered *as the a*ffaiRs *of others with more* foRce *of character have* prospered. *But* | *the* chances were missed, *and the* unfortunate *ones are a*mazed *at their* failuRe. They *a*ffect *to* blame *their* want *of* | luck, *when, as a* matter *of* fact, *their* failuRe *is the* effect *of their* own *care*lessness. Now, *it is remarkable* | *that those who are* most v*o*luble *in a*ffiRming *the* necessity *for* foRming *a* rapid judgment *and* taking *immediate* action *when* (2) favourable *opportunities* occur, *are* invariably successfuL men *who have, in* most instances, *a*ttained *an a*ffluent position *by* dint *of* haRd | woRk *and* industry, *or, as* they declaRe *in their* own fluent way, *by* reason *of putt*ing *in*to *practice the* theory | *we have* just explained. *Without, however,* seeking *to a*dvance *a* defence *of* laziness *or* SHEER incapacity, *it may be* doubted | *whether all who* faiL *to a*mass wealth, *or a*ttain even *to a* competency, *are to be* blamed *for their* want | *of* success. *There are, a*las, *too* many men *who* appeaR *to be u*tterly unable either *to* devise *their* own means (3) *of a*dvancement, *or to* follow *the a*dvice *of others who are* better qualified, *and of* such weak persons perhaps *the* | less said *the* better. *But there are others whose* want *of* success *can be a*ttributed *to no* fault *of their* | own. They *have not had equal* chances *with others. The* conditions *of their* eaRly life, *from which* they *could not* | escape, *have* doubtLess *a*ffected *their* bodies, *their* minds *and* temperament, *and no* amount *of* energy *or* zeal *on their* part | *would* enable *them to* extract *as much from their opportunities as might be* extracted *by others* reared *under more* favourable (4) conditions. *There is no* denying *the influence of* environment *in giving* tone *to the* mind, *and it is very difficult* | *in* later life *to a*tone *for the* mischief *done by* unhealthy surroundings *or a* banefuL atmosphere *in* childhood *and in* | youth. *But, however much opinions may* differ *with* regard *to the* inequality *of the* chances offered *to* men, *and the* | manner *in which one's* surroundings *may o*perate *in the* foRmation *of character and thus* affect *the* part played *by the* | man, *it will be* agreed *that everyone has* some *opportunities, and that, if he* desiRes, *he can* create *others.* (500)

EXERCISE 191.

Figures.

Very much more interest may be derived *from the* study *of* figures, such *as the* Board *of* Trade Returns, than | *at first* sight appears likely. *It* does *not* require *a very great* effort *of* imagination *to* suppose *that* behind *these* | figures *there may be* stories *of* self-denial, suffering *and* misery, undreamt *of by the* thoughtless reader. *Lord* Russell *of* | Killowen produced *in* 1898 facts *and* figures *to* prove *that in* seven *years* £28,000,000 *had* | *been* lost *in* company liquidation, *and that of this* amount £20,000,000 *had been* lost *by* shareholders *and over* (1) £7,000,000 *by* creditors. *Is it* unreasonable *to* suppose *that these great* losses were *the immediate* cause *of much* | suffering *and* hardship *that the out*side world *never* heard *of?* *Or,* take *the* statement *that in* 1894 *the* | capital invested *in* limited companies *in this* country alone amounted *to more* than £1,000,000,000, *being* £315,000,000 | *more* than *was* invested *in the* companies *of* France *and* Germany combined. *Is it not* likely | *that a large* part *of this* enormous sum *represented the* fruit *of care,* industry, *and* perseverance *on the* part *of* (2) many men *and* women *whose* names were unknown *to the* world around *them?* *And* wherein lies *the* secret *of* | England's superior wealth, whereof *these* figures offer such convincing proof? Herein, surely, *is* food *for* profitable reflection, *and* hereon *might* | *be* based many *interest*ing discourses wherewith thoughtful men *would be* both edified *and* instructed. *Or,* again, *who can* fail *to* | *be* both *interested and* amused *at the* statement *of the* Registrar *of* Limited Companies, *that, in* 1891, *a* | company *was* registered *with a* nominal capital *of* £10,000, divided *in*to 9,600,000 shares *of* ¼d. (3) each, *and that the* total *subscribed* capital *was* 1¾d.? *The* Act *of* 1862 requires | *that at* least seven shares *shall be subscribed, and is it not interesting to see how* scrupulously *the* strict letter | *of the* law *was* complied *with?* Further, cheques *and* bills *of* exchange amounting *to not* less than £20,000,000, | *and* often exceeding £40,000,000, pass *through the* London Bankers' Clearing House *every* day. *What* labour *of* brain *and* | muscle *is represented by these* figures! *To what* distant parts *of the* earth *will the* fruits *of that* labour *be* (4) *for*warded! 'Tis *an* enormous sum. *What an* amount *of good might be done* therewith, whereat thousands *would* rejoice, *and* whereof | *the* world *might* feel proud! Lastly, *the* value *of the* British imports *for the* four months ended 30th April, 1903, | amounted *to* £117,385,167. | *The* commodities *represented by this* sum were supplied *by* peoples *of* various hues *and* customs *in different* parts | *of the* world. Picture *to your*self *the* gathering *and for*warding *of these* commodities, *and you cannot* fail *to be interested.* (500)

EXERCISE 192.

Negative Prefixes.

The italic type indicates that both consonants must be written.

Many *ill*iterate persons, *and others who can* only *be* described *as ill*iberal-minded, appear *to be imm*ovably convinced *that there* | *is no advantage to be* derived *from the* study *of* such *a subject as* astronomy, and that any attempt to | number bodies which are admitted to be innumerable, or to measure space which is simply immeasurable, is but a waste | of time and energy. Such a view is at once irrational, illogical, and immoderate. Indeed, it is almost irreconcilable with the spirit of the age in which we live. The conclusion is irresistible that persons who hold such opinions are (1) in an almost irredeemable state of ignorance as to the value of mental training. None but the most immature intellect | can for a moment suppose that the contemplation of the illimitable space above and around us, with the innumerable crowd | of unnamed and unknown stars, can be anything but beneficial to any man, or can fail to irradiate the mind | of the observer and render him better fitted for the performance of even the ordinary duties of life. No man | will be unneighbourly because of his study of the immutable laws of nature. He is much more likely to be (2) known as an irreproachable member of society; moderate in his views; mature in his judgment; kind and generous to his | fellows. But apart from these considerations, it has been shown that from a purely legal point of view the study | of astronomy is far from being an unnecessary branch of learning. Thus, there is recorded an instance of a man | who was summoned to appear at a court of law held in Carlisle, and punctual to the minute, according to | the local time, he was in his place, only to find that the court had met according to Greenwich time (3) before his arrival, and had decided the case against him. The decision was afterwards declared to be illegal, and there | was another trial. More over, as a direct result of the illegality of the first trial an Act of Parlia ment was | passed with the object of preventing such a hardship in the future. It has been proved beyond a doubt that | were the labours of the astronomical observers suspended for any length of time, innumerable inconveniences and immeasurable, indeed, irretrievable mischief | would speedily result. The running of railway trains, now so marvellously methodical, would become quite immethodical; long sea voyages, now (4) so common as to be unnoticed, would have to be abandoned, and, in consequence, much of the merchandise now readily | movable from any one part of the world to another, would become practically immovable. In other directions, also, there would | be an almost inconceivable disarrangement of the affairs of life. Such considerations should serve to strengthen our conviction that no | branch of human learning can truly be said to be utterly useless, and should result in nerving us to greater | and better efforts towards self-improvement. Learning does not necessarily bring all happiness, but it certainly helps to alleviate much misery. (500)

EXERCISE 193.

Reporting Grammalogues.

I do not know that you will approve of my contention, *but I have special* reasons *which* lead *me to* | *speak as I do, and the strength of my opinion ought not to be influenced by any objection which you* | *may* take *to my belief. I believe* then, *and I have* always *believed, that* curiosity *is a very much* stronger | feeLing *in the* minds *of most of the* men *I have met* than perhaps, *they would be willing to own.* | *I believe that it is this* feeLing *which has sent* adventurous men *in every generation to* exploRe regions *of the* (1) worLd *whither* man *had not* traveLLed before. *I have no* doubt *that it is the* same feeLing *that* impels men | *to the* study *of* history, *that they may* find *out the religious and* political views *of their* predecessoRs *on this* | earth, *the* struggles *they had, and the* sufferings *they* enduRed *for the* sake *of religion and the Holy Scriptures ; that* | *they may* trace *the* rise *and* progress *of Christianity in the* days *when the word* "*Christian*" *was* taken *to signify* | *a* traitor *to the* State *itself ; and that they may* learn *something of what was signified by the* downfaLL *of* (2) heathenism, *the* gradual dawn *of* freedom *of* worsHip, *and the* growth *of a larger* measure *of liberty to practise the* | teachings *of the Saviour. When I speak thus, however, I do not* intend *that my words should be* taken *to* | *signify that this* curiosity *is in any* sense *to be* deprecated *or* blamed. *On the* contrary, *I glory in the* | possession *of a larger* sHaRe *of the* feeLing than *most young* men *can* lay claim *to.* Indeed, *I go so* | faR *as to* say *that the great* men *of the* past, *who have glorified the* age *in which they* lived, (3) were *remarkable for the* possession *of this* quality *of* curiosity; *and the* same *may be* said *of the* men *who* | *are* likely *to glorify the* present age. *Tell me, ye* doubters, *what* led SiR Isaac Newton *to the* discoveries *which* | *have* revolutionized *the* scientific worLd, both *as* regards theory *and practice? What* induced SiR Isaac Pitman, *when a mere youth,* | *to* devote *himself to the* study *of* phonetics, *and* brought *him, at* last, *to* invent *a* system *of short*hand *that* | *is* now *practised by* hundreds *of* thousands *in all* parts *of the* EngLish-*speak*ing worLd? *What was the* feeLing *that* (4) *first* impeLLed Edison *and* Marconi *to* experiment, *and,* uLtimately, *to* woRk such wonders *with the* subtle foRce *of* eLectricity? *Was* | *it not, in all these* cases, *a* feeLing *of* laudable curiosity *to know more* than *they* previousLy knew, *which* prompted | *these* men *to* studies *which have had* such striking effects *upon the* worLd *at large? And if we* look *at* | *the most* prominent men *in the House of* Commons, *we shall* find *that they, too, have* turned *to advantage this* | feeLing *of* curiosity *which is* inherent *in us all. It is the* indulgence *of an* idle curiosity *that is* blameworthy. (500)

EXERCISE 194.

Reporting Grammalogues (continued).

According to the general opinion or belief, a country *cannot be* defended *with any great* measure *of* success *by a* | population *that has been, on whatever account,* degraded. "*They who are to* resist *with* success," says *one high* authority, "*must* | *first be* moulded *by equal* laws *into a* due sense *of* national pride *and* personal *importance.*" *It was from the* | lack *of these* feeLings *of* pride *in their nation and in themselves that the* Britons suffered *during the* Roman occupation, | *so* many *generations ago. It is quite true that after the* Romans *had been called away to the* defence *of* (1) *their own* capital, *the* Britons made *a much more* stubborn resistance *to their* new enemies than *the* latter *could have* | *thought or believed* possible, *yet there can be no* doubt *at all that the* Britons lost *their liberty a* second | time, *and* feLL *under the* sway *of the* men *from the* northern *nations, because the* sentiments *which had* animated *those* | *who met the first* invaders *of our* island *had* died *away and given* place *to a* sense *of* infeRiority. *When* | *the very principles of* freedom—*which should be the* life *and spirit of the* manhood *and youth of the* country (2) —*when these are* broken, *there is but* little hope *for the* future *glory of the nation. It was thus with* | *the* Britons. *Their young* children *and youths of* both sexes, *had been* accustomed, *year after year, and generation after generation,* | *to* accept *without a word of* reply *the* assumption *of* superiority *by their* conqueroRs, *the* Romans, *whose* residence heRe, *while* | *it improved the* face *of the* country *and* tended *to improve the* minds *of its* native inhabitants, certainLy destroyed *in* | *them those principles of liberty to which I have* referred. *They, therefore, cared* less than *they ought to have cared* (3) *what might be the* result *of their* struggles *with the* fresH invaders. *It is not difficult to believe that this* | lack *of true spirit* affected *somewhat the* issue *of the* struggle. *What might not have happened if the* Britons *had* | *but* preserved *in all its strength that spirit of* | freedom *which did so much to glorify the* deeds *of their* | predecessoRs! *How different it might all have been! And what a difference it would have* made *to us and to* | *the* worLd *at large! Let us think over these things in this way for a short* time, *and we shall* (4) *see how significant may be our own* actions, *and what significance they may have for generations yet* unborn. *Remember, ye* | students *upon whose* eaRs *these words may* faLL, *that if you are to* receive *the* fuLL *weight of the advantage* | *and improvement which may be* drawn *from the important* Lessons *of* history, *you must know what those* Lessons *signify to* | *you, and what they have signified to your* forefathers. *This is a truth that must ever be remembered by every* | *member of* society *who* desiRes *to be able to speak with special knowledge of the great importance of* historical study. (500)

EXERCISE 195.

Reporting Grammalogues (continued).

A gentleman, who was himself the principal manager *of one of the most important* railways *in this* country, *once remarked* | *that the secret of good* management *in any* business *or trade was to* attend strictly *to one thing at a* | time. *He never tried to do two things at once, and we are told that he* resisted, *too, any* attempt | *on the* part *of other gentlemen to* make *him* alter *his* ruLe. *If he had a meeting with one* person, | *whether that* person *was a* chief *of a* department, *a* medical *doctor, a scripture* reader *for* some *religious* society, *or* (1) *an* advocate *for* some new woRk *of the Christian religion—it* mattered *not; he would see no one* else untiL | *he had done with the* business *in hand. If others called they had to wait till the first* visitor *went* | *away, which might be in* ten minutes *or in half an hour; or they could call* again *upon a more* | favourable *opportunity.* "*One at a* time, *and let each* take *his* turn" *was the* ruLe *he put down for* himself, | and by following it steadily he got through an amount of work that I believe would have been altogether above and (2) beyond the powers of most gentlemen. The number of people who interviewed him each week was almost incredible, and though | they did not all go away equally well pleased with themselves and with him, yet they seldom failed to thank | him for his courtesy of manner and language, and they never accused him of want of thought. To be sure, | he would not always see eye to eye with those who came to meet him, nor could he approve of | the methods of all who worked near him. In several instances he was known to send out for an official (3) that he might tell him his duties, and give him a warning if he had done wrong. He never made | light of a serious offence, but no man was ever called upon to explain a mere slip, and no one | was sent away, however serious his fault might be, till it was impossible to doubt his guilt. The manager usually | took particular pains to show the culprit that if it was necessary to punish him, the evil was brought about | by his own fault; that it was owing principally to a want of care on the offender's part; and that (4) it gave his superior no pleasure to have to use the authority he had for the purpose of chastisement. "Why | will you not apply your mind to study, and so build up a future for yourself?" was a question he | often put to the clerks in the building wherein his office was situated. And he would continue: "Won't you now | decide to make use of the powers which have been given you to help you toward a better and more | happy life? Whither do you go after the day's work is over? Is it your usual plan to take the (5) chair at some convivial meeting, or do you usually keep out of such societies and spend your time in your | own house, effecting improvements in one direction or another? Use your time wisely and well, for it cannot be extended." (540)

EXERCISE 196.

Reporting Grammalogues (concluded).

My dear Mr. Green,—It may not be out of place to remind you, and I am sure you will | pardon me for doing so, that though one may have difficulty in earning a good character, it is quite an | easy thing to lose it, as has been done over and over again by men specially lacking in strength of | will. I do not wish to deliver a sermon, or to suggest that my remark applies to you personally. Oh, | dear no; I should owe you an apology, if I even thought of such a thing. I threw out the (1) remark merely to remind myself, as well as you, that it requires prudence to guard the good names we have | won among our fellows. Our fair names are prized by us both, and had not we deserved them we should | not possess them. The old epigram is as true now as ever, and it puts the same truth in a | different way, thus:

> See thou thy credit keep; 'tis quickly gone;
> 'Tis gained by many actions; but 'tis lost by | one.

This epigram should be delivered to every student of Phonography a third and a fourth time; aye, and repeated (2) till it is deeply graven in his mind *and* heart. *The delivery of a truth* like *the one* contained *in* | *the* couplet just quoted *may not* appeal *to him who has his* ideas confined *within a* narrow circle, *and who* | looks *with a cold eye upon anything* requiring *a larger* mental scope. *But it will* appeal *to the* healthy, *able* | man *who* looks *with awe and* reverence *upon everything that is good and holy and* sublime. *And, surely, his is* | *the* right attitude *of* mind, *according to the* tenets *of Christianity and the* teachings *of the Saviour, now glorified in* (3) *heaven. A good* name *is his by* right, *and as his* actions *have* deserved, *it is generally given to him.* | *Ah, my* friend, *not every lord is a* noble man, *but every* poor man working *at his art or trade* | *may cheer himself and child with the thought that it is the* manner *of using the* faculties *given him by* | *God that* makes *the true* man *and the gentleman. The* possession *of gold in itself is of no use. It* | *may* even *do* harm *by* hardening *a* man's kind *nature. Remember,* thou wealthy man, thou canst *buy a house, a* (4) horse *or a cart; but* thou canst *not buy a good* name. Thou canst *build thyself a house with thy* | *gold which shall not be equalled by any, and* fashion *it according to thy* desire; *but* thou canst only *build* | *up a good* name *by good* deeds, *and the* labourer *in thy yard may have a* better name than thou | hast. *Ah, remember these truths, and* thou *shalt be happy!* Proceed *upon principle; give all the weight of thy influence* | *to the* furtherance *of truth, religion, and* justice; *and* thou *shalt be thanked and* blest *by all who know* thee. (500)

EXERCISE 197.

Reporting Contractions (Section 1).

A brief *observation or inspection is sufficient to* show *anyone, irrespective of his professional* standing, *that productive and* non-*productive* wages | *respectively* require *special* treatment *from the efficient* book-keeper. Only *an inefficient accountant, deficient in the organization of financial* affairs, *and* | *imperfect or defective in his knowledge of commercial* matters, *could* make *the mistake of* supposing *that it would be sufficient* | *in every circumstance to* regard both classes *of* expense *as of the* same *description. No controversial* discussion *can be* held | *on the* point, *which is beyond controversy. Generalization in the preservation of accounts may be* termed *unconstitutional, from the* point (1) *of* view *of anyone who has organized or knows how to organize a* set *of accounts, whether* relating *to passenger* | traffic *or any other* business. Such *generalization would* denote *inefficiency in the* book-keeper, *and would be prejudicial to the interests* | *of his* firm. *It would be destructive of* accuracy, *and it might* result *in substantial* loss *and the* consequent *indignation* | *of the* management *or executive, who would naturally be indignant at a deficiency in their* profits brought about *by the* | *insufficient knowledge of anyone under their jurisdiction or subjection.* Imagine *their large prospective* dividend reduced *to an insignificant or unsubstantial* (2) *amount, and you will understand the signification of* such *a mistake as I have* mentioned. *I* fear *they would cross-examine* | *the* inefficient book-keeper on his inefficiency, and when they had cross-examined him sufficiently, the result of the cross-examination would probably | be that the executive would exercise their prerogative, and, without prejudice to his personal character, would dismiss him for his | want of proficiency. He might plead abstraction on his own part, or obstruction on the part of another as a | reason for the insufficiency of circumstantial detail in his book-keeping; but this would not cover the imperfection of his knowledge (3) of the construction of accounts. The chaRtered accountant must have undergone an examination, both subjective and objective, in the theory | of accounts. After his credentials have been inspected, he must inscribe a foRm of adhesion to the constitution of the | association, and when this is inscribed the inscription is taken as binding upon him. He must be a constitutional member | and must never behave in an unconstitutional way. He must act constitutionally himself and must restrain others from acting unconstitutionally, | or so as to lead to the degeneration of the association. He need know nothing about perspective or the doctrines (4) of transubstantiation, regeneration, jurisprudence, or the transmission of energy; but he must be proficient in accounts; must know how to | draw up a deficiency account, explain the insufficiency of the debtor's funds, and how there might have been a sufficiency | instead of an insufficiency. His assistants must woRk efficiently, too. He must check anyone whose woRk is inefficiently done, who | is insubordinate himself, or whose conduct leads to insubordination in others. The apparent insignificance of obstructive tactics must not deceive | him, and if he can transcribe shorthand and make an accurate transcription on the writing macHine so much the better. (500)

EXERCISE 198.

Reporting Contractions (Section 2).

Among the distinguished personages present at the thanksgiving service in a metropolitan church last January was an archbishop; a benignant | Nonconformist preacher, with benignity in every feature; a professor of Nonconformity from a neighbouring Tabernacle; a benevolent Presbyterian, famous for | his benevolence, especially to those connected with Presbyterianism; a leading Episcopalian and several members of the Episcopal bench, and a philanthropist, who in philanthropy and philanthropic zeal sets an example of unexampled unselfishness to the worLd. There was also an ecclesiastic, | whose name I was unable to ascertain, but whose dignified, yet melancholy, appearance attracted me. A fine, tall man he (1) was, in whom every baseR feeLing seemed extinguished. Holiness and dignity sHone in every line of his face. The majesty | of his figure helped to dignify his whole appearance and stamp him as an ecclesiastic incapable of selfishness or meanness. | A man with a high appreciation of the dignity of the sacred ministry; who would not hesitate to remonstrate with | any offender against ecclesiastical orthodoxy, and who would insist upon an orthodox observance of the ecclesiastical laws with all the | poweR which he was evidentLy capable of sHowing, should occasion requiRe it through a breach of orthodoxy *by anyone subject* (2) *to his jurisdiction. The* strong resolute mouth *of the stranger* convinced *me that he was an administrator who would demonstrate* | *his strength of will in any tribunal over which he might be called upon to* preside. *I could well* imagine | *him to be a* man *who would discharge the* duties consequent *upon his appointment,* regardless *of any disappointment or displeasure* | *he might give* either *to a plaintiff or a defendant.* Doubtless then *his* present air *of resignation and contentment would* | *give* place *to dissimilar* appearances, *and he would* simply *be the* judge *and administrator of the* law *as he* found (3) *it.* Clearly, *he was a* man *who would distinguish himself in any* position, either *as a plenipotentiary representing a* powerful | *cabinet in an arbitration, or as an executor and* trustee *for a* deceased friend. *For th attainment of a* worthy | *object, or the atonement of a* supposed fault, *that* man *would relinquish any* position *and extinguish any* private ambition. *I* | *should* like *to* hear *him* preach *on the resurrection and the celestial entertainment waiting for all who give up selfish* | *ways, and* live *henceforth a* life *distinguished for* virtue. *I* noticed, also, *Lieutenant-Col.* Smith, *Captain* Brown, *and a non-commissioned* (4) *officer who has been* promised *a lieutenancy as a* reward *for* bravery *in the* field last *November and December. Near* | *them was an evangelical* minister, formerly connected *with Methodism, and also a* statesman *who was baptized a Baptist and* holds | strong views regarding *Baptism and the* right *to baptize* infants. *He* addressed *a public meeting* last *February, and is to* | *speak in* Manchester *next September. I* observed, also, Lady Nemo, *who is an administratrix and executrix under the will of* | *a* lady *whose* estates were *so* heavily *mortgaged that she could* obtain *no* further *mortgage upon them under any circumstances.* (500)

EXERCISE 199.

Reporting Contractions (Section 3).

Sir Isaac Newton, *the extraordinary mathematician whose wonderful and unquestionable* genius *astonished the* world *and* raised *him from obscurity into* | *a* position *proportionate to his* talent, *and whose* name *has the singular* power *of* arousing *the enthusiasm of all enthusiastic* | lovers *of original and independent* research, *was the* son *of a* farmer, *who was* devoted *to agriculture and agricultural* pursuits. | Isaac Newton *was* always *an enthusiast* as regards *mathematics, and was able to astonish those who assembled in his* father's | *house by the imperturbable and impregnable* patience *he* exhibited, *and by his* skill *as a mechanic in the manufacture of* (1) *mechanical* toys. *His* life *was a perpetual* study *of subjects which are repugnant to most* men. *He* felt *no repugnance* | *for them, however, and he was perpetually* exercising *his intelligence in* attempts *to* reduce *the expenditure of* energy, *to* make | *the* forces *of nature subservient to* man *and applicable to every contingency, and to substitute mechanical* power *for* manual labour. | *It is unquestionably true that the applicability of* many *of the* inventions *used by the manufacturer at the* present day, | *though he may not suspect it, is* due *to the preliminary* experiments *of* Newton. *His* name *is* among *the highest* (2) *in the aristocracy of the* scientific worLd. Both *the aristocratic* statesman *and the democratic* leader advocating *the* cause *of the* | *democracy owe a* debt *to the indefatigable* labours *of* Newton. *Magnetism and magnetic* phenomena attracted *him, and we are informed* | *that the* simple *observation of an* apple faLLing *in a perpendicular* direction *was sufficient to inform him of a* universaL | law. *He was the great informer of the* worLd *of* science. *He manufactured no* theory *without care, and no* ChanceLLor | *of the Exchequer could* bestow *more* pains *on his* Budget than Newton bestowed *on the* statement *of a* discovery. *To* (3) *the inconsiderate and extravagant individual* devoid *of sensibility, to* whom *expensive* attiRe *and extravagance in* living *are indispensable, the indescribable* | simplicity *of* Newton's life *is not intelligible. Indiscriminate expenditure of his revenue was antagonistic to his sensible,* well-*proportioned and* | *intelligent nature, and intemperance was never suspected in him.* Indeed, *it* found *in him an antagonist whose antagonism was proportionate* | *to his enthusiasm for* learning. *He* recognised *his responsible* position *and the responsibility* attaching even *to his extemporaneous* utterances, *and* | *not in his most familiar* moments, *and with those whose friendship and familiarity he* prized, *would he* sanction *intemperance. He* (4) *would superscribe no suspicious recognizance, and, though he* liked *journalism, he did not* favour *it as an investment. His superscription* | *on any indenture or certificate was sufficient to advertise its* genuineness. *He never advertised himself at an assembly, and he* | resented *advertisement by others.* Isaac Newton, *Esquire, was* title enough *for him, but* Queen Anne bestowed *on him the* honour | *of* knighthood, *and,* certainLy, *his* merits were *no more* than *proportionately* rewarded. *The magnetism of his example, and the magnetic* | *influence he* exercised, were *extraordinary. He* died *in* 1725, *at the* ripe age *of* eighty-five. (500)

EXERCISE 200.

Advanced Phraseography (Section 1).

I-am about *to* say *something which I*-hope-*you-will-not* take *as-if-it*-were meant *to be* | dis*respect*ful *to-the* authors *whos* woRks *you*-love, *and-the* accuracy *of whose opinions I*-am-*not* disputing—*at-all*-events, *not for-the*-moment. *I-can quite understand that I-may-be* wrong; *I-cannot*-hope *to be* right | *at-all*-times; *but, at-the*-same-time, *you-should-not, you-must-not, and-I*-hope-*you-will-not,* | condemn *me* unheaRd. *I-cannot-be* led *to-believe that-you-are so* unfaiR. *I*-trust-*not, and-I-shall-* (1) *be* disappointed *if-it-is* proved *that I*-am-*mistaken. I-did-not, and-I-do-not, expect to*-find | *that I*-am. *I-shall-be*-glad, then, *if-you-will-tell-me if-it-has* occurred *to-you that-* | *there-are*-some readers *who never* take-*the* trouble *to* verify-*the* statements *which they see from*-time-*to*-time | *in-the* books *they* read? *I-do-not*-say—*I-cannot*-say—*that-they-believe a* statement *because-they-think* | *that-the* book *in-which-it-has*-appeaRed *is an* inspiRed voLume; *for, as you-must-be*-aware, *here-is-* (2) onLy *one* such voLume. *But I-do* say, *and-I-think-you-will-not* deny *it, that, at-any-*rate, | *they* act *as-if-they-thought so. I-may-not-be* right, *but I-think I-shall-not-be mistaken* | *in* saying *that-you-must-have come* across instances *of* assertions *in* books *of-which-it-must-be-*said, *and* | *of-which-it-has-been-*said repeatedly, *that-they-are* absolutely incorrect. *You-will, I-think,* agree *with me that-* | *we-have all, at-some-*time *in-the-*course *of-our* reading, *met* such instances. *Moreover, you-should-not-be* (3) unwilling *to* allow *that for a* reader *to* accept *every-*statement *of an* author *as-if-it-*were heresy *to-* | doubt *it or to-*check *it, is, and must-be,* opposed *to* common-sense *and-the* right *use of-one's* | reasoning poweRs. *If-the* statement *is* found *to be* correct, *surely you-*weRe-*not* wrong *in* proving *its truth. If-* | *it-is-not* proved *to be* accurate, then *you-cannot-be* blamed *for* avoiding *the* trap *in*to *which-you-*weRe | *so very near*Ly faLLing. *The* faculties *by-which-it-was* possible *for-you* to-discover-*the* inaccuracy *were given to-* (4) *you in-*order-*to-be used, and you-can* scaRcely *be* wrong *in* using *them. You-may-not have-thought* | *of-this* before, *but I-*trust *that for-*some-time *to-come you-will* watch *more* closely *the* statements *you-* | read, *and-if-it-*does *happen that-you-can* verify *them I-*hope-*you-will. You-may* then say *I-* | *was-not* wrong, *and-that I-had* reason *for-these remarks. I-had-not thought of-*extending *this* chat *to-* | such *a* length, *and I-cannot-do* better-than conclude now. *I-shall-not* trouble *you* again *for-*some-time. (500)

EXERCISE 201.

Advanced Phraseography (Section 2).

I-think-there-will-be few, *or-rather, I-know-there-will-be* few, *who-will* deny *that if-there-* | *is-one thing more-than-*another *upon-which* some-men pride *themselves* before-*their* friends *whenever-there-is a* chance | *of-doing-so, it-is what in-their-own-language they-call their* liberality *of-thought and* extent *of information.* | *As-*soon-*as a subject is* started *in-their-*presence, *they-are* anxious *to-*prove *how-much* they *know* about | *it; what, in-their-opinion, should-be-done or* avoided; *how, in-their-*case, *hey would-have* acted *in-*such (1) *and-*such *a way; and so on. And, as-we-have-*seen, *they expect their* heaRers *to be interested in-* | *their-*statements, *and to-*accept *them as* authoritative. *We-know-their-ways as-well-as-can-be, and-we-have-* | *their* names before *our* minds *just-*now, *have-we-not?* Now, *I-am-sure-there-is* always *a* desiRe *on-* | *the-*part-*of sensible* people *to-*heaR *a* schoLar *speak on a subject which he knows as-well-as-*possible; | *for-there-is sure to be-*something said *that-is-*worth Listening *to.* Such-men *are* decidedly worth heaRing *for-* (2) *their-own-*sake, *and for-the-*sake-*of-the* wisdom *which* faLLs *from-their* lips. *But, I-wish-there-*weRe | *more-*men *who* realized *that though-there-is* such *a* desiRe *as I-have-*mentioned, *it-is* restricted *to-the* | utterances *of-those* whom *we-call* thinkers. *I-know-there-is a* deep-rooted antipathy *in most-*men *to-be-* | *told-that, after-all, their knowledge is very* limited; *but,* then, *I-know-there-is-not-one of us who-* | *can* truthfully assert *that-he* possesses fuLL *information* even *on-the most* simple-matters, *and-I-think-there-is-no* (3) haRm *in* reminding *ourselves* sometimes *of*-some (of the) *things* about *which-we* neither *know anything nor can* readily get | *to know anything*. *For*-instance, *I-see-there-is a* statement *that* wild ducks *will* readily follow *a* red dog | *as*-soon-*as-they see it*. *Why is-this?* *There-may-be an* answer, *but*, *if-there-is*, *I* confess | *I-do-not-know it*. Again, *I-think-there-will-be*-some *of-my* hearers *who-will-have* noticed *in*- | *their* country walks *that-the* scarlet runner always twines *to-the* right, *while-the* honeysuckle *as* invariably twines *to-the* (4) left. *If-you-are as-well-as-usual in-the*-morning *we-will go out* and-verify-*the* statement. *Can*- | *you* explain *these* simple facts? *There-is*-another-instance *which I-may*-refer *to*, *while we-are on-this-subject*. | *As-soon-as-the* spring comes, *we-know as-well-as-can-be, that-the* swallow *and-the* cuckoo *will* | *come to-this*-country, *as-we-have*-seen-*them come in-the* past, *and as*-soon-*as-they* feel *that* | autumn *is upon them they-will* leave *us* again. *What* brings *them*, *and how do they* find *their way* here? (500)

EXERCISE 202.

Advanced Phraseography (Section 8).

(*a*) *Dear*-Madam,—*In*-reference-*to your*-letter (of the) 10th-inst., *I-have* further-considered-*the* point raised, and-*I*- | *am*-certain-*that-you-are mistaken in-your* view. *I*-am-confident *that when-the*-matter *has-been* fully-considered, | *and-after-the* peculiar-*circumstances in*-connection-*with-the* case *have-been* taken-*into*-consideration, *you-will-see that*, *having*- | regard-*to-the* possible consequences, *it-will-be* better, *under-the-circumstances*, *to*-leave-*the*-matter where *it-is*. *On* | further-consideration *you-may think-this an unsatisfactory*-conclusion; *but when you* take-*into*-consideration *the* necessary-consequences *of*-legal (1) measures, *which-must-be*-considered, *I-think-you-will-agree that*, *all-circumstances* considered, submission *will-be-the* best. *I*- | am-inclined-*to-think-that-the peculiar-circumstances-of-the*-case *must-be*-considered, *and-the*-matter dealt *with in*- | such-*a*-manner *as to* avoid *all*-further friction, *if*-possible. *After*-due-consideration *of-every-circumstance*, *I-have*-concluded | *that-the*-course *I* advise *is-the* best, *and-I*-hope *that-that*-conclusion *will meet with your* approval. *What* | attitude does-*the* local-authority take *in*-relation-*to the* proposed new *buildings in* Morton Road? *Yours*-truly, ALFRED OLIVER. (200)

(*b*) *Dear*-Sir,—*I-have*-received *your*-letter *with*-reference-*to-the* dispute about *which I*-wrote *to-you*, *and-I*- | *will*-consider-*the*-matter *care*fully before taking action. *Every*-point *shall-be*-considered; *every*-possible consequence *shall-be*-taken-*into*- | consideration, before *I*-decide. *At-the*-same-time, *I*-feel bound *to* say *that I*-fear *your* counsel *will-not* | lead *to a satisfactory*-conclusion (of the) matter. *On-the*-contrary, *I-think-it-is a* course *which-will-be*- | considered *by-the other*-side *as an* evidence *of* weakness *in-my* attitude *with*-relation-*to the* trespass, *and-the*- (1) contrary result *to-the one you-expect is very*-likely *to* follow *in*-consequence. *In-this*-manner-*the* trouble *will*- | *be* aggravated, *and-the*-provocation *I-have*-received *in-the* past *will-be* small *in*-comparison *with what I-may*- | *be-called-upon to put up with. However, I*-am-*very*-glad *I*-wrote *to-you with*-regard-*to-this*- | matter, *and-I-will*-consider *your* counseL before *going* further. *With*-reference-*to-the* proposed new *houses in* Morton Road, | *I-have*-received *a* letter *from-the* surveyoR *to-the* local-authority, stating *that-it-is*-considered *essential that I* (2) *should* alter *the* plans *in-several important respects, and-that with*-regard-*to-the* drainage scheme, *the* local-authority *will*- | *be*-glad *to*-receive fresH plans, *which-will-be*-taken-into-consideration, *and, if*-possible, *approved. I-have*-seen *my*- | brother *in*-relation-*to this*-Letter *and, after*-due-consideration, *we-have*-concluded *to* abandon-*the* idea, *in*-view (of | the) opposition *we-have*-received, *and-in-this*-manner answer-*the* surveyoR's letter. *You-will-probably remember that I-was* | treated *in-the*-same-manner last-*year, and-in*-Like-manner *I*-gave *up-the* project. *Yours*-truly, TERESA DRIVER. (300)

EXERCISE 208.

Advanced Phraseography (Section 4).

In-all-parts-*of-the*-worLd educational-authorities *are* vying *with-one*-another *in-their* efforts *to* encourage *commercial* students | *to*-dive deeper-*and*-deeper *in*to-*the* theory *of* business *on-the-one-hand, and to-give more-and-more*- | attention *to-the* application *of-that* theory, *on-the-other-hand. In*-point-*of*-fact, *there-is*-now, *for-the*- | *first-time, a general* recognition (of the) need *for* preparation *for* business life. *The* fact-*of-the*-matter *is* that- | *the-example* (of the) foreigneR *has* set *us thinking, with-the*-result *that, whether it-be* right-*or*-wrong, *the* (1) *commercial* schools *are with us, and it-would*-now *be more-or*-less *impossible to*-close-*them. That-they-are* | appreciated *at-the*-present-day *is* proved *by-the large-numbers in* attendance *at-them, notwithstanding-the* comparatively *short*-space- | *of*-time *which-has* elapsed since-*they*-were *first established.* The facts-*of-the*-case *in-their*-favour *have-been* | *put* forward again-*and*-again *by* prominent *commercial*-men, both *in-this*-country *and on-the-other*-side (of the) | Atlantic ; *but never more* foRcibly than *by* "Punch" *when-he*-said "Incompetency *is a* gift *of heaven, but* business habits (2) *can-be* acquiRed." *This-is*-now widely recognised, *and* men *send their* sons *and* daughters *to-commercial* schools *quite as*- | *a*-matter-*of*-course. *From-first-to*-last, *all-the-way through-the* course, *the* students *are* taught *on practical* | lines. Imaginary transactions *are* carried *on with*-clients *all-over-the*-worLd, *and, by-the-way, there-is* almost *as*- | *much* keenness displayed *by-the* students *as there-is in* actuaL business. *As-a*-matter-*of*-fact, *the* rivalry *that* | exists *between-them accounts in-a-great*-measure *for-the* successfuL sHow *they-are able-to*-make, *first in-the* (3) examinations, *and*, sooner-*or*-Later, *in* business also. *Prejudice, however*, dies haRd, *and-though-the number* grows less-*and*-less | *every*-day, *there-are* still *a* few people *who-are, to-a-great*-extent, opposed *to-the* idea *of* teaching | business methods *in* school. *It-is difficult to* say *what-is-the*-matter *with*-such people. *I-shall-be*-glad- | *to-know, in-the-first*-instance, *or in-the-first*-place, *what-is their objection to a youth* learning, say, | *the* theory *of* Banking *and-the* Exchanges? *In-the*-second-place, *I would* ask "*Do-you*-mean-*to*-say *that*- (4) such *knowledge will* interfeRe *with a youth's* progress *in* business life?" *In-the-third*-place, *I*-ask *what-would-be*- | *the* present condition *of*-BritisH *trade* were *it not for-the* theories *of-thought*ful men *in-the* past? *In-the*- | *next*-place, *we-shall-be*-glad-*to*-heaR *if-it-has-not-been* proved again-*and*-again *that* ignorance *of* | theory *on-the*-part-*of* merchants *has-been-the* cause *of* failuRe? *And-in-the*-last-place, *I* would point- | *out that-the* ideal trader, like-*the* ideal artisan, *is-he who most* successfully combines perfect theory *with* prudent *practice.* (500)

EXERCISE 204.

Business Phrases and Contractions (Section 1).

(*a*) *Dear*-SiR, — *I-am-in*-receipt-*of-your*-letter, *and-I*-am-instructed *by-the*-directors *to* ask *why you* | *did-not* report *with*-reference-*to* Brown's position eaRlieR? *I-am*-directed also *to-forward you-the* enclosed-letter, *and* | *to*-request *an immediate* explanation (of the) same. *I-am*-directed-*to*-state further, *that* untiL *these*-matters *are* cleaRed | *up, you-must*-consider *yourself* suspended *from* acting *on* behalf (of the) company. *I-can*-assure-*you that I*-regret | *having to*-write-*you in*-such *a* strain. *I-am-surprised that-you-should-be*-placed *in*-such *a* position, (1) *and-I-do-not-understand how it-has come* about. *I*-hope-*you-will-be-able*-to explain *what I*- | regard *as an* awkward state *of* affaiRs. *You-may*-consider *it* best *to-come to*-London, *and-I-think-you*- | *may-as-well do-so as*-Long-*as you-are-at-liberty*. Enclosed-please-find cheque *for* last-week's expenses. | *I*-beg-*to-call-your*-attention *to-the* deduction, *which I*-regret-*to*-state *I-was*-obliged-*to*-make, *as*- | *it-is* against *the* ruLes *to* allow *for*-such items. *I-have-to-call-your*-attention *to-the* small cheque (2) dated 15th September, *which* apparently *has-not-been* presented. *I*-am-requested *to* ask-*you to-present this at-once*, | *so-that our* books *may-be* cleaRed. *With*-regard-*to* Patterson's oRder, *you-will-be*-glad-*to-know that-we*- | *are-in-a*-position *to*-make *delivery next*-week. *I-have-the-pleasure to* enclose-herewith *the particulars you*-requiRe, | *and-I*-hope-*you-will-be-able-to* cleaR *up-the* present-*difficulty*. *Yours*-faithfully. (275)

(*b*) *Gentlemen*,—*I*-am-*in*-receipt-*of-your*-favour *of-yesterday, and-I*-am-*rather-surprised that-you-should* consider *me* | *in* fault *with*-regard-*to* Brown's affaiRs. *I*-beg-*to*-enclose-herewith *for-your*-consideration copy *of-my*-report (of | the) 2nd August, *from which-you-will-see that I* advised caution *in* dealing *with-this* man. *I-beg-to*- | *inform-you* also, *and-I-think-you-will-be-surprised to*-heaR, *that I* repeated *this* advice *in-my* interview | -*with-the*-manager last-month. *Under-these-circumstances, I-do-not-understand-the* tone *of-your*-favour *of-yesterday, and*- (1) *I*-propose *to-wait upon you at-once, so-that-this and-the-other* matter *may-be* gone *into* thoroughly. | *I*-enclose-*account for* expenses *to* date, *and-I* also enclose-statement sHowing *that-the* items deducted *from* last-week's | *account* were authorized *by-the* terms *of-my* agreement. *I-have,* therefore, included *these* items *in-the*-present *account.* I- | enclose-cheque *for* Smithson's *account, and-I*-hope-*you-are*-satisfied *with-the*-oRders *for*warded *to-you yesterday. I*-am- | *much*-obliged *for-the-particulars you sent me.* Faithfully-youRs. (190)

(*c*) *Dear*-SiR, — *I*-beg-*to-acknowledge*-receipt-*of-your*-letter *of-yesterday, and to* confiRm-*the* telegram *sent you this-* | morning, asking *you to*-wait instructions. *Your*-letter *was* considered *by-the*-directors *at-their* meeting *this*-morning, *and-I-* | am-directed-*to-inform-you that-they-will-be*-pleased *if-you-will* resume *your* duties forthwith, *and* leave-*the-* | matters requiRing explanation untiL *you-are* heRe *in-the usual* course. *I-am*-requested *to* add *that-the*-directors *have-* | *no*-doubt *that a* personal interview *will satisfactorily* cleaR *up-the* position. *I*-enclose-invoice *for* Grayson *and* Blackstone, *and* (1) also cheque *for-the-amount* deducted *in* eRROR *from-your* last-week's expenses *account. Yours*-obediently. (116)

EXERCISE 205.

Business Phrases and Contractions (Section 2).

(*a*) *Dear*-SiRs,—*In*-reply-*to-your*-esteemed-favour *of-yesterday, we*-regret *that-we-are*-unable *to*-quote *special*-rates | *for-the* quantity *of* Petersburg Deals *you*-mention, *but-we-shall-be*-glad-*to* supply *you at-the* oRdinary-rates | *if-you* favour *us with-the*-oRder. *These-are-the* best-terms *we-are-in-a*-position *to*-offer *for-* | such *a* small lot. *Our* lowest-terms *for* 150 standaRds *would-be* £10 5s. | per standaRd. *The goods are* (of the) best-quality, *and-if-you-can let-us have an* oRder *for-this* (1) quantity *by*-return-*of*-post, *or by*-wire-*at-once, we-shall-be*-pleased *to*-make-*the* necessary-arrangements *to-* | *deliver-the* deals *in*-accordance-*with your*-requiRements. Kindly *give our* quotation *your* eaRly-consideration, *and*-oblige *us with an* | eaRly-reply, *as there-is a* brisk demand *for-these-goods, and-we-cannot* make *this* offer fiRm *beyond* Saturday *next.* Referring-*to-your*-letter (of the) 5th-inst., *the* specimens *of* mouLdings *will-be-for*warded *to-you by*-parcel- | post *as*-soon-*as* ready, *and-we*-hope *they-will-be*-found suitable *for-your* purpose. *We-could forward-the* (2) quantity *you*-requiRe *by-goods*-train *on*-receipt *of-your instructions, and-if-you* desiRe *it we-could send on* | *a* small quantity *by* passenger-train *to* ALLendale station. *We-will*-arrange-*the*-matter *any-way to-meet your* convenience, | *and, in-any*-case, *you-may*-rely *upon your*-oRder *being* promptly executed *to-the* best-*of-our*-ability. Please | accept *our* best-*thanks for-your*-kind enquiry.—*Yours*-faithfully. (270)

(*b*) *Gentlemen,—In*-reply-*to-your*-letter (of the) 3rd inst., *I-will-forward-the* books *by-first*-post *to*-morrow, *and-* | *the* bill-*of*-sale *and* bill-*of*-exchange *by* registered-letter *as*-soon-*as*-convenient. *The* balance-sHeet *and* statement- | *of-account are-not-yet* ready, *but will-be for*warded *as*-soon-*as*-possible. Referring-*to-your*-favour (of the) | 26th ult., *I-have-sent Mr.* Miles *a* copy *of-your*-last-letter *to-me, as* desiRed. *I*-enclose- | herewith copy-*of-my*-last-letter *to* Brown, *together* with postal-order received *from-him in* payment-*of-account yesterday.* (1) *I* heaR *he-has-been* speculating *on-the* Stock-Exchange, *and-has* lost heavily. Rider promises *to-send-the* balance- | *of-your-account at-the* week-end. *According-to-my* notes *the* balance-due *is* £40 10s. 0d. *Is*- | *this* correct ? Rider asks *me if-we-can* supply *him with* two dozen paiRs (of the) vases *with* tulip decoration, | *in*-exchange *for an equal* number decorated *with a* rose, *delivered to-him* six-months-*ago, and for-which he* | finds *he-has-no* sale. *He-is willing to* pay *the* cost *of* carriage, *if-you* agree *to-the* exchange. (2) Please instruct *me on-the* matter, *or* write-*him* direct, *sending me a* copy *of-your*-reply. *The other* matters | *you*-refer *to are having my* best-attention. *Yours*-faithfully. (230)

EXERCISE 206.

Business Phrases and Contractions (Section 3).

(*a*) *Dear*-SiR,—*We-are-in*-receipt-*of-your*-favour (of the) 2nd inst., *and-in*-reply beg *to*-quote-*you* | 3s. 9d. peR-lb. *for first*-quality, Scotch yarns. *We-could-deliver-the first*-instalment *by-the* | 18th-inst., *and-the* remainder *according-to*-agreement. *We should-be*-pleased *to* instruct *our* | makers-up *to* add *your* | *trade*-mark *to-the* labels, *but-this would* entail *a* little additional-expense. *We should, of*-course, onLy charge *you*- | *the* net *amount* (of the) additional-cost. Please-*let-us-know by* Wednesday-evening, *if*-possible, *if-we-may* book (1) *your*-oRder *on-these* terms. Referring-*to*-your-favour (of the) 1st-inst., *this-is-the first*-notice *we-have*- | received *of any* defect *in-the-goods, though-we for*warded last-week *over* fifty lots *to* various customeRs, besides fulfilling | *a large-number of*-oRders *this-week. In*-addition-*to-this, we-have-just*-received *a large* oRder *for immediate* | *delivery in-the*-north. *It-is*-just-possible *that yours was-the* onLy lot affected. *We-expect a call from*- | *the* finisHer *on-the* Tuesday-afternoon *of next*-week, *and-we-will* take-*care to-go* into-*the*-matter *with* (2) *him.* Please-*let-us-know by*-Monday-morning *the* fuLL extent (of the) damage, *together-with any* further-*particulars you*- | *may-have as-to-the* apparent cause. *You-will, of*-course, estimate *the* loss *at-first*-cost. *If-you-care* | *to*-make-*an-appointment for next* Tuesday-morning, *we-shall-be very*-pleased *to see-you on-the* matter. Please- | note-*that-the* catalogue *you*-refer *to as having-been sent* last-week *is not-yet-to-hand. Yours*-faithfully. | (280)

(*b*) *Gentlemen,*—*I*-regret *to inform-you that* Grinwell's *financial*-affaiRs *have* turned *out to be in a* worse muddle *than* | *I*-anticipated *from-the*-last-report *I*-received. *It*-appears-*that not*-onLy *has-he been* selling *first*-class *goods* | *at* considerably less than *trade*-price, *but-that, in*-order-*to* obtain ready money, *he-has* sold *them much under* | *first*-cost. *This, of*-course, *could-not* last long, *but-the* end came, apparently, sooner-than *he* expected. *The* trustee | hopes *to* declare-*a*-dividend *of* about 5s. 6d. *in-the* £. *Mr.* Grinwell *was* eLected *to-* (1) *the* board-*of-* directors (of the) Print Finishing Company, Limited, *two-years-ago; but he* seldom attended *a* directors'-*meeting,* | *and-his* name onLy appeaRed *in-one* directors'-report. *He-has-no interest in-the* concerRn *at-the*-present-time. | Please-forward *me the* necessary authority *to-* receive-*the-amount of* dividend *on-your* behalf. *I* heaR *that-there-is* | likely *to be* trouble *with-the* leaders (of the) local Trades-Union heRe. *According-to-their*-statement, *it*-appears-*that-* | *the* EmployeRs' Federation *have-not* kept *to-the*-terms *of-their* agreement *with-the*-men *in-* regard-*to an* advance (2) promised *them* last spring. *I*-hope-*the* dispute *will-be* settled amicably, *as-the* whole district *would* feeL *the* effects | *of a* strike *or* lock-out. *Yours*-faithfully. (227)

EXERCISE 207.

Political Phrases.

The party-leaders *in-the-House-of*-Commons *met* last-week *to* discuss-the Act-*of-Parliament, or-rather the* | Acts-*of-Parliament,* relating *to* free-*trade with-the* colonies, *the* freedom-*of-trade in*-EngLand, *and-the* freedom-*of-* | *the*-Press throughout-*the* BritisH EmpiRe. *There-was a large* gathering *of* right-honourable-*gentlemen from-the House-of-* Commons, | *and-one* right-honourable-*member is* reported *to-have called it-the most* successfuL *meeting of-the* kind *he had* | attended since *he first* entered-*the House-of*-Commons *as a member-of-parliament* many *years-ago.* *The* Prime-Minister, (1) *as* Leader-*of-the-House and* Leader-*of-the-* Party, presided *over-the-meeting, and was* supported *by-the* Chancellor- | *of-the*-Exchequer, *the First Lord-of-the*-Treasury, *the First Lord-of-the-* Admiralty, *the* Secretary-*for*-War, *and* | *other* prominent *members* (of the) *Government.* *It-is-understood that-the*-speech *of a well*-known *member* (of the) *House-* | *of-Lords, who-is a* pronounced free-trader, *was-the-subject of* discussion, *and it-is* rumoured *that a* bill | *will shortly be* introduced *in-the-House-of-Lords* dealing *with-the* question *of* taxation. *The* Army-*and*-Navy both (2) came *in for*-consideration, *and it-is-* said *that a Parliamentary*-Committee *is-to-be* appointed *to* inquiRe *into-the-* | *subject* (of the) training *of* officers *for* both branches (of the) service. *The* Secretary-*of*-State *is thought to* favour- | *the appointment of-members of* both Houses-*of-Parliament on-the* proposed committee. *With a Chairman-of*-Committee *who-has* | *had practical* experience *of* military *or* naval affaiRs *the* suggested committee *would-be*-likely *to* achieve beneficial results. *As-the* | President-*of-the*-Board-*of-Trade* said *in-his* speech *at* Manchester, *very-much-more information can-be* obtained *in-* (3) committee than-*the* majority *of* people *would* suppose. Another matter *which-is* stated *to-have* occupied *the* attention *of* right- | honourable-*members at-the meeting was-the* conveyance (of the) mails *to* Canada *and-the* United-States, *on-which* question | *the* Postmaster *General and-the* Secretary-*of*-State-*for-the*-Colonies both hoLd strong-views. *The* Leader-*of-the*-Opposition | *has* stated *his* intention *of*-raising-*the* question *in*-Committee-*of*-Supply, *and-the public will* look *forward with interest* | *to-the next* move. *The* Secretary-*of*-State-*for-the*-Home-Department *and-the* honourable-*and*-learned-*member for* Northwich (4) *are* said *to be* drafting *a* bill *for-the more* stringent regulation (of the) tobacco *trade*, *with a* view *to*- | *the* prevention *of* juveniLe smoking. *It-is probable that very-little interest will-be* displayed *at-the-first*-reading (of the) bill, *but at-the*-second-reading *there-should-be a good* debate, *as-the* Anti-Tobacco League *are* making *every* effort *to influence the* voting *upon-the* measure. *Those* engaged *in-the-trade are of opinion that though-the* bill | *may* pass-*the* second-reading, *it-will-be so* altered *that at-the-third*-reading *it-will-be quite* haRmless. (500)

EXERCISE 208.

Law Phrases.

The Articles-*of*-Association *are-the* ruLes *for-the* regulation *of a* joint-stock-company, *and-according-to-the opinion* | *of a* King's-Counsel (*who-was* recentLy counsel-*for-the*-defence *in an important* case tried *before-the Lord*-Chief- | Justice, *in-which-the* learned-counsel succeeded *in* obtaining *a* verdict-*for-the*-defendant), *the* Articles-*of*-Association *may-be* | produced *as* documentary-evidence aLong *with circumstantial*-evidence *in-the* Chancery-Division (of the) High-Court-*of*-Justice, *or* even | *in-the*-Central-Criminal-Court, *should a* case aRise *in-that* court. *The* Memorandum-*of*-Association, *on-the-other-hand*, (1) contains *a* statement (of the) *objects for-which a* joint-stock-company *is* foRmed, *and-the* conditions *of-its* incorporation. | *The* secretary *of a* joint-stock conceRn *should* make *it his* business *to be* acquainted *with-the principal* Acts-*of*- | *Parliament* relating *to* joint-stock-companies, *so-that if-he-should-be called-upon to-give* evidence *in a* court- | *of*-justice, *he-may* acquit *himself well*, *whether under-the* examination-*in*-chief *by* counsel-*for-the*-plaintiff, *or-the* | cross-examination *by-the* counsel-*for-the*-defendant. *He should remember that* fuLL *knowledge gives* calmness *and* nerve *to a* (2) witness, *and-that-the*-man *who-knows* both-*the* law *upon-the*-matter *and-the circumstances-of-the*-case need | feaR *no* question *from* learned-counsel. Then-*the* joint-stock-company's secretary *should* also *have a general knowledge of* County- | Court procedure, *so-as-to know how to* enfoRce payment *of a* debt *by-the* issue *of a* judgment-summons, | *should* such *an* extreme method become necessary *in-the*-course-*of* business. *If-the*-company *for-which he-is* secretary | *is a manufacturing* conceRn, *he-should* make *himself* acquainted *with-the*-main provisions (of the) Workmen's-Compensation-Act *and-the* (3) Employers'-Liability Act, *remembering that at* common-law *an* employeR *is-not* liable *for an* injury *to-one-of-his* | servants unLess personal negligence *on-the* employeR's part *is* proved *to-have* caused *the* accident. *It-should* also *be* borne | *in* mind *that in*-cases *of*-claim *for* compensation *under-these* acts *there-is a* right *of* appeal *from-the* | County-Court *to the* Divisional-Court (of the) High-Court-*of*-Justice, *and-afterwards*, *by* leave, *to-the* Court-*of*- | Appeal *and to-the-House-of Lords*. *Of*-course, *every* business man *should-know how to*-deal *with a* dishonoured (4) bill-*of*-exchange, *and-the circumstances in-which-the* services *of a* notary-*public may-be* dispensed *with; and-as* | *he-may*-requiRe *to* act *under a* power-*of*-attorney, *he should-be familiar with-the* foRm *of-this* authority. | *The* terms bill-*of*-sale, personal-estate, real-estate, *and* reversionary-bonus, *should-be* known *and-understood, and-there-should* | also *be*-some acquaintance *with-the-principal* duties *of an* official-receiver. *It-will-be* gathered *from-the* foRegoing *that*-| *there-are*-many *things* besides actuaL *knowledge of-his* business *which it-is very* desirable *the commercial* man *should-know.* (500)

EXERCISE 209.

Theological Phrases.

On-Christmas-Day, followeRs (of the) *Christian*-faith, *whether they be members* (of the) Church-*of*-England, *the* Church-*of*-IReland, *the* Church-*of*-Rome, *or-the* Episcopal-Church, *have-their*-attention directed *to-the-great* event *which-the* day | commemorates, *and-the* whole Christian-Church, *the* Church-*of*-Christ throughout-*the* whole woRLd, unites *in* celebrating *with* joy *the* | anniversary (of the) birth *of*-Christ-Jesus, *the* Son-*of*-God, *the* Lamb-*of*-God, *who*-came *in* obedience *to* | *the will of-His* Heavenly-Father, *to establish-the* Kingdom-*of*-Christ *upon* earth, *to* teach *the* children-*of*-God (1) *how to*-grow *in* grace *and* obtain everlasting-life *in-the* kingdom-*of-heaven.* *On-this*-day *every* minister (of | the) gospel, *whether a* Roman-*Catholic, a* Wesleyan-Methodist, *or a member* (of the) Established-Church, directs *his thoughts and*- | *his words to-the Child who-was* born (of the) Virgin-Mary, *and who-was* destined, *in-the*-providence-*of*- | God, *to*-preach *the* gospel *of*-peace, *and* woRk *a* stupendous change *in-the religious beliefs and practices* (of the) nations- | *of-the*-earth. *It-is* safe *to* say *that on-this*-day *every* Right-*Reverend*-Bishop *in-the*-Church, *every* (2) preacher *in-the* United-Free-Church-*of*-Scotland, *every* Sunday-School teacher, *who speaks* (of the) Word-*of-God,* mentions | *the* glad-tidings referred *to in-the* passage-*of*-Scripture *which* relates *the* birth *of-our-Lord.* *There-is-not* | *a* preacher *of-Christianity, whether* engaged *in* woRk *on-the* home-missions *or* serving *the* cause *of-God by* spreading- | *the knowledge of-His Holy-Word* among-*the* heathen *in* foreign-missions, *who-could* allow *this*-day *to* pass *without* | congratulating *himself and-his* fellow-creatures *upon-the* advent *of*-Christ, *our-Lord-and-Saviour.* *In a* similaR *way, it*- (3) *is-impossible to* pass *a* Good Friday *without* reverting *to-the-Great* Tragedy narrated *in-the* New-Testament-Scriptures, *when*- | *He who*-came *to* bestow *upon-the* people *of-this*-woRLd everlasting-life *in a* woRLd-*without*-end, *was himself* | *put to* death. *Thus, too, the* resurrection-*of*-Christ *and-His* ascension *to-the* right-*hand-of-God-the*-Father, | reminds *us* (of the) *doctrine* (of the) resurrection-*of-the*-dead *and-the* continued existence (of the) soul *in a* | future-state. *Surely one* (of the) *great* Lessons *to be* learned *from-the* life *of*-Christ *is-the* Lesson *of* (4) kindness *towards* others! *Every true* believer *in*-Christ *who* reads *and* reflects *upon our-Lord's* Sermon-*on-the*-Mount *must*- | *be* struck *with-the* beautiful Lessons *of* charity, mercy, *and* forgiveness-*of*-sins, *which it* teaches. "*When God,*" said *a* | *great* preacher, "made *the* heart *of* man, *His first* gift *to-it was* kindness," *and-if-this* gift *has-not-* | *been* actively employed previously, *it-must-be* roused *into* life *by-the* reading *and* consideration (of the) Lessons *of-* | *this wonderful* Sermon-*on-the*-Mount. *The* goodness-*of*-God appears *in every word, and* exhorts *us,* also, *to goodness.* (500)

EXERCISE 210.

Intersected Words.

It-is-to-be deplored *that* some *members of-every* political-party *in-the Houses-of-Parliament, whether the* Liberal- | Unionist-Party, *the* Conservative-Party, *the* Liberal-Party, *or any other* Parliamentary-Party, *are too-much* inclined *to*-make *a* | party-question *of al*most *every* proposal *that comes* before *them. I quite believe that* party-*government is, on-the* whole, | *the* best system; *but it-has, I-think,* some drawbacks, *and-this-is one-of-them. Should-the Government, for-* | instance, ask-*the House to-give* serious-attention *to a* new bill *for-the* better management *of*-some *Government*-department, (1) *as, for*-instance, *the* Local-Government-Board; *or should-they* propose *a change in-the* regulation (of the) shipping-department | (of the) *nation*; some *members of-one or-other* (of the) political-parties *in-the-House would* treat *the* proposal | *as a* party-question, whereas, *as-a*-matter-*of*-fact, *a* few-minutes' *special*-attention *given to-the*-matter *would* | show *it to be nothing* (of the) kind. *Government* officials *are* conscious *of-this* defect *in-the*-system *of* English- | -Government, *and-they* hesitate, *I*-fear, *to*-suggest *improvements in-their*-departments, *because-they-do-not wish- their* suggestions *to* (2) *be* treated *as* party-questions. *The* same flaw exists, *I-believe, to*-some-extent *in our* system *of* municipal-government. | *Thus,* suppose-*that* some *members* (of the) local-authority *are in*-favour *of*-granting facilities *to-the* military-authorities (of | the) neighborhood *for* exercising-*the* troops *on* ground belonging *to-the* local-authority; *others—members* (of the) opposite political-party— | *object, not-so-much because-they* disapprove (of the) proposal, *but because-it* originated *with-the* opposite-party. *They* treat- | the matter *as a* party-question, *and*-vote *accordingly. Why, if-these* methods were followed *in-the* joint-stock-companies, (3) *the* steamship-companies, *or the* railway-companies (of the) country, *these* companies *would* lose many (of the) advantages *they* now | enjoy. *But it-is-not-so. On-the*-contrary, *if a* railway-official *of,* say *the* Great-Western-Railway-Company | were *to*-suggest *an improvement in-the*-method *of* signalling, *his* suggestion *would*-receive proper-attention, *and, if approved, it-* | *would-be put into practice, without* regard *to-the* position (of the) man *who*-made-*the* suggestion. Local managers *would-* | *be* instructed *to*-make-arrangements *for* carrying *out-the* idea, *and-when satisfactory*-arrangements *had-been* made *the public would-* (4) *be informed* (of the) change. *Why cannot the* same method *be* adopted *in-the-House-of*-Commons *and-by every* | local-authority? *I* raised *the* point *at-the* recent debate *in our Short*hand-Writers'-Association, *but I*-found little support | *for-my* views. *My* motion *for an* inquiry *was* seconded *by-our* president, Major-Jones (of the)Volunteers, *merely as*-| *a*-matter-*of*-form *and in*-order-*that-it-might be* discussed. *In-the opinion* (of the) majority *the* methods | *of*-procedure *in-the-House-of*-Commons, *and-in-the* various County-Councils *and* Town-Councils, *had* reached *high*-water- (5) mark, *as-they put it, and could-not-be improved.* Professor-Morgan *and-the* Managing-Director (of the) General-Omnibus- | Company *who*-came *to*-heaR-*the* debate, were invited *to-speak*, *and-they*-were both against *me*. *In*-fact, *the* | onLy men *who* agreed *with me* were-*the* local managers (of the) Life-Assurance-Company *and-the* General-Insurance-Company, | *who* both spoke *very* strongLy *in*-support *of-my* views. (570)

THE END

ARITHMETIC.

FIRST STEPS IN COMMERCIAL ARITHMETIC. By ARTHUR E. WILLIAMS, M.A., B.Sc. Specially compiled and adapted to cover the syllabuses of the Elementary Examinations of the Lancashire and Cheshire Union of Institutes, the Midland Union of Institutes, and other examining bodies. In crown 8vo, limp cloth, 80 pp., net 8d.

BUSINESS ARITHMETIC. Part I. In crown 8vo, cloth, 120 pp., 1s.
CONTENTS.—Simple and Compound Rules, Reduction of Weights and Measures, Vulgar and Decimal Fractions, Proportion and Square Root—Short methods in Multiplication and Division of Decimals to a small number of places, together with a knowledge of the degree of approximation possible—Short methods in Multiplication, Division, Prices of Articles, Practice Interest and Discount, Percentages and Averages, Commission and Brokerage—Areas and Quantities—The Metric System and Coinage of France.

ANSWERS TO BUSINESS ARITHMETIC. Part I. Cloth, 1s.

BUSINESS ARITHMETIC. Part II. In crown 8vo, cloth, 144 pp., 1s. 6d.
CONTENTS.—Stocks and Shares—Profit and Loss—Bills Receivable and Bills Payable, Interest, True Discount and Bankers' Discount. The Use of Logarithms more particularly for Problems on Compound Interest, Insurance, and Annuities—The more important European Weights and Measures other than the Metric—The Coinage of Germany and the United States—and the Weights Measures and Coinage of India.

ANSWERS TO BUSINESS ARITHMETIC. Part II. Cloth, 1s.

PITMAN'S COMPLETE COMMERCIAL ARITHMETIC. In crown 8vo, cloth, 264 pp., 2s. 6d.
Contains Part I and II above mentioned.

ANSWERS TO PITMAN'S COMPLETE COMMERCIAL ARITHMETIC. Whole cloth, 1s. 6d.

PITMAN'S SMALLER COMMERCIAL ARITHMETIC. By C. W. CROOK, B.A., B.Sc. This volume includes those parts of Arithmetic which are necessary in commercial life. In crown 8vo, cloth, net 1s.

ANSWERS TO SMALLER COMMERCIAL ARITHMETIC. Net 1s.

RAPID METHODS IN ARITHMETIC. By JOHN JOHNSTON. In crown 8vo, cloth, 87 pp., net 1s.
Gives the quickest methods of obtaining solutions to Arithmetical questions of a business character.

EXERCISES IN RAPID METHODS IN ARITHMETIC. By JOHN JOHNSTON. In crown 8vo, cloth, net 8d.

METHOD IN ARITHMETIC. By G. R. PURDIE, B.A. A guide to the teaching of Arithmetic. In crown 8vo, cloth, 87 pp., 1s. 6d.

METHOD ARITHMETIC. Illustrates the principles explained in "Method in Arithmetic." 324 pp. 3s.

ARITHMETIC (continued).

ANSWERS TO METHOD ARITHMETIC. 67 pp. Net 2s. 6d.

CIVIL SERVICE AND COMMERCIAL LONG AND CROSS TOTS. In crown 8vo, 48 pp., 6d.

Contains 1,200 tests and numerous examples.

BOOK-KEEPING.

FIRST STEPS IN BOOK-KEEPING. By W. A. HATCHARD, A.C.P., F.B.T. Specially compiled and adapted to cover the syllabuses of the Elementary Examinations of the principal examining bodies. In crown 8vo, limp cloth, 80 pp., net 8d.

PITMAN'S PRIMER OF BOOK-KEEPING. Thoroughly prepares the student for the study of more elaborate treatises. In crown 8vo. 144 pp., cloth, 1s.

PRINCIPAL CONTENTS.—The entering up and posting up the Cash, Purchases, and Sales Books—Ledger—Making the Trial Balance and preparing the Balance Sheet—Explanation of Bills of Exchange and their Uses—The Treatment of Bad Debts, Dishonoured Bills, Consignments Outwards and Inwards, Partnership Accounts, etc.—Many fully-worked Examples, carefully graduated additional Exercises, Facsimiles of Commercial Documents and Definitions of Business Terms.—The rulings and balances are shown in red ink.

ANSWERS TO PITMAN'S PRIMER OF BOOK-KEEPING. In crown 8vo, cloth, 1s.

EASY EXERCISES FOR PITMAN'S PRIMER OF BOOK-KEEPING. This work provides useful additional exercises for students of the Primer of Book-keeping, and may be used either with or without that text-book. The answers to the exercises are given at the end of the book. In crown 8vo, 48 pp., 6d.

BOOK-KEEPING DIAGRAMS. By JAMES McKEE. These diagrams show most graphically how the varied items in a set of transactions should be entered in the books of account, how the Ledger Accounts are closed, and the Profit and Loss Account and Balance Sheet drawn out. Real, Personal, and Nominal Accounts are illustrated, and useful notes and reference numbers are added. In crown 8vo, 36 pp., 6d.

BOOK-KEEPING SIMPLIFIED. A text-book covering all business requirements and affording a thorough preparation for certificate and professional examinations. Special features of the book are the large number of examples worked in full, and the printing of rulings and balances in red ink. New Edition, enlarged, and thoroughly revised. In crown 8vo, cloth, 272 pp., 2s. 6d.

PRINCIPAL CONTENTS.—The Ledger—Journal—Posting—Trial Balance and Balance Sheet—Closing Entries—Cash Books, various forms—Cheques—Purchases and Sales Books—Bad Debts—Bills of Exchange—Returns and Allowances—Capital and Revenue Accounts—Trading Account—Consignments Outward and Inward—Purchases and Sales on Commission—Joint Accounts—Partnerships—Branch and Departmental Accounts—Contracts—Sectional

BOOK-KEEPING (continued).

BOOK-KEEPING SIMPLIFIED—(contd.)

Balancing Ledgers—Reserves—Inaccurate Trial Balances and their Correction—Business Abbreviations—Business Terms and Their Meanings—Upwards of 100 Exercises, including Examination Papers of the Royal Society of Arts, London Chamber of Commerce, Lancashire and Cheshire Union of Institutes, etc., etc.

ANSWERS TO BOOK-KEEPING SIMPLIFIED. Revised Edition. In crown 8vo, cloth, 1s.

PITMAN'S ADVANCED BOOK-KEEPING. In crown 8vo, cloth, 187 pp., 2s. 6d.

PRINCIPAL CONTENTS.—Auditing—The Preparation of Profit and Loss Accounts and Balance Sheets—Bankruptcy, Insolvency Accounts and Statements of Affairs—Joint Stock Companies' Accounts, the Register of Members and Share Ledger, and the Register of Transfers, etc.—The Trading Accounts of Joint Stock Companies, and the Profit and Loss Account and the Balance Sheets—Liquidation—The Tabular System in General—The Tabular System as used in Hotels, etc.

ANSWERS TO PITMAN'S ADVANCED BOOK-KEEPING. In crown 8vo, cloth, 1s.

PITMAN'S HIGHER BOOK-KEEPING AND ACCOUNTS. By H. W. PORRITT and W. NICKLIN, A.S.A.A. In crown 8vo, cloth, 304 pp., with many up-to-date forms, and facsimile documents, 2s. 6d.

This book is absolutely self-contained; that is to say, it gives the answers to the varied exercises given in illustration of the text. Exactly suited to the requirements of students preparing for examinations in the advanced stages of Book-keeping and Accounts.

SHORT SYNOPSIS OF CONTENTS.—Single Entry—Double Entry—Statement of Affairs and Balance Sheet—Trial Balance—Manufacturing and Trading Accounts—Profit and Loss—Profit and Loss Appropriation Account—Balance Sheet—Partnership Accounts—Limited Partners—Limited Companies—Special Undertakings—Double Account System—Abstract and Revenue and Net Revenue Accounts—Deeds of Assignment—Bankruptcy—Departmental Accounts—Branch Accounts—Foreign Exchange and Foreign Branch Accounts—Bills of Exchange, Inland and Foreign—Consignment and Joint Venture, Account Sales—Average Due Date, Current Accounts—Contract Accounts—Hire Purchase of Wagons; Royalties; Dead Rents; Leases, etc.—Bank Accounts—Income and Expenditure Accounts—Receipts and Payments—Voyage Accounts—Self-Balancing Ledgers—Income Tax—Cost Accounts—Executorship Accounts—Various matters in connection with Accounts, etc.

PITMAN'S COMPLETE BOOK-KEEPING. A thoroughly comprehensive text-book, dealing with all departments of the subject, and embracing practically every kind of account. With about 20 facsimiles of Company Forms, etc. Enlarged Edition. In crown 8vo, cloth, 424 pp., 3s. 6d.

BOOK-KEEPING (continued).

COMPLETE BOOK-KEEPING—(contd.)

The FIRST PART gives full explanation of Single Entry—Method of Converting Books from Single to Double Entry—Complete Instruction in the Preparation of Balance Sheet—How to Deal with Receipts and Payments by Cheques and Bills—Principal Laws governing use of Paper Money—Returns and Allowances—Bad Debts—Dishonoured Bills, etc.

The SECOND PART deals with Agency Accounts—Productive Wages Account—Brewery and Colliery Accounts—Accounts for Professional Services—Hotel Book-keeping—Accounts to be kept in hospitals and other charitable institutions—Theoretical and Practical use of the Journal—Joint Stock Company Book-keeping—Insolvency and Bankruptcy Accounts—Executors' and Trustees' Accounts—The Double Account System employed in Railways, Public Works, etc.

The THIRD PART gives thorough explanations of various kinds of Shipping Accounts, and the terms, books, and forms connected therewith. Inward and Outward Consignments—Accounts Current Book—Bankers' Account Current—How to draw Bills against Shipment—The Compilation of Shipping Invoices and Account Sales—Letters of Hypothecation and Letters of Lien, with Specimens of these important documents—Orders by Telegraph Code—Calculations of C. I. F. Invoices, etc., etc.

ANSWERS TO PITMAN'S COMPLETE BOOK-KEEPING. Enlarged Edition. In crown 8vo, cloth, 213 pp., 2s. 6d.

Contains answers to all the questions, and fully worked solutions to all the exercises in the text book.

BOOK-KEEPING FOR RETAILERS. By H. W. PORRITT and W. NICKLIN, A.S.A.A. (See page 14.)

INCOME TAX ACCOUNTS AND HOW TO PREPARE THEM. Notes on Income Tax Law and Practice.

This practical book, with its notes on Income Tax Law and Practice, and its clear instructions with regard to the preparation of the returns to be presented to the commissioners, has been thoroughly revised and brought up-to-date, so that it is a reliable guide for the book-keeper, accountant, or auditor, whose duty it is to compile these important and rather difficult statements. Second Edition, Revised. In crown 8vo, cloth, 2s.

ADDITIONAL EXERCISES IN BOOK-KEEPING. Nos. I and II. In crown 8vo, 48 pp., each 6d.

Containing papers recently set by the leading Examining Bodies; College of Preceptors; National Union of Teachers, Elementary, Junior and Senior; Civil Service; London Chamber of Commerce; Society of Accountants and Auditors; Institute of Chartered Accountants; Institute of Bankers; Union of Lancashire and Cheshire Institutes, etc., etc.

ANSWERS TO THE ABOVE EXERCISES. Nos. I and II. Each 6d.

BOOK-KEEPING (continued).

PITMAN'S BOOK-KEEPING TEST CARDS. A series of carefully graded tests in book-keeping by which the student's progress can be satisfactorily gauged. There are three sets, Elementary, Intermediate, and Advanced, and each set contains 20 cards with a varying number of questions on each card selected from those actually set by the different examining bodies. Each set is graded in difficulty, printed on stout cards and put up in a strong cloth case with two sets of answers arranged in book form.' The Answers are full and explicit, detailed workings being given and explanations where required. Per set, 1s. 6d.

PITMAN'S BUSINESS BOOK-KEEPING TRANSACTIONS. No. 1. 1s. Including 52 forms for Invoices, Cheques, etc., and 8 blank Exercise Books enclosed in envelope. This work is planned to teach the principles of Book-keeping and at the same time furnish an insight into actual business methods. This is accomplished by the employment of a text-book giving particulars (with copious explanatory notes) of the transactions of a trader, accompanied by facsimiles of all documents which would be received, and of blank forms such as Invoices, Cheques, Bank Paying-in Slip Book, Account Books, etc.

PITMAN'S BOOK-KEEPING TRANSACTIONS. No. 2. This new work is arranged on a plan very similar to that which has proved so successful in the case of Book-keeping Transactions, No. 1; but, of course, the transactions include items of a rather more advanced character. There is a concisely-written text-book, giving clear and explicit instructions in the principles of Book-keeping, full particulars regarding the transactions of a trader, and the traders' books of account, forms, documents, etc., the whole enclosed in a stout envelope. The new work is arranged so as to give not only instruction in Book-keeping, but also a good deal of reliable information relating to business methods. Price 2s.

PITMAN'S HOTEL BOOK-KEEPING. A practical text-book explaining the principles of Book-keeping as applied to Hotel accounts. With illustrative forms and exercises. In crown 8vo, cloth, 72 pp., 2s. 6d.

HOW TO TEACH BOOK-KEEPING. By H. W. PORRITT and W. NICKLIN, A.S.A.A. The authors of this valuable book are professional accountants who have also a large and varied experience in the conduct of classes and the coaching of candidates for Book-keeping examinations. The book abounds with practical hints as to the management of classes, the treatment of backward pupils, the examination and marking of papers, etc. There are also specimen courses of lessons suitable for elementary, intermediate, and advanced students, with fully-worked keys, balance sheets, and so on. While primarily appealing to teachers, this book will also be found useful to the learner who is unable to attend a class or who wishes to extend his knowledge beyond what he is able to gain in a class. In crown 8vo, cloth, 180 pp., net 2s. 6d.

BOOK-KEEPING (continued).

PITMAN'S BOOK-KEEPING (EXAMINATION PAPERS) ANNUAL. This volume contains the actual papers set at the 1909 Examinations of the principal Education authorities, with answers thereto, and full answers to the many questions on Commercial Law and Business Practice. In crown 8vo, cloth, 212 pp., 2s. 6d.

THE ROYAL SOCIETY OF ARTS BOOK-KEEPING EXAMINATION PAPERS FOR THE YEAR 1910. Test Papers with fully worked Keys and Answers to the Questions on Law and Business Practice. In envelope, 6d.

THE LANCASHIRE AND CHESHIRE UNION OF INSTITUTES BOOK-KEEPING EXAMINATION PAPERS FOR THE YEAR 1910. Test papers with fully worked Keys and Answers to the Questions on Law and Business Practice. In envelope, 6d.

PITMAN'S EXAMINATION NOTES ON BOOK-KEEPING AND ACCOUNTANCY. By J. BLAKE HARROLD, A.C.I.S., F.C.R.A., Lecturer in Accountancy at the Birkbeck College, London; Candidates for the Book-keeping and Accountancy Examinations cônducted by the Royal Society of Arts, London Chamber of Commerce, College of Preceptors, Union of Lancashire and Cheshire Institutes, etc., will find much valuable information in this little book. Cloth, 6½ in. by 3¼ in., net, 1s.

HOW TO BECOME A QUALIFIED ACCOUNTANT. By R. A. WITTY, A.S.A.A. A guide for those who intend to take up accountancy as a profession and for those who are already accountants, with full guidance respecting examinations. Second Edition. In crown 8vo., cloth, 120 pp., net 2s.

ACCOUNTANCY. By F. W. PIXLEY, F.C.A. Barrister-at-Law. The student of Book-keeping, who has thoroughly mastered his subject, cannot do better than devote himself to the higher branches of the work, and study what is described under the general head of Accountancy. The present work deals with Constructive and Recording Accountancy, and treats the subject on a scientific basis. All the principal statements of account are reviewed and discussed, and the law relating to them is epitomized and explained. In demy 8vo, cloth, 318 pp., net 5s.

IDEAL MANUSCRIPT BOOKS FOR BOOK-KEEPING. Specially ruled and adapted for working the exercises contained in the Primer of Book-keeping. The sets consists of:—Cash Book and Journal; Purchase Book; Sales Book; Ledger. Each 2d.

AVON EXERCISE BOOKS FOR BOOK-KEEPING. Specially adapted for the exercise in "Book-keeping Simplified" or "Advanced Book-keeping." Fcap. folio. Journal, 3d.; Cash Book, 3d.; Ledger, 6d.

DOUBLE ENTRY IN ONE LESSON. By R. FLEMING, A.C.I.S. Price 6d.

BUSINESS TRAINING.

OFFICE ROUTINE FOR BOYS AND GIRLS, 1st STAGE. In crown 8vo, 64 pp., 6d.

Deals with the treatment of outgoing and incoming letters, Postal arrangements, means of remitting money and forwarding goods.

OFFICE ROUTINE FOR BOYS AND GIRLS, 2nd STAGE. In crown 8vo, 64 pp., 6d.

PRINCIPAL CONTENTS.—Business Forms, such as Invoices, Credit Notes, etc.—Telegrams—The Telephone—Banks and Banking, Joint-stock and Private Banks, Post Office Savings Bank, etc.

OFFICE ROUTINE FOR BOYS AND GIRLS, 3rd STAGE. In crown 8vo, 64 pp., 6d.

Deals with explanation of Terms—Promissory Notes and Discount—Terms used in Payment of Accounts, etc.—Bills of Exchange—Stocks, Dividends, etc.—Government Securities—Business Correspondence.

COUNTING-HOUSE ROUTINE. 1st Year's Course. In crown 8vo, cloth, 144 pp., 1s.

COUNTING-HOUSE ROUTINE. 2nd Year's Course. In crown 8vo, cloth, 144 pp., 1s. 6d.

FIRST STEPS IN BUSINESS TRAINING. By V. E. COLLINGE, A.C.I.S. Specially written and adapted to cover the syllabuses of the Elementary Examinations of the Lancashire and Cheshire Union of Institutes and other examining bodies. In crown 8vo, limp cloth, 80 pp., net 8d.

GUIDE TO BUSINESS CUSTOMS AND PRACTICE ON THE CONTINENT. By A. E. DAVIES. Contains information of the utmost value to all who have business relations with Continental firms, or who have to visit the Continent for business or pleasure. In crown 8vo, cloth, 154 pp., net 2s. 6d.

HOW TO GET A SITUATION ABROAD. By ALBERT EMIL DAVIES. Gives information of the most reliable character to those who desire to obtain an appointment in a foreign country. Also states the prospects of advancement in such a position; the varying conditions of life in different countries; the cost of living; the opportunities afforded of perfecting one's knowledge of the foreign language, etc. In crown 8vo, cloth, net 1s. 6d.

MASTERS' NEW READY RECKONER. PITMAN'S EDITION. Contains 63,000 calculations. In foolscap 8vo, cloth, 358 pp., net 1s.

PITMAN'S DISCOUNT, COMMISSION, AND BROKERAGE TABLES. By ERNEST HEAVINGHAM. Contains upwards of 18,000 workings of the kind which are in constant use in warehouses, offices, shops, and other places of business of whatever nature, and shows at a glance the discount on any sum of money from 1d to £1,000 at from 1/16% to 95%, and from £1 to £25,000 at from 1/8% to 4½%. Size 3 in. by 4½ in. 160 pp., cloth, net 1s.

BUSINESS TRAINING (continued).

GEOGRAPHICAL-STATISTIC UNIVERSAL POCKET ATLAS. By Professor A. L. HICKMAN. Second Edition. This handy Atlas contains sixty-four splendidly coloured maps and tables, including pictorial charts of the heavens, the races of mankind, religions and languages of the World, statistics of productions, educational tables, coinage, public debts, shipping, coats of arms, railways and telegraphs, imports and exports, principal towns of the World, and a mass of other useful information. In demy 18mo, cloth, net 5s.

HOW TO START IN LIFE. By A KINGSTON. In crown 8vo, cloth, 128 pp., 1s. 6d.

A Popular Guide to Commercial, Municipal, Civil Service, and Professional Employment. Deals with over 70 distinct kinds of Employment.

THE JUNIOR CORPORATION CLERK. A Guide to Municipal Office Routine. By J. B. CARRINGTON, F.S.A.A., Borough Accountant of Paddington; Member of the Institute of Municipal Treasurers and Accountants (Incorporated); etc., etc. This book consists of a series of articles for the guidance of Junior Clerks or for young persons who desire to become Junior Clerks in the service of Municipal Corporations. Much useful and practical advice is given as to the duties of a Junior in the various departments. In crown 8vo, cloth gilt, with illustrations, net 1s. 6d.

PITMAN'S MANUAL OF BUSINESS TRAINING. Contains fifty-seven maps and facsimiles. Seventh Edition, thoroughly revised and considerably enlarged. In crown 8vo, cloth, 282 pp., 2s. 6d.

PRINCIPAL CONTENTS.—Conditions of Commerce—Inward Correspondence—Outward—Postal Information—The Telegraph and Telephone—Business Letter Writing, etc.—Office Books and Business Forms—Market Reports—Railways and Canals—Forwarding Goods by Rail—Channels of Commerce—Customs and Excise Duties—Importing—Exporting—Insurance—Private Firms and Public Companies—The World's Currencies—Banks and Banking—Bills of Exchange—Bankruptcy and the County Court—Two hundred Questions on the Chapters.

PITMAN'S BUSINESS TERMS, PHRASES AND ABBREVIATIONS, with equivalents in French, German, Spanish and Italian, and Facsimile Documents. Fourth edition, revised and enlarged. In crown 8vo, cloth, 280 pp., net 2s. 6d.

MERCANTILE TERMS AND ABBREVIATIONS. Containing over 1,000 terms and 500 abbreviations used in commerce, with definitions. 126 pp., size 3" × 4¾", cloth, net 1s.

COMMERCIAL TERMS IN FIVE LANGUAGES. Being about 1,900 terms and phrases used in commerce, with their equivalents in French, German, Spanish, and Italian. Cloth, 3in. × 4¾ in., cloth, 118 pp., net 1s.

BUSINESS TRAINING (continued).

GUIDE TO INDEXING AND PRÉCIS WRITING. (See page 14.)

INDEXING AND PRÉCIS WRITING. A text-book specially adapted to the present requirements of Candidates for Examinations. By A. J. LAWFORD JONES, of H.M. Civil Service, Medallist and First Prizeman, Society of Arts, 1900. In crown 8vo, cloth, 144 pp., 1s. 6d.

EXERCISES AND ANSWERS IN INDEXING AND PRÉCIS WRITING. By WM. JAYNE WESTON, M.A. (Lond.). A carefully selected list of actual exercises and test papers with model workings. The author's notes on the various exercises contain many useful hints and some sound advice for the student. In crown 8vo, cloth, 144 pp., 1s. 6d.

HOW TO TEACH BUSINESS TRAINING. By F. HEELIS, F.C.I.S. This book contains chapters on teaching methods, the presentation of the subject, the illustration of the lesson, home work, examinations, individual and class tuition, tuition by correspondence-apparatus required, etc., etc. There are also valuable and suggestive notes of lessons, specimen courses, exercises, specimen forms, etc. In crown 8vo, 160 pp., net 2s. 6d.

QUESTIONS IN BUSINESS TRAINING. By F. HEELIS, F.C.I.S. Questions taken from the actual examinations of such authorities as The Union of Lancashire and Cheshire Institutes. The West Riding County Council, and similar important bodies. With 540 original questions specially framed for the purpose of testing a student's knowledge. In crown 8vo, cloth. 108 pp., 1s.

ANSWERS TO QUESTIONS IN BUSINESS TRAINING. By the same author. Crown 8vo, cloth, about 160 pp., 2s.

QUESTIONS AND ANSWERS IN BUSINESS TRAINING. By the same author. Crown 8vo, cloth, 269 pp., 2s. 6d.

DIGESTING RETURNS INTO SUMMARIES. Graphical methods, etc. A text-book especially adapted to the requirements of candidates for the examinations of the Civil Service. By A. J. LAWFORD JONES, of H.M. Civil Service. In crown 8vo, cloth, 84 pp., net 1s. 6d.

PITMAN'S CIVIL SERVICE GUIDE. By A. J. LAWFORD JONES, of H.M. Civil Service; Medallist and First Prizeman, Society of Arts, 1900. Mr. Lawford Jones gives in this book complete guidance to the candidate, besides offering a good many useful hints and suggestions which should be of the greatest assistance to him in his examinations. The volume may be recommended not only to intending candidates, but to teachers and others entrusted with the coaching of Civil Service Students. In crown 8vo, cloth, 100 pp., net 1s.

PITMAN'S TRADERS' HANDBOOKS.

The new volumes have been prepared with the idea of assisting the earnest business man who is engaged in trade to render himself more efficient in his work. Each volume deals with every matter in which a trader desires information, and is in crown 8vo. cloth. 260 pp., net 2s. 6d.

DRAPERY AND DRAPERS' ACCOUNTS. By RICHARD BEYNON.

GROCERY AND GROCERS' ACCOUNTS. By W. F. TUPMAN.

IRONMONGERY AND IRONMONGERS' ACCOUNTS. By S. W. FRANCIS.

COMMON COMMODITIES OF COMMERCE SERIES.

Each book in crown 8vo. cloth, with coloured frontispiece and many illustrations, maps, charts, etc., net 1s. 6d.

In each of the handbooks in this series a particular produce i treated by an expert writer and practical man of business. Beginning with the life history of the plant, or other natural product, he follows its development until it becomes a commercial commodity, and so on through the various phases of its sale in the market and its purchase by the consumer.

TEA. From Grower to Consumer. By A. IBBETSON. Of Messrs. Joseph Travers & Sons.

COFFEE. From Grower to Consumer. By B. B. KEABLE. Of Messrs. Joseph Travers & Sons.

COTTON. From the Raw Material to the Finished Product. By R. J. PEAKE.

SUGAR, CANE AND BEET. By GEO. MARTINEAU, C.B., Secretary to the British Sugar Refiners' Committee 1872-92. Adviser to the British Delegates at the International Conferences of 1875-6-7, 1888, 1898, and 1901-2. Assistant British Delegate on the Permanent International Sugar Commission at Brussels, 1903-5.

OIL, ANIMAL, VEGETABLE, ESSENTIAL, AND MINERAL. By C. AINSWORTH MITCHELL.

RUBBER: Production and Utilisation of the Raw Product. By C. BEADLE and H. P. STEVENS, M.A., Ph.D., F.I.C.

IRON AND STEEL. Their production and manufacture. By C. HOOD, of the well-known firm of Messrs. Bell Brothers, Limited.

SILK. Its production and manufacture. By LUTHER HOOPER. Weaver, Designer, and Manufacturer.

Other volumes in preparation.

PRACTICAL PRIMERS OF BUSINESS.

Each in crown 8vo, cloth, about 120 pp., net 1s.

BOOK-KEEPING FOR RETAILERS. By H. W. Porritt and W. Nicklin, A.S.A.A. The authors of this new book have had in their professional capacity a great amount of experience in retailers' accounts, and in this handy little volume they present a system of book-keeping for retailers designedly simple easy in operation, and accurate in its results. The adaptation of the system to various retail businesses is clearly discussed and explained. Numerous illustrations and examples simplify the treatment. Additional chapters deal with "Incidental Matters," such as leases, rates, assessment, and stock-taking, the various necessary forms of insurance, the making out of income tax returns, partnerships and limited companies.

ENGLISH COMPOSITION AND CORRESPONDENCE. By J. F. Davis, D.Lit., M.A., LL.B. (Lond.). The purpose of this book is by means of a few simple rules, to enable a writer of either sex to express himself or herself clearly and correctly in the mother tongue as it ought to be written. The first part contains chapters on accidence with examples from Commercial Correspondence. The second part deals with syntax, parsing, analysis, and punctuation. The third part treats of the construction of sentences; precision and order, and the choice of words; and closes with specimens of business letters. The author, from his experience as examiner in English to the University of London and the Institute of Bankers, is peculiarly fitted to deal with this subject.

THE ELEMENTS OF COMMERCIAL LAW. By A. H. Douglas, LL.B. (Lond.). In the present volume the general principles of commercial law are presented. Examples and illustrations are freely used, in order that the subject may be made as intelligible and interesting as possible. In the first portion of the book the general principles of contract are discussed in comprehensive fashion, and later chapters deal with commercial relationships, partnerships, the sale and carriage of goods, and negotiable instruments. The author is a barrister-at-law who has attained the highest academic distinction both at the Inns of Court and London University.

GUIDE TO INDEXING AND PRÉCIS WRITING. By William Jayne Weston, M.A., and E. Bowker. The present little work is intended primarily for candidates for the Civil Service, the Society of Arts, and similar examinations in the subject of Indexing and Précis Writing. The whole of the exercises included in the book are reproductions of actual examination papers.

PRACTICAL PRIMERS OF BUSINESS (continued).

THE MONEY, AND THE STOCK AND SHARE MARKETS. By Emil Davies. The idea of the author of this volume is not so much to give information to experts, but rather to assist the uninitiated in the somewhat complicated subjects of stock and share transactions. The author has for many years been actively engaged in the higher branches of finance, and makes the present primer as comprehensive and practical a work as possible.

SHIPPING. By Arnold Hall and F. Heywood. This book constitutes a reliable guide to the routine in connection with the shipment of goods and the clearance of vessels inwards and outwards. Part I describes the work of a shipper, and explains his duties after the receipt of the indent, in packing, forwarding, and insuring the goods, making out and sending the invoices telegraphing, the routine of obtaining payment, customs formalities, claims for insurance, etc. Part II gives precise information regarding the work of a ship-broker, the entry and clearance inwards, the details in connection with the Custom House and the Shipping Office, the entry outwards, riggers, runners, and pilots, the Docks, Warehousing, Shipping, Exchange, etc., etc. With 27 shipping forms.

THE ELEMENTS OF BANKING. By J. P. Gandy. Besides giving a brief history of Banking, this book deals practically with such matters as Opening an Account, the various forms of Cheques, Crossings, Endorsements, Bills of Exchange, the Rights of Holders, of those instruments, Promissory Notes, the Pass Book, and the Collecting Banker. There are also chapters explanatory of the Bankers' Clearing House, the necessary steps to be taken in the case of dishonoured bills and cheques, etc. The Bankers' obligations to his customers, the rights and duties of agents and trustees, Partnership Accounts and Companies' Accounts are all fully dealt with, while Circular Notes and Letters of Credit receive adequate attention.

THE ELEMENTS OF INSURANCE. By J. Alfred Eke. This new work presents in a brief form a vast amount of information with regard to the principles and practice of the important business of insurance. Workmen's compensation insurance is fully dealt with, and the book also treats of baggage insurance, bad debt insurance, live-stock insurance, stock insurance, etc., etc. There are chapters on carriage insurance, burglary insurance, marine, fire, and life insurance, with full explanations of the various kinds of policies, and in many cases reproductions of the documents.

PRACTICAL PRIMERS OF BUSINESS (continued).

ADVERTISING. By HOWARD BRIDGEWATER. The author of this little work is the Advertisement Manager of a well-known daily paper, and the writer of many articles on the subject of advertising. He speaks, therefore, with the authority which comes of long experience. In the present work, Mr. Bridgewater sets forth the principles to be observed in drawing up advertisements, points out the errors that are to be avoided, gives hints on the preparation of "copy," and the choice of suitable media, describes the processes employed in reproducing illustrations of various kinds, and discusses the questions of type display and the frequency of insertion, etc., etc. The book is illustrated by examples of good and bad advertisements, representative of various businesses.

THE CARD INDEX SYSTEM. Its Principles, Uses, Operation, and Component Parts. By R. B. BYLES. The author deals with practically every possible adaptation of the system and illustrates his explanations with facsimiles of the most modern apparatus. The book may be recommended to those who desire to equip themselves with a perfectly satisfactory method of keeping their correspondence, etc. With 30 illustrations.

MODERN LIBRARY OF PRACTICAL INFORMATION.

Each in foolscap 8vo, cloth, about 128 pp., net 1s.

WILLS, EXECUTORS, AND TRUSTEES. With a chapter on Intestacy. By J. A. SLATER, B.A., LL.B. (Lond.), A complete guide clearly and succinctly written.

THE TRADER'S GUIDE TO COUNTY COURT PROCEDURE. By F. H. B. CHAPMAN. The object of this book is the presentation to the ordinary lay reader of a full and clear account of the proceedings which are necessary to be taken in the County Court for the recovery of small debts. The procedure is set out in full for all ordinary cases, and the creditor will learn from the forms in the text what is expected from him at each stage.

CLERKS: THEIR RIGHTS AND OBLIGATIONS. By EDWARD A. COPE. This book deals with such matters as termination of engagements, summary dismissal, bankruptcy, secret commissions, compensation, etc. It is a complete guide for the clerical worker written in a plain and sensible manner.

MODERN LIBRARY OF PRACTICAL INFORMATION (continued).

THE LAW RELATING TO TRADE CUSTOMS, MARKS, SECRETS, RESTRAINTS, AGENCIES, ETC., ETC. By LAWRENCE DUCKWORTH, Barrister-at-law. The subjects dealt with have been handled with great skill by the author whose reputation as a legal writer ensures the reliability of the statements made in the book.

BALANCE SHEETS. How to Read and Understand Them. A complete Guide for Investors, Business Men, Commercial Students, etc. By PHILIP TOVEY. In the course of his business life the author of this little book has had to examine and report upon thousands of balance sheets, and he offers the result of his experience and knowledge in the present volume. With 26 inset balance sheets.

THE HOUSEHOLDERS' LEGAL RIGHTS AND DUTIES with respect to his Neighbours, the Public, and the State. By J. A. SLATER, B.A., LL.B. (Lond.). This book may be generally described as an attempt to set out the duties imposed by law upon every individual when he is away from his own house, and which he owes to the State and to the public.

THE HOUSEHOLDERS' GUIDE TO THE LAW with respect to Landlord and Tenant, Husband and Wife, Parent and Child, and Master and Servant. By the same Author. The taking of a house, either on lease or otherwise, the common obligations as to the conditions of the house, the legal duties imposed as to the relationship with one's neighbours, are among the subjects dealt with in this book, and full information is given as to the procedure to be adopted in the case of births, marriages, and deaths.

BUSINESS MAN'S HANDBOOKS.

PITMAN'S BUSINESS MAN'S GUIDE. Fifth Edition, Revised. With French, German, and Spanish equivalents for the Commercial Words and terms. Edited by J. A. SLATER, B.A., LL.B., of the Middle Temple, Barrister-at-Law, and author of "Commercial Law of England." The information is of such a character as will assist a business man in an emergency and will clear up doubts and difficulties of everyday occurrence. The work includes over 2,000 articles. In crown 8vo, cloth cover of special design, 500 pp., net 3s. 6d.

PITMAN'S PUBLIC MAN'S GUIDE. A Handbook for all who take an interest in questions of the day. Edited by J. A. SLATER, B.A., LL.B. (Lond.). The object of this book is to enable its readers to find within a comparatively compact compass information on any subjects which can possibly bear upon matters political, diplomatic, municipal, or imperial. There is no book of a similar nature published, and this will be found invaluable to all public men and platform speakers. In crown 8vo, cloth gilt, 444 pp., net 3s. 6d.

BUSINESS MAN'S HANDBOOKS (continued).

OFFICE ORGANISATION AND MANAGEMENT, INCLUDING SECRETARIAL WORK. By Lawrence R. Dicksee, M. Com. F.C.A., and H. E. Blain, Tramways Manager, County Borough of West Ham.

This volume gives in detail, with the aid of specially selected illustrations and copies of actual business forms, a complete description of Office Organisation and Management under the most improved and up-to-date methods. It has been specially written so as to be of service either to those who are about to organise the office work of a new undertaking, or to those who are desirous of modernizing their office arrangements so as to cope more successfully with the ever increasing competition which is to be met with. New Edition, Revised. In demy 8vo, cloth gilt, 306 pp., net 5s.

THE STUDENT'S GUIDE TO MARINE INSURANCE. Being a Handbook of the Law and Practice of Marine Insurance Policies on Goods. By Henry Keate. In crown 8vo., cloth gilt, 200 pp., net 2s. 6d.

INSURANCE. By T. E. Young, B.A., F.R.A.S., ex-President of the Institute of Actuaries; ex-Chairman of the Life Offices' Association, etc., etc. A complete and practical exposition for the Student and the Business Man of the principles and practice of Insurance presented in a simple and lucid style, and illustrated by the author's actual experience as a Manager and Actuary of long standing. This book has been written expressly for (1) The Actuarial student, (2) The student of Fire, Marine, and Insurance generally, (3) The Insurance Clerk, (4) The Business Man. It treats in an elementary and intelligible manner of the principles, processes and conduct of Insurance business as a key to the interpretation of the accounts and practice of offices and as a comprehensive foundation for maturer study. Second Edition. In demy 8vo, cloth gilt, 408 pp., net 5s.

INSURANCE OFFICE ORGANISATION, MANAGEMENT, AND ACCOUNTS. By T. E. Young, B.A., F.R.A.S., and Richard Masters, A.C.A. Second Edition, Revised. In demy 8vo, cloth gilt, 146 pp., net 3s. 6d.

SHIPPING OFFICE ORGANISATION, MANAGEMENT, AND ACCOUNTS. By Alfred Calvert. Full information is given in this new book of the methods of securing orders, getting in patterns, circularising foreign firms, conditions of sale, fulfilling contracts, making up and packing goods for shipment, arranging for insurance, shipment and freight, chartering of vessels, pricing and invoicing the goods, preparing the bills of lading, etc., etc. The book contains many and varied shipping documents in facsimile. Put in a few brief words, the new work gives an accurate insight into the thousand and one technicalities associated with the intricate business of a shipping house. In demy 8vo, cloth gilt, 203 pp., net 5s.

BUSINESS MAN'S HANDBOOKS (continued).

SOLICITOR'S OFFICE ORGANISATION, MANAGEMENT, AND ACCOUNTS. By E. A. COPE, and H. W. H. ROBINS. This handbook is full of useful hints by practical and experienced men. The first part covers all the details of management, such as the staff, business records, correspondence, and so forth; while the second part goes very fully into accounts on the columnar system. In demy 8vo, cloth gilt, 176 pp., with numerous forms, net 5s.

DICTIONARY OF BANKING. A Complete Encyclopædia of Banking Law and Practice. By W. THOMSON, Bank Inspector. The object of this Dictionary is to bring together in commercial form the rules of practice in the banking profession as well as the law relating to the subject of banking generally. To the Bank manager the "Dictionary" cannot fail to be invaluable, as it will form a handy volume of reference on every conceivable occasion. In a sense, however, it will be equally invaluable to the subordinate officials of a bank, who are anxious to gain a practical knowledge of their routine work. The highest authorities have been consulted in the preparation of this unique work, and the author has had many years' practical experience with every branch of banking work. In crown 4to, half leather gilt, about 550 pp., net 21s.

MONEY, EXCHANGE, AND BANKING. In their Practical, Theoretical, and Legal Aspects. Second Edition, Revised. By H. T. EASTON, of the Union of London and Smiths Bank, Ltd. A practical work covering the whole field of banking and providing new and valuable features of great use to the student, bank clerk, or man of business. Second Edition, Revised. In demy 8vo, cloth, 312 pp., net 5s.

BANK ORGANISATION, MANAGEMENT, AND ACCOUNTS. By J. F. DAVIS, M.A., D.Lit., LL.B. (Lond.), Lecturer in Banking and Finance at the City of London College. The present volume is an exposition of the whole practice of banking, chiefly in its commercial aspect, for the special benefit of younger members of bank staffs who wish to get a comprehensive view of business while they are yet in personal touch with only the initial stages. The duties of the various members of a bank staff, from the board of directors down to the junior clerk, are described, and details are given as to the methods of keeping accounts and the various books necessary to them. A section is also devoted to the working of the machinery of the head office. In demy 8vo, cloth gilt, 165 pp., with forms, net 5s.

BANK BALANCE SHEETS AND HOW TO PREPARE THEM. By J. F. G. BAGSHAW, Member of the Institute of Bankers. First medallist Advanced Book-keeping, National Union of Teachers; Fourth Gilbart Prizeman in Banking, etc. In demy 8vo, net 6d.

BUSINESS MAN'S HANDBOOKS (continued).

PITMAN'S BILLS, CHEQUES, AND NOTES: A HANDBOOK FOR BUSINESS MEN AND COMMERCIAL STUDENTS.

The attempt has been made in this book to trace the principal negotiable instruments, viz., bills of exchange, cheques and promissory notes, from their inception to their discharge, and to point out the exact position occupied by every person who is in any way connected with these documents. The Bills of Exchange Act, 1882, and the Amending Act, Bills of Exchange (Crossed Cheques) Act, 1906, are printed *in extenso* in the Appendix. In demy 8vo, cloth gilt, 206 pp., net 2s. 6d.

THE HISTORY, LAW, AND PRACTICE OF THE STOCK EXCHANGE. By A. P. POLEY, B.A., Barrister-at-Law, and F. H. CARRUTHERS GOULD, of the Stock Exchange. A complete compendium of the law and the present practice of the Stock Exchange. Special attention is devoted to the Rules of the Stock Exchange, and these are given in full. Second Edition, Revised. In demy 8vo, cloth gilt, 348 pp., net 5s.

PITMAN'S MERCANTILE LAW. By J. A. SLATER, B.A., LL.B. As a practical exposition for law students, business men, and advanced classes in commercial colleges and schools, this volume will be found invaluable. Without being a technical law book, it provides within moderate compass a clear and accurate guide to the Principles of Mercantile Law in England. Second, Revised, and Cheaper Edition. In demy 8vo, cloth gilt, 448 pp., net 5s.

INCOME TAX AND INHABITED HOUSE DUTY LAW AND CASES. By W. E. SNELLING. This book contains a complete statement of every provision of the Income Tax and House Duty Acts still in force. Statements of some 240 cases determined thereunder are included, together with many extracts from judgments. Arranged under headings, in alphabetical order, all the enactments and cases on a particular subject are grouped together with suitable sub-headings. House Duty is dealt with, and a full index, with Tables of Acts and Cases complete a handbook of extreme usefulness to Solicitors, Accountants, Householders, and others. In demy 8vo, 278 pp., cloth gilt, net 5s.

ENCYCLOPÆDIA OF MARINE LAW. By LAWRENCE DUCKWORTH, Barrister-at-Law. In the present edition the text has been carefully revised, all the most recent decisions on Shipping Law and Marine Insurance having been incorporated therein. Recent legislation has also been attended to by the addition of certain Statutes in the appendix, and the main provisions of the much discussed Declaration of London is also set out. Second Edition, Revised and Enlarged. In demy 8vo, cloth gilt, 386 pp., net 5s.

BUSINESS MAN'S HANDBOOKS (continued).

THE LAW OF HEAVY AND LIGHT MECHANICAL TRACTION ON HIGHWAYS IN THE UNITED KINGDOM. By C. A. Montague Barlow, M.P., M.A., LL.D., and W. Joynson Hicks, M.P. Containing the text of all the important Acts on the subject and a summary of the English and Scotch Reported Cases on Extraordinary Traffic. In demy 8vo, cloth gilt, 318 pp., net 8s. 6d.

THE STUDENT'S GUIDE TO COMPANY LAW. By R. W. Holland, M.A., M.Sc., LL.B. (Hons.). Designed for candidates preparing for the examinations of the Chartered Institute of Secretaries, Accountants' Societies, etc., Secretaries and other officers of Companies. Contains the elementary principles of Company Law without dealing in detail with the Companies (Consolidation) Act, 1908. In crown 8vo, cloth gilt, 203 pp., net 2s. 6d.

COMPANIES AND COMPANY LAW. Together with the Companies (Consolidation) Act, 1908. By A. C. Connell, LL.B. (Lond.). In the present volume the law of Companies is treated on the lines adopted by the new Consolidation Act. In demy 8vo, cloth gilt, 344 pp., net 5s.

THE LAW OF CARRIAGE. By J. E. R. Stephens, B.A. Of the Middle Temple, Barrister-at-Law. A clear and accurate account of the general traders' rights and liabilities in everyday transactions with carriers, whether by land or by water. Cases are quoted and statutes cited and a complete index renders the book easy of reference. In demy 8vo, cloth gilt, 340 pp., net 5s.

HOUSEHOLD LAW. By J. A. Slater, B.A., LL.B. (Lond.). In demy 8vo, cloth gilt, 316 pp., net 5s.

THE STUDENT'S GUIDE TO BANKRUPTCY LAW AND WINDING UP OF COMPANIES. A manual for business men and advanced classes in schools, with "test" questions. By F. Porter Fausset, B.A., LL.B., *Barrister-at-Law.* In crown 8vo, cloth gilt, 187 pp., net 2s. 6d.

BANKRUPTCY AND BILLS OF SALE. An A B C of the Law. By W. Valentine Ball, M.A., Barrister-at-Law. In this volume special attention has been paid to those branches of the subject which are of general interest to Chartered Accountants, and the volume contains many practical notes which cannot fail to be of great advantage to any person who acts as a trustee in Bankruptcy. Another prominent feature is that portion of the work which deals with the preparation of Deeds of Arrangement. There are numerous references to case law and all the latest decisions connected with the subject are incorporated. Second Edition, Revised and Enlarged. In demy 8vo, cloth gilt, 386 pp., net 5s.

BUSINESS MAN'S HANDBOOKS (continued).

FARM LAW. By M. G. JOHNSON. This is a handy volume which cannot fail to be of the greatest use to farmers, and agents, surveyors, and all other persons who have to deal with land and landed interests. In demy 8vo, cloth gilt, 160 pp., net 3s. 6d.

THE FARMER'S ACCOUNT BOOK. A Simple and concise System of Account Keeping specially adapted to the requirements of Farmers. Compiled by W. G. DOWSLEY, B.A. Size, 15½" by 9½", half leather, 106 pp., with interleaved blotting paper, net 6s. 6d.

THE PERSONAL ACCOUNT BOOK. By the same author. Size, 15½" by 9½", half leather, 106 pp., with interleaved blotting paper, net 6s. 6d.

THE STUDENT'S GUIDE TO COMPANY SECRETARIAL WORK. By O. OLDHAM, A.C.I.S. Couched in simple language, this book aims at giving concisely, yet clearly, a true explanation of the multifarious matters that have to be dealt with by the company secretary, and the idea throughout has been to show the student how to deal with matters and not merely to tell him with what matters he has to deal. Covers syllabus of the Chartered Institute of Secretaries in regard to Secretarial Work. In crown 8vo, cloth gilt, 256 pp., net 2s. 6d.

PITMAN'S GUIDE FOR THE COMPANY SECRETARY. A Practical Manual and Work of Reference with regard to the Duties of a Secretary to a Joint Stock Company. By ARTHUR COLES, A.C.I.S., Sometime Lecturer in the Technological Schools of the London County Council. With an Introduction by HERBERT E. BLAIN. The author has had many years' practical experience of Company Secretarial work, which is dealt with very exhaustively and freely illustrated with fifty-four facsimile forms. In demy 8vo, cloth gilt, 346 pp., net 5s.

THE CHAIRMAN'S MANUAL. Being a guide to the management of meetings in general, and of meetings of local authorities, with separate and complete treatment of the meetings of Public Companies. By GURDON PALIN, of Gray's Inn, Barrister-at-Law, and ERNEST MARTIN, F.C.I.S. The object of this book is to supply in a concise and readily-found form, all the information and advice necessary to enable a Chairman of any Meeting to conduct the proceedings effectively, smoothly and expeditiously. The rules of debate are clearly explained; legal considerations are discussed; and every contingency a Chairman may have to deal with is provided for. The authors have brought to their task a large and varied experience of meetings. In crown 8vo, cloth gilt, 192 pp. net 2s. 6d.

BUSINESS MAN'S HANDBOOKS (continued).

PITMAN'S SECRETARY'S HANDBOOK. Edited by HERBERT E. BLAIN, joint author of "Pitman's Office Organisation and Management." An entirely new work, written on an original plan, and dealing in a concise yet sufficiently full manner with the work and duties in connection with the position of Secretary to a Member of Parliament or other public man; to a Country Gentleman with a landed estate; a Charitable Institution; with a section devoted to the work of the Lady Secretary, and a chapter dealing with secretarial work in general. In demy 8vo, cloth gilt, 168 pp. net 3s. 6d.

HOW TO TAKE MINUTES. Being a Reliable Guide to the best method of noting and recording the Minutes of a Business Meeting. The object of this book is to assist Secretaries and others who may be called upon to record the Minutes of Meetings. Full instructions are given as to the proper way to take and record Minutes, whether of Directors' or Shareholders' Meetings, and model Agenda, Minutes, etc., are given. A copy of Table A of the Companies, Consolidation Act, 1908, is also included. In demy 8vo, cloth, 80 pp., net 1s. 6d.

COST ACCOUNTS IN PRINCIPLE AND PRACTICE. By A. CLIFFORD RIDGWAY, A.C.A. This work sets out clearly and briefly the method of costing suitable for a small manufacturer or a big engineer, the whole being illustrated with upwards of 40 forms specially drawn up for the book. In demy 8vo, cloth gilt, 120 pp., net 3s. 6d.

SALESMANSHIP. A Practical Guide for Shop Assistant, Commercial Traveller, and Agent. By W. A. CORBION and G. E. GRIMSDALE. The authors deal at length with the influence of character upon salesmanship, the relation of the salesman to the buyer, the knowledge and care of stock, suggestive salesmanship, the avoidance or rectification of mistakes, system, etc. The lessons for the guidance of the salesman are illustrated by concrete examples, so that the work is eminently practical throughout. In crown 8vo, 186 pp., net 2s. 6d.

THE THEORY AND PRACTICE OF ADVERTISING. By WALTER DILL SCOTT, Ph.D., Director of the Psychological Laboratory of North-Western University, U.S.A.

The author of this work has made advertising the study of his life and is acknowledged as one of the greatest authorities on the subject in the United States. The book is so fascinatingly written that it will appeal to many classes of readers. In large crown 8vo, cloth, with 61 illustrations, 240 pp., net 6s.

THE PSYCHOLOGY OF ADVERTISING. A Simple Exposition of the Principles of Psychology in their Relation to Successful Advertising. By the same author. Professor DILL SCOTT has made a very lengthy and careful examination of his subject, a task for which his special training and his wide experience eminently qualify him.

BUSINESS MAN'S HANDBOOKS (continued).

THE PSYCHOLOGY OF ADVERTISING—(contd.)

In view of the publication of the present work he prosecuted extensive enquiries as to the effect of various styles of advertising, etc., receiving replies from about 2,300 business and professional men. He gives us the result of his researches in this book. In large crown 8vo, cloth gilt, with 67 illustrations, 282 pp., net 6s.

THE PRINCIPLES OF PRACTICAL PUBLICITY. Being a Treatise on "The Art of Advertising." By TRUMAN A. DE WEESE. The author was in charge of special Publicity for the Louisiana Purchase Exposition at St. Louis (1904), and is Director of Publicity for one of the largest advertising firms in America. The book will be found a comprehensive and practical treatise covering the subject in all its branches, showing the successful adaptation of advertising to all lines of business. In large crown 8vo, cloth, with 43 full-page illustrations, 266 pp., net 1s. 6d.

GROCERY BUSINESS ORGANISATION AND MANAGEMENT. By C. L. T. BEECHING, Secretary and Fellow of the Institute of Certificated Grocers. With Chapters on Buying a Business, Grocers' Office Work and Book-keeping, and a Model Set of Grocer's Accounts. By J. ARTHUR SMART, of the Firm of Alfred Smart, Valuer and Accountant; Fellow of the Institute of Certificated Grocers. This book contains a mass of invaluable information with regard to the buying of stock, the design of the shop front, fixtures, etc., etc. In demy 8vo, cloth gilt, about 160 pp., with illustrations, net 5s.

THE WORLD'S COMMERCIAL PRODUCTS. A descriptive account of the Economic Plants of the World and of their Commercial Uses. By W. G. FREEMAN, B.Sc., F.L.S., Superintendent, Colonial Economic Collections, Imperial Institute, London, and S. E. CHANDLER, D.Sc., F.L.S., Assistant, Colonial Economic Collections, Imperial Institute, London. With contributions by numerous Specialists. In demy 4to, cloth gilt, with 12 coloured plates, 12 maps, and 420 illustrations from photographs. 432 pp., net 10s. 6d.

DICTIONARY OF THE WORLD'S COMMERCIAL PRODUCTS. With French, German, and Spanish equivalents for the Names of the Products. By J. A. SLATER, B.A., LL.B. Second Edition, Revised. In demy 8vo, cloth, 163 pp., 2s. 6d.

PITMAN'S OFFICE DESK BOOK. Contains most of the matters upon which information is constantly required in an office. Gives reliable information on points of Commercial Law, Banking, and Bank Notes, Bills of Exchange, the Board of Trade, Joint Stock Companies, Deeds, Taxes, Weights, and Measures, Insurance, Importing and Exporting, Foreign Exchanges, Methods of Calculation, etc., etc., and also a useful Ready Reckoner. Second, Revised and Cheaper Edition. In crown 8vo, cloth, 309 pp., net 1s.

BUSINESS MAN'S HANDBOOKS (continued).

THE "COLE" CODE, OR CODE DICTIONARY. A simple, safe and economical method of cabling verbatim commercial, technical and social messages, complete and up-to-date, with unlimited facilities for extensions to suit any kind of business, including cabling from books, catalogues, price lists, etc. With two extra vocabularies of 10,000,000 words each, arranged in alphabetical and numerical order. Size 7½ in. by 10 in., 272 pp., cloth, net 15s.

WHERE TO LOOK. An easy guide to the contents of certain specified books of reference. Fourth Annual Edition, revised and augmented with the assistance of a prominent Public Librarian. Including a list of the principal continental and American books of reference with a note of their contents. In crown 8vo, cloth, 140 pp., net 2s.

ECONOMICS FOR BUSINESS MEN. By W. J. WESTON, M.A. (Lond.), B.Sc. (Lond.). In this useful and readable volume Mr. Weston, in a lucid and entertaining style, strives to bring into harmony the theory of the great economists, and the practice of the busy world of men. In crown 8vo, cloth, net 1s. 6d.

OUTLINES OF THE ECONOMIC HISTORY OF ENGLAND. A Study in Social Development. By H. O. MEREDITH, M.A., M.Com. Fellow of King's College, Cambridge; Professor of Economics, Queen's University, Belfast; Sometime Russell Research Student and Lecturer in the London School of Economics; Sometime Lecturer in Economics at Cambridge University. Beginning with the Economic development of Britain during the Roman occupation, the work traces the progress made down to the present day. The author deals with the genesis of capitalism, money and taxation, the growth of trade and industry, the trade union movement, the law and the wage-earning classes, finance and national welfare, etc. In demy 8vo, cloth gilt, 376 pp., net 5s.

SYSTEMATIC INDEXING. A complete and exhaustive handbook on the subject. By J. KAISER, *Librarian of the Tariff Commission.* In royal 8vo, cloth gilt, with 32 illustrations and 12 coloured plates, net, 12s. 6d.

CONSULAR REQUIREMENTS FOR EXPORTERS AND SHIPPERS TO ALL PARTS OF THE WORLD. Including exact copies of all forms of Consular Invoices, with some hints as to drawing out of Bills of Lading, etc. By J. S. NOWERY. In crown 8vo, cloth, 82 pp., net 2s. 6d.

A COMPLETE GUIDE TO THE IMPROVEMENT OF THE MEMORY: or the Science of Memory Simplified, with practical Applications to Languages, History, Geography, Prose, Poetry, Shorthand, etc. By the late Rev. J. H. BACON. In foolscap 8vo, cloth, net 1s.

HOW TO STUDY AND REMEMBER. By B. J. DAVIES. Third Edition. In crown 8vo, net 6d.

COMMERCIAL CORRESPONDENCE AND COMPOSITION.

FIRST STEPS IN COMMERCIAL ENGLISH. By W. Jayne Weston, M.A. (Lond.), B.Sc. (Lond.). Intended principally for candidates preparing for the elementary examinations conducted by the Lancashire and Cheshire Union of Institutes, the Midland Union of Institutes, the Royal Society of Arts, and similar examining bodies, this book contains exercises, skilfully selected and carefully graded so as to provide a continuous course. In crown 8vo, limp cloth, 80 pp., net 8d.

PITMAN'S GUIDE TO COMMERCIAL CORRESPONDENCE AND BUSINESS COMPOSITION. By W. Jayne Weston, M.A. Intended for beginners in the study of commercial education, this book gives simple but practical instruction in the art of business composition and the writing of commercial letters, and is suitable either for private study or for use in class. Cloth, 146 pp., with many facsimile commercial documents, 1s. 6d.

INDEXING AND PRÉCIS WRITING. (See page 12.)

PUNCTUATION AS A MEANS OF EXPRESSION. By A. E. Lovell, M.A. A complete guide to the accurate use of stops in writing. In crown 8vo, cloth, 80 pp., 1s 6d.

THE AVON ENGLISH GRAMMAR PRIMER. Cloth, 219 pp., 1s.

ENGLISH GRAMMAR. New Edition, Revised and Enlarged by C. D. Punchard, B.A. (Lond.). Without altering the former plan, the reviser has brought the contents of this book into closer harmony with the requirements of modern examinations, and has brought together a number of exercises comprising many questions given in recent examinations, and specimen papers set by the College of Preceptors and the Joint Scholarships Board. In crown 8vo, cloth, 142 pp., net 1s.

A GUIDE TO ENGLISH COMPOSITION, with Progressive exercises. By the Rev. J. H. Bacon. 112 pp., paper, 1s.; cloth, 1s. 6d.

NOTES OF LESSONS ON ENGLISH. A comprehensive series of lessons, intended to assist teachers of English Composition and Grammar. In crown 8vo, cloth, 208 pp., 3s. 6d.

GRAMMAR AND ITS REASONS: For Students and Teachers of the English Tongue. By Mary Holland Leonard. This book is a series of essays, dealing with the more important parts of English Grammar. In crown 8vo, cloth, 392 pp., net 3s. 6d.

COMMERCIAL CORRESPONDENCE, ETC. (continued).

PITMAN'S STUDIES IN ELOCUTION. By E. M. CORBOULD (*Mrs. Mark Robinson*). A guide to the Theory and Practice of the art of Public Speaking, Reciting, and Reading. With over 100 selections for Reciters and Readers. Cloth gilt, gilt top, net 2s. 6d.

ENGLISH COMPOSITION AND CORRESPONDENCE. (See page 14.)

HOW TO TEACH COMMERCIAL ENGLISH. By WALTER SHAWCROSS, B.A. A Practical Manual dealing with *methods of teaching* English to Commercial students. The divisions of the subject—Grammar, Vocabulary, Spelling, Style, Essays, Reports, Correspondence, etc.—are considered in turn, the parts essential to commercial students picked out, and methods of treatment outlined. There are in addition separate chapters on General Teaching Methods, the Essentials of Grammar, Common Errors, and the Teaching of Précis Writing. Outline courses of lessons for both elementary and advanced classes are given together with suggestions on Home Work, Test Examinations and Choice of Text-books. In crown 8vo, cloth gilt, 160 pp., net 2s. 6d.

MANUAL OF COMMERCIAL ENGLISH. Including Composition and Précis Writing. A Handbook covering all the requirements of students of English for commercial purposes. Adapted for use in class or for private study. By the same author. In this book every important part of the subject is dealt with, including style and construction of sentences, correspondence, drafting reports, resolutions, amendments, etc., and indexing and précis writing. There are also separate chapters on the Essentials of Grammar, and an appendix containing an analysis of the chief rules governing English spelling. The book is specially intended for candidates entering for the examinations of the Royal Society of Arts, the Chartered Institute of Secretaries, the Institute of Bankers, and similar bodies. In crown 8vo, cloth gilt, 234 pp., net 2s. 6d.

PITMAN'S COMMERCIAL CORRESPONDENCE AND COMMERCIAL ENGLISH. A new and practical Manual of Commercial Correspondence in two divisions: first, Commercial Correspondence, including about 340 letters; and, second, Commercial English. In crown 8vo, cloth, 272 pp., 2s. 6d.

PITMAN'S COMMERCIAL CORRESPONDENCE IN FRENCH. This work gives all the letters of "Pitman's Commercial Correspondence" in French, and also contains a List of French Commercial Abbreviations, French coinage, weights, measures, and other matter of importance to the student of Commercial French, together with a number of reduced facsimiles of actual French business forms and documents. In crown 8vo, cloth, 240 pp., 2s. 6d.

PITMAN'S COMMERCIAL CORRESPONDENCE IN GERMAN. Uniform with the above. In crown 8vo, cloth, 240 pp., 2s. 6d.

COMMERCIAL CORRESPONDENCE, ETC. (continued.)

PITMAN'S COMMERCIAL CORRESPONDENCE IN SPANISH. Uniform with the above. In crown 8vo, 240 pp., 2s. 6d.

PITMAN'S COMMERCIAL CORRESPONDENCE IN SHORTHAND (Reporting Style). This work gives in beautifully engraved Shorthand all the letters included in "Pitman's Commercial Correspondence," with a chapter on the Shorthand Clerk and his Duties. In crown 8vo. cloth, 240 pp., 2s. 6d.

PITMAN'S INTERNATIONAL MERCANTILE LETTERS. In five volumes, crown 8vo, cloth gilt; each about 250 pp.

English-German ...... 2s. 6d. English .... 2s. 6d.
English-French ...... 2s. 6d. English-Italian .... 3s. 0d.
English-Portuguese .... 3s. 6d.

Each volume contains a very large and widely varied collection of business letters, arranged in groups and in series, and dealing at length with (*a*) Business in Goods; (*b*) Banking, etc.; (*c*) Commission and Consignment Business; and (*d*) The Transport and Insurance of Merchandise. Each set of transactions is first presented in the form of a précis or summary, and then the same transactions are fully illustrated by letters. In the English-Foreign volumes the information respecting the particular business treated, the précis of the transactions, and the letters are given in English and in either French, German, Italian, or Portuguese, according to the language dealt with in the volume.

ELEMENTARY GERMAN CORRESPONDENCE. By LEWIS MARSH, B.A. (Hons.). Cantab. Intended for students who are just beginning the study of Commercial German. Facsimiles are furnished of German commercial correspondence and business documents. In crown 8vo, cloth, 143 pp., 2s.

THE FOREIGN CORRESPONDENT. By ALBERT EMIL DAVIES. For the student, the youthful commercial aspirant, or the clerk wishful of bettering his position, the book is a guide and counsellor. In crown 8vo, cloth, 80 pp., net 1s. 6d.

PITMAN'S DICTIONARY OF COMMERCIAL CORRESPONDENCE IN FRENCH, GERMAN, SPANISH, AND ITALIAN. This volume which has just undergone a very thorough revision, has been limited to the most common and ordinary terms and phrases of a commercial nature. Second, Revised and Cheaper Edition. In demy 8vo, cloth, 502 pp., net 5s.

ENGLISH-GERMAN AND GERMAN-ENGLISH DICTIONARY OF BUSINESS WORDS AND TERMS. A new pocket English-German and German-English Dictionary, with a list of Abbreviations in general use, by FRITZ HUNDEL. Size 2 by 6 in., rounded corners, roan, net 2s. 6d.

ENGLISH-FRENCH AND FRENCH-ENGLISH DICTIONARY OF BUSINESS WORDS AND TERMS. 2 ins. by 6 ins., rounded corners, roan, net 2s. 6d.

COMMERCIAL CORRESPONDENCE, ETC. (continued.)

A NEW DICTIONARY OF THE PORTUGUESE AND ENGLISH LANGUAGES. Based on a manuscript of JULIUS CORNET, by H. MICHAELIS. In two parts. First Part: Portuguese-English. Second Part: English-Portuguese. Colloquial, commercial and industrial terms have been plentifully introduced throughout the book and irregularities in the formation of the plural and in the conjugation of verbs have been carefully noted. Second Edition. Two volumes, 15s. each, net.

ABRIDGED EDITION. Two parts in one volume, net 15s.

PITMAN'S POCKET DICTIONARY of the English Language. This Dictionary furnishes in a form suitable for ready reference, a guide to the spelling and meaning of words in everyday use, and it is a trustworthy authority on the best modern English usage in spelling. The definitions—though necessarily concise—are thoroughly accurate. A List of Abbreviations in General Use is given. Royal 32mo, 5 in. by 3 in., cloth gilt, 362 pp., net 1s.; also in leather, net 1s. 6d.

COMMERCIAL DICTIONARY. In this book univocal words which present no difficulty as to spelling are omitted, and abbreviations, signs, anglicized foreign expressions, etc., are placed in their alphabetical order in the body of the book. The appendix contains forms of address, foreign coinage, weights and measures, etc. In crown 8vo, paper boards, net 9d.; cloth, net, 1s.

STUDIES IN ESSAY WRITING. By V. P. PEACOCK. This book deals, in a very attractive manner, with the higher stages of the art of English Composition. In crown 8vo, paper, net 6d., cloth, net 9d.

COMMERCIAL GEOGRAPHY.

FIRST STEPS IN COMMERCIAL GEOGRAPHY. By JAMES STEPHENSON, M.A., B.Com. An entirely new volume intended principally for candidates preparing for the elementary examinations conducted by the Lancashire and Cheshire Union of Institutes, the Midland Union of Institutes, the Royal Society of Arts, and similar examining bodies. There are 16 maps and diagrams included. In crown 8vo, limp cloth, 80 pp., net 8d.

THE WORLD AND ITS COMMERCE: A Primer of Commercial Geography. Contains simply written chapters on the general geography of the world, the seven great industries, the commercial geography of the British Empire at home and abroad, and of foreign countries. The information conveyed is quite up-to-date. In crown 8vo, cloth, 128 pp., with thirty-four maps, 1s.

PRINCIPAL CONTENTS.—PART I.—The World Generally—The Surface of the Earth—Zones and Heat Belts—Distribution of

COMMERCIAL GEOGRAPHY (continued.)

Life—Agriculture—Herding and Ranching—Fishing—Lumbering—Mining—Manufacturing—Commerce.

PART II.—The British Empire—The United Kingdom—The British Empire Abroad.

PART III.—Foreign Countries.

A thorough description is given of the commercial position, the mineral, agricultural and manufactured productions, and chief commercial towns of each country.

PITMAN'S COMMERCIAL GEOGRAPHY OF THE BRITISH ISLES. New edition, revised and enlarged. In crown 8vo, cloth, 150 pp., with 34 coloured maps and plates, three black and white maps, and other illustrations, 1s.

PRINCIPAL CONTENTS.—INTRODUCTION.—Kinds of Commerce—Exchange and Exchanges—Imports and Exports—The Metric System — Manufactures — The World generally. COMMERCIAL PRODUCTS.—Common Metals and Minerals—Commercial Products of Animal Origin—Common Plants and their Commercial Products. THE UNITED KINGDOM.—Position, Configuration and Coast Line—Manufactures—Imports and Exports—Means of Transport—Commercial Towns—Trade Routes. ENGLAND AND WALES.—SCOTLAND.—IRELAND.—Mountains—Metals and Minerals—Productions—Animals—Geographical Structure — Climate — Bogs—Lakes—Fisheries.

PITMAN'S COMMERCIAL GEOGRAPHY OF THE BRITISH EMPIRE ABROAD AND FOREIGN COUNTRIES. New edition, revised and enlarged. In crown 8vo, cloth, 205 pp., with 35 coloured maps and plates, 11 black and white maps, and end-paper maps, 1s. 6d.

PRINCIPAL CONTENTS.—THE BRITISH EMPIRE ABROAD.—Naval and Military Stations—Canada and Newfoundland—Australia, Tasmania, and New Zealand—the British Empire in Asia and Africa—the British West Indies, etc. FOREIGN COUNTRIES.—Europe generally: France, Germany, Holland, Russia, Belgium, Spain, Denmark, Sweden, Norway, Italy, Switzerland, Austria-Hungary, Portugal, Turkey, and Greece—Minor European Countries—Asia generally—North America generally, the United States—Mexico and the Republics of Central America—South America generally, and the States of South America.

PITMAN'S COMMERCIAL GEOGRAPHY OF THE WORLD. New edition, revised and enlarged. For Principal Contents see Books I and II immediately above. In crown 8vo, cloth, 350 pp., with about 90 maps and plates, 2s. 6d.

THE WORLD'S COMMERCIAL PRODUCTS. (See page 24.)

GEOGRAPHICAL STATISTIC UNIVERSAL POCKET ATLAS. (See page 11.)

COMMERCIAL HISTORY.

COMMERCIAL HISTORY. An Introductory Treatise for the use of advanced classes in schools. By J. R. V. MARCHANT, M.A., formerly Scholar of Wadham College, Oxford, Examiner in Commercial History to the London Chamber of Commerce. In crown 8vo, cloth gilt, 272 pp., 3s.

PART I.—The History of Commerce down to the end of the Middle Ages—Coloured Maps, Plates, Maps in black and white, fully illustrated from ancient tapestries, sculptures, etc., etc., 1s. 6d. PART II.—The History of Commerce from the Middle Ages to the Present Time.—Maps, Plates, etc. 2s.

THE EVOLUTIONARY HISTORY OF ENGLAND. Edited by OSCAR BROWNING, Fellow of King's College, Cambridge. 125 illustrations, beautiful reproductions of eleven famous historical paintings, genealogical tables, glossary, summary. 272 pp., 1s. 10d.

COMMERCIAL LAW.

THE ELEMENTS OF COMMERCIAL LAW. By A. H. DOUGLAS, LL.B. (Lond.). (See page 14.)

THE COMMERCIAL LAW OF ENGLAND. A Handbook for Business Men and Advanced Classes in Schools. By J. A. SLATER, B.A., LL.B. (Lond.), of the Middle Temple and North-Eastern Circuit, Barrister-at-Law. This work is intended for the service of advanced students in schools; but it has been designed in an equally important degree as a constant desk companion to the modern man of business. It is believed that the method of treatment will render the work a useful text-book for the various examinations in Commercial Law. With five facsimiles. Fourth Edition. In crown 8vo, cloth, 227 pp., 2s. 6d.

QUESTIONS AND ANSWERS IN COMMERCIAL LAW. By J. WELLS THATCHER, Barrister-at-Law. This new book contains the whole of the questions in Commercial Law set at the examinations of the London Chamber of Commerce and the Royal Society of Arts, for the years 1900 to 1909 inclusive, with the correct answers thereto. In crown 8vo, cloth gilt, 2s. 6d.

EXAMINATION NOTES ON COMMERCIAL LAW. By R. W. HOLLAND, M.A., M.Sc., LL.B., Barrister-at-Law; Lecturer in Commercial Law at the Manchester Municipal School of Commerce. This work is primarily intended to assist candidates who are preparing for the Commercial Law examinations of such bodies as the Royal Society of Arts, London Chamber of Commerce, National Union of Teachers, the Union of Lancashire and Cheshire Institutes, etc. Cloth, 6½ in. by 3½ in., net 1s.

COMMERCIAL LAW (continued).

PITMAN'S HANDBOOK OF LOCAL GOVERNMENT LAW. Specially designed for students for the Examination of the Institute of Municipal Treasurers and Accountants (Incorporated), as well as for all students engaged in the offices of Local Authorities in England and Wales. By J. WELLS THATCHER, of the Middle Temple, Barrister-at-Law. In large 8vo, cloth gilt, 250 pp., net 3s. 6d.

ELEMENTARY LAW FOR SHORTHAND CLERKS AND TYPISTS. The plan followed in this work is that of giving such an account of various branches of English law as shall serve to bring out the precise significance of the chief terms customarily used by lawyers, and often used by laymen. In crown 8vo, cloth, 213 pp., 2s. 6d.

LEGAL TERMS, PHRASES, AND ABBREVIATIONS. For typists and Shorthand and other Junior Clerks. This work is supplementary to "Elementary Law," and its chief object is that of enabling junior clerks in English legal offices to gain an intelligible grasp of the meaning of the terms that they are called upon to employ every day. In crown 8vo, cloth, 200 pp., 2s. 6d.

PITMAN'S SOLICITOR'S CLERK'S GUIDE. By E. A. COPE. This work is designed to serve for beginners and junior clerks in solicitors' offices the purpose served as regards other callings by office guides and other introductory technical books. In crown 8vo, cloth, 2s. 6d.

CONVEYANCING. By E. A. COPE. Explains the essentials of a contract relating to land, illustrates the nature, the form, and the structure of the modern deed, the order of its contents, the importance of recitals, the clauses implied by virtue of the Conveyancing and other Acts, the appropriate use of technical expressions, and numerous other points. In crown 8vo, cloth, 206 pp., net 3s.

PITMAN'S BILLS, CHEQUES, AND NOTES. (See page 20.) Net 2s. 6d.

PITMAN'S MERCANTILE LAW. By J. A. SLATER, B.A., LL.B. (See page 20.) Net 5s.

THE LAW OF HEAVY AND LIGHT MECHANICAL TRACTION ON HIGHWAYS IN THE UNITED KINGDOM. By C. A. MONTAGUE BARLOW, M.A., LL.D., and W. JOYNSON HICKS. (See page 21.) Net 8s. 6d.

ENCYCLOPÆDIA OF MARINE LAW. By LAWRENCE DUCKWORTH, Barrister-at-Law. (See page 20.) Net 5s.

THE STUDENT'S GUIDE TO BANKRUPTCY LAW. By F. PORTER FAUSSET, LL.B. (see p. 21). Net, 2s. 6d.

BANKRUPTCY AND BILLS OF SALE. By W. VALENTINE BALL, M.A., Barrister-at-Law. (See page 21.) Net 5s.

THE STUDENT'S GUIDE TO COMPANY LAW. By R. W. HOLLAND, M.A., W.Sc., LL.B. (see p. 21.) Net 2s. 6d.

COMPANIES AND COMPANY LAW. By A. C. CONNELL, LL.B. (See page 21.) Net 5s.

THE LAW OF CARRIAGE. By J. E. R. STEPHENS, B.A. (See page 21.) Net 5s.

COMMERCIAL READERS.

PITMAN'S COMMERCIAL READER (Intermediate Book). A splendidly illustrated reading book, written on the same general plan as the Senior Book, in the same series, but intended for younger readers. It is divided into nine sections, dealing with the chief branches of Modern Industry, such as Paper-making and the Production of Books and Newspapers; Steam and Machinery; Shipping; Mining and Metal Works; Electricity and its Uses; Cotton and what is made from it; Woollen Manufactures, etc. Each section ends with the life story of some notable industrial pioneer. In crown 8vo, cloth, 240 pp., 1s. 9d.

PITMAN'S COMMERCIAL READER (Senior Book). An Introduction to Modern Commerce. The most important and valuable Reading Book yet published for use in the Upper Classes in Day Schools and in Evening Continuation Schools. Crown 8vo, cloth, 272 pp., 2s.

Contains over 160 black and white illustrations, which include reproductions of famous pictures by Lord Leighton, P.R.A., Vicat Cole, R.A., Sidney Cooper, R.A., and Marcus Stone, R.A., together with portraits (reproduced from photographs) of Lord Rothschild, Lord Armstrong, Lord Masham, Sir Alfred Jones, Sir George Williams, Guglielmo Marconi, etc., etc., etc.; six black and white maps, and a coloured quarto Map of the World, showing the British Empire, the chief Telegraph Cables and Steamer Routes, etc.: Glossary.

PITMAN'S FRENCH COMMERCIAL READER. Deals in an interesting manner with the leading Commercial and National Institutions of France. The reading matter is most carefully selected, and while the student of French is improving his mastery of the language, he is at the same time getting a good insight into French commercial methods. Thus, while reading about invoices, the actual document is brought under his notice. Additional value is given to the book by the inclusion of questions and exercises. Maps, illustrations, and facsimiles of French commercial documents illustrate the text, and, in addition, the book contains a selection of commercial letters, a full list of commercial abbreviations in current use, and an exhaustive vocabulary. In crown 8vo, cloth, 208 pp., 2s. 6d.

PITMAN'S GERMAN COMMERCIAL READER. Prepared on similar lines to the French Commercial Reader above. It furnishes a practical introduction to German commercial institutions and transactions, with questions and exercises which render it well suited for use in schools. Students are afforded the fullest help possible from plates, illustrations, maps, and facsimiles of German commercial documents. The text has had the benefit of revision by modern language masters in well-known schools. In crown 8vo, cloth, 208 pp., 2s. 6d.

HANDWRITING.

PITMAN'S COMMERCIAL HANDWRITING AND CORRESPONDENCE. A complete and reliable guide for the student of any kind of handwriting, designed for use in class or self-tuition. In fcap. quarto, quarter cloth, 2s.

Contains carefully graduated Exercises, together with Plain and Practical Instructions for the Rapid Acquirement of a Facile and Legible Business Style of Handwriting—Furnishes also Explicit Directions for the Formation of the Recognised Civil Service Style—Text Hand—Legal Style—Engrossing Style—Block Lettering, as Required for Business Purposes—Valuable Hints on Business Composition—Specimens of Written Business Letters and Various Commercial Documents, such as Account Sales, Accounts Current, Bills of Exchange, Promissory Notes, I.O.U.'s, Invoices, Statements, Receipts, etc.—Lists of Business Abbreviations, and Particulars of the Examination Requirements of the Society of Arts, Union of Lancashire and Cheshire Institutes, Midland Union of Institutes and other Examining Authorities.

The whole of the numerous exercises, copies and illustrations are facsimile reproductions of the author's actual handwriting.

BUSINESS HANDWRITING. The object of this work is to enable students to acquire the habit of writing with ease and rapidity, in such a manner that the meaning of even careless writing may be at once evident to the reader. The many illustrations and exercises form a special feature of the work, and these are photographic reproductions of the actual writing of the author and his professional friends. Seventh Edition, revised. In crown 8vo, cloth, 84 pp., 1s.

PITMAN'S COMMERCIAL COPY AND EXERCISE BOOKS. These Copy Books contain carefully graded sets of exercises in business work. The copies are engraved in a clear style of writing, for the purpose of guiding the student to a rapid and legible commercial hand. In fcap. folio, 32 pp., each 6d.

No. 1.—Documents and Exercises relating to the Home Trade.

PRINCIPAL CONTENTS.—Commercial Terms and Abbreviations—Copying and Docketing Letters—Copying and Arrangement of Addresses—Subscriptions and Signatures of Letters—Letter-Writing—Composing Telegrams—Home Invoices, Cheques, and Receipts.

No. 2.—Documents and Exercises relating to the Import and Export Trade.

PRINCIPAL CONTENTS.—Shipping Invoices of various kinds—Account Sales—Statements of Account—Credit Notes—Inland Bill and Promissory Note—Account Current—Balance Sheets—Bills of Exchange—Bank Deposit Slips—Bills of Lading—Advice Notes—Customs Declaration Forms and Despatch Notes for Parcels Post—Brokers' Notes—Market Reports—Price Lists—Letters of Advice—Insurance Accounts, etc., with blank forms to be filled up by the student, and also a list of Commercial Terms and Abbreviations with their meanings.

PITMAN'S "NEW ERA" BUSINESS COPY BOOKS. By F. HEELIS, F.C.I.S. Civil Service Style. In three books, Junior, Intermediate, and Senior. This series of Copy Books is designed to give pupils training and practice simultaneously in the art of writing and addressing business letters, making out receipts, bills, credit notes,

HANDWRITING (continued).

"NEW ERA" BUSINESS COPY BOOKS—contd.

and invoices, drafting Bank slips, and Postage Accounts. Model extracts from the Petty Cash Book occur, and useful information is supplied showing how best to make memoranda, fill in Delivery Notes, Telegraph Forms, Money Orders, Freight Notes, Order and Bearer Cheques, Promissory and Contract Notes, and Shipping Advice Forms. All the business technicalities, a knowledge of which is indispensable to the youth of to-day, are dealt with in detail. Each in stout paper covers, large post 4to, 32 pp., 4d.

EXERCISE BOOKS OF FACSIMILE COMMERCIAL FORMS. Designed for the dual purpose of a copy book of commercial handwriting and to enable the student to familiarize himself with the filling up of business documents, etc. Among the forms given are:—Accounts Current, Account Sales, Invoices, Bills of Lading, Bills of Exchange, Cheques, Consignment Notes, etc. In large post 4to, printed in red and black, in wrapper, 32 pp., 6d.

PITMAN'S FACSIMILE COMMERCIAL FORMS. A collection of the most common forms in everyday use in business to be filled up by the student. 26 separate forms in envelope. 6d. Forms separately, per doz. 3d.

PITMAN'S OFFICE ROUTINE COPY BOOK, No. 1. In large post 4to, 24 pp., 3d.

CONTAINS.—Specimen Addresses—Clerical, Commercial, Express Delivery, French, German, Italian, Miscellaneous, official, Private, Railway, Registered, and Spanish, with forms of Transmitting Money or Goods by Post or Rail.

PITMAN'S OFFICE ROUTINE COPY BOOK, No. 2. In large post 4to, 24 pp., 3d.

CONTAINS.—Inland Invoices—Statements of Accounts—Receipts—Telephone Message and Reply—A Credit Note—Export Merchant's Invoice—Telegrams—Cheques—Letters Advising and Acknowledging Payment.

PITMAN'S OFFICE ROUTINE COPY BOOK, No. 3. In large post 4to, 24 pp., 3d.

CONTAINS.—Letters Ordering Goods—Letters Advising Travellers, Call—House Agent's Letters—Reply to an Inquiry—Letter enclosing Copy of Advertisement—Application for Shares—Letter Advising Despatch of Catalogue—Letter Advising Delivery of a Cycle—Letter Requesting a Special Favour—Letter of Recommendation—Dunning Letters—A Promissory Note—Order for Advertisement and Reply—Banker's Receipt for Share Deposit.

CIVIL SERVICE AND COMMERCIAL COPYING FORMS. A collection of papers set at various examinations, with suggestions for obtaining the best results. In crown 8vo, 40 pp., 6d.

RULED FORMS for use with the above. Books I and II. Each fcap. folio, 40 pp., 8d.

FRENCH.

PITMAN'S FRENCH COURSE, Part I. Grammar, with exercises, carefully selected conversational phrases and sentences, correspondence, short stories from French authors, and judiciously chosen vocabulary with imitated pronunciation. In crown 8vo, paper, 6d.; cloth, 8d.

PITMAN'S FRENCH COURSE, Part II. In crown 8vo, paper, 8d.; cloth, 10d.

KEY TO PITMAN'S FRENCH COURSE, Parts I and II. In crown 8vo, each 1s. 6d.

PITMAN'S PRACTICAL FRENCH GRAMMAR and Conversation for Self-Tuition, with copious Vocabulary and Imitated Pronunciation. In crown 8vo, 120 pp., paper, 1s.; cloth, 1s. 6d.

PITMAN'S COMMERCIAL FRENCH GRAMMAR. By F. W. M. Draper, B.A., B. ès L. Of Queen's College, Cambridge, and Licencié of the University of Paris; also Assistant Master at the City of London School. In this book French grammar is taught on normal lines, with the addition that all grammatical points are illustrated by sentences in commercial French. The exercises are written with a view to enabling the student to read and write business letters in French, and to understand without difficulty commercial and financial articles in French books and newspapers. Accidence and Syntax have been, as far as possible, blended. In crown 8vo, cloth gilt, 166 pp. net 2s. 6d.

A CHILD'S FIRST STEPS IN FRENCH. By A. Vizetelly. An elementary French reader with vocabulary. Illustrated. In crown 8vo, limp cloth, 9d.

FRENCH BUSINESS LETTERS. First Series. A Practical Handbook of Commercial Correspondence in the French Language, with copious notes in English. In crown 4to, net. 6d.

FRENCH BUSINESS LETTERS. Second Series. By A. H. Bernaardt. In crown 8vo, 48 pp., net 6d.

COMMERCIAL CORRESPONDENCE IN FRENCH. (See page 27.)

FRENCH COMMERCIAL READER. (See page 33.)

RENCH COMMERCIAL PHRASES and Abbreviations with Translation. In crown 8vo, 6d.

FRENCH BUSINESS INTERVIEWS. With Correspondence, Invoices, etc., each forming a complete Commercial Transaction, including Technical Terms and Idiomatic Expressions, accompanied by a copious vocabulary and notes in English. In crown 8vo, 80 pp., paper, 1s.; cloth, 1s. 6d.

EASY FRENCH CONVERSATIONAL SENTENCES. With literal interlinear translation and imitated pronunciation. In crown 8vo, 6d.

ADVANCED FRENCH CONVERSATIONAL EXERCISES. Consisting of everyday phrases, dialogues, proverbs, and idioms, with translation, for the use of schools and private students. In crown 8vo, 6d.

EXAMINATIONS IN FRENCH, AND HOW TO PASS THEM. Examination Papers recently set at some of the Chief Public Examinations fully solved. In crown 8vo, 6d.

FRENCH (continued).

EXAMINATION NOTES ON FRENCH. By F. W. M. Draper. Compact notes for candidates preparing for Examinations of the London matriculation, Central Welsh Board, Northern Universities Joint Board, College of Preceptors, Chamber of Commerce, and Society of Arts. Size, 6½ in. by 3½ in., cloth, 50 pp., net 1s.

TOURIST'S VADE MECUM OF FRENCH COLLOQUIAL CONVERSATION. A careful selection of every-day phrases in constant use, with Vocabularies, Tables, and general rules on Pronunciation. An easy method of acquiring a knowledge of French sufficient for all purposes of Tourists or Business Men. Special attention has been devoted to the section on Cycling and Photography. Handy size for the pocket, cloth, net 1s.

FRENCH TRANSLATION AND COMPOSITION. By Lewis Marsh, B.A. (Hons.), Cantab., Med, and Mod. Languages Tripos, Late Exhibitioner of Emmanuel College; White Prizeman; Assistant Master, City of London School; and Special Instructor in French and German to the London County Council. Students preparing for public examinations will find this book exceedingly helpful. It is divided into four parts. In Part I the chief difficulties met with in translation are classified and arranged, and the hints conveyed are summarized in a number of "Golden Rules" at the end; while in Part II the author works through a good selection of representative extracts according to the methods previously described, and finally gives in each case a finished translation, the aim throughout being to teach the student to deal intelligently with different styles of prose and verse. Part III consists of 100 carefully graduated extracts to be worked out by the student himself, all taken from classical French authors; and these are followed in Part IV by exercises in French composition based on the extracts in the preceding part. At the end is a French-English and English-French vocabulary. In crown 8vo, cloth, 187 pp., 2s. 6d.

FRENCH PHRASES FOR ADVANCED STUDENTS. By Edward Kealey, B.A. A collection of useful phrases compiled on a new system which will be of the utmost utility and assistance to advanced students of French. In crown 8vo, 1s. 6d.

PITMAN'S INTERNATIONAL MERCANTILE LETTERS. English-French. (See page 28.) In crown 8vo, cloth, 2s. 6d.

ENGLISH-FRENCH AND FRENCH-ENGLISH DICTIONARY of Business Words and Terms. Contains many terms used in commercial correspondence which are not found in ordinary dictionaries. Size, 2 in. by 6 in., cloth, rounded corners. Price, net 2s. 6d.

LE BOURGEOIS GENTILHOMME. Molière's Comedy in French, fully annotated. Price 1s.; cloth, 1s. 6d.

GERMAN.

PITMAN'S GERMAN COURSE. Part I. Grammar, with exercises, carefully selected conversational Phrases and Sentences, Correspondence, short stories from German authors, and vocabulary with imitated pronunciation. In crown 8vo, paper, 6d.; cloth, 8d.

KEY TO PITMAN'S GERMAN COURSE. Part I. In crown 8vo, 1s. 6d.

PITMAN'S PRACTICAL GERMAN GRAMMAR and Conversation for Self-Tuition, with Copious Vocabulary and imitated pronunciation. In crown 8vo, paper, 1s.; cloth, 1s. 6d.

PITMAN'S COMMERCIAL GERMAN GRAMMAR. By J. BITHELL, M.A., Lecturer in German at the Birkbeck College, London; Recognised Teacher of the University of London. This book teaches the rules of German grammar on the basis of a commercial vocabulary. In crown 8vo, cloth gilt, net 2s. 6d.

GERMAN BUSINESS INTERVIEWS, Nos. 1 and 2. With Correspondence, Invoices, etc., each forming a complete Commercial Transaction, including Technical Terms, Dialogues for Travellers, and Idiomatic Expressions used in Shipping and Mercantile Offices, accompanied by a copious marginal Vocabulary and Notes in English. In crown 8vo, each, paper, 1s.; cloth, 1s. 6d.

ELEMENTARY GERMAN CORRESPONDENCE. By LEWIS MARSH, B.A. (See page 28.) In crown 8vo, cloth, 2s.

COMMERCIAL CORRESPONDENCE IN GERMAN. (See page 27.) In crown 8vo, cloth, 240 pp., 2s. 6d.

GERMAN COMMERCIAL READER. (See page 33.) In crown 8vo, cloth, 208 pp., 2s. 6d.

GERMAN BUSINESS LETTERS. With copious maginal vocabulary and notes in English, and some letters in German script characters. In crown 8vo, 6d. net.

GERMAN BUSINESS LETTERS. Second Series. By G. ALBERS. In crown 8vo, 48 pp., net 6d.

GERMAN COMMERCIAL PHRASES. With abbreviations and translation. In crown 8vo, 6d.

GERMAN EXAMINATION PAPERS with model answers. In crown 8vo, net 6d.

EASY GERMAN CONVERSATIONAL SENTENCES. With literal interlinear translation and imitated pronunciation. In crown 8vo, 6d.

ADVANCED GERMAN CONVERSATIONAL EXERCISES. In crown 8vo, 6d.

TOURIST'S VADE MECUM OF GERMAN COLLOQUIAL CONVERSATION. With vocabularies, tables, etc., and general rules on pronunciation; being a careful selection of phrases in constant use. In crown 8vo, cloth, net 1s.

DER NEFFE ALS ONKEL. Schiller's Comedy, fully annotated. In crown 8vo, paper, 6d.; cloth, 1s.

GERMAN (continued).

ENGLISH-GERMAN AND GERMAN-ENGLISH DICTIONARY OF BUSINESS WORDS AND TERMS. (See page 28.) Size 2 by 6 in., rounded corners, cloth, net 2s. 6d.

PITMAN'S DICTIONARY OF COMMERCIAL CORRESPONDENCE IN FRENCH, GERMAN, SPANISH AND ITALIAN. (See page 28.) In demy 8vo, cloth, 500 pp., net 5s.

PITMAN'S INTERNATIONAL MERCANTILE LETTERS. English-German. (See page 28.) In crown 8vo, cloth, 2s. 6d.

ITALIAN.

TOURISTS' VADE MECUM OF ITALIAN COLLOQUIAL CONVERSATION. Uniform with the French, German, and Spanish volumes. Cloth, net 1s.

INTERNATIONAL MERCANTILE LETTERS. English-Italian (see page 28). In crown 8vo, cloth, 3s.

ITALIAN BUSINESS LETTERS. A practical Handbook of Modern Commercial Correspondence, with copious notes in English. By A. VALGIMIGLI. In crown 8vo, 48 pp., net 6d.

PITMAN'S ITALIAN COMMERCIAL GRAMMAR. By LUIGI RICCI, Professor at the University of London. Deals exclusively with commercial Italian, although it includes all the information and the rules for learning the language thoroughly. The explanatory exercises and phrases which number over 1,300, deal with practical information about business; and are full of technical commercial words, a complete list of which, at the end of the volume, supplies the student with a very useful commercial Italian Dictionary. In crown 8vo, cloth gilt, net 2s. 6d.

SPANISH AND PORTUGUESE.

SPANISH BUSINESS LETTERS. A handbook of commercial correspondence in the Spanish language. In crown 8vo, net 6d.

SPANISH BUSINESS LETTERS. 2nd Series. By E. MCCONNELL. In crown 8vo, 48 pp., net 6d.

SPANISH BUSINESS INTERVIEWS. With Correspondence, Invoices, etc. In crown 8vo, paper, 1s.; cloth, 1s. 6d.

EASY SPANISH CONVERSATIONAL SENTENCES. With literal interlinear translation and imitated pronunciation. In crown 8vo. 6d.

ADVANCED SPANISH CONVERSATIONAL EXERCISES. Consisting of everyday phrases, dialogues, proverbs, and idioms, with translation. In crown 8vo, 6d.

PITMAN'S PRACTICAL SPANISH GRAMMAR. With Conversation for Self Tuition, copious vocabulary, and imitated pronunciation. In crown 8vo, paper, 1s., cloth, 1s. 6d.

SPANISH AND PORTUGUESE (continued).

PITMAN'S SPANISH COMMERCIAL GRAMMAR. By C. A. Toledano, Spanish Master at the Manchester Municipal School of Commerce, Manchester Athenaeum, etc. Contains in its exercises and conversations an abundant commercial phraseology, and at the same time a thorough treatise on Spanish grammar. Rules and illustrations are given in appendixes. A synopsis of Spanish conjugations compiled on an original plan will be of great use in mastering the Spanish irregular verbs. In crown 8vo, cloth gilt, 250 pp., net 2s. 6d.

SPANISH COMMERCIAL PHRASES. With abbreviations and translation. In crown 8vo, 8d.

TOURIST'S VADE MECUM OF SPANISH COLLOQUIAL CONVERSATION. With vocabularies, tables, etc., and general rules on pronunciation. Cloth, net 1s.

COMMERCIAL CORRESPONDENCE IN SPANISH. (See page 28.)

A NEW DICTIONARY OF THE PORTUGUESE AND ENGLISH LANGUAGES. (See page 29.)

PITMAN'S INTERNATIONAL MERCANTILE LETTERS. English-Portuguese. (See page 28.)

SHORTHAND AND TYPEWRITING.

See separate catalogue (H), post free on application.

PERIODICALS.

PITMAN'S JOURNAL. Contains six pages of Shorthand in the Learner's, Corresponding, and Reporting Styles, with Key, besides special articles of interest to all connected with commercial education. Subscription, which may begin at any time, 6s. 6d. per annum, post free. (Estab. 1842.) 32 pp. Weekly 1d., by post 1½d.

PITMAN'S COMMERCIAL TEACHER'S MAGAZINE. This new magazine caters for the teacher who is engaged in giving instruction either in day or evening schools. 32 pp. Monthly. Price 1d.

BOOK-KEEPERS' MAGAZINE. Edited by F. J. Mitchell. Organ of the Association of Book-keeping Teachers. Monthly, 2d.; post-free 2½d.

COMMERCIAL TEACHER. Edited by W. H. Lord and H. H. Smith. Organ of the Incorporated Society of Commercial Teachers. Quarterly, 3d. post-free 4d.

INSTITUTE OF COMMERCE MAGAZINE. Edited by Egbert P. Booth. Monthly, 2d., post-free 2½d.